# INSTRUCTIONAL MESSAGE DESIGN

## Principles from the Behavioral and Cognitive Sciences

### SECOND EDITION

# INSTRUCTIONAL MESSAGE DESIGN

## Principles from the Behavioral and Cognitive Sciences

### SECOND EDITION

**Malcolm Fleming**
**and**
**W. Howard Levie**
**EDITORS**

#### CONTRIBUTORS

Anne Bednar
Ernest Burkman
Michael J. Hannafin
Simon R. Hooper
John Keller
Richard E. Mayer
Alexander J. Romiszowski
William Winn

**EDUCATIONAL TECHNOLOGY PUBLICATIONS**
**ENGLEWOOD CLIFFS, NEW JERSEY 07632**

**Library of Congress Cataloging-in-Publication Data**

Instructional message design : principles from the behavioral and
    cognitive sciences / Malcolm Fleming, W. Howard Levie, editors :
    Anne Bednar ... [et al.], contributors. — 2nd ed.
        p. cm.
    Rev. ed. of: Instructional message design / Malcolm Fleming and W.
Howard Levie. 1978.
    Includes bibliographical references and index.
    ISBN 0-87778-253-9
    1. Instructional systems—Design. I. Fleming, Malcolm L.
II. Levie. W. Howard. III. Fleming, Malcolm L. Instructional
message design.
LB1028.38.I58 1993
371.3—dc20                                                     92-30916
                                                                  CIP

Printed in the United States of America.

Library of Congress Catalog Card Number:
92-30916.

International Standard Book Number:
0-87778-253-9.

*First Printing: January 1993.*

# DEDICATION

## to

## R & D

# Preface

## From the First Edition

Our purpose in this book is to narrow the gap between research and practice in instructional message design.

The research utilized here is generally not research that has dealt with message design *per se*. Rather we have sampled broadly from across the spectrum of research on human behavior relevant to the teaching/learning process.

We have attempted to maximize the usefulness of this research by offering sets of generalizations stated as principles. The principles are: (1) based upon empirical evidence, (2) selected for their relevance to practical instructional design problems, and (3) expressed in non-technical language. Further, numerous examples for practice are offered.

We do not treat the step-by-step process of instructional design, but instead assume the reader has a basic familiarity with procedures for analyzing learners and subject matter, stating objectives, and evaluating outcomes. We believe that such systematic analyses of an instructional problem, though necessary, are not a sufficient basis for synthesis of a remedy. Our concern is how to move from well-defined instructional problems to effective solutions through the application of research-based principles.

There is no necessary order in which this book should be read. A practicing professional can access relevant principles by first deciding which cognitive process is primarily involved in the instructional problem and then referencing the appropriate chapter. Other users may find a straight-through reading better at first, and may then continue using the book as a reference when the need arises.

Consistent with the design process we espouse, all users are urged to send evaluative feedback regarding the design and utility of this book to the authors.

We acknowledge our debt to the large number of investigators and reviewers from whose findings and generalizations we have selected the substance upon which the principles are based. They are the discoverers and summarizers, we are the translators and disseminators.

## For this Second Edition

The purpose of this second edition is the same as that noted in the earlier Preface.

This edition was undertaken as a revision and update of the 1978 work authored by Fleming and Levie. When the publisher requested a revised edition about ten years later, neither author, both by then retired, felt up to the task. However, they agreed to be editors of a new edition, provided appropriate new authors could be found for each chapter.

Dr. Howard Levie's untimely death prevented his active involvement as editor, but his name has been retained as an honorary editor in recognition of his essential role in the first edition and his informed and analytical approach to the research literature which characterizes this revised edition.

The result is an excellent revision and update of the four original chapters: Perception Principles, Memory Principles (now Learning Principles), Concept-Learning Principles, and Attitude-Change Principles. Additionally, three entirely new chapters have been created: Motivation Principles, Psychomotor Principles, and Problem-Solving Principles.

In this edition, each principle can be identified by chapter and number, i.e., "Learning principle 3.2" is the second principle in the third section of the Learning chapter. (Alternatively, one can add the chapter number, e.g., 4.3.2, for Chapter 4, Section 3, Number 2.)

Three aspects of this revised edition are important to note here:

1. The recent research literature did not so much question the findings and principles reported earlier as it did refine them and enrich our theoretical understanding and explanation of them.

2. Very important new principles have been gleaned from the recent literature in the areas previously covered, and whole new bodies of research have yielded the many additional principles found in the several new chapters.

3. This update reflects the pervasive change in the research literature from the earlier behavioral emphasis to the current cognitive orientation. It also reflects the fruits of new research technology as well as the explosion of new instructional technologies.

The eight new authors are, in the judgment of the editors, recognized authorities on the pertinent research literature as well as successful researchers, teachers, and instructional designers and developers in their own right. In short, they are experts in relating research to practice, precisely what this book is all about.

Malcolm Fleming
W. Howard Levie
Bloomington, Indiana

# Introduction

## Malcolm Fleming

This book is for teachers and instructional developers who want to make appropriate choices among numerous instructional methods and materials, and who have found that knowing the subject matter and the learners is insufficient for making those choices wisely.

Our specific focus is on the neglected area of study that John Dewey (1900) referred to as a "linking science" between learning theory and educational practice. My interest in this area began in the 1960s as I attempted to bridge for students the gap between the research and theory of educational psychology courses and the concrete task of planning effective instruction and producing useful instructional materials.

The basic mechanisms we have found for bridging the chasm between educational research and practice are *principles*, dozens of them, that state research-based links between instructional condition and learning outcomes, and that do so with a minimum of technical terminology.

Reigeluth (1983) makes a pertinent distinction between descriptive and prescriptive principles. Though both involve instructional conditions and outcomes, descriptive principles merely describe certain processes of learning, while prescriptive principles translate these into prescribed methods of instruction. Clearly, the latter is of greater utility to teachers and instructional developers because it links means and ends, i.e., it links instructional methods with learning outcomes. The instructional design task, for both teachers and developers, is directly facilitated by principles that indicate which instructional methods are likely to lead to the designers' intended outcomes.

The intent of the authors of this book was to be as prescriptive, i.e., as precise regarding instructional conditions and methods, as the present research literature allows. However, the desire to make the principles as widely applicable as possible across subject matters and learners has limited the specificity of the principles. Where principles appear more descriptive, the provision of specific examples of their uses has added a more prescriptive dimension.

Thus, the book provides the designer some reliable guidelines for answering the key design question: What is the best way of teaching this? Or more generally, What instructional *conditions* will most likely lead to the desired *outcome*? A relevant design principle should, in a parallel statement, indicate what *conditions* have been found in research to be associated with the *outcome*.

However, we have carefully avoided making a book of rules, a cookbook. Applying the principles will require careful analysis of learners, content, and intent, as well as making creative and intuitive leaps from general principles to specific practice. Further, in as complex and multifactored a process as human learning, the authors can make no guarantees. It is the responsibility of users to test their designs and redesign as necessary.

## What Is Instructional Message Design?

Reigeluth (1983) defines the broader term "instructional design" as "...the process of deciding what methods of instruction are best for bringing about desired changes in student knowledge and skills for a specific course content and a specific student population." This book goes beyond his "methods" of instruction toward specifying the characteristics of appropriate instructional "messages."

A "message" is a pattern of signs (words, pictures, gestures) produced for the purpose of modifying the psychomotor, cognitive, or affective behavior of one or more persons. The term does not imply any particular medium or vehicle of instruction.

"Design" refers to a deliberate process of analysis and synthesis that begins with an instructional problem and concludes with a concrete plan or blueprint for a solution.

Instructional message design can occur either before or during instruction. Teachers typically do both, i.e., they plan instruction ahead of time—predesign—and they also modify it during execution—extemporaneous design (Gagné, 1970). Many principles in this book would be useful in both situations. Nunan (1983) makes the distinction between teacher design and professional design, i.e., design "from the classroom" in contrast to design from a distance. Our view is that designers in both contexts can benefit from principles that inform the kinds of decisions each makes. This book is written primarily in the spirit of predesign (whether by teacher or developer), for predesign permits more careful consideration of more factors. It also facilitates pre-testing, evaluation, and re-design.

"Instruction" as used here will refer not only to relatively formal classroom contexts in which the acquisition of particular skills and concepts is central, but also will include much of what the term "communication" implies, including informal contexts of various types where attitudes as well as skills and concepts are communicated.

## Limitations

Some words of caution are necessary here. Despite the utility and validity of the research-based principles that follow, the reader may not find clear-cut or easy answers to design problems. The complexity of practical instructional problems is greater than can be adequately encompassed by present-day research-based principles of human behavior.

The first edition used the qualifier: Aotbe, which meant: all-other-things-being-equal. This caution also applies to this edition. It means that while the principles hold under controlled research conditions, they may vary under applied conditions, i.e., other factors may reduce, enhance, or otherwise change their expected effect.

Adherence to the procedures and principles offered in this book will not automatically result in better learning, and these ideas are not offered as substitutes for the teacher/designer's experience and creativity.

It is expected, however, that this information will guide the insightful designer to analyze problems from more than one point of view, and may suggest effective solutions that would otherwise have been overlooked. The message designers who gain here a richer understanding of the diversity of factors that influence human behavior should be less prone to overconfidence in their ability to teach with unerring fidelity, but should also, in fact, be much more likely to be successful teachers and instructional developers.

# References

Dewey, J. (1900). Psychology and social practice. *The Psychological Review, 7,* 105–124.

Gagné, R. M. (1970). *The conditions of learning.* New York: Holt, Rinehart, & Winston.

Nunan, T. (1983). *Countering educational design.* New York: Nichols.

Reigeluth, C. M. (1983). Instructional design: What is it and why is it? In C. M. Reigeluth (Ed.), *Instructional design theories and models: An overview of their current status* (pp. 3–16). Hillsdale, NJ: Lawrence Erlbaum Associates.

# Table of Contents

# INSTRUCTIONAL MESSAGE DESIGN

## Principles from the Behavioral and Cognitive Sciences

**SECOND EDITION**

# Chapter 1

# Motivation Principles

## John Keller and Ernest Burkman

### Florida State University

## Introduction

The design of an instructional message is not complete without considering its motivational appeal. The extent to which an instructional stimulus will be received, acquired, and applied depends on the student's *willingness* to learn and perform in addition to his or her *ability* to do so. Most designers would agree with these assertions, but many would think of motivation as a consideration to be brought up late in the design process—an embellishment of a draft design to make it more interesting. Yet, *for the learner*, motivation is an initial determining factor that colors all that follows in a learning event. Motivation should be considered throughout the design and development process (Okey & Santiago, 1991), not just as an embellishment.

It is because of the primacy of motivation for the learner that this chapter is placed first. It serves as a signal to the designer to give these principles both early consideration and constant attention throughout the design process.

The principles contained in this chapter are divided into two parts. The first includes principles that apply generally to designing courseware that will be motivating regardless of the medium. Examples are included from various media. The second part focuses on text and graphics with a primary emphasis on text. This is still the most common medium, yet very little has been written on its specific motivational properties.

In the remainder of this introduction, several topics appear that are related to the concept of motivation; the parameters of the contents of this chapter; and several assumptions concerning the motivational principles.

### The Concept of Motivation

In its most general sense, motivation is defined as that which determines the magnitude and direction of behavior. Magnitude is generally regarded as degree of effort, and direction is generally defined in terms of goal orientation. Historically, there have been many approaches, theories, and constructs used to explain motivation, or aspects of it. For example, researchers have attempted to explain motivation in terms of *attitudes, beliefs, values, expectancies, attributions, needs, motives, deprivations,* and *incentives,* or *reinforcements.* Reviews and syntheses of these various approaches may be found in Beck (1990), Good and Brophy (1986), Keller (1983), Weiner (1985), and Wlodkowski (1985). The principles in this chapter are derived from these and secondary sources, and, for the most part, are based on reasonably well-established findings. However, it is often necessary to extrapolate based on the nature of the research, and to include principles based on validated practices rather than theories.

In considering ways to use media to motivate, it is difficult to draw firm conclusions from the empirical research. Many designers believe that effective use of communication media can contribute to increasing motivation to learn (Burbank & Pett, 1986). Their assumption is supported by some research, but rests heavily on conceptual frameworks and the opinion and experience of skillful practitioners (Macdonald-Ross, 1978a, 1978b; Duchastel, 1982). Formal studies on print materials of the effects of manipulating variables like graphics, typography, language, and page design have yielded contradictory results, and most were done in non-instructional contexts. Achievement, not motivation, is the dependent variable in most studies of how best to use media in instruction, and most experiments are single-variable studies with often contradictory results. Furthermore, much of the applied media research has dealt with optimizing the impact of brief messages with limited content, like television commercials and print advertisements, and so does not relate easily to instructional materials. This means that we must draw upon the experience and opinions of media professionals and instructional materials developers. Message design is still an art as well as a science (Duchastel, 1982).

As a means of defining the focus of this chapter, given the vastness of the literature on motivation and the potential influences of motivation on learning, several assumptions and parameters guided our work. They provide both the rationale and the framework for the approach taken here to the incorporation of motivation in message design.

## Assumptions

The motivation to learn depends largely on the learner's personality, the nature of the thing or skill to be learned, and the learner's perceptions of the value and difficulty of learning it. Since courseware designers have little control over the personalities of their audience, this implies that their best chance to motivate learners is simply to select carefully what they teach, and to teach it well. This is the position of many instructional design authorities (Gagné, 1985, p. 309).

In contrast to this attitude, our first assumption is that the motivation to learn is, in large part, a courseware designer's responsibility. One could also say that it is an instructor's responsibility or, more broadly, an educator's responsibility. This assumption is important because educators, both designers and instructors, all too often assume that motivation is the *student's* responsibility. "I can design (or teach) a good course," we often hear, "but it's up to the students to decide if they want to learn it." It is true that an educator cannot totally control a learner's motivation, but it is easy to demonstrate that poor instruction can demotivate an otherwise motivated learner, or that excellent instruction can inspire an otherwise demotivated learner.

The second assumption, which is implied by the phrase *motivation to learn*, is that in a context of message design, learner motivation is a means, not an end; that is, the goal in message design is to use principles of motivation to stimulate the *motivation to learn*. This stands in contrast to the inclusion of principles and strategies whose primary effect is *entertainment*. There is a tendency among educators to assume that they must be entertaining to be motivating. It is true that one can use entertaining approaches to stimulate the motivation to learn, but it will be apparent from the principles in this chapter that the motivation to learn is affected more profoundly by factors other than entertainment.

The third assumption is that designing instruction to be motivating can be a systematic process; it is not totally an art, or an intuitive process. The use of a systematic process of audience motivation analysis, and motivational design, development, and evaluation (Keller, 1987a, b) can lead predictably (Bickford, 1989) to more motivating instruction. The emphasis in this chapter is on the principles to use in the process, and not on the process itself.

Assumption four is that motivation must be considered in all parts of an instructional message. Gagné (1985) includes motivation as the first event of instruction, but it is limited primarily to gaining student attention. One also needs to consider the motivational appeal of every part of the message—the beginning, the middle, and the end—in addition to considering various types of motivational effects as included in the principles in this chapter.

The fifth and final assumption is that motivational design interventions can be studied in terms of their effects on motivation independently of their effects on performance, although this has not typically been done adequately in the instructional design literature. Motivation is intertwined with effectiveness and learner performance, and more effective instructional materials will generally motivate more students more strongly than ineffective ones. As discussed elsewhere (Keller, 1979, 1983), many principles that have been accepted in the instructional design literature describe effects in which there is a motivational relationship that has not been identified as such. For example, informing students of the goals or objectives can have an attention-getting, or energizing, effect as well as an attention-focusing, or information-acquisition, effect. Furthermore, the motivational effect can be positive or negative depending on how the objectives are presented and how they relate to the learner's expectations.

## Parameters

The primary focus of this chapter is on principles related to stimulating and sustaining the motivation to learn. The goal is *not* to provide principles on how to change personalities, or to teach specific motivational values or attitudes, although both of these are important to overall learner motivation The work of McCombs (1984) focuses on the problem of how to help students become self-motivated to learn. With respect to the teaching of attitudes, or what is sometimes called values education, Martin and Briggs (1986) have provided a comprehensive view of teaching for attitude change. (Attitude change principles follow in Chapter 7.) In the present chapter, there are principles concerned with attitude change, but the focus is on the development of positive attitudes and behaviors toward learning. Consequently, we will generally refer to the motivation to learn as opposed to motivation in general.

The second parameter concerns the audience, or population, to whom these principles apply. Although there are commonalities among people with respect to motivation, individual motivation is also highly idiosyncratic, and attributes that motivate one learner will not necessarily appeal to another. This means that courseware designers cannot expect to use media in any particular way to reach all members of a diverse audience. It also means that our topic is too complex to deal with comprehensively. Instead, we have chosen to focus primarily on ways to motivate what we call *typical* learners.

We define typical learners as those who are within a response range of moderately low to moderately high in regard to their willingness to respond positively to a learning event, or conversely, to lose interest if the instruction becomes boring or irrelevant. Efforts to use motivational tactics to stimulate and sustain the interest of these learners will usually have a positive effect on the group as a whole.

The situation is different with students who have severe motivational problems, or who have extremely high levels of self-motivation. The students with severe problems will usually require specialized, individualized assistance before their curiosity and achievement will improve. In these cases, the work of McCombs (1984) provides guidance on how to improve self-motivation.

The situation is usually quite different with premotivated learners—capable students who are studying a topic or skill that they want or need to learn. These learners will usually try very hard to learn from any relevant instruction no matter how the medium is used (i.e., medical students will study any textbook that they believe will help them pass a required anatomy course). In fact, studies have shown that efforts to make instructional materials *motivating* by adding unnecessary enhancements can distract premotivated learners and actually reduce their interest (Wilson, Pfister, & Fleury, 1981).

# I.  General Motivational Principles

## 1.  Variation and Curiosity

### 1.1.  *Changes in the organization and presentation of content can stimulate the learner's attention and curiosity.*

First impressions have an important influence on a person's attitude toward an object or situation. If you can stimulate a student's curiosity during the first few minutes of instruction, you are more likely to have a motivated student. Berlyne (1966) makes a distinction between perceptual and epistemic curiosity. Perceptual curiosity is aroused by unusual or unexpected stimuli that impact directly on a person's senses with little cognitive activity occurring between the perception and the response. This includes reflexive responses to stimuli, and the immediate impressions people form based on their cultural conditioning and training. The second major section of this chapter, *Text and Graphics*, contains several variations on this principle.

In contrast, epistemic curiosity is aroused by a perceived gap or incongruity based on the characteristics of a stimulus and a person's existing knowledge or expectations. When epistemic curiosity is aroused, a person is motivated to seek more information to resolve the incongruity. This can range from a brief investigation to years of study. The following principles incorporate this and other characteristics that influence the attention span of an audience.

### 1.2. Variation in sequencing of the elements (events) of instruction helps maintain attention.

A typical sequence of instructional events is the rule-example-practice approach to organizing instruction. It is, in most situations, the most efficient approach to teaching in that students are quickly introduced to the content, provided with examples, and then given learning exercises. It is also a very effective approach.

However, variations of this structure can be highly motivating, both as approaches in themselves, or as variations of the basic model. To begin with an exercise that students attack with their existing knowledge and skill stimulates student interest and involvement and also creates a desire to know the content that will follow. When the instruction then moves into explanations and examples followed by another opportunity to work on the same or a similar exercise, students get to satisfy their curiosity and feel rewarded by the immediate growth in their knowledge or skill.

### 1.3. Provoking mental conflict stimulates epistemic curiosity.

Mental conflict, at an appropriate level, is a useful way to stimulate the motivation to learn. Mental conflict can take many forms, some of which are highly stressful. In the present context, mild levels of mental conflict that do not threaten the mental well-being of the students can be used productively to stimulate curiosity. Following are three variations on this basic approach.

### 1.3a. Introduce topics problematically to stimulate an attitude of inquiry.

When students are presented with a problem that catches their interest, the stage is set for learning. Suchman (1966) developed a technique called *inquiry teaching*, not to be confused with discovery learning, which engages students in a process of creating problems that they then try to solve. For example, in a middle-school science class, the teacher might task students what purpose the leaves serve on a plant. Someone might know that oxygen is released by the leaves. The teacher might then ask, "How important to the plant is it for the leaves to be able to release oxygen?" Students might say a variety of things such as they do not know, the plant will die, or it does not matter. The teacher could then ask, "How could we find out?" This process could continue until, perhaps, the students decide to cover various amounts of leaves on a plant with wax, cover only the tops of leaves, cover tops and bottoms, etc., in order to find out what happens under various conditions. The inquiry approach can be used to launch a group into a large project, or it can be used for a period of minutes to create awareness of the problem for which the subsequent instruction is the solution. It can also serve as a bridge to relevance. As illustrated by the case in Figure 1.1, a problematic approach combined with some analogies (Principle 2.2b) and an application to a familiar situation (Principle 2.2a) helped build relevance for the unfamiliar situation.

### 1.3b. Use facts that contradict past experience, paradoxical examples, conflicting opinions or facts, unexpected opinions, or humor to stimulate curiosity.

People look for congruence among the facts and opinions in their lives (Festinger & Carlsmith, 1959), and when faced with contradiction they try to resolve it. Whether it is the child reading *Ripley's Believe It or Not* or a scientist trying to resolve conflicting explanations of a phenomenon, people are stimulated by conflict. In an instructional environment, the paradoxes, etc., should be used to stimulate interest in the instruction, and not become an end in themselves. Also, there are ethical considerations regarding the types of contradictions (real or apparent) to present, especially if the instructor is moving into a values dimension. Unless values exploration is part of the instructional goal, it is best to use conflictual situations that avoid such issues. One teacher of elementary school children begins one of her classes by asking, "What poisons did you eat today?" The children say, "None." She says, "Yes, you did." She then goes on to talk about nutrition and how some of the minerals that are necessary to sustain life are also poisonous *if* you eat too much of them. This leads to a discussion of other polluting and poisonous substances.

Humor can be an effective attention-getting tactic, but its effects are difficult to predict (F.E. 4.36[*]). People enjoy humor that is not destructive, but it can distract from the instructional aims and interfere with comprehension (Markiewicz, 1974; Sternthal & Craig, 1973).

### 1.3c. Invoke a sense of mystery by presenting unresolved problems which may or may not have a solution.

This principle is of the same type as the preceding ones. It varies only in the specific nature of the approach. Kaplan and Kaplan (1978) have shown how an attitude of inquiry can be simulated by evoking a sense of mystery in an environment. In an instructional setting, graphic illustrations that reveal only

---

[*]References to principles in the first edition (Fleming & Levie, 1978) will be indicated by *F.E.*, for *first edition*, and the principle number in that volume.

---

**CASE: THE SOCIAL STUDIES CHALLENGE**

*In his ninth grade social studies class, Gil Perkins had to teach a thematic unit on cities. It focused on politics, economics, education, and other aspects of a city's infrastructure such as distribution systems (food and merchandise) and communications. He had trouble motivating the interest of the students in his rural midwestern school with respect to this module. Almost none of them had ever been to a large city. Their impressions were formed by the excitement, drama, and usually, violence of television programs set in large cities. In contrast, this social studies information was not interesting or relevant to them.*

*After reading some material about "inquiry teaching," Gil began his unit this year by asking the class, "What would happen in a town of 12,500 people if the food supply were cut in half overnight?" The students were both surprised and intrigued by this question, which referred to a town the size of theirs. A lively discussion followed in which speculation turned into thoughtful discussion based on their knowledge of the close interactions of people in the town and the surrounding farms, ranches, and dairies.*

*After 20 minutes, Gil interrupted and asked the class what would happen if the food supply were cut in half overnight in a city of 1,250,000 people, and he named some cities of that approximate size. The discussion took a very different turn. It was much more speculative and reflected the values and beliefs of the students based on their home backgrounds, travel experience, and television preferences. It soon became obvious that they were dealing purely in speculation and could not meaningfully analyze the situation.*

*At that point Gil introduced the new module and explained how the things they would learn would help them better understand what might happen. Before beginning the module, he and the class summarized a list of their key questions and predictions. As he taught the material, Gil had the students relate it to the small town situation and to the list of questions and predictions.*

**Figure 1.1.** A technique for stimulating curiosity and building relevance. This case illustrates how curiosity and relevance can be increased by using a problematic opening combined with relating the new material to something already familiar to the students.

---

parts of the stimulus and then use progressive disclosure to reveal the rest can evoke a mild sense of mystery, especially when the visual has various parts that are revealed in a non-liner manner. The mysteries of the dinosaurs, the ancient Egyptians, and the pre-Columbian civilizations of Central and South America have been used countless times to stimulate curiosity in school projects, mystery novels, and adventure films.

# 2. Need Stimulation (Relevance)

### *2.1.* *Strengthen the students' motivation to learn by building relationships between the content and objectives of the instruction and the learner's needs and desires.*

This principle, at some levels, is both intuitively obvious and supported by research (Keller, 1983). People make decisions about how to spend their time based on both necessity and desire. Teachers know that their content will be more appealing if they can bridge it to the needs or goals of the students.

The importance of this principle of relevance is illustrated by many areas of research, including the traditional studies of needs and motives (e.g., Murray, 1938; McClelland, 1976). Relevance is the central concept of a theory of communication and cognition (Sperber & Wilson, 1986), and it can help explain the research on selective attention. The structure and content of one's existing cognitive, linguistic, and experiential foundation gives direction, or goal orientation, to one's motivation, and to a person's perception of meaningfulness in behavior.

How does the instructional designer deal with this phenomenon in an instructional environment? The following principles represent several aspects of relevance that can be influenced in the design of messages.

### *2.2* *People are usually most interested in things that are related to their existing knowledge and skills.*

People tend to be most interested in things which build upon existing interests, and they tend to notice and understand things which confirm or build upon their existing knowledge base. This does not contradict the influence of novelty and curiosity, as indicated in some of the principles listed under Principle 1. People vary in their level of activation, sensation-seeking, and curiosity, but their exercise of these characteristics tends to be contextual. That is, people who are interested in sports cars and have a high level of curiosity will order magazines, go to trade shows, and do other things to find the novel experience or unusual piece of information related to sports cars. People tend not to become interested in whole new categories of things, unless something happens in their lives to make them relevant. For example, the person who experiences the death of a friend or relative may become interested in reading and learning about the grieving process. The point is that relevance and curiosity work together in helping people build meaningful yet stimulating life experiences. The case in Figure 1.1 illustrates this principle.

### *2.2a.* *Use explicit statements about how the instruction builds on the learner's existing skills or knowledge.*

When the connection of new instruction to existing knowledge or skill is not self-evident, a simple verbal description of the relationship can help build the bridge from the new to the old. Trigonometry, for example, is not nearly so foreign looking, with its strange-sounding concepts such as *cosine,* if the teacher illustrates how some of the simple mathematical skills already possessed by the students will help them get off to a good start.

This process will succeed if the students are already interested in math, but it will not establish relevance. To do that, the teacher may be able to relate the subject to hobbies or other interests of the students. A traditional example in trigonometry is to show how it can be used to estimate distances that cannot be directly measured. The height of trees or mountains, or the distance across a lake can be estimated easily by using trigonometry. This could be of interest to anyone interested in orienteering, mountaineering, or navigation.

### 2.2b. *Use analogies or metaphors to connect the present material to processes, concepts, skills already familiar to the learner.*

People often use metaphor when attempting to describe events for which they lack literal language. This is one of the ways in which we expand the boundaries of our knowledge (Wheelwright, 1962). Metaphor and analogy are also effective ways of improving motivation (Curtis & Reigeluth, 1984). A good analogy, like a good bridge, helps connect the unknown to the known. The case in Figure 1.1 illustrates how students' interest in a topic lacking in personal relevance can be stimulated by building an analogical comparison between a local situation and the remote one.

### 2.3. *The motivation to learn is greater when there is a clear relationship between the instructional objectives and the student's goals.*

In contrast to the previous set of principles, which refer to the established interests and knowledge of the students, this principle is more future oriented. Together with the previous set, it probably constitutes the most frequently used technique for establishing relevance. This principle is also supported by the literature on persuasion, which demonstrates that arguments are more effective if they are relevant to the receiver's needs (Ch. 7, 1.6*). In both school and non-school settings, instructors look for ways to connect their content to the goals that their students are likely to have. Typically this is easier in a vocational than a basic school or liberal arts setting, but often there is a way to make the connections to existing student goals, or to inspire the creation of new goals.

---

*References to principles in Chapter 7 of this edition will be indicated by Ch. 7, followed by principle number.

> ***2.3a.*** *To stimulate goal orientation, provide explicit statements describing how the given instruction is or can be related to meaningful goals in the student's future.*

As in Principle 2.2a, this principle indicates that simple verbal statements can be used to help students make the connections. By relating the instructional goals to the requirements of jobs, subsequent educational goals, or professional development, the instructor can help the student see connections that were not self-evident. It is best not to try to use this strategy in an artificial or forced manner. If there is no clear connection, then some of the other principles in this section can be used to establish relevance.

> ***2.3b.*** *Use examples and exercises that are related to the student's present or future area of application to increase the student's perception that the instruction has relevance.*

Examples and exercises from an area of application that is related to the student's goals provide more convincing evidence of relevance than explicit statements used by themselves. Sometimes, for purposes of economy, *generic* courses in areas such as statistics or management are offered for majors from all disciplines rather than having separate courses in different colleges. However, Ross (1983) has shown that in regard to statistics, for example, there are motivational and learning benefits to offering versions of the course that have examples from the discipline in which they are taught. At other times, an instructor might not know what the learners' areas of application are. An exercise such as the one in Figure 1.2 allows the instructor to find points of relevance while actively engaging the students, which is a preferred learning style for most people (Principle 2.4b).

> **2.4.**   *Stimulate the motivation to learn by giving students the opportunity to satisfy high-valence motives.*

As a substitute, or supplement, to stimulating relevance based on goals, as in the preceding examples, it is possible to build relevance by using strategies that appeal to the basic motive structure of the students. The traditional need- or motive-based theories of motivation demonstrate (Atkinson & Raynor, 1974; McClelland, 1976) that people have rather stable sets of motivational proclivities that lead them to consistently seek the same kinds of experiences. These desires do not become satiated in the ways that one would expect from a conditioning theory of behavior. On the contrary, people who are high in need for achievement, for example, tend to be energized by opportunities to exercise that motive.

In this regard, it is best to present need-arousing information prior to need-satisfying information (F.E. 4.29). Cohen (1964) found that students were more responsive to information about the characteristics of a particular grading

**HAVE YOU EVER HAD A PROBLEM
WITH STUDENT MOTIVATION?**

What kinds of motivational problems do you encounter in the classroom or
with the materials you produce?  List three or more motivational problems
faced by you or other developers or instructors in the courses you deliver.
In other words, what kinds of motivational problems are presented by the
participants (students) or the situation?

1.

2.

3.

4.

5.

**Figure 1.2.** A relevance-building activity. After having the participants list problems, the
instructor can relate the workshop content to the audience's concerns.

method after they had been told that grading standards might be toughened.
This technique is consistent with Principle 1.3a in that students are engaged in a
problem-oriented perspective which then stimulates their desire to learn the
solution.

### 2.4a. *Use personal language to stimulate human interest on the part of the learner.*

Flesch (1948) and Flesch and Lass (1949) demonstrated that people prefer
writing that is high in terms of personal interest. Specifically, it was found that
people prefer text that uses personal pronouns and names of specific people. The
use of action words or vivid modifiers did not seem to make a difference.

A primary interest of people is people, especially themselves. As a
consequence, many authorities stress the importance of referring to people as a

technique for making prose interesting (Keller & Suzuki, 1988). One suggested way to do this in written text is to link events with people and to refer to people directly by name or indirectly through the use of personal pronouns or other personal references, such as uncle, sister, or grandfather (Flesch, 1948). Another is to include direct quotes (Murray, 1938).

One way to accomplish this is to add a human interest story to technical material. For example, physics textbooks often contain a section on the laws of motion that features descriptions of rolling objects and colliding masses. For non-scientists this material is not terribly exciting, but the human touch might be added by including text that describes the kind of person that Issac Newton was and how he came to discover the laws of motion. Naturally, the writer would have to be careful that students do not get distracted so much by Newton's life that they lose the point of the instruction.

Gunning (1968), Trimble (1975), and many others feel that another form of human interest is especially important for writers—using a conversational tone or "writing as if you were talking to the reader." Flesch and Lass (1949) describe this as "making the reader feel that he or she is listening to a friend." Two important elements of a conversational tone are using personal pronouns extensively (e.g., "you," "we") and using everyday words rather than formal English.

### 2.4b. *Improve relevance by adapting your course requirements and teaching style to the learning style of the students.*

The research on aptitude-treatment interactions (Cronbach & Snow, 1976) suggests that there are no effects strong enough to support prescriptions for differential approaches to teaching, but other approaches to defining and studying learning styles do support this principle, especially those that are defined in terms of a specific learner characteristic, such as the need for achievement or the need for affiliation. Learners with a high need for achievement tend to prefer (Altschuler, 1973; deCharms, 1976) situations where there are clearly defined standards of quality and success (defined either by themselves or others), and a degree of moderate challenge. Also, they like to have a great deal of personal control in working to achieve the goals. When they require assistance, they look for experts, whether or not the expert is a friend. From a persuasion perspective, credible sources are those with high perceived expertise (Ch. 7, 1.1, plus discussion).

In contrast, many students prefer a cooperative group environment (Slavin, 1984) in which they do not have to experience competition. They enjoy the opportunity to work in a friendly, helpful environment. Credibility, from their perspective, comes largely from the trustworthiness of the source (Ch. 7, 1.1).

### 2.5. *Role modeling of the value, utility, and interest of the instruction can stimulate intrinsic motivation and personal goal setting.*

This type of motivational stimulation results in the formation of new or reinforced attitudes; consequently the principles of modeling that apply in attitude formation also apply here. The strength of modeling on the formation of attitudes is demonstrated in the extensive work of Bandura (e.g., 1977), and the frequent use of testimonials and role models in advertising and marketing.

### 2.5a. *The enthusiasm of an instructor or speaker can stimulate positive motivation from the students.*

People respond to their environments as well as to their internal motives, goals, and attitudes. Most current theories of motivation involve assumptions or principles that account for the interaction of the person with the environment in relation to the formation and continued stimulation of individual motivation. Consequently, it is possible to inspire motivation in students even when they do not initially perceive relevance based on outcomes or process (style of teaching).

An enthusiastic teacher, or textual materials that convey a sense of enthusiasm in the writing style, or other media such as video that model the desired behavior, can stimulate a motivated response from the learners. In the long run, other aspects of relevance will have to be activated to sustain the perception of relevance, but this is an excellent approach to helping the students develop a new area of interest.

### 2.5b. *Increase personal interest by including anecdotes or vignettes about noteworthy people in the area of study, the obstacles they faced, their accomplishments, and the consequences.*

Another type of modeling that can stimulate motivation is provided by the use of anecdotes. To know that other human beings have experienced certain achievements, and to know what they were thinking, feeling, and facing as challenges, helps a person develop personal goals and direction. McConnell (1978), in conducting developmental tryouts of his psychology text, found a definite positive effect for the insertion of vignettes, with photographs, of famous people in psychology, and personal-interest information about them.

### 2.5c. *Increase the motivation to change behavior by including the learners as role players in a role modeling episode.*

Active participation in a learning activity that requires one to demonstrate a given behavior or attitude increases the likelihood of acquiring the new behavior or attitude (Ch. 7, Section 2). As illustrated by the story (Ch. 7, 2.4), the subjects who had to role-play smokers who were receiving news of a malignant tumor in their lungs, and would require immediate surgery with only a moderate chance for a successful outcome, reduced their smoking behavior more than the control subjects who only listened to a recording of one of the role-playing sessions (Miller & Burgoon, 1973).

### 2.6. *Use images, values, and other features of the course materials or instructors that are similar to those of the learners to increase perceived relevance.*

People tend to respond most positively to other people or sources of information that reflect their perceptions of their own appearance, values, and circumstances. Much of the research support for this principle is located in the literature on persuasion, advertising, and communication, and is represented in several principles in Chapter 7 (e.g., 1.2, plus discussion, 1.3, and 1.5). This principle supports the concerns of many groups that illustrations include the variety of ethnic backgrounds and gender balance that are found in the student audience for a given set of course materials.

# 3. Challenge Level

### 3.1. *Design the challenge level to produce an appropriate expectancy for success.*

If the actual or perceived challenge level in an instructional situation is either too high or too low, students will be improperly motivated. If the actual challenge level is too high, then an appropriate response is for the student to quit trying and to seek help or to work to build the necessary prerequisites. If the challenge level is too low, it suggests that the student already knows a great deal of the material, and the student will lose interest or not notice the specific areas in which there is something new to be learned.

If the perceived challenge level is too high, the student is likely to have a low level of persistence, and to quit trying to succeed, even though he or she has the ability to succeed. Conversely, if the perceived challenge level is too low, the student is overconfident and tends not to believe that there is anything new to be learned.

The relationship between perceived challenge level and performance tends to follow the shape of an inverted U-curve. Known as the Yerkes-Dodson law (Yerkes & Dodson, 1908), it indicates that when motivation, or arousal, is too low then performance will be low due to boredom or indifference. When motivation, or arousal, is too high, performance will be low, again due to excessive stress. This principle was included in the first edition of this book in relation to anxiety and attitude change (F.E. 4.33).

A key point in this research is the importance of the performer's perceptions of the challenge level of the task. In this regard, the research on attribution theory (e.g., Weiner, 1985) and other factors that influence an individual's perceptions of control and expectancy for success (see Keller, 1983, for a review) apply to the principles in this section.

### 3.2. *People are more confident in their likelihood of reaching a goal if they know where they are going.*

A highly supported principle in instructional design is that students will learn more effectively if they have advance information that helps them focus their study on the concepts and skills that ultimately will be tested. This relationship is supported by many areas of research, such as that on objectives, adjunct questions, and advance organizers.

In addition to its positive effect on learning, by helping the students focus on what to learn, it improves motivation. When a person knows what has to be achieved, providing the perceived challenge level is appropriate, the person will have a higher degree of expectancy for success. The increased level of effort combined with actual successes then support each other in sustaining motivation.

### 3.2a. *Describe goals and performance requirements to help learners set realistic expectations for success.*

In instruction the goals are usually provided. Typically the instruction has been designed to lead the student toward the accomplishment of prespecified goals. Frequently, however, students will respond to inquiries about the purpose and performance requirements of a course by saying that they do not know. Somehow this information is not transmitted effectively to the students. A simple statement of the objectives is not usually sufficient, as indicated by the inconsistent results of research on informing students of objectives. The goals and performance requirements have to be presented, reiterated, and supported by the examples and exercises in the instruction.

Often, students will not be able to anticipate what their questions or sources of confusion will be until after they have begun working on an assignment. A professor who knows from past experience that this will happen, and whose course meets only once a week, can use a "motivational message" (Visser & Keller, 1990) to give additional guidance and support when they are needed. A motivational message is a greeting card type of note which can be prepared easily even with simple graphics and text software. The message in Figure 1.3, which the professor placed in student mailboxes or mailed to their homes, had a positive effect on confidence. It also increased relevance by modeling the value that the professor placed on this topic, and demonstrated his concern for the students' success (Principle 2.5).

### 3.2b. *Increase self-direction by providing ways for learners to set their own goals.*

Learners who have well-defined goals, and the maturity to study independently, respond well to setting their own goals. Providing that these

**Figure 1.3.** A group motivational message. This message, sent individually to each student as a potential confidence booster, reaches the students outside of class at a time when the instructor knows they might be having problems.

conditions are met on the part of the learner, and the course of instruction lends itself to individualization, personal goal setting can be an effective way of helping students to build a positive expectancy for success and increase the personal relevance of the instruction.

### *3.3     Persistence in learning activities is enhanced if learners attribute their success to their own effort and ability.*

Attribution theory (Nicholls, 1984; Weiner, 1985) indicates that people interpret the outcomes of their behavior in terms of causality. That is, they make assumptions about whether their successes and failures were due to external factors such as luck, powerful others, or task difficulty, or to internal factors such as ability and effort. Some of these factors, such as ability and task difficulty, are fairly stable and not easy to change. Others, such as effort, luck, and powerful others, are more unstable, or unpredictable.

### *3.3a.    Build confidence and persistence by using easy to difficult sequencing of content, exercises, and exams, especially for less able and low-confidence students.*

When students face a series of difficult tasks, including some which are too difficult, they will quit trying at some point. Furthermore, they may develop the perception that the work is too difficult or that they do not have the ability to do it. When this happens, they may fail at relatively easy tasks because they have already developed the expectancy of failure. Good students usually learn to scan the material and look for easier problems to do first. But less able students have trouble with this tactic. For one thing, they often cannot readily tell the difference between an easy and a difficult problem. In contrast, sequencing from easy to difficult helps students develop confidence as they have a series of successes, and it can help them be more persistent at difficult tasks, which leads them further into success.

The perceived challenge level can inhibit learners even when they are able to do the work. The case in Figure 1.4 illustrates how an instructor divided a task into two parts to build a less threatening sequence of instruction.

---

### CASE: A PROBLEM OF STRESS INDUCED ERRORS

*The trainees for a one-day course on a new computerized accounting system consisted of bookkeepers and secretaries responsible for entering travel receipts and other financial items. The instruction was on-line so that it would have high relevance to the actual performance conditions.*

*Lucille, the instructor, noticed that many trainees were making mistakes because of their nervousness about learning the new procedures and about working on the computer. Lucille knew that the mistakes were not due to lack of ability because the new procedures were actually simpler than the old ones.*

*She revised her approach by having the trainees learn and practice small parts of a more complex procedure off-line using pencils and worksheets. Then she had them do the procedure on the computer. Their confidence in their ability to do the accounting process and in using the computer increased more rapidly, and stress related errors decreased immediately.*

---

**Figure 1.4.** Reducing the perceived challenge level. In this case the trainees perceived the task to be more challenging than it actually was. The *motivational* tactic in this case was to reduce the perceived challenge level by revising the *instructional* strategy. This increased the trainees' expectancies for success, and their performance improved.

### 3.3b. Use design principles of internal consistency to build learner trust and confidence.

Exercises and measurements should be consistent with the objectives, content, and examples. This helps avoid the perception among students that their success is going to be influenced heavily by luck or powerful others. That is, when internal consistency is lacking, students worry about whether they will be "lucky" enough to study the right material, and whether the teacher or professor will choose to like the work they have done. Using "trick" or excessively difficult questions as a means of creating challenge conveys the impression that the student's success or failure is at the whim of the instructor. When there is internal consistency, the student can make more accurate predictions of the likelihood of success based upon his or her own effort and ability.

### 3.3c. Provide criteria for success and answers to exercises to encourage students to use self-evaluation of performance.

People like to be and appear competent to themselves and others (White, 1959). However, it is normal during the learning process to be "incompetent" in a sense. That is, the student is trying to learn something he or she does not already know. Consequently, if students can work on exercises and get feedback without attracting the attention of others, it helps avoid the anxiety that is aroused by the possibility of making mistakes and seeming to be incompetent. It also helps students build more of an internal attribution of success. After completing a set of learning activities and evaluating their results, the students can then take criterion tests that include external evaluations.

In some situations this principle does not apply. Some learning activities do not lend themselves to self-evaluation, and some students are not sufficiently motivated or confident to benefit from this opportunity. In these situations, it is important to try to create a supportive psychological climate during the learning phase so that students are not afraid to try new skills.

### 3.3d. Help students build confidence by providing confirmational feedback for acceptable responses, and corrective feedback for responses that do not meet criteria.

During the learning process, it is very demotivating to never know how well you are performing. People with a high need for achievement have a strong desire for feedback regarding how well they are progressing. Confirmational feedback simply tells people when they are correct, and has been shown to have a beneficial influence on learning when the correct response is not self-evident. Corrective feedback tells the student what is wrong with a response, not just that it is wrong.

### 3.4    Include learner options to promote an internal sense of control on the part of the learner.

The opportunity to have some control over the outcomes of one's behavior, combined with the perception of control, generally results in less stress for a learner or decision-maker (Weiss, 1972), yet it is difficult to predict how people will respond to the availability of control. This is due in part to the fact that people's perceptions of control diverge from the objective level of control in a set of situations. Some people consistently underestimate their control, while others overestimate (Bandura, 1977; deCharms, 1976; Rotter, 1972). It most often appears to be beneficial to help develop perceptions that are on the positive side, because this creates a positive "self-fulfilling prophecy" (Livingston, 1969) and higher levels of performance (Perlmuter & Monty, 1977). Negative expectations lead toward underachievement and feelings of helplessness (Seligman, 1975).

### 3.4a.  Allow learners to go at their own pace to increase motivation and performance.

Working under pressure can be energizing when performing a task at which you are competent and when you are confident about your chances of success. However, when acquiring a new skill, stress tends to result in a deterioration of performance. Carroll's (1963) theory of school learning posits that time is a key variable in learning. If people are given the time they require, they can succeed at most learning tasks. Part of the reason for this is that there is more opportunity for rehearsal and other cognitive and psychomotor activities that are necessary for acquisition and retention. But, there is also a motivational component. Knowing that time is not a source of pressure, especially during the early phases of learning new content or skills, the student will experience a lower stress level and work at a more optimal level of motivation. If time pressure is part of the final performance requirement, introduce it gradually as the students master the basic content and skills.

### 3.4b.  Develop self-direction by providing a well-defined, but not rigid, structure that gives learners options for assignments, modes of study, and modes of testing.

A classic study on leadership style demonstrated that when students are working under a democratic, or participative, style of leadership they are very productive and their productivity does not diminish when the leader leaves the classroom. Both authoritarian and laissez-faire styles did not work well. This study focused on organizational structure, which is an important aspect of classroom management.

With respect to studies of learner control over instruction, the research is not clear. At this point, there is no clear picture of what the parameters of learner control are. However, there are some types of learner control that learners tend to enjoy. In classroom settings, students appreciate the opportunity, whether or not they exercise it, for alternative approaches to testing, and for individualizing assignments such as term papers. In a context of computer-based instruction, Merrill (1975) found that learner control over the sequencing of instructional events did not influence motivation or learning. Other studies indicate that learner control over certain aspects of computer-based instruction does result in more positive attitudes.

A degree of learner control appears to be an important motivator for the person who is self-motivated and has clearly defined personal goals, or at the other extreme, the person who can't perform well under the prescribed conditions.

### 3.5.   *Learner confidence and efforts to succeed are increased in proportion to the perceived credibility of the source.*

Learners will be more motivated to learn if they believe in the truth and appropriateness of the materials presented to them. The credibility of an instructor or a set of course materials is influenced by several factors concerning the qualifications of the instructor, the reputation of the publisher, the quality and structure of the arguments in a message, and the correspondence of values and beliefs between the learners and the source of information. As with Principle 2.6, much of this research is found in the communication literature, particularly in the areas of persuasion and advertising, and there are several principles on this topic in Chapter 7 (e.g., 1.3, plus discussion, and 1.4).

## 4. Positive Outcomes

### 4.1.   *Use intrinsically satisfying outcomes and positive rewards to produce continuing motivation to learn.*

To have a group of students succeed in accomplishing the objectives of a course is not necessarily to succeed as an instructional designer or teacher. Consider the following dialogue.

Tom:   "That was a great class. I passed it and I'm looking forward to taking the next course on this subject."

Mary:   "The class was okay. I passed it too, but I never want to study this subject again!"

Jack:   "What are you saying, Tom? It was a terrible class. I'm glad I passed it, but I'm not happy with it, and I certainly do not want to take another class on this subject."

All three students were motivated enough to finish the course, but only Tom has continuing motivation which, according to Maher (1976), is characterized by a voluntary effort on the part of the student to continue learning in a given topic area. Mary was satisfied with the course, but her satisfaction was lukewarm, and she has no continuing motivation for the subject. Jack was minimally satisfied in that he did pass, but his overall dissatisfaction was high, and he certainly has no continuing motivation.

Research under several topics (e.g., continuing motivation, intrinsic motivation, and behavioral psychology) illustrates that the appropriate use of intrinsic and extrinsic reinforcers facilitates the development of learner satisfaction and continuing motivation. Extrinsic rewards, such as awards, grades, money, promotion, or tokens, are useful when the students lack intrinsic motivation, or to supplement, but not overwhelm, intrinsically satisfying consequences.

### 4.2. The opportunity to apply newly acquired skills in a meaningful way contributes to intrinsic satisfaction.

To be able to apply something that you have learned, to discover a new level of competence (White, 1959), is reinforcing. There are two aspects to this principle that make it intrinsic rather than extrinsic as a reinforcer. The first is that the learner is doing something meaningful, which means that the task has positive value to the learner. Secondly, the learner is doing something at which success in and of itself is satisfying, and it does not involve the receipt of an external reward or a controlling influence by another person.

This principle also supports the tactic of engaging students in a problem-oriented perspective (see 1.3a and 2.3) before presenting information related to a solution. After the students are engaged, it becomes important to have an outcome that confirms the anticipated relevance and provides a meaningful solution to the problem.

This type of outcome is also satisfying because it provides confirmation of the perceived relevancy and positive expectancy for success that were presumably established earlier.

### 4.2a. Promote feelings of accomplishment by including, in the instructional materials, exercises or problems that require the application of the new knowledge or skill to solve.

The use of instructionally relevant exercises means that the student will receive an exercise that is congruent with the knowledge and skills that were acquired in the lesson, and that could not be solved without that knowledge and skill. This is an obvious example of the principle stated in 4.2, but there is an assumption that the exercise not be trivial; that is, that it not be a duplicate of the kinds of problems or exercises solved in the learning activities. Too often, a student will finish pages of practice problems only to receive identical problems in the final exercise. This might provide a satisfying consequence to insecure or relatively unmotivated learners; indeed, it is a better situation than when the students receive problems that are unrelated, deceivingly tricky, or that require excessive degrees of inference to leap from what was actually learned to the requirements of the test. In the present example, however, the exercise must require the *application* of the new knowledge and skills to the exercise situation and not be simply a repetition of an already learned response.

### 4.2b. Produce a perception of natural consequences by using an exercise or simulation that resembles the real world application of the new knowledge or skill.

This is similar to the preceding principle, differing only in the degree of verisimilitude relative to the actual job or other post-course application. Lab exercises, as in scientific or vocational education classes, simulations when a lab would be unfeasible or too expensive, and role plays in soft-skill areas have all been shown to increase transfer, and to have a positive motivational consequence in the form of increased learner confidence, satisfaction, or other positive affective indicators.

### 4.3. Reward accomplishment by using positive feedback following success at a challenging task.

A key word in this principle is *challenging.* The challenge is relative to the abilities and perceptions of the learner. For one learner, the difficulty level would have to be quite high before the learner would feel a sense of challenge and accomplishment. For another student, simply completing an assignment, without regard to quality, would be a rewardable challenge. A critical factor is to acknowledge, by means of positive comments, the effort that went into succeeding at a task that is challenging relative to the abilities and confidence of the performer. This requirement, together with several others related to the effects of positive outcomes, was included in the first edition. (F.E. 4.39, 4.46, and 4.58).

### 4.3a. To build learner satisfaction, use congratulatory comments for performances that meet the criteria for success.

This principle refers to positive, or motivational, feedback, not corrective feedback. This distinction, which grew out of behavioral psychology and programmed instruction research, is critical in distinguishing between the use of feedback to stimulate motivation versus learning. As formulated by Tosti (1978), motivational feedback should occur as soon as possible after a performance, and should pertain to those aspects of performance that have met the criteria for success. Corrective feedback, which can negate motivational feedback if offered simultaneously, should be delayed until it is immediately useful. That is, corrective feedback should be offered when the learner is ready to use the feedback in a new effort to succeed at the task. The individualized motivation message (Visser & Keller, 1990) in Figure 1.5 illustrates how a teacher rewarded an improving student while avoiding the negative effect of simultaneous criticism.

At this point, in contrast to the use of confirmatory or corrective feedback (see Principle 3.3d), the emphasis is on personal reinforcement for successful task completion. The affective aspects of expressing positive attitudes toward the student are the focus rather than supporting the student's cognitive

**Figure 1.5.** An individual motivational message. A personal written message may have a more lasting influence on a student's feelings of satisfaction than a verbal comment or a brief comment on the assignment itself.

understanding of outcomes (hence, the student's formation of effort–success expectancies) as in Principle 3.3d.

### 4.3b. Stimulate the learner's feelings of pleasure by including enthusiastic comments which model positive feelings associated with goal accomplishment.

Being successful in school learning, or in any other endeavor, is a state of mind as well as an accomplishment. People high in need of achievement sometimes underrate their achievements, which leads to greater anxiety about future successes. Consequently, the motivation to continue to succeed and feelings of high self-esteem are stimulated by the modeling of positive feelings associated with achievement. This is true whether the feelings are modeled by an instructor or presented through media. This is particularly important for learners who have been anxious or who tend to undervalue their accomplishments.

### 4.3c.  *Reward self-directed actions by including statements which acknowledge actions, student characteristics, risks, or challenges that were necessary for success.*

Satisfaction increases following success when a student attributes success to his or her personal abilities and efforts. Consequently, statements which overtly make the attributional connection between student actions and personal characteristics and which contribute to overcoming risks and obstacles either reinforce or help the student develop internal attributions.

### 4.4.  *Extrinsic rewards help maintain motivation to learn repetitive material, or material that is in other ways intrinsically uninteresting.*

Although the research on intrinsic motivation and cognition has led to revisions of the traditional assumptions of behavioral psychology, there are learning situations in which simple extrinsic reinforcement is beneficial as a satisfying reward for sustained effort or achievement. This is particularly true when the learning task involves rote learning of verbal information or procedures, and there is little that can be done efficiently to present the material problematically or to otherwise increase its intrinsic interest. The rewards do not have to be of significant value, such as grades or money. Token rewards, such as extra play time for young children and certificates or mementos for older children and adults (Figure 1.6), can be very effective if used contingently with appropriate reinforcement schedules.

### 4.4a.  *Games with scoring systems can add an extrinsically motivating outcome to instruction.*

Games are popular with many people. Witness the sales of board games, and the numbers of people found in video arcades. In instruction, games can be used effectively as rewards in several ways. They can be used purely as diversions after the students have achieved a preset criterion for time on task or task accomplishment. In this case, the game is not likely to bear any relationship to the instruction, but simply serves as an enjoyable alternative to instruction. A second example is when the game is used in conjunction with the instruction. For example, Malone (1981) used a game of *Darts* to support a  drill and practice form of instruction. Each time the student answered an estimation question, a dart would be fired at a measuring stick. If the answer was correct, the dart would burst a balloon. A third example is the embedded game that, apart from the actual scoring mechanism and other management features, is part of the instruction, or criterion test, itself. A traditional example is a spelling contest performed individually or in teams. Each person or team accumulates points for correct answers and is rewarded by either getting the highest score or achieving a preset total.

**Figure 1.6.** Examples of token rewards. Extrinsic rewards, ranging from extra play time for children to a corporate coffee cup for adults, can be very effective when used appropriately.

The use of games in this context is similar to their use to build relevance through motive-matching. The difference is their use as an extrinsically rewarding outcome following sustained learning activity, versus an embedded device to support the learning process and to appeal to the need for achievement.

### 4.4b. *Use extrinsic rewards such as privileges or tokens when it is difficult to develop or sustain intrinsic motivation.*

This principle is based on a straightforward application of reinforcement theory. In most learning situations the students' overall motivational profiles will include expectations of external rewards such as access to jobs, promotions, access to college, etc., and hopefully an intrinsic interest in the overall course of study. These macro-level rewards provide important incentives to the overall learning experience, but they do not provide a sustaining level of motivation for specific learning events within the overall course of instruction. Consequently, it is beneficial to use extrinsic rewards to provide a satisfying outcome for students when a specific sequence of instruction, or the overall course, is boring or irrelevant to the students. However, cautions are in order. Research on the use of extrinsic rewards, as in token reinforcement systems, shows that although they can be beneficial, they can lead to undesirable outcomes in that students start working purely for the rewards. This can easily heighten the levels of superficial learning and cheating that occur. Also, there can be a spread of effect; the students' desire for extrinsic rewards can expand beyond the original boundaries, and they will lose their intrinsic interest in other areas of study which they now want to be rewarded for studying. One effective use of extrinsic rewards is to reinforce desired classroom behavior rather than achievement (except for grades and other normal outcomes of achievement). This is a common practice among elementary and secondary teachers, and the case in Figure 1.7 illustrates how an instructor applied this principle with adults.

### 4.5.   To sustain positive feelings of satisfaction, provide an equitable relationship between learner expectancy, performance assessments, and rewards.

People evaluate the information they process, and when they find discrepancies, they resolve them through rational and emotional means. This phenomenon is at the basis of curiosity as discussed earlier in this chapter, and it is also at the basis of cognitive dissonance (Festinger & Carlsmith, 1959) and equity theory (Adams, 1965), which explains how people react to conflicting versus congruent items of information. The following principles describe how to promote satisfaction and continuing motivation by using equity in course delivery and outcomes.

### 4.5a.   Exams and other performance activities should be consistent in content and level of difficulty with the objectives, instructional content, and learning activities in order to confirm students' feelings of control over outcomes.

Dissatisfaction with a course can occur very quickly if students feel that they have been deceived, whether deliberately or by mismanagement. Internal consistency is important, not only as a feature of good design in almost any context, but because of its effects on motivation and performance. Exams that do not cover the appropriate content or are set at the wrong difficulty level obviously can result in lowered performance. But even if the student manages to succeed, there is still a negative effect on the student's affective response to the course, and it could have a negative effect on the student's continuing motivation.

---

### CASE: A GAMBLE FOR ATTENTION

*The five instructors who shared responsibility for a five day workshop offered by their company for customers who purchased a network system along with a block of their computers had filled the course with relevant exercises that were graduated in difficulty. However, they still had trouble maintaining the students' attention during the entire day, especially as they moved into the middle part of the week. After discussing the situation, they decided that the sheer amount of material and its technical nature made it difficult to keep it intrinsically interesting at all times despite having numerous applied exercises. Some instructors would tell "war stories" to make it more interesting, but one can only tell so many "war stories" regarding highly technical information, and even they become boring after a while.*

*One instructor remembered a gimmick used at the end of a one day workshop she had taken, and she decided to try adapting it to this course.*

*On the first day of the next offering, she gave each student a "personal I.D." number. During the first hour of the workshop, she introduced a computer game called "Bandit." It was a simulation of a Las Vegas style one-armed bandit. Each time she "pulled the handle," a different student's number appeared, and the student received a prize such as a pen, coffee cup, or tablet binder with the company's logo. During the day, the game was played several more times at seemingly random intervals.*

*By noon of the second day, students realized that it was not totally random. They got to play the game two to four times during the first hour in the morning and two or three times during the first hour after lunch. It was also played whenever they had been actively paying attention and participating, but not every time. The game was never played when their attention waned or they were totally passive. In those cases, the instructors might introduce an extra exercise as a diversion to the lecture or a short break. This "gimmick" resulted in a dramatic improvement in the overall consistency of attention and interactivity of the students.*

**Figure 1.7.** Using extrinsic rewards to improve attention. The instructors were focusing on attention, and they accomplished their goal, but they were using a satisfaction tactic to do it. The extrinsic reward value of the prizes was very high. The students were happy to receive these items with the corporate logo that they could take back to their companies and universities. The prizes provided extrinsic rewards for active participation, and did so without detracting from the intrinsic rewards associated with success in achieving the course learning objectives. The intermittent nature of the reward process was very effective.

> **4.5b.** *To promote a sense of equity, extrinsic rewards, such as grades, tokens, public acclaim, or other awards, should be consistently related to performance, and to expectations that have been established earlier in the course.*

A student might feel very good about a particular achievement and outcome, such as earning a *B* in a difficult course. But if the student learns that someone else, who performed at a lower level, received an *A*, the feeling of satisfaction will instantly turn to anger. In designing and implementing an extrinsic reward system, equity within the course (i.e., relative to established expectations) must be maintained as well as equity in treatment of all individuals.

# II. Text and Graphics

Up to this point we have focused upon ways to motivate learners by means of teaching methods and manipulating the content to be taught. Now we turn our attention to possible ways to use text and graphics, particularly in the print medium, as motivational tools. We have chosen to focus on printed text for two reasons: (1) print is probably the most widely used medium of instruction; (2) since text is incorporated at some point into most media, principles for using text can be applied to most instruction.

This section is based on the assumption that the careful use of text features such as type, graphics, page design, and language can help influence motivation to learn, although primary emphasis remains on teaching methods and the content to be taught. Since the research base regarding motivating learners via the courseware media (whether print, video, computer, or other means) is not adequate, we must draw upon the experience and opinions of expert practitioners for principles relating motivation to text and graphics. Such experts include writers, graphic designers, and designers of print instructional materials.

## Typical Learners

It is also important to emphasize again the "typical" learners who form the target group for discussion. Previously, we defined the typical learner as falling in the mid-range of motivation (neither severely under- or over-motivated). In designing text, however, one must take into consideration reading skills and interest in reading. Most of the principles and tactics that apply to low-average learners also work with above-average learners, but the converse is not true. Therefore, our typical learner will fall into the low-average to average range with respect to reading skills and interest in reading.

## Motivational Principles

The majority of the motivational text, graphic, and print prescriptions relate to (1) gaining and maintaining attention, (2) relating the content of materials to learner interests, goals, or past, and (3) building and maintaining learner confidence in ability to use the material. Each prescription will be presented, followed by an explanation and examples.

# 5. Positive Impression

### 5.1. *Give print courseware a comfortable image to gain and maintain learner attention and to build confidence.*

Commercial producers have found that users' first impressions of a media product are very important to getting them to adopt (buy) it. Consequently, they spend a lot of time and money in giving their products a favorable feel or "image." Common sense and the experience of teachers suggest that first impressions can play a similar role in shaping learners' attitudes toward print instructional materials, and there is some evidence that they do (Felker, 1980).

Many typical learners check out courseware that they are expecting to use by quickly thumbing through it and reading a few excerpts. In part this scan is aimed at identifying the topic of the materials and assessing whether it is likely to be interesting. But many typical learners have a second important goal—to assess their chances of reading and using the materials without too much of a struggle. That quick judgment often determines whether typical learners approach their work optimistically or with dread, or may cause some of them to decide not even to try.

Designers of print materials for typical learners would probably be wise to systematically design their products to create a favorable first impression. That means making potential users who browse through them feel confident that they can easily read and understand what is there. A comfortable image may help to gain and keep learner attention and to build confidence that they can successfully use the material. Here are some further prescriptions related to this.

### 5.2. *Make initial perception of print courseware seem easy, rather than difficult, to read and use in order to gain and maintain attention and to build confidence.*

It is obvious that people would rather do pleasant tasks than unpleasant ones. Consequently, learners are more likely to be confident and enthusiastic about tackling instructional materials that appear to be easy to use than those that do not. And the way that print courseware is formatted can contribute to making it appear to be easy to use (and to actually be easy to use).

### 5.2a. *Use relatively short books and text segments to convey a less formidable image than long books or segments in order to maintain attention and to build confidence.*

Typical learners who lack confidence in their learning skills often associate long books and books with lengthy chapters or segments with difficult reading. Concise chapters can be frightening too if several of them must be read completely and in order before their meaning becomes clear. On the other hand, relatively short books, and concise, self-contained segments tend to suggest fairly easy reading to typical learners and can therefore be reassuring to them. Similarly, books with soft covers may convey a less rigorous image than those with hard covers.

When feasible, designers can make print courseware seem less formidable to typical learners by packaging it as separately bound, short booklets rather than as a single large book. Using soft rather than hard covers would probably help as well. If separately bound booklets are inappropriate, designers can create a similar effect by dividing a lengthy volume into visually distinct segments (Smith & Orr, 1985; White, 1987).

Naturally, the content of a book may restrict a designer's chances for breaking the text into sequential chunks. It has been well established that prerequisite knowledge and skills should be identified and taught before introducing more complex topics (Gagné *et al.*, 1962), and doing this inevitably results in sequential text. For this reason it is most difficult to thoroughly present complex topics to typical learners in a way that is both effective and motivating. However, a designer interested in motivation should be sure that prerequisites included in text are really prerequisite before using them to build long sequences of instruction. Unnecessary sequencing should be eliminated.

### 5.2b. *Make the instructional text well-organized and explicit to maintain learner attention and to build confidence.*

When applied to text, the terms "structuring" and "organizing" refer to making sure that topics and subtopics are sequenced logically. They also relate to making sure that relationships among text elements like illustrations and blocks of text are clear and that elements that are not related are perceived that way. "Text organizers" are devices that graphic designers use to make the structure of text explicit. Headings, typographic cuing, and use of white space on a page are examples of text organizers.

It is generally accepted that printed instructional materials are enhanced by making it easy to perceive their structure. Expert graphics designers who work with instructional text universally stress the importance of using text organizers to label text elements and highlight the way that text is organized (White, 1987). And many empirical studies have established the importance of easily perceived organization and structure to learning from print materials (Brooks & Dansereau, 1983; Resnick, 1981; Shimmerlik, 1978).

It seems fairly clear that explicit text organizers actually **do** make instructional text easier to learn from. But they also make text **appear** to be easier to understand, which may be an important motivator for typical learners, especially those who lack confidence in their learning skills. This possibility is intuitively appealing and is supported by a few studies that have shown that the more organized instructional text appears, the more students seem to prefer it (Grabinger, 1985).

In any case, print courseware designers who wish to motivate typical learners should probably take care to carefully organize their products and to make their organization explicit.

### 5.2c. *Use a reasonably open text display rather than a constrained display in order to maintain learner attention.*

Sometimes designers of print courseware try to cram as much information into as little space as possible. The result can be a crowded text display with small type, few graphics, and very little white space. Such a display is likely to keep printing costs down and so be easy on the pocketbook, but it is not likely to appeal to typical learners.

Most graphic designers strongly favor using a fairly spacious or "open" text display. By this they mean including pages in which type consumes only part of the total space with the rest devoted to white space and, if appropriate, graphics that are used as text organizers, to add meaning to the text, and to prevent monotony. This preference is defended on two grounds: (1) the content of the text will be easier to follow and understand, and (2) such a display tends to be more aesthetically pleasing and therefore attractive to the reader.

The graphic designers' view is supported by the experience of commercial publishers, who have found that typical consumers prefer (buy) print products with fairly open displays (novels and publications for conservative consumers excluded). Even some publishers of scholarly journals have concluded that their readers would prefer a more open format and have recently given their publications new looks. Formal research on the importance of open formats in the area of instruction is not adequate or convincing, but Grabinger (1985) found that students prefer text designs with "lots of white space and openness."

Although the evidence is more intuitive than empirical, it suggests that designers of courseware for typical learners who aim to build a favorable image into their products should use a fairly open text display. Naturally, the content to be taught may limit chances for doing this, as may resource constraints. However, the open display is more likely to gain and maintain attention and to build confidence. (The open space around principles in this book helps relieve the otherwise compact text.)

### 5.3. *Make the physical attributes of the product consistent with learner experience and expectations to maintain learner attention and to build confidence.*

Publishers of textbooks have found that many people react to print matter as they do to other products—they prefer materials that fit their expectations (put another way, they tend to dislike materials that fail to meet their expectations). And, it seems that their expectations extend to language, typography, graphics, and page layout as well as content.

To optimize sales, market-driven publishers have learned to identify the attributes that their customers prefer and then try to match those preferences. For example, *The Wall Street Journal*, a publication that is intended for conservative business persons, features text written in a fairly formal writing style and uses a parsimonious format with text in regular columns, few graphics, no color, and a small number of quite conventional typefaces. On the other hand, these days most magazines and newspapers that are designed for mass consumption (i.e., typical learners) feature text that is very easy to read, and a lively format with large type, prominent headings in several type faces, flexible column widths, and extensive use of color and graphics.

Although the empirical evidence is slim, it is probably safe to assume that users of instructional materials react in much the same way as other readers—in line with strong preferences as to language and format. So, instructional designers who wish to create a favorable first impression should probably consider their audiences' preferences when deciding on a format and writing style. The next few principles provide some guidelines for making the choice when the audience is typical learners.

### 5.3a. Use appropriate color, graphics, and high-quality typesetting and printing for print products to gain and maintain learner attention.

These days, people are flooded with advertising and other print matter, and much of it is of high quality and done in full color. As a result of this deluge, the average person has gotten used to high-quality print material and now expects it. Consequently, many people will pay little attention to print products that feature lackluster printing or that lack color. That is why monochrome products have practically disappeared from the mass market.

There is some evidence that people's strong preference for color and quality printing applies to instructional materials as well. Market research has convinced publishers of pre-college textbooks and other printed courseware that using high-quality printing and including color are necessary to generate sales in most markets (university professors and others who select tertiary courseware seem to pay less attention to these attributes). Despite the fact that publishers' market research focuses on teachers and other purchasers of materials more than on learners, this experience suggests that designers who generate print courseware for typical learners should try to include color and use high-quality printing even if they are not essential to the instruction. (Note! One has to be careful that using color improperly does not distract learners' attention and actually interfere with learning.)

### 5.3b. *Use a familiar typeface and size that follow standard typesetting conventions to maintain learner attention.*

Most graphic designers believe that the readability of text type depends upon a balance among its size, the distance between the lines of type, and the width of the type column. Consequently most of them follow the same informal typographic rules when specifying type. As a result, readers are repeatedly exposed to text that is typographically similar. Over time, many readers have become accustomed to standard typesetting and most tend to favor the norm.

Many graphic designers also share common beliefs about the desirability of certain typefaces. For example, today the text type in most books features tiny horizontal projections called "serifs." This is probably because many designers believe that serifs make letters easier to discern and help to guide a reader's eye along a line of type and therefore make the type more readable (Lichty, 1989). Although the evidence for this notion is not convincing, it has become more or less standard to use a text type with serifs. So, whether serifs really help reading or not, many people are used to seeing them and find it uncomfortable to read long stretches of sans serif type (type without serifs) (Hvistendahl & Kahl, 1975). In similar ways, particular typefaces have become widely accepted by readers and therefore by publishers (i.e., Times Roman type and its variations are used widely for text).

Given most readers' bias in favor of conventional typefaces and typesetting, designers of print courseware for typical learners are probably wise to abide by major typographic conventions. Doing otherwise is likely to lead to materials that will be less appealing to typical learners. (Note—some departures from the norm may be required to prevent boredom.)

### 5.3c. *Make each line around eight to ten words and 10- to 12-point type to make text easier to read, maintain learner attention, and increase confidence.*

Although there are many exceptions, the general principle is—wider columns call for larger type and more space between lines. One rule of thumb for determining type size for easy reading is to use 10- to 12-point type for typical readers and to make each line of type fifty to seventy characters long (eight to ten words) (Felker *et al.*, 1981). It is considered better to err on the side of larger rather than smaller type, more rather than less space between lines, and shorter rather than longer lines (White, 1987).

There are literally thousands of typefaces, and most graphic designers agree that some faces make text more readable than others (White, 1987). Since we lack convincing evidence to the contrary, designers of print courseware for typical learners should probably use one of the readable faces. Generally, this means choosing a face that is (1) widely used and therefore likely to be familiar, and (2) legible (i.e., the letters are easy to distinguish. Old English is not a legible face). Naturally, a typeface must also be available and include all characters that are likely to be needed.

# 6. Readable Style

### 6.1. *Use a readable writing style to maintain learner attention and increase confidence.*

Most people have developed preferences with respect to writing style as well as format and typography. People who write for newspapers, magazines, and other publications designed for mass consumption have developed a writing style that features short, familiar, image-provoking words, the active voice, and a number of other standard elements. There is considerable evidence that this style of writing communicates very well and is efficient if not carried to extremes (magazine writers are accused by writing teachers of using too many image-provoking words). Perhaps more important, the average person has come to prefer and expect a readable style. Consequently, virtually all print products for mass distribution incorporate a highly readable style. Designers of print instructional materials should follow suit if their products are targeted for typical learners.

It would seem to be self-evident that designers who generate materials for poor readers should try to insure that their text is perceived as easy to read. Obviously, print courseware with hard-to-read text is not likely to encourage poor readers. But, there has been considerable controversy about this. (See the discussion in Klare, 1982.)

The problem stems from evidence that poor readers must be challenged if their reading is to improve (Chall, 1979). With this in mind, many people feel that if courseware is made too easy to read we will destroy poor readers' chances to advance. On the other hand, it is certainly true that poor readers will never be able to learn subjects like science and history if they cannot read their textbooks.

Both of these arguments are compelling, which means that there is a necessary trade-off between teaching poor readers to read better and adjusting existing text to improve chances that poor readers can read it. Authorities differ on what the balance should be, and we will not try to resolve that issue here.

### 6.2. *Use readable language to gain and maintain learner attention.*

We have seen that using readable language may help to give print materials a favorable image with typical learners. But, there is a more important reason for making text readable. Making text readable also helps typical learners be successful and, over time, success can increase both learners' confidence and motivation. But first, we must think briefly about what the process of reading entails.

Today, most experts think of reading in terms of an information-processing model for learning and memory. Modern information-processing models (IPMs) are fairly complex and differ in their details, so it is not possible to deal with them in detail here. See Gagné (1985) for an example of a typical IPM. However, most IPMs include steps similar to these:

**Step 1.** During reading, the eye moves across a line, stopping periodically to process what is seen. Processing is limited to about ten or so letters or spaces per stop.

**Step 2.** The brain converts what is seen into a coded "chunk." To a poor reader a chunk may be a letter. Good readers generate chunks in the form of words, i.e., c-a-t becomes cat.

**Step 3.** The reader consults a sort of dictionary of previously encountered chunks that are linked with familiar words. Chunks that are linked to commonly used and frequently encountered words are easiest to find. With experience, identifying chunks can become automatic.

**Step 4.** Identified chunks are temporarily stored in short-term memory. Unidentified chunks are lost. A chunk can be a letter, syllable, word, phrase, or even a sentence. Short-term memory can hold only about 7 chunks. Too many chunks cause it to erase. Short-term memory unloads at ends of sentences or clauses or when part of a sentence seems to convey meaning.

**Step 5.** Information moves quickly to long-term memory, where it is given meaning and is stored as a gist or scenario. The gists or scenarios are called "schemata" (singular, schema). For storage, schemata are entwined in an interlocking network. If no appropriate schema is present, chunks from short-term memory are lost.

As we shall see, IPMs suggest many things that a writer can do to make text easier to read. And, the recommendations that emerge from IPMs correspond quite closely to what many good writers and researchers have suggested as procedures for authoring readable text (Hartley, 1987; Felker *et al.*, 1981; Becker, 1978). The following principles include those that are most commonly recommended.

> *6.2a. Use action verbs, words that are familiar, concrete, and specific, and avoid jargon in order to maintain learner attention.*

## Action Verbs

Many experts emphasize that writers should use action verbs and avoid using nouns that are created from verbs (nominals). "Specification" is an example of a nominal that is derived from the action verb "specify." Consequently, the phrase "The company specifies that" is better usage than the "specification of the company is."

From an information processing point of view, there are two main advantages to using action verbs rather than nominals: (1) action verbs are more direct and therefore more easily processed than nominals, and (2) using action verbs results in sentences with the subject and verb close together and early in the sentence, which makes it easier to sort out their meaning.

### Familiar, Concrete, and Specific Words

According to IPM, words that are familiar to learners and that are concrete and specific tend to be more quickly and easily processed than abstract ones. Most people use mostly short words of few syllables, so writers of courseware for typical learners should probably do the same. IPM models suggest that words that are used frequently by a reader tend to be processed more quickly and easily than infrequently used ones. A number of studies confirm that using unfamiliar words tends to impede comprehension (Clark and Clark, 1977).

This suggests that it normally pays to be as specific as possible when writing for typical learners. For example, "plow" is more concrete than "farm equipment." Similarly, "almanac" is more specific than "book" which, in turn, is more specific than "publication" or "print matter."

An easy way to identify nominals is to look for the endings -tion, -al, -ance, -ence, -ment, or -ure. Also look for the phrase "the _____ of." Here are seven examples of nominals along with the verbs from which they derive: (1) decide-decision, (2) refuse-refusal, (3) assign-assignment, (4) rely-reliance, (5) verify-verification, (6) disclose-disclosure, (7) participate-participation.

### Technical Terms and Jargon

Technical words should be used sparingly because they tend to be unfamiliar to many people and, therefore, difficult to process. A technical term is useful only if it adds needed precision to text and if the reader can process it automatically. If an everyday word is just as precise, then a writer should use it. If the reader may not be able to process an essential technical word, then a writer should define the word before using it. Educators might process AERA as one chunk that means "American Educational Research Association." But, to a typical learner, AERA is probably four chunks that have little collective meaning.

#### *6.2b. Use a natural word order to maintain learner attention.*

Keeping the subject and verb close together and early in a sentence tends to simplify processing because, collectively, they carry most of the meaning. Conversely, anything that separates the subject and verb or pushes them back in the sentence tends to make reading harder.

One way to promote a natural word order is to use the first or second person. Using the pronouns "I" or "You" forces a writer to place the subject and verb close together (and early in the sentence if the active voice is used). This promotes easy processing and happier readers. (If "I" is inappropriate, "We" can be substituted.)

Another advantage is that first and second person words are hard to modify. This helps to reduce clutter and keep the subject close to the verb. Using too many modifiers does the opposite. Contrast this phrase: "We found out from recent intelligence reports that—" with this one: "The annual regulatory monitorship review of intelligence reports from various federal agencies with agricultural oversight responsibilities has been made." Notice how the many modifiers in the second version causes stilted text that is hard to follow.

There are still other advantages to using the first and second person. "I" and "you" are common and concrete words, so typical learners can process them easily. Finally, the words "I" ("we") and "you," like all personal pronouns, make a sentence more interesting and so help to hold the reader's attention.

### 6.2c.  Use the active voice to maintain learner attention.

In the active voice the subject of a sentence does what the verb says. For example, "Fred hit the ball." In contrast, in the passive sentence "The ball was hit by Fred." the subject (the ball) does not do the acting.

The main problem with passive sentences is that a lot of key information is usually pushed to the end of the sentence. This complicates processing for the reader. Also, using the passive voice tends to replace high-frequency words like "I" and "we" with low frequency abstract nouns.

Some people use passive construction to hide responsibility, i.e., "A penalty was called" versus "I called a penalty." Also, passive sentences avoid the appearance of self-promotion, i.e., "The base-stealing record was broken" versus "I broke the base-stealing record." This kind of imprecision appeals to some lawyers, politicians, and academics, but it is likely to frustrate most people and does not help typical learners to process text.

### 6.2d.  Use sentences that are of moderate length to maintain learner attention and to build confidence.

IPM suggests that short sentences should make processing easy because they restrict the number of "chunks" that a reader has to contend with. This tends to be true but not if essential information is deleted. Here are some suggestions for being brief without complicating the reader's task.

A.  Do not delete pronouns and/or conjunctions such as "that" and "which"! Doing so often makes sentences harder to interpret. Contrast "I want the book written by Paul" with "I want the book that was written by Paul."

B.  Avoid using strings of modifiers to explain complex relationships. Contrast "The committee responsible for examining the institution" with the shorter but more difficult revised version, "The institution examination committee." Note that the reviser placed the three most difficult words (institution, examining, committee) next to each other. He or she also took out two important words that explained relationships (responsible for), and, by converting the verb "examining" to the nominal "examination," further obscured relationships.

C.  Do not overuse acronyms and abbreviations in an effort to be concise.

D.   Avoid forcing readers to make inferences in order to get the meaning of a sentence. To accurately infer a meaning often demands schemata that a reader may not have. Consider the sentence pair: "The principal held a lot of meetings. Many teachers resigned." The sentences are short but it is not clear what happened. It would take a lot more information (words and sentences) to explain, but the conciseness gained by leaving out the information is not worth the likely miscommunication.

E.   Don't leave out the examples. Often, writers (and editors) try to achieve conciseness by removing the examples of the thing or process being described. Doing this usually hurts rather than helps communication because the examples tend to be the part of text that is the most concrete, interesting, and easy to read. Consequently, examples serve to make reading easier, especially for poor readers. Often, the way to make text easier to follow is to add examples, not delete them.

### 6.2e. *Use macrosignals to make it easier for a reader to understand relationships in the text which will help maintain learner attention and build confidence.*

Evidence suggests that writers can make text easier to understand and less frustrating by providing introductions of various kinds (Gagné, 1978; Resnick, 1981) and by giving the reader frequent clues as to how parts of the text fit together and especially, what comes next (Pace, 1982). We will discuss this subject again in the next section but it is appropriate to list a few suggested procedures here.

A.   Use headings and start long sections of text with an overview paragraph. Try to tell the readers where they are headed and why they are going there. Include periodic summaries to tell them where they have been.

B.   Start paragraphs with a topic sentence that foreshadows what the paragraph is about. In general, include the big ideas first followed by the details rather than the other way around. To see this technique in polished form, check the way newspaper stories are written.

C.   Help readers by using "signal words" often. These are noncontent words that emphasize the structure or emphasis of a passage. For example, words like "however," "but," and "on the other hand" signal that two or more things are being compared. And, "first," "second," and "another reason for" imply the structure of an argument. "A better example" does the same thing. Words like "therefore," "so that," and "because" signal a causal relationship.

> ### *6.2f.* *Vary the vocabulary and the complexity of the sentences to maintain learner attention.*

In the first part of this chapter we showed that including a variety of elements (or avoiding sameness) is one way to create interest in courseware. Experts seem to agree that principle applies to the way a writer says things as well as to the things he or she says. To attract average adults' interest they advise that prose should feature a mix of sentences that vary in length and syntax (Flesch & Lass, 1949). Authors can also liven up text by including a rich variety of words (providing that they are words that the intended readers can process).

Note that there is some tension between writing for interest and writing for readability. Being concise is high on almost every expert's list of ways to write effectively, as is keeping the vocabulary simple, but these things affect interest as well. To children and poor readers, reading uncomplicated prose can be quite exciting, but reading a long string of very readable sentences like "John hit the ball" is deadly for most people. Similarly, it helps readability to keep the subject and verb close together and early in a sentence, but too much of that can also result in prose that will bore many people.

# 7. Graphic Illustrations

> ### *7.1.* *Include graphics that make courseware easier to interpret and use in order to maintain learner attention and to build confidence.*

For purposes of this discussion we will define "graphics" as alternatives to prose for conveying information. Some examples of graphics that fit this definition are: illustrations (photographs, drawings, and paintings), tables, maps, and graphs. Devices like rules and boxes that are used to organize information will not be considered graphics.

Although the results of research on the effects of using graphics are neither consistent nor compelling, most authorities and professionals are convinced that in many circumstances graphics help readers (especially poor readers) to use and understand instructional text (Levie & Lentz, 1982; Hartley, 1987). Greater ease of use helps to maintain attention and promotes greater confidence. In fact, graphics are almost essential for cognitive processing of print-based instruction on identifying things or carrying out procedural tasks.

The "before" and "after" examples in Figure 1.8 illustrate how graphics can add visual appeal and meaning to a visual. In contrast to the list in the top panel, the graphics in the bottom panel illustrate several of the relationships inherent in the theory covered.

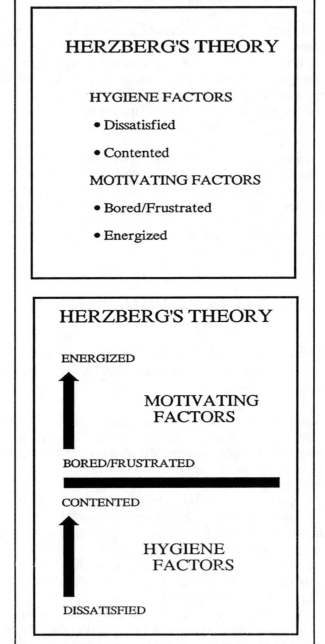

**Figure 1.8.** Graphic enhancements. The organization of material and the graphics on the bottom panel show relationships in addition to enhancing visual appeal.

## Pictures

Pictures have an important place in print courseware. But it is hard to generalize about how designers can make the most effective use of pictures because pictures can do many things in text, and there are good and bad pictures (Hartley, 1987, p. 81). We are particularly constrained here because we are interested in effectiveness only as it influences motivation. However, a few things about using pictures seem to stand out. First, learners do not automatically associate pictures with the corresponding text or focus on the relevant parts of pictures. According to Brody (1982) and many others, effective ways to direct learners' attention include direct references in the text, i.e., "See Figure 2," captions, and visually linking each picture with its associated text.

Once learners have focused on a picture and its related text, they must be able to process the information. How well they do this depends partly on the complexity of the picture, which means the number of elements it contains (i.e., a picture of two houses with several shade trees is more complex than a picture of one house with no trees because it contains more elements). The trick is to include all elements that learners need for understanding but not so many that they are distracted or overwhelmed (Brody, 1982).

Getting the number of elements right often means using several simpler pictures rather than one complicated one to communicate a complex idea. On the other hand, pictures that are too simple tend to be boring and those that lack critical elements are likely to be ineffective.

It appears that the format of a picture also affects its effectiveness. Line drawings seem to work better than photographs in conveying some kinds of ideas (the reverse is true also). Felker *et al.* (1981) have provided guidelines for choosing an appropriate format for different purposes.

## Maps, Tables, Charts, Graphs, Diagrams

Almost without exception, good writers and experts on written communication recommend the use of maps, tables, charts, graphs, and diagrams in dealing with quantitative data, complex relationships, and large data sets. For example, a graph or chart can show what the weather is like across the fifty states (Felker *et al.*, 1981). In such situations words alone are usually inadequate because readers tend to get lost in the details. Furthermore, graphic devices make it much easier for a reader to find a particular piece of information, i.e., what the weather is like in Arizona.

Obviously, the key to using these kinds of graphic devices is to make them easy to interpret. A good deal of research has been devoted to ways to do this, and several lists of practical guidelines are available (Felker *et al.*, 1981; Hartley, 1987). These design attributes seem to be the most important: (1) keep graphics simple—don't include too many elements or variables; (2) label important elements of the graphic (i.e., graphs axes) clearly and legibly; and (3) be sure that the reader understands how to interpret the graphic (carefully explain any codes used and train inexperienced learners how to use the graphic).

# 8.  Helpful Formatting

**8.1.**   *Make the layout of print courseware easy to perceive in order to maintain learner attention and build confidence.*

Gradually designers of print courseware are coming to realize that most users of their products do not start on page one and then proceed sequentially through the text at one sitting. Instead, they take breaks, skip sections that are unimportant, and turn back to segments they studied earlier. This makes formatting courseware much more difficult than dealing with novels and other books that are read from cover to cover (Waller, 1982).

Typical learners need help in finding their way through print courseware. They need to be able to quickly locate parts of a book such as particular pages, sections, topics, and figures. And, as they read, learners need to know what is important and where to go and what to do next. They also need to be sure of such things as which illustrations go with which text and which questions are to be answered in writing. In this section we discuss principles that provide the necessary help.

To ease a reader's task, designers should locate repeating elements, such as page numbers, headers, and footers, in the same place on each page of a book. Similarly, margin widths, indenting, and vertical and horizontal spacing of page elements should be consistent.

Designers can easily and conveniently accomplish the needed consistency by designing an appropriate reference grid and using it to organize the elements on each page. Hartley (1987) presents an excellent summary of procedures for designing and using reference grids for instructional text.

Designers can facilitate the way users actually get information from text by organizing the instruction into logical chapters, sections, lesson topics, or subtopics, and by keeping the segments or lessons as short and sequentially independent of each other as possible.

Most designers are convinced that good organization of text helps learning, and many studies confirm this (Glynn & Britton, 1984; Meyer, 1981; Singer, 1985). But, maximum help is unlikely unless the writer makes the organization of the text explicit to the learner (Jonassen & Kirschner, 1982). Here are some suggested ways to identify, highlight, and label text elements.

## White Space

Careful use of white space is an important tool for making the structure of instructional text explicit. In a seminal work on designing instructional text, Hartley (1987) emphasizes the importance of consistently indenting certain text elements and leaving vertical space between them so as to set them visually apart. The Hartley book also provides guidelines for effectively using white space.

Many graphic designers emphasize the importance of another way of using white space effectively—"chunking" or tying related elements together visually, e.g., a text segment and a related photograph. One important way to chunk is to place related elements close together and separated by white space from unrelated elements (Felker *et al.*, 1981). Doing so probably helps to motivate typical learners not only by making the structure of the materials more explicit, but also by making the text display seem less formidable (more spacious).

## Headings

Another way to make the structure of print courseware explicit is to foreshadow the content of text elements by labeling them with prominent titles and headings. Most graphic designers are convinced that headings are very important for directing readers' attention (White, 1987), and many studies have shown that using headings can improve learning from prose materials (Doctorow, Wittrock, & Marks, 1978; Holley *et al.*, 1981; Hartley, 1987).

## Typography

Typographic cues can also tell a reader what is important in text. Boldface type, italics, underlining, all capital letters, lines (rules) and boxes, and using a highlight color are examples of typographic cuing devices. Research and the experience of professionals generally support using typography for emphasis. Authorities differ on the details but many seem to prefer using boldface over other ways of making type stand out (Hartley, 1987). To avoid confusing learners, designers should take care not to use too many of these devices.

In courseware the same elements sometimes appear repeatedly, which creates another labeling problem. For example, self-tests or inserted questions that a student is expected to answer overtly may be scattered through a text. To make such elements effective, it is important to direct learners' attention to them. One way to do that is to consistently label each element with its own marker, such as a unique type size, font, or style, a numeral, or a symbol (i.e., a bullet). Markers of this kind should not be overused! Too many kinds of markers on a page can be confusing and distracting.

## Page Layouts

Page "layout" refers to the way that type, illustrations, other graphics, and white space are arranged on a page. Layouts for courseware should be designed primarily to make the structure of the text explicit—that is, to help the student see at a glance which elements on a page are most important and which ones go together. But it is clear that graphic designers can create interest through page layout as well.

The aesthetic aspects of page layout are more art than science, and graphic designers cannot follow rigorous "rules" in spurring reader interest (Turnbull & Baird, 1964, 1975). However, there is fairly good agreement on the very general guidelines that are summarized below.

Novelty is important in creating interesting page layouts. The idea is to avoid making the pages of a book look too much alike. On the other hand, a certain amount of consistency in placing elements on the pages of a book makes it easier for readers to use and provides a comfortable feeling that is often welcome. One trick is to inject novelty into individual pages but to retain an overall pattern of consistency.

Most page designers assume that readers' perceptions of a page as "pleasing" depend upon inherent preferences for arrangements that feature "proportion," "balance," "contrast," "unity," "rhythm," and "harmony." Consequently, they try to reflect these design basics in their designs (Lichty, 1989). Use of these basics seems consistent with principles of perception, but because they are interrelated and difficult to define precisely, their actual importance has not been convincingly verified by research. However, designing for proportion, balance, contrast, unity, rhythm, and harmony has become so pervasive that many readers have probably become conditioned to prefer this kind of design.

# 9.  Interesting Pictures

### 9.1.  *Use interesting pictures to gain and maintain learner attention in instructional text.*

Although research has failed to demonstrate conclusively that using pictures in courseware is related to motivation, their instincts tell many designers that good pictures really do motivate learners. For example, the pictures in the motivational messages (Figures 1.3 and 1.5) attract attention and contribute to curiosity. Duchastel (1980) and others suggest that good designers' advice is probably more useful than research, given the inadequacies of the research. We will assume that it is and will focus on identifying attributes that a designer should look for when searching for pictures that will stimulate interest as well as be effective.

Earlier we saw that the complexity of a picture may affect how well it communicates. If a picture contains too many elements, the learner may have trouble finding the thing that is intended, and leaving out important elements reduces effectiveness. Keller and Suzuki (1988) suggest that complexity also helps to determine how interesting a picture is. They posit that simple pictures with few visual elements tend to be uninteresting and, conversely, that too many elements make a picture "busy" and also uninteresting. They conclude that a picture should be "moderately" complex to generate maximum interest.

### 9.2.  *Include pictures that include novelty and drama to maintain learner attention.*

There is wide acceptance of Berlyne's (1966) notion that people tend to be attracted to things or events that are novel or dramatic, and many designers use it in designing illustrations for text. Studies have shown that learners are drawn to pictures that include unique or dramatic elements, different or dramatic placements of elements, and novel ways of using color, tone, and other picture qualities.

Without doubt, a designer can overdo variety and novelty in selecting illustrations. Most designers agree that too much novelty can be distracting or confusing and therefore counterproductive. There is little doubt that the illustrations in text displays for typical learners should be varied and should contain novel elements. But they must also be consistent and familiar enough to promote ease of use and to create a sense of comfort.

### 9.3. *Include pictures that include people to gain and maintain learner attention.*

Many designers believe that readers are more interested in pictures that include people than those that do not. Consequently, they recommend that editors use people-oriented pictures in print products. This recommendation can be easily applied to illustrated text, and theory supports doing just that (Keller & Suzuki, 1988). For example, a picture of a teen-aged boy rolling a ball down an inclined plane is likely to be more interesting to a teen-aged learner than a picture of the same ball simply rolling down the plane. Assuming the two pictures are equally effective in teaching mechanics, it would be wise to include the boy (or girl) in a picture destined for a junior high school text.

### 9.4. *Colored pictures tend to be more interesting to most readers than those without color.*

Unless the instruction requires learners to discriminate among colors, color alone does not seem to make print courseware more effective. Even so, most people prefer products that include color over those that do not. Furthermore, as a result of being bombarded with color products, the public has come to expect color as a matter of course. So, unless their audience is limited to premotivated learners, it is probably advisable for designers to incorporate color illustrations into print courseware as long as they do not distract attention from the main point of the instruction.

## 10. Early Interest

### 10.1. *Create interest as early as possible to gain learner attention.*

It is important that typical learners become engaged and successful from the start. As discused earlier, the usual way to do this is to begin with a topic or activity that is sure to interest the target learners. A high-interest activity often involves confronting learners with some dramatic or unexpected event (Berlyne, 1966; Kagan, 1972). Generally, the best topics to start with are those in which the learners have previously shown interest.

Sometimes, however, sequence considerations force a designer to open with uninteresting content. When that happens, print courseware designers should make a special effort to creatively use language, type, graphics, and page layouts to generate interest. For example, an overhead transparency can combine many of these features. Figure 1.9 illustrates how interesting graphics can be used with the technique of progressive disclosure to reveal each of several concepts at the appropriate moment.

**Figure 1.9.** Stimulating curiosity with progressive disclosure. In this overhead transparency, each sign is covered with a non-permanent sticky label. The instructor removes each as it is discussed. In the final one, the word "surprise" is upside down, which has a surprising and mildly amusing effect.

# Chapter Summary

The key goal in education is effective learning, which leads to effective performance. However, learning is not a one-time event. Educators endeavor to help students become self-motivated and self-directed learners. Virtually all employers in the private and public sectors are spending increasing amounts of money to develop and sustain a competent and competitive workforce. The rapidity of change in both technical knowledge and cultural perspectives leads to increasing demands for ongoing education. The motivation to learn impacts on both the effectiveness and the efficiency of instruction. Consequently, the importance of motivational design is growing, as is our knowledge about the processes, strategies, and tactics to promote the motivation to learn. However, this is still an emerging area relative to our knowledge of instructional design, and there is much to be learned. The principles and prescriptions presented in this chapter are based on both research studies and practitioners' experience. They represent the beginnings of focused, practical guidelines for designing motivating instructional programs and materials.

# References

Adams, J. S. (1965). Inequity in social exchange. In L. Berkowitz (Ed.), *Advances in experimental social psychology* (Vol. 2). New York: Academic Press.

Altschuler, A. S. (1973). *Developing achievement motivation in adolescents: Education for human growth.* Englewood Cliffs, NJ: Educational Technology Publications.

Atkinson, J. W., & Raynor, J. O. (Eds.) (1974). *Motivation and achievement.* Washington, DC: V. H. Winston.

Bandura, A. (1977). Self-efficacy: Toward a unifying theory of change. *Psychological Review, 84,* 191–215.

Beck, R. C. (1990). *Motivation: Theories and principles.* Englewood Cliffs, NJ: Prentice-Hall.

Becker, F. (1978). *The making of a textbook.* Morristown, NJ: Silver Burdett.

Berlyne, D. (1966). Curiosity and exploration. *Science, 153*(3731), pp. 25–33.

Bickford, N. L. (1989). *The systematic application of principles of motivation to the design of printed instruction.* Unpublished doctoral dissertation, Florida State University.

Brody, P. (1982). Affecting instructional textbooks through pictures. In D. H. Jonassen (Ed.), *The technology of text.* Englewood Cliffs, NJ: Educational Technology Publications.

Brooks, L. W., & Dansereau, D. F. (1983). Effects of structural schema training and text organization on expository prose processing. *Journal of Educational Psychology, 75*(6), 211–220.

Burbank, L., & Pett, D. (1986). Designing printed instructional materials. *Performance and Instruction Journal, 8,* 5–9.

Carroll, J. B. (1963). A model of school learning. *Teachers College Record, 64,* 723–733.

Chall, J. S. (1979). Readability: In search of improvement. *Publisher's Weekly,* October 29, 40–41.

Clark, H. H., & Clark E. V. (1977). *Psychology and language.* New York: Harcourt, Brace, Jovanovich.

Cohen, A. F. (1964). *Attitude change and social influence.* New York: Basic Books.

Cronbach, L. J., & Snow, R. E. (1976). *Aptitudes and instructional methods.* New York: Irvington.

Curtis, R. V., & Reigeluth, C. M. (1984). The use of analogies in written text. *Instructional Science, 13,* 99–117.

deCharms, R. (1976). *Enhancing motivation change in the classroom.* New York: Irvington.

Doctorow, M., Wittrock, M. C., & Marks, C. (1978). Generative processes in reading comprehension. *Journal of Experimental Education, 46,* 109–118.

Duchastel, P. C. (1980). Research on illustration in text: Issues and perspectives. *Educational Communications and Technology Journal, 28*(4), 283–287.

Duchastel, P. C. (1982). Textual display techniques. In D. H. Jonassen (Ed.), *The technology of text.* Englewood Cliffs, NJ: Educational Technology Publications.

Felker, D. (1980). *Document design: A review of relevant research.* Washington, DC: American Institutes for Research.

Felker, D. B., Pickering, F., Charrow, V. R., Holland, V. M., & Redish, J. C. (1981). *Guidelines for document designers.* Washington, DC: American Institutes for Research.

Festinger, L., & Carlsmith, J. M. (1959). Cognitive consequences of forced compliance. *Journal of Abnormal and Social Psychology, 58,* 203–210.

Fleming, M., & Levie, W. H. (1978). *Instructional message design: Principles from the behavioral sciences.* Englewood Cliffs, NJ: Educational Technology Publications.

Flesch, R. (1948). A new readability yardstick. *Journal of Applied Psychology, 32,* 221–233.

Flesch, R., & Lass, A. H. (1949). *A new guide to better writing.* New York: Harper and Row.

Gagné, E. D. (1978). Long term retention of information following learning from prose. *Review of Educational Research, 48,* 629–665.

Gagné, R. M. (1985). *The conditions of learning* (4th ed.). New York: Holt, Rinehart, & Winston.

Gagné, R. M., Mayor, J. R., Garstens, H. L., & Paradise, N. E. (1962). Factors in acquiring knowledge of a mathematical skill. *Psychological Monographs: General and Applied, 76* (Whole No. 526).

Glynn, S. M., & Britton, B. K. (1984). Supporting readers' comprehension through effective text design. *Educational Technology, 24*(10), 40–43.

Good, T. L., & Brophy, J. E. (1986). *Educational psychology: A realistic approach.* New York: Longman.

Grabinger, R. S. (1985). *Relationships among text format variables in computer generated text.* Paper presented at the 1985 annual convention of the Association for Educational Communications and Technology, Las Vegas, NV.

Gropper, G. L. (1991). *Text displays: Analysis and systematic design.* Englewood Cliffs, NJ: Educational Technology Publications.

Gunning, R. (1968). *The technique of clear writing.* New York: McGraw-Hill, p. 120.

Hartley, J. (1987). *Designing instructional text.* London: Kogan Page.

Holley, C. D., *et al.* (1981). Utilizing intact and embedded headings as processing aid with nonnarrative text. *Contemporary Educational Psychology, 6*(3), 227–236.

Hvistendahl, J., & Kahl, M. (1975). *Roman vs. sans serif body type: Readability and reader preference.* News research bulletin, No. 2. Washington, DC: American Newspaper Publishers Association.

Jonassen, D. H., & Kirschner, P. A. (1982). Introduction to section 2: Explicit techniques for structuring text. In D. H. Jonassen (Ed.), *The technology of text.* Englewood Cliffs, NJ: Educational Technology Publications.

Kagan, J. (1972). Motives and development. *Journal of Personality and Social Psychology, 22*(1), 51–66.

Kaplan, S., & Kaplan, R. (1978). *Humanscape: Environments for people.* North Scituate, MA: Duxbury Press.

Keller, J. M. (1979). Motivation and instructional design: A theoretical perspective. *Journal of Instructional Development, 2*(4), 26–34.

Keller, J. M. (1983). Motivational design of instruction. In C. M. Reigeluth (Ed.), *Instructional-design theories and models: An overview of their current status.* Hillsdale, NJ: Lawrence Erlbaum Associates.

Keller, J. M. (1987a). Strategies for stimulating the motivation to learn. *Performance & Instruction, 26*(8), 1–7.

Keller, J. M. (1987b). The systematic process of motivational design. *Performance & Instruction, 26*(9), 1–8.

Keller, J. M., & Suzuki, K. (1988). Use of the ARCS motivation model in courseware design. In D. H. Jonassen (Ed.), *Instructional designs for microcomputer courseware.* Hillsdale, NJ: Lawrence Erlbaum Associates.

Klare, G. R. (1982). Readability. In H. Mitzel (Ed.), *Encyclopedia of educational research,* Vol. 3 (pp. 1520–1531). New York: The Free Press.

Levie, W. H., & Lentz, R. (1982). Effects of text illustrations: A review of research. *Educational Communications and Technology Journal, 30*(4), 195–232.

Lichty, T. (1989). *Design principles for desktop publishers.* Glenview, IL: Scott Foresman Computer Books.

Livingston, J. S. (1969). Pygmalion in management. *Harvard Business Review, 47* (July–August), 81–89.

Macdonald-Ross, M. (1978a). Graphics in text. In L. Shulman (Ed.), *Review of Educational Research,* Vol. 5. Itasca, IL: Peacock.

Macdonald-Ross, M. (1978b). Language in text. In L. Shulman (Ed.), *Review of Educational Research,* Vol. 6. Itasca, IL: Peacock.

Maher, M. L. (1976). Continuing motivation: An analysis of a seldom considered educational outcome. *Review of Educational Research, 46,* 443–462.

Malone, T. W. (1981). Toward a theory of intrinsically motivating instruction. *Cognitive Science, 4,* 335–369.

Markiewicz, D. (1974). Effects of humor on persuasion. *Sociometry, 37,* 407–422.

Martin, B. L., & Briggs, L. J. (1986). *The affective and cognitive domains: Integration for instruction and research.* Englewood Cliffs, NJ: Educational Technology Publications.

McClelland, D. C. (1976). *The achieving society.* New York: Irvington Publishers.

McCombs, B. L. (1984). Processes and skills underlying continuing intrinsic motivation to learn: Toward a definition of motivational skills training. *Educational Psychologist, 4,* 190–218.

McConnell, J. V. (1978). Confessions of a textbook writer. *American Psychologist, 33,* 159–169.

Merrill, M. D. (1975). Learner control: Beyond aptitude-treatment interactions. *AV Communications Review, 23,* 217–226.

Meyer, B. J. F. (1981). Basic research on prose comprehension: A critical review. In D. F. Fisher & C. W. Peters (Eds.), *Comprehension and the competent reader: Interspecialty perspectives.* New York: Praeger.

Miller, G. R., & Burgoon, M. (1973). *New techniques of persuasion.* New York: Harper and Row.

Misanchuk, E. R. (1992). *Preparing instructional text: Document design using desktop publishing.* Englewood Cliffs, NJ: Educational Technology Publications.

Murray, H. A. (1938). *Explorations in personality.* New York: Oxford University Press.

Nicholls, J. (1984). Conceptions of ability and achievement motivation. In R. Ames & C. Ames (Eds.), *Research on motivation in education,* Vol. 1. Orlando, FL: Academic Press.

Okey, J. R., & Santiago, R. S. (1991). Integrating instructional and motivational design. *Performance Improvement Quarterly, 43*(2), 11–21.

Pace, A. J. (1982). Analyzing and describing the structure of prose. In D. H. Jonassen (Ed.), *The technology of text.* Englewood Cliffs, NJ: Educational Technology Publications.

Perlmuter, L. C., & Monty, R. A. (1977). The importance of perceived control: Fact or fantasy? *American Scientist, 65,* 759–765.

Resnick, L. B. (1981). Instructional psychology. *Annual Review of Psychology, 32,* 659–704.

Ross, S. M. (1983). Increasing the meaningfulness of quantitative material by adapting context to student background. *Journal of Educational Psychology, 75,* 519–529.

Rotter, J. B. (1972). In introduction to social learning theory. In J. B. Rotter, J. E. Chance, & E. J. Phares (Eds.), *Applications of a social learning theory of personality.* New York: Holt, Rinehart, & Winston.

Seligman, M. E. (1975). *Helplessness.* San Francisco: Freeman.

Shimmerlik, S. M. (1978). Organization theory and memory for prose: A review of the literature. *Review of Educational Research, 48*(1), 103–120.

Singer, H. (1985). Comprehension instruction. In T. Husen & T. N. Postlewaite (Eds.), *The international encyclopedia of education,* Vol. 2. Oxford: Pergamon Press.

Slavin, R. (1984). Students motivating students to excel: Cooperative incentives, cooperative tasks, and student achievement. *Elementary School Journal, 85,* 53–64.

Smith, J., & Orr, J. (1985). Some basic writing concepts. *Performance and Instruction Journal, 5,* 5–7.

Sperber, D., & Wilson, D. (1986). *Relevance: Communication and cognition.* Cambridge, MA: Harvard University Press.

Sternthal, B., & Craig, C. S. (1973). Humor in advertising. *Journal of Marketing, 37* (October), 12–18.

Suchman, J. R. (1966). A model for the analysis of inquiry. In H. J. Klausmeier & C. W. Harris (Eds.), *Analysis of concept learning.* New York: Academic Press.

Tosti, D. T. (1978). Formative feedback. *NSPI Journal,* October, 19–21.

Trimble, J. (1975). *Writing with style: Conversations on the style of writing.* Englewood Cliffs, NJ: Prentice-Hall.

Turnbull, A. T., & Baird, R. N. (1964). *The graphics of communication: Typography, layout, design.* New York: Holt, Rinehart, & Winston.

Turnbull, A. T., & Baird, R. N. (1975). *The graphics of communication.* New York: Holt, Rinehart, & Winston.

Visser, J., & Keller, J. M. (1990). The clinical use of motivational messages: An inquiry into the validity of the ARCS model of motivational design. *Instructional Science, 19,* 467–500.

Waller, R. (1982). Text as diagram: Using typography to improve access and understanding. In D. H. Jonassen (Ed.), *The technology of text.* Englewood Cliffs, NJ: Educational Technology Publications.

Weiner, B. (1985). *Human motivation.* New York: Springer-Verlag.

Weiss, J. M. (1972). Psychological factors in stress and disease. *Scientific American, 226,* 104–113.

Wheelwright, P. (1962). *Metaphor and reality.* Bloomington, IN: Indiana University Press.

White, J. (1987). *The grid book.* Paramus, NJ: Letraset, pp. 37–52.

White, R. W. (1959). Motivation reconsidered: The concept of confidence. *Psychological Review, 66,* 297–323.

Wilson, T. C., Pfister, F. C., & Fleury, B. B. (1981). *The design of printed materials: Research on illustrations and typography.* Syracuse, NY: ERIC Clearinghouse on Information Resources.

Wlodkowski, R. J. (1985). *Enhancing adult motivation to learn.* San Francisco: Jossey-Bass.

Yerkes, R. M., & Dodson, J. D. (1908). The relation of stimulus to rapidity of habit formation. *Journal of Comparative and Neurological Psychology, 18,* 459–482.

# Chapter 2

# Perception Principles

## William Winn

### University of Washington

## Introduction

In 1982, David Marr published his book *Vision*. In it, he described a theory of vision that is compatible with current theories of cognition but is at the same time innovative. The ideas contained in this book have had a great impact on research in human perception in subsequent years and therefore contribute significantly to the formulation of principles for the message designer.

There are several reasons why it is useful to begin our discussion of perception with Marr's theory, apart from its influence on recent research. The first is that it exemplifies both the tenets and the methodologies of what is referred to generically as "Computational Psychology" (Boden, 1988; Pylyshyn, 1984). Like many of us, Marr was dismayed by the problems confronting those who would like to explain perception and cognition in terms of how the brain works. Instead, he proposed an approach in which these problems are bypassed in favor of the development of functions and algorithms that describe how perceived information is transformed as it passes through various stages of perceptual processing. For example, imagine that you are looking at a bright figure on a dark background. The intensity of the image and the level of activation of the light-sensitive cells in the retina change as the boundary between figure and background is crossed. This change can be represented by a simple mathematical function which, in effect, describes what happens when we detect an edge in the visual field. Marr built sophisticated mathematical models of perception from functions like this which allowed him to simulate perceptual processes mathematically. When he compared the results of these simulations with data representing the electrical activity associated with the perception of forms, he found that his mathematical functions predicted actual neurological activity with a high degree of accuracy (Marr & Ullman, 1981). In other words, he demonstrated that, given the right functions from which to compute results, it is possible to account for perceptual phenomena without understanding how the brain works.

What this means for the message designer is that it is how information is processed that is of primary interest, not cerebral functioning. This should come as something of a relief to readers of this chapter! However, it carries with it a responsibility. The message designer needs to understand how message form and structure influence information processing. Many of the principles presented in the chapter deal with this issue head on.

A second reason for beginning with Marr's work is that he shows that much of the computational action of perception takes place preattentively. This means that we have no control over it. It is involuntary and automatic. Try looking at an edge somewhere in your environment, perhaps the edge of the paper that you are now reading. There is no way in which you can will yourself not to see it as an edge. What is of greatest importance is that Marr (and others, e.g., Pomerantz, 1981, 1986; Treisman, 1986, 1988; Treisman & Gelade, 1980) has shown that a great deal of perceptual organization occurs preattentively. We used to think that perception is strongly influenced by what we already know, what we need to find out, and what we expect to see (Neisser, 1976). What Marr has demonstrated in effect is that the "top-down" effects of knowledge, needs, and expectations do not exert their influence until most of the organization of what is seen has taken place (that is, all of it except for the recovery of some depth cues). As we shall see later in this chapter, perceptual organization strongly predisposes people to make one interpretation of what is seen rather than another. The net result is that, in spite of the top-down influences that operate once attention is brought to bear, preattentive organization is a powerful determinant of what is actually understood in the perceived message.

For message designers, this means that great care should be given to the structural properties of messages that affect perceptual organization. These include, but are not limited to, the relative placement, size, and dominance of objects in the visual field, and the way the eye is "led" over the image by various techniques of composition. The message designer cannot assume that people will see what they are told they are looking at, and cannot easily compensate for a poorly designed message with instructions on how it is to be perceived. For this reason, many of the design principles we shall be discussing are concerned with designing messages for appropriate preattentive processing.

I hope that I have not given the impression that Marr has been the only serious recent contributor to our understanding of perception. Far from it. As we shall see, the study of perception is in a period of great activity and abounds with exciting and provocative ideas. However, the computational approach and the belief in the importance of preattentive processing are fundamental to an understanding of current thinking about perception and to the development of message design principles. The work of Marr encapsulates these ideas in a manageable fashion.

We move now to our examination of recent research and theory about human perception. The reader will notice that the implications of the computational approach and of preattentive processing are far-reaching in both the scholarly literature and in the principles for message design. This chapter is divided into two parts. The first proposes principles derived from basic mechanisms that are responsible for the perception and interpretation of messages. The discussion is drawn largely from basic psychological research. The second part presents principles derived more from educational literature that have a closer relationship to more specific factors involved in message design.

# I. Basic Mechanisms:
# Preattentive and Attentive Processing

Perception can be thought of as a set of physiological and psychological processes by means of which we make sense of our environment. All living organisms respond to changes in the environment—to changes in light and temperature, to threats of danger, and to information leading to a source of food or to a mate. In many species, from planarian worms to humans, these responses have to be *learned*, either through experience or as a result of instruction.

To understand perception is to understand why and how information in the environment that is directly available to the senses gives rise to certain behaviors. In lower animals, changes in behavior as a result of the perception of events in the environment are readily observed and therefore easy to study and understand. In many species of coral, the polyps extend their tentacles to feed at night, when the light level falls below a particular threshold. Moths are drawn to their mates when they detect certain chemicals in the air. In the case of human perception, however, the response to perceived changes in the environment is often not apparent. Humans are thinking and feeling creatures, and their thoughts and emotions are not directly observable. The effects of perceptual processes on inner, cognitive phenomena are therefore often undetectable, making them difficult to study and understand. Even when observable behaviors do result from perceptual experiences, they are often mediated by memory, meaning that they can occur well after the event was perceived—weeks, perhaps years later.

In order to understand the effects of perception, it is therefore necessary to understand all of human cognitive activity. Fortunately, the scope of this book is such that most major aspects of cognition are addressed. However, for the message designer, the fact that the earliest stage of cognition, namely perception, predetermines much of what goes on in later stages is clearly an indication that the nature and effects of the earliest processes are important to consider and to influence. Because people's behavior may not immediately reveal what they learn from what they perceive, a message may be misinterpreted without anyone knowing about it. The designer therefore needs to take all necessary steps to ensure that the message is constructed so as to make it easy to perceive in the way it was meant to be.

Fortunately, at one level, perceptual processes are among the most tractable of the processes people use to organize and interpret information. This is because early perception is not under the control of attention, proceeding automatically under the control of physiological as much as psychological processes. Our pupils dilate and contract to adapt to different levels of light in ways that we cannot willfully control. Our attention is automatically drawn to loud noises or rapid movement. Manipulations of message components that the designer undertakes to influence these early stages of perception are therefore more likely to have predictable results than manipulations done to influence the later stages of information processing.

A useful place to begin our examination of human perception is therefore to examine the differences between preattentive and attentive processing. At what point do sensory data become information? Opinions on this have varied. On the one hand, Gibson (1979) has proposed that information exists in the environment, in the very light that enters our eyes. All humans have to do is pick it up and use it. Others have claimed that nothing can make any sense to us at all until it has been processed, top-down, by conscious attention; even that which we perceive in the first place is determined by what we know and therefore expect to perceive (Neisser, 1976). Recent research suggests a middle ground. While existing knowledge and attentive processing are important for recognition, identification, and so on, a great deal of organizing goes on preattentively. This means that conscious attentional processes are given data to work with that already have an organization that can predispose the perceiver toward particular interpretations.

Our quest for message design principles based upon research on human perception will therefore begin with preattentive perceptual organization. It will then move to attentive selection and those cognitive processes that further organize perceived information in preparation for its assimilation to existing schemata in memory. All the time, however, it must be remembered that preattentive processing does determine what happens later, but also that an understanding of early perceptual processes, while necessary, is by no means sufficient for the message designer to create effective instructional messages.

## 1. Preattentive Perceptual Processing

**1.1.**   *A great deal of perceptual organization occurs preattentively, not under cognitive control. The way a message is organized will therefore have an important effect on the way the perceptual system structures what it detects and, in ways that the perceiver will not be aware of, on how that information is interpreted.*

The work of Marr (1982) and his colleagues has given us a very fine account of what happens, in vision, as neurophysiological processes operate on the retinal image and begin to organize it. Because these early processes are not under the control of attention, they do not draw on cognitive resources at all. They occur in parallel and rapidly. As a result, people cannot willfully alter them or control them. Indeed, people are not even aware of them. This means that changes in the instructional message that are likely to affect early processing may predispose students to quite different interpretations of messages in ways that are unknown to the student or the designer. The message designer therefore needs to be aware of what these early perceptual processes are and of the factors that influence them.

### 1.2. *Human perception is only sensitive to CHANGES in stimulation.*

The message designer therefore should pay particular attention to making such changes clear. Examples would include making sure that the boundaries of figures or the onsets of sounds are unambiguous. It is generally understood that information is processed in the central nervous system through the firing or inhibition of neurons. Once a neuron has fired, it needs to be re-stimulated before it can fire again. Thus, information that the senses detect in the environment can only be conveyed to the brain when the level of stimulation changes. However, not only must stimulation change, but also it must change to a sufficient degree to cross the threshold below which a neuron cannot fire.

In vision, such changes in stimulation occur when there is a fairly abrupt change from light to dark and vice versa, or from one color or texture to another. Phenomenologically, we experience these changes as edges. Physiologically, the neurons that are sensitive to light, or to a particular color, will fire on that side of the edge that is above the threshold. The pattern of firing is transmitted to the visual cortex by the optic nerve.

Marr has drawn attention to the importance of edge-detection in his theory of vision. Scenes are initially reduced to patterns of edges that look like line drawings. The pieces that the lines outline form "primitives," that include edges, bars, dots, and blobs, which have such characteristics as position, length, and width. Figure 2.1 illustrates this. Perceptual organization is based on the subsequent processing of these primitives. If the edges are not clear, neither will the formation of primitives be clear, and perceptual organization will not lead to well-structured and interpretable messages.

### 1.3. *Distinguishing between figure and ground is one of the most basic perceptual processes. Early perceptual processes are active in figure-ground organization. Message designers should make figure-ground distinctions as clear as possible.*

The mechanisms of early perception often give rise to the creation of figures that stand in contrast to a background. In all cases, such figures are delimited by a boundary. Boundaries may be continuous edges that enclose a space, or may be created when areas of different texture (Julesz, 1981), or groups of primitives having a common characteristic such as orientation, are juxtaposed or superimposed. These types of organization are implicit in much of Marr's theory. Ullman (1985) describes "visual routines" that apply more directly to figure-ground distinctions. Three routines in particular are relevant. First, Ullman proposes that boundary-tracing is a necessary capability of the human perceptual system. It is a routine that operates on data provided by the earliest stages of perception, and allows people to determine where boundaries around an area lie.

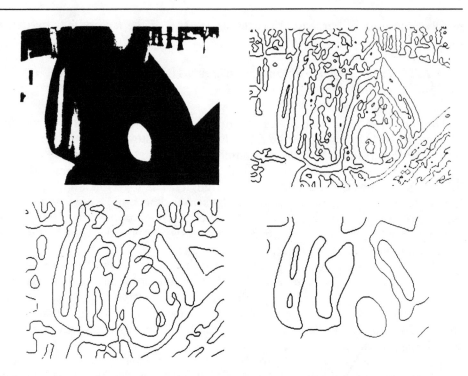

**Figure 2.1.** How Marr proposes that early perception computes perceptual primitives from a retinal image. The line drawings illustrate edge-detection at different scales (Marr, 1982).

Second is a routine, "coloring," that in effect allows the viewer to fill in an area that is surrounded by a boundary. It is the perceptual equivalent of coloring in shapes using a typical computer "paint" program. The color "runs" across the image until a boundary is encountered, where it stops. Third is a routine that allows us to judge whether a location is inside or outside a figure. This is something that people are generally very good at; but "insideness" is not something that is explicit in the perceptual data themselves.

It follows from this that message designers stand a better chance of constructing "good figures" if the boundaries that surround them are not only clear but also complete. However, people are capable of completing boundaries for themselves if they are not too seriously degraded. This process, usually referred to as "closure," is also apparent in the early stages of perceptual processing. Both Marr and Ullman describe processes in which primitives or tokens are grouped on the basis of colinearity. In other words, tokens that line up in a straight line or on a curve are grouped together. In this way, shapes with gaps in their boundaries are perceived as complete shapes, provided that what remains of their boundaries aligns in geometrically relatively simple ways.

***1.4a.*** *Configuration of parts into potentially meaningful units is an important feature of preattentive perceptual organization. It occurs whenever the parts are not attended to selectively.*

Beyond edge detection, the forming of primitives, and figure-ground discrimination, preattentive perceptual processes impose organization on perceptual data in a number of important ways. One of these has to do with how primitives are put together to form configurations that can be treated subsequently as single perceptual units.

Pomerantz (1986) and Pomerantz, Pristach, & Carson (1989) have described perceptual grouping in terms of the failure of selective attention. This means that a perceptual unit can be defined as the largest collection of parts in which the parts are not attended to separately. Pomerantz's experimental materials illustrate this. In a number of studies, he found that pairs of parentheses such as ( ( and ( ) were perceived as one unit, while pairs such as ( ∩ or )∩ were perceived as two units. Reaction times in a task requiring the classification of the first kind of parenthesis pair were longer when the classification had to be made on the basis of one of the two parentheses than on the basis of the pair as a whole. For the second kind of pair, there was no difference in reaction times. This suggested that having to break apart two elements that configured to form a single perceptual unit, as in ( ( and ( ), interfered with the task. In the case of ( ∩ and )∩, the parts were already attended to separately, so reaction times were not affected.

It is clear that the two types of stimuli used by Pomerantz are qualitatively different from a phenomenological point of view. One readily senses that ( ( and ( ) have a property, symmetry perhaps, that makes it easier to see them as one unit, than ( ∩ and )∩. While such an observation lacks in prescriptive precision, it is nonetheless important for the message designer to realize that, for certain aspects of an instructional message, some arrangements of parts will allow them to configure into perceptual units, while others will not. The design of effective icons for use in computer interfaces is a case in point.

***1.4b.*** *The configuration of parts into perceptual units takes place when such a configuration permits an "emergent property" to become evident.*

The idea of "emergent property" (Rock, 1986) comes very close to the Gestalt psychologists' principle of "Prägnanz" (Wertheimer, 1938), or parsimony, in perceptual organization. Perception tends to look for the simplest organization of the parts of a display. If tokens can therefore be configured to form a single perceptual unit, perceptual processes will tend to "see" the unit rather than its parts. In the case of Pomerantz's parentheses, symmetry was an emergent property of ( ( and ( ) that allowed the two parts to be seen as one unit. In other research (Pomerantz, Sager, & Stover, 1977), other emergent properties were identified. For instance, a diagonal line, a vertical line, and a horizontal line, presented in that order, did not configure to form a single perceptual unit.

However, as can be seen from Figure 2.2, when the same three lines were arranged to form a triangle or an arrow, the three lines were perceived as a single perceptual unit. In this case, "triangleness" and "arrowness" were emergent properties that defined the unit of analysis. These conclusions were derived from reaction-time studies using a similar methodology to the parentheses studies. Breaking apart an arrow or a triangle interferes with the classification of arrows or triangles on the basis of the orientation of the diagonal line.

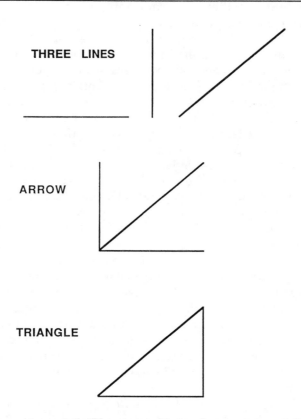

**Figure 2.2.** "Emergent properties" become apparent when parts are configured into more elaborate forms. The three lines on top are perceived separately. The arrow and triangle, in which the same lines are configured to reveal emergent properties, are seen as single forms.

The idea of emergent properties of configurations is extremely important for message designers. Used with skill, emergent properties can help designers to create configurations that lead to the association of parts in the precise perceptual units on which subsequent interpretation of a message is to be based. Ignored, unforeseen configurations may appear that bias interpretation in ways that the designer never anticipated, let alone desired.

> **1.4c.** *The configuration of parts into perceptual units, arising from the presence of an emergent property, is influenced by the physical proximity of the parts to each other, in time as well as in space.*

Message designers therefore need to make sure that parts that are intended to be perceived as perceptual units are close to each other in the display. Pomerantz and Schwaitzberg (1975) demonstrated that moving the parts of a perceptual unit farther apart made configuration less likely, thus increasing the likelihood of selective attention to individual parts and destroying the integrity of the unit. This demonstration confirms, for preattentive perception, the Gestalt principle of proximity that is usually considered in the context of attentive processing. For the designer, it confirms that the parts of a message that are perceived as being close together will be processed together as one entity. Our example described spatial proximity. The proximity principle applies to time as well. Sounds that rapidly follow each other, followed by a pause, and then another succession of rapid sounds, will be "configured" into two perceptual units (Deutsch, 1986).

> **1.5a.** *Early processing organizes perceptual units into groups, and groups into other groups in a hierarchical manner. The way the elements of a message are clustered by the designer may therefore have an important influence on perceptual organization.*

The configuration of parts into perceptual units takes place on a variety of scales in the message. Just as selective attention to separate parts fails when they are in close proximity and bound together by some emergent property, larger perceptual units can be formed when smaller units are clustered together and configured in some particular way.

The question that now becomes extremely important for the message designer is the level at which the perceiver "enters" the hierarchy of the message's components. Does the perceiver start by seeing the details and then synthesize them, working up the hierarchy, until the whole message emerges; or does the perceiver see the "big picture" first, analyzing it into its component parts? Early research (Navon, 1977; see Figure 2.3) seemed to provide evidence that the latter was the case, that perceivers work top-down from the whole message to its details, from global to local elements. However, subsequent studies showed that global precedence may not occur when the message is presented for relatively long periods of time. (Navon presented stimuli tachistoscopically for very short durations.) Global versus local precedence also seems to be affected by whether or not the parts are connected in some way (Lesaga, 1989) or are separated from each other, by the size of the parts within a group, and by the discriminability of the parts from each other.

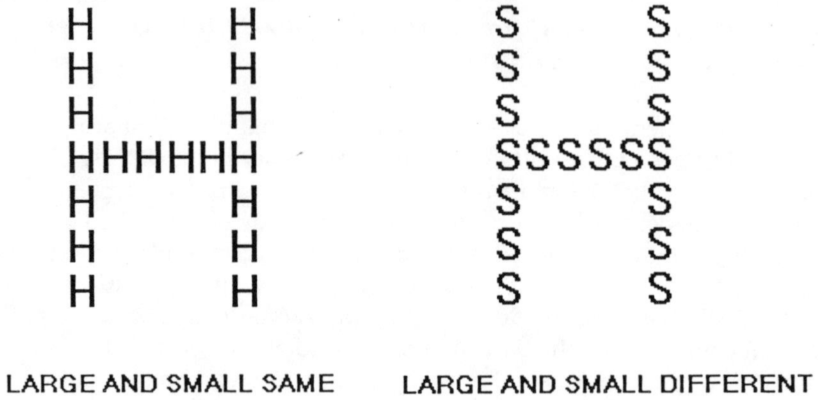

```
H        H              S          S
H        H              S          S
H        H              S          S
HHHHHH                  SSSSSS
H        H              S          S
H        H              S          S
H        H              S          S
```

LARGE AND SMALL SAME        LARGE AND SMALL DIFFERENT

**Figure 2.3.** Which do you see first, the small h's and s's, or the large H? Navon (1977) used figures like these in his demonstration of "global precedence" in perception.

> *1.5b.  Whether people see the "big picture" or details first depends primarily, in visual perception, on the size of the visual angle, that is, on the size of the image relative to the whole visual field. This means that, typically, neither global nor local precedence dominates, but rather that people enter the image at a level of detail that is somewhere between the two extremes.*

Perhaps most important is the evidence presented by Kinchla and Wolfe (1979) for a "middle out" approach to the question of precedence. In a study of local versus global precedence along the lines of Navon's work, they found that people attended first to local details when the image subtended a large visual angle, and that they attended first to the whole image when it subtended a small visual angle. This result clearly tied global and local precedence to the size of the retinal image relative to the visual field. People tend to look at small pictures first of all as wholes and first at the details in large pictures. Given that people tend to look at pictures that cast an average-sized image on the retina, it seems reasonable to conclude that normally people first perceive a middle level of detail in a message and work out from there, up to a coarser-grained level and down toward finer and finer detail.

Subsequent research has added an important refinement to this conclusion. Antes and Mann (1984) confirmed Kinchla and Wolfe's finding that precedence was determined by visual angle. However, they explained this finding in terms of what they called a "critical sampling bandwidth" which determines the level at which people start viewing an image. Simply put, processing priority does not depend absolutely on the size of the image, but on the density of the detail. Size only appears to determine precedence because when small pictures are enlarged, the details become less compact. The manipulation of the size of images relative to the visual field or the density of details in an image is something that the message designer can use to increase the chance of a person starting his or her examination of a message at a particular place. This in turn will influence the subsequent stages of processing and interpretation.

### 1.6. *A horizontal-vertical reference system seems to be fundamental to perceptual organization. There is also a natural tendency for people to partition images into left and right fields.*

There is evidence that humans possess a natural internal frame of spatial reference that is oriented toward the horizontal and the vertical rather than the diagonal. Both the classification of dot patterns (Cecala & Garner, 1986) and judging whether dot patterns that had undergone a variety of geometric transformations were the same or different (Kahn & Foster, 1986) were easier when the dots were aligned along the horizontal or vertical axis rather than the diagonal axis. There is a suggestion that this preference is the result of the fact that human beings tend to deal with their world in terms of its vertical and horizontal dimensions. We walk upright and lie down to sleep. Objects aligned vertically and horizontally tend to be stable, which is often the state we want them to be in. However, there is reason to suppose that preferred frames of reference may vary across cultures. The evidence for this comes from studies of such things as representational and decorative arts and architectural styles of different cultures, and not from the controlled study of basic perceptual mechanisms.

Nicoletti and Umilta (1989) suggest that our internal frame of reference arises from the fact that humans have bilateral symmetry, that is to say, the two "halves" of a person around the vertical axis are roughly mirror images of each other (as is indeed the case in all vertebrates). They found that responses to stimuli presented to the left of the point of fixation were quicker when made by the left hand, with those made by the right hand being quicker to stimuli to the right of the fixation point. Most important, this was true regardless of whether or not the display was obviously divided into left and right halves, or where attention was focused, or whether the display was partitioned into right and left fields at a point other than the obvious central division. In other words, the internal frame of reference was sufficiently influential to override factors, such as obvious divisions or focusing attention, that are usually considered to be powerful determinants of perception, interpretation, and behavior.

The suggestion in this research that our internal frames of reference are somatically rather than perceptually or psychologically based is important. It means that they will be quite resistant to change by the message designer, and must therefore be considered a constraint on design. Fortunately, the designer is a human being too, and will tend naturally to follow the same frames of reference when designing messages as students will when perceiving them. (But this will not be the case when message design is performed by computers, which is certainly now within the realms of possibility.)

## 2. Attentive Perceptual Processing: Selection and Organization

**2.1.** *The way in which cognitive processes operate on perceptual data is in large measure directed by the organization that has been imposed preattentively.*

This principle summarizes a theme that has been woven throughout our discussion of preattentive perceptual organization in the previous section. It has been treated as a fundamental assumption, although there is direct empirical evidence that it is true. Studies by Calis, Sterenborg, and Maarse (1984) and Owen (1985a, 1985b) both demonstrated that a picture presented very rapidly before another, which replaced it before the first could be scrutinized by focused attention, nonetheless influenced the way in which the second picture was processed and interpreted under the control of attention.

In this section we begin our examination of research concerning the second major phase of perception, that is, processing under the control of focused attention. Unlike preattentive processing, which is parallel, rapid, and does not draw upon cognitive resources, attentive processing is serial, slower, and draws heavily on short-term memory. People are usually aware of what they are seeing, and can deliberately influence the processes that are occurring.

**2.2.** *Attentive processing draws directly on cognitive resources. Attentive perception is therefore constrained in its ability to handle information, and is highly selective as a result.*

Once percepts become available to conscious attention, an important change occurs in the way information is processed. What we already know, what we expect to see, our various mental abilities and perceptual "styles" begin to influence our interpretation of the information before us. The interface between perception and cognition, thus created, is bi-directional; it operates top-down and bottom-up, in a way described by Neisser (1976). Our existing knowledge leads us to anticipate, top-down, what we see or hear in the data before us. Our anticipatory schemata guide our scrutiny of the data, which influence in turn, bottom-up, what we look for next. This interaction of data-driven and schema-driven processing is a theme that we will keep coming back to as we examine attentive processing.

Of more immediate concern are the implications of these processes for perceptual capacity. Because all attentive processing is in some way concerned with the apprehension, temporary storage, and elaboration of information, it involves short-term memory, a notorious bottleneck in the human information processing system. The capacity of short-term memory is generally considered to be about five items. Moreover, the contents of short-term memory require constant refreshing through rehearsal, otherwise they will be lost. It follows that only a few of the items presented to attentive processing can be dealt with at once. Therefore, cognitive scrutiny of what is perceived must be serial. This has three important implications. First, because it is serial, it is slow. Second, because it is serial, some things are considered before others, so the order in which items are attended to becomes crucial to comprehension of the message. Third, because it is constrained both in terms of memory capacity and processing speed, recognition, interpretation, and comprehension will take place without the inspection and elaboration of every piece of information that is available. Indeed, it is likely that most of the information that is organized preattentively will not be attended to at all. Attentive perception is very selective. The message must therefore not contain much irrelevant information, for that may be attended to in preference to what is really important. It is crucial that the message designer control which parts of the message are attended to and the order in which items in a message are examined.

> **2.3a.** *Attention is drawn to the parts of a message that stand in contrast to the others. Such contrasts can exist in just about every aspect of the message's content, organization, and modality.*

The attention-drawing power of those parts of messages that stand in contrast to the rest of the message is something we have all experienced. In visual messages, attention can be directed by the use of contrasting brightness, color, size, shape, type style, and motion. This is why the use of some color in a black-and-white picture, bold type in a text, and animation of just one object on a screen is so effective at drawing attention. In auditory messages, attention can be directed by contrasts in pitch, tempo, loudness, and timbre. Thus, a loud sound draws attention, as does switching from a low male voice to a higher-pitched female voice in a narration. The change of tempo, background music, or narration will likewise draw the listener's attention. Finally, any change in visual or auditory stimulation that has an abrupt rather than a smooth onset will attract attention. This means that message designers can affect how much attention is paid to a certain part of a message by varying the rate at which changes occur. An instantaneous change in brightness or loudness will be more successful at attracting attention than changes that take place gradually over a longer period of time. Indeed, over very long periods, changes in brightness and loudness may not be noticed at all.

> **2.3b.** *Contrasts among different levels of sensory stimulation are most noticeable in the middle ranges of stimulus intensity and harder to detect at extreme ranges.*

Changes and differences in brightness are hard to detect when the overall brightness of an image is either very high or very low. However, when the image is of average brightness, the same degree of difference or change would be more noticeable. The same is true of sounds. It is harder to detect differences between two soft sounds or two loud sounds than between sounds of average loudness. In order to use contrast to manipulate attention, the message designer should therefore take care that the level of perceptual stimulation provided by the message is neither very high nor very low.

> ### 2.4a. The sequential flow of attention to the parts of a message is determined by the sequence in which information is presented.

Many messages have a built-in sequence, meaning that information is presented a piece at a time. Examples include motion pictures (film, television, videodisc in "play" mode, animated computer graphics), any auditory message (lecture, narration, music), and written text (although some people have a tendency to hop about in books and on the page, and hypermedia technologies are designed deliberately to "liberate" information from the necessity of sequential presentation). In many of these cases, the control the designer has over the order in which information is attended to is absolute. Any perceptual access, preattentive or attentive, to the next piece of information is denied until the current piece has been presented and examined.

> ### 2.4b. The rate at which sequential information is presented should be slow enough to allow accurate perception, attentive scrutiny, elaboration, and comprehension. It should also be rapid enough to prevent attention from wandering. Under some circumstances, the rate of presentation can be determined by the learner.

Although the message designer has control over the rate at which the parts of a message are presented, and thus indirectly over how the message is processed, too rapid a presentation will not allow enough time for the learner to perceive and interpret the message. Just how much time is necessary for decoding and interpretation, beyond the time needed for the acquisition of the message, is difficult to determine. However, Belland, Taylor, Canelos, Dwyer, and Baker (1985) found that adding seven seconds of "processing time" to the time estimated as necessary to read text on a computer screen produced significantly better performance. Overdoing it, though, can lead to decrements in performance. If the pace is too slow, then the necessary attention and processing effort will have been spent on a message segment long before it is replaced with the next part. During this time, attention may wander to other, irrelevant matters which actively interfere with processing the current message, meaning that it may be partially forgotten before the next piece is presented.

This poses something of a dilemma to the designer. Some (for example, Hannafin, 1984) have suggested that giving the learner control over the rate of presentation is the solution. However, Tennyson (1981) cautions us that this causes other problems. Because learners cannot know the extent of what is to be mastered before they have been exposed to it, there is a tendency for students using learner control to skim over or omit important parts of what they are to study. Tennyson recommends that learners be given specific advice about how to proceed through instruction, while maintaining their control over pace.

> **2.4c.** *When the sequence in which message elements are to be processed is not controlled by the order in which they are presented, sequence can still be influenced by the relative attention-drawing capability of individual items, and by devices such as lines, arrows, and the message's composition.*

In many messages, such as still pictures, graphs, charts, diagrams, maps, and so on, all of the parts are available to the perceptual system simultaneously. Preattentive perception will deal with them in parallel, as we have seen. This means that the order in which they are attended to is not determined by their being made accessible to perception in a particular order. The cognitive mechanisms that guide attention are therefore largely responsible for where attention is directed. The message designer can influence these processes in several ways.

We saw above that attention is drawn to parts of messages that stand in contrast to the rest of the message. If the message is constructed with different degrees of contrast among its parts, then attention will be drawn to the greatest contrast first, to the next greatest contrast second, and so on. Thus, by presenting items in three different sizes, the designer can be reasonably sure that the student will attend to them in order from largest to smallest.

The sequence in which parts of a message are inspected can also be influenced by showing those sequences explicitly through the use of such graphic devices as lines and arrows. Winn and Holliday (1982) and Rankin (1986) have demonstrated the effectiveness of these techniques for determining processing sequence. Some are illustrated in Figure 2.4. Since attentional sequence is determined largely by where the eye is looking (though shifts in attention can occur without changes in eye fixation points; Umilta, 1988), then the guiding of eyeflow over an image by means of such devices will guide attention along a similar path. Joining perceptual units with lines helps them to configure into groups for the same reasons that we examined in the first section of this chapter. The eye tends to follow lines and contours, and thus message elements that "line up" in a noticeable way will be attended to in sequence.

If we take this notion one step further, we find that various rules for the composition of pictures, derived more from aesthetic than psychological inquiry, are relevant to message design. The eye is influenced by the "balance," "harmony," and general composition of a picture, as the classical studies of Yarbus (1967), illustrated in Figure 2.5, have clearly demonstrated. The message designer may therefore use these principles for guidance.

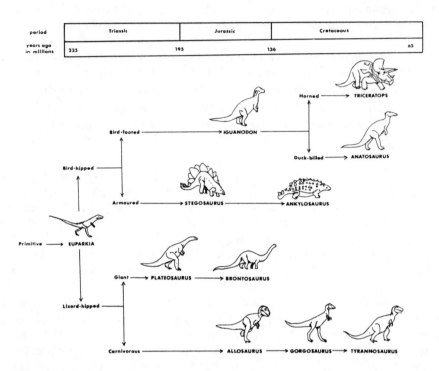

**Figure 2.4.** A number of devices suggest the sequence of dinosaur evolution: the arrows, the time scale, the "sideways" hierarchical arrangement, and the direction in which the animals appear to be walking (Jonassen, 1982).

2.5.    *If none of these factors come into play, there is a tendency for literate viewers to "read" visual messages in the same way they read text—for English speakers, that means from left to right and top to bottom.*

In cases where neither the sequence in which information is presented, nor the organizational and compositional factors we have just examined are present, people seem to read images in the same way that they read text. This means, for speakers of English and many other languages, that all other things being equal, the information in the top left part of a visual display will be attended to first, with attention shifting to the right and toward the bottom of the image. However, this is admittedly a weak design principle. Even if the designer wants to, it is extremely difficult to construct a visual message that is completely neutral as to the influence of the factors that affect where attention is directed. And even in cases where the left-right, top-bottom principle is deliberately violated, people quickly adapt to the new format (Winn, 1983). It is therefore best for designers to construct messages in which the devices we have been examining

 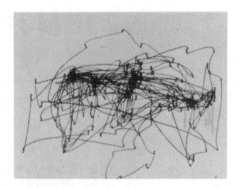

**Figure 2.5.** These tracks of eye movements were taken by Yarbus over a three-minute period while the subject viewed the picture. Notice the greater number of fixations on the people in the picture, around whom the composition of the picture is built (Yarbus, 1967).

are deliberately applied to direct attention, and not simply to assume that viewers' attention will shift reliably from left to right and top to bottom.

### 2.6a. *Information is processed and remembered in "chunks" that are organized hierarchically.*

One way in which the constraints placed on attentive processing by the limitations of short-term memory and processing capacity can be reduced is by organizing perceived information in clusters, or "chunks," that can be dealt with subsequently as single units (Anderson, 1983; Miller, 1956). Figure 2.6 shows examples of this. The way in which chunks are formed is something that the message designer should attend to, and over which it is possible to exercise a measure of influence by capitalizing on message structures that assist both preattentive perceptual organization and where and how attention is directed.

### 2.6b. *Message structure determines how chunks are formed and thus how memory for the content of the message is organized.*

Does Reno lie to the east or the west of San Diego? Think about it for a moment, and then look at Figure 2.7. The reason most people think it lies to the east of San Diego is as follows: Reno is in Nevada; San Diego is in California; Nevada is to the east of California; therefore Reno is to the east of San Diego.
Reno and all cities in Nevada form one chunk of information. San Diego and all other California cities from another chunk. To answer the question, the chunks rather than the individual cities are compared, and in this case the wrong answer is usually produced. The greater storage and recall efficiency obtained by chunking is therefore sometimes traded off against accuracy in the details within each chunk. But this is the exception rather than the rule.

# IBMJFKCBS

**Easy to chunk in groups of three.**

# BVEFTOPZA

**Harder to chunk.**

**Figure 2.6.** When strings of letters form well-known sets of initials, as in the top string, each set can be encoded as a single "chunk," which makes it easier to remember.

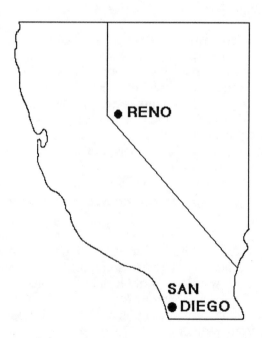

**Figure 2.7.** Yes, Reno is west of San Diego. People misjudge its position because it belongs to a larger unit, Nevada, which lies generally to the east of California, the larger unit to which San Diego belongs.

Chunking not only helps circumvent the limited capacity of short-term memory, but also it reduces the number of items that need be placed into long-term memory, making storage and retrieval more efficient (McNamara, 1986). However, it does mean that, to recall the details stored in each chunk, a greater amount of processing has to be done to "unpack" (Anderson, 1983) the contents of each one. McNamara has claimed, in fact, that spatial memory is only partially hierarchical. Sometimes relationships among perceptual groups are attended to and remembered. At other times, relationships among details are processed one-to-one. (You will probably now remember for a while that, although Nevada is east of California, Reno is west of San Diego. The former fact involves a chunk that includes all of the items that belong in each state; the latter a one-to-one relationship between a single item from each.)

> *2.6c. The formation of chunks is facilitated by factors that encourage the clustering of perceptual units into groups. These include the relative proximity of elements to each other, enclosing groups in boundaries, and arranging them so that emergent properties, such as easily recognizable shapes, are evident.*

It should be clear from looking at Figure 2.8 that the organization of a message into chunks has an important influence on how it is processed and understood. It should also be clear that how this organization takes place under attentive cognitive control is considerably affected by such factors as the configuration of parts into perceptual units, the formation of groups and local versus global precedence that we examined earlier in this chapter. Now we can assert with some confidence that the direct manipulation of these aspects of a message's structure by the designer can control how chunks are formed. There are direct parallels at this attentional level of processing with processes that operate preattentively.

As we saw in the case of Reno and San Diego, items surrounded by a clear boundary, in this case a state line, form readily into chunks. The same is true of items that are close together in space or time. Features in a picture or on a map that are physically close tend to be processed and remembered as one unit. Sounds, notes, and spoken words that follow close after each other likewise form chunks. Thus, varying layout or pace will affect how information is organized. Finally, arranging elements so that they form shapes that have nothing to do with the sense of the message helps their organization and memory. Bellezza (1986) found this to be true of words arranged in various configurations on the page. Other mnemonic techniques involving the loci method (where items to be remembered are associated with features in a familiar environment through which a person takes a mental "walk"; Weinstein, 1978) and pictorial imagery (Levin, Anglin, & Carney, 1987) have likewise shown that spatial arrangements in mental images organize lists of words or text passages in ways that facilitate their recall and comprehension.

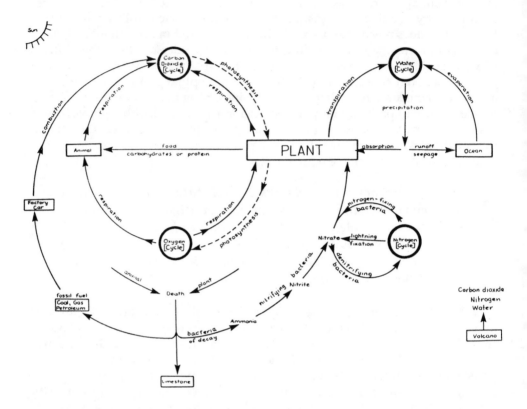

**Figure 2.8.** The two main chunks comprise the circular configurations lying on either side of the word "Plant." Each may be subdivided into smaller subordinate pieces, the Carbon Dioxide/Oxygen cycle, the Water cycle, and the Nitrogen cycle. Within each of these are even smaller structures, the smallest components of which are the individual concept names enclosed in boxes, circles, or simply standing on their own (Jonassen, 1982; originally, Holliday *et al.*, 1977).

# 3. Interpretation

3.1.    *The recognition and understanding of what is perceived are affected primarily by the relationships between messages and people's internal representations of what they entail, and not by the way messages relate to their referents.*

Message design has long been dominated by a concern for the degree to which messages resemble what they stand for. This is not to say that designers put much stock any more in the primacy of realism, as earlier scholars such as Dale (1946) and Carpenter (1953) would have us do. It was more than twenty years ago that Knowlton (1966) convinced us that a picture was often not worth a thousand words. Nonetheless, a great many researchers have told us that the relationship between a message and what it makes statements about is the primary factor whose successful manipulation by the designer can determine what a message means (Dwyer, 1972, 1978; Levie & Dickie, 1973). In other words, message designers have been concerned with "sign-referent" relationships (Ogden & Richards, 1946), and have failed to consider how messages affect what they mean to the individual who receives them in interaction with each person's knowledge of the world.

We saw in the previous section that an important feature of cognitive theories of perception and learning is the interaction between schemata and data, between what we know and believe and what our perception presents us with. Because of this, Salomon (1979) has argued that what a message means to a person is determined by that person's internal representation of the message's content and how that matches relevant knowledge that the person already possesses. Because everyone's knowledge of the world is different, the same message can mean very different things to different people. This puts the message designer on somewhat shaky ground, for it follows that the way a message is designed may have no regular and predictable effect on its meaning at all, unless the designer knows a lot about an individual at the time the message is perceived. Yet the designer can make some valid assumptions about people's knowledge on the basis that people agree about the meaning of many message elements, be they written or spoken words, conventional signs, or even aspects of pictorial composition. What is more, preattentive processing is not open to the influence of individual variations in world knowledge. It is "cognitively impenetrable" to use Pylyshyn's (1984) term. This means that at the preattentive level the results of the manipulation of message variables are reasonably predictable, and in many cases even at the attentional level of processing certain message manipulations are reasonably certain of producing consistent interpretations. The point is, however, that these are not just because the message resembles what it stands for.

The reader might be forgiven for concluding that the attention to each individual's world knowledge, recommended here, makes the message designer's job an impossible one. That is not really the intention. However, what is intended is to stress the need for the designer to consider the message's audience more seriously than is often the case (see Sless, 1981, for a discussion of this in the context of visual communication). What is more, it is now technologically possible to design certain aspects of messages dynamically in interaction with the user (Weyer & Borning, 1985; Winn, 1988b). This means that the messages presented to students using intelligent computer-assisted learning software can, in principle, be adapted to changes in students' knowledge from moment to moment. This calls for the development of powerful and flexible tools for learner analysis that the message designer can use.

### 3.2.    *The assimilation of perceived information to existing schemata, and the accommodation of those schemata to new information, require effort.*

The top-down processing of messages draws heavily on cognitive resources. As a result, effort is required by the perceiver to interpret messages. The greater the discrepancy between the message and the perceiver's knowledge of what the message is about, the greater the effort will have to be, and the process of interpretation and understanding will become more demanding. As Salomon has shown (1983), the willingness and ability of people to invest mental effort in these tasks depend on a number of factors, including their belief in their own ability to succeed and their belief about how much effort is typically required of them for interpreting the medium by means of which the message is presented to them. Ideally, the message should be designed with these factors in mind. However, this is difficult to do.

### 3.3.    *Sometimes, interacting with messages presented in ways that require a modest degree of mental effort will allow people to develop a greater ability in the mental skills necessary for decoding the message. Also, the way the message is presented can model these skills for the perceiver.*

Salomon (1976) has shown that simple exposure to messages presented in ways that require the development of skills the perceiver does not yet possess is sufficient to develop those skills. Television-naïve children have developed a variety of visual skills after exposure to "Sesame Street." But we should note that the exposure was relatively lengthy, and it is unlikely that these skills would have developed over a shorter period.

In some instances, the way a message is presented can overtly model the mental operations perceivers need to develop in order to interpret what they perceive. Salomon's classic "zooming" study (Salomon, 1974) illustrates this. It was found that a presentation in which details were zoomed in on produced better recall of details in a picture than a presentation that simply showed cuts from long shot to close-up and vice versa. Salomon argued that the dynamic property of zooming demonstrated to the viewer how *mental* "zooming" should be performed, and thus improved performance. Later research by Bovy (1983) found the same effect for *irising*, which suggests that zooming is in itself only a sufficient condition for improved recall of details, and that what is really necessary is some form of attention-focusing within a context. Any such device would have worked. Nonetheless, the designer can construct messages in such a way that they are perceived to demonstrate cognitive techniques that students can practice and learn in order to improve how they interpret messages.

The reader has probably noticed that these last three principles have not been so much prescriptions of what the message designer can do in order to facilitate the perception and understanding of messages, but rather have drawn attention to what the designer cannot do with any great precision. Although the cognitive paradigm has enormous advantages over behavioral theory in terms of what it can account for in human perception and learning, it also insists that a great deal of cognition is individual, private, and therefore inaccessible to control, and often even to inspection. These principles reflect this problem. They are offered in the belief that it is nonetheless useful for the message designer to understand what factors have an impact on perception and understanding, even though they are largely intractable.

3.4. *Expectations concerning the degree to which different media and messages require different amounts of effort in order to be understood are as important to learning as the perception of the message itself.*

This principle will doubtless be seen as somewhat controversial. It is derived from the observation (Salomon, 1984; Clark & Salomon, 1985) that people attribute different degrees of difficulty to learning from different forms of presentation. Thus, most people believe that television is easier to learn from than text. They will therefore invest less effort into learning from television, and consequently will learn less. The message designer could therefore present messages in such a way, or using such a medium, that students realize they are going to have to invest effort to learn from them.

3.5a. *Perception of objects is such that they are identifiable even when they have undergone considerable transformation.*

A major puzzle for scholars of perception has always been how it is possible for someone to recognize and correctly identify an object that he or she has never seen before. A variation of this puzzle is the uncanny ability of people to identify objects perceived from novel, even unlikely, points of view. How can the objects in Figure 2.9 be recognized as the same object? How does someone identify a new species of duck as a duck? How can someone recognize an umbrella seen from a variety of different angles? Explanations of this ability that rely on the matching of perceived objects to stored memories of the object are now generally discredited (Pinker, 1985; Uttal, 1988). The efficiency with which object recognition is executed would simply be impossible if it relied on the storage in long-term memory of images of every object we have ever perceived from every possible angle.

3.5b. *The identification of perceived objects requires the accurate perception and identification of their parts.*

Current thinking about object identification seems to converge on the idea that we identify things in terms of their parts. The first difficulty with this is the matter of what distinguishes the parts from each other in the visual field. We

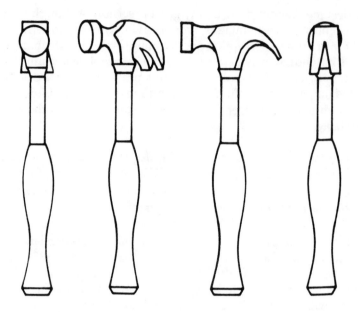

**Figure 2.9.** This is a hammer whichever way you look at it. We recognize objects easily even when they are shown in unfamiliar and unusual orientations (Fleming & Levie, 1978).

have already seen one answer to this question. Pomerantz's work on the configuration of parts into perceptual units told us that parts are seen as units when they are attended to simultaneously, when they give rise to an emergent property, and when they are physically close. But this research has been by and large at a level of detail that does not enter directly into the identification of whole objects. In the latter case, we are dealing with perceptual analysis under the control of attention rather than preattentive synthesis.

Hoffman and Richards (1984) have proposed a theory of how what we perceive is partitioned into parts. When two objects interpenetrate, concave discontinuities in the apparent contour are created, as shown in Figure 2.10. These "cusps" mark where the parts join. Human perception, being sensitive to such discontinuities, therefore uses the information they provide as a basis for dividing what is perceived into parts. The theory is extended to permit the development of rules for the partitioning of smooth surfaces. Once the parts or partitions of what is perceived have been established, knowledge of the world is inferred inductively from them.

### 3.5c.  *Accurate identifications can be made from the correct perception of just a few parts.*

Once the parts have been isolated, how do they permit us to identify objects? Marr (1982; Marr & Nishihara, 1978) suggests a way that is consistent with the

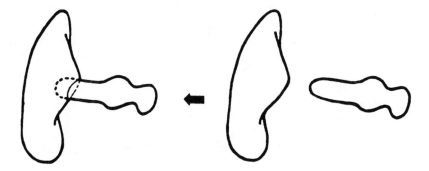

**Figure 2.10.** When two objects are joined together, or when one occludes the other, discontinuities are created in smooth outlines. Here, these appear as concave angles. Hoffman and Richards (1984) have proposed that these discontinuities are the basis for the perceptual system's ability to identify the correct parts of objects that we see (Hoffman & Richards, 1984).

theory of preattentive visual processing. It involves the top-down analysis of shapes into configurations of cylinders, and is illustrated in Figure 2.11. For example, a person might be thought of as having the general shape of a vertical cylinder. However, that person would only become distinguishable from other vertical cylinders, such as utility poles, wine bottles, and penguins, once further analysis had broken the general form into parts consisting of other cylinders representing the torso, arms, and legs. Yet only at the next level of detail, where the length of the limbs and the configuration of the fingers of the hand, also represented as cylinders, would the person be distinguishable from a chimpanzee. In this way, we do not need to match a perceived person to a stored memory of a person in order to make an identification. After only two levels of analysis, we have narrowed the object down to primates, purely on the basis of a very generalized representation of the parts (cylinders) and how they fit together. At this point, it might be possible even to distinguish a person from a chimpanzee on the basis of context, making further analysis unnecessary (more of which later).

Another account of how parts enable us to identify objects is provided by Biederman (1987). His approach does not involve a top-down analysis of what is perceived. Rather, he has proposed what amounts to a perceptual "alphabet" of 36 "geons" from which what we perceive can be constructed. Geons, a sample of which is shown in Figure 2.12, are primitive shapes out of which can be built representations of anything that a person is likely to perceive. Recognition requires the identification of the geons from which a perceived object is composed, and the retrieval of its identification on the basis of a representation in long term memory that has the same geons. As with Marr's theory, identifications can be made readily on the basis of very generalized representations.

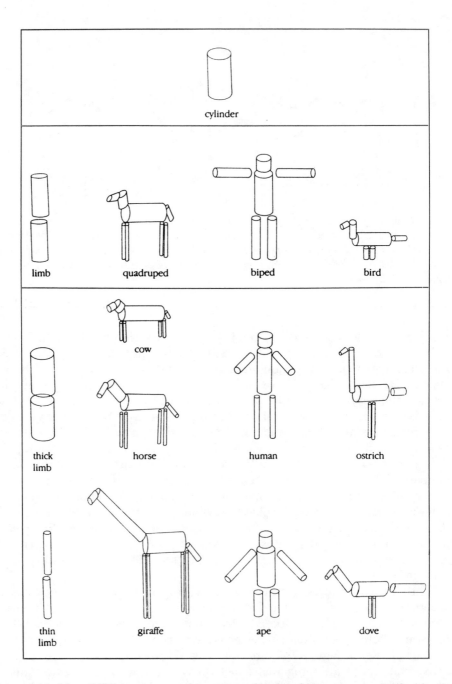

**Figure 2.11.** Marr (1982) has proposed a system whereby objects are perceived as having parts that have the general form of cylinders. As you can see, this allows the recognition of objects from very simple and very abstract representations (Marr, 1982).

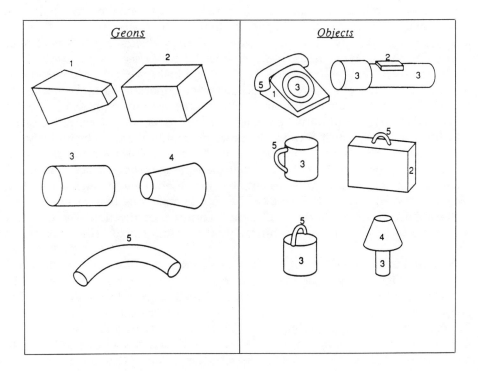

**Figure 2.12.** Five of Biederman's geons are shown on the left. On the right, you can see how objects can be constructed from them. Again, the representations are simple and abstract (Biederman, 1990).

*3.5d. The identification of perceived objects is greatly facilitated through the representation of information as relatively abstract schemata embodying propositional knowledge. Too much detail may therefore obscure attributes that are critical to identification.*

Both of these theories, along with others (for example, Pentland, 1986), lead one to believe that correct identifications are made from rudimentary, abstract, even sketchy perceptual data. Importantly, this is consistent with schema theories of memory, and particularly with propositional accounts of the representation of what is perceived (Pylyshyn, 1981; Winn, 1982). These maintain that we retain information in memory in the form of abstract structures, "schemata," which contain certain key features of the information. It is from these that our identifications are derived not from a direct match of a percept with a mental image. For example, if we know that, in a person, the hands hang above the knees while in a chimpanzee they hang below them, then when we perceive an image in which it is possible to determine where the hands hang, even if that image only represents hands and knees in the crudest way, we can make a correct identification. This would not be possible if we were required to make a perfect match with an accurate representation of either person or ape. Thus, as long as we can identify a few parts, we can identify objects, regardless of their orientation and often regardless of whether we have ever seen them before.

The tolerance that these theories allow when identifying what we perceive is not absolute. When images are degraded, as when important parts are omitted or occluded, or when we have nothing in long-term memory with which we can associate even a minimum configuration of parts, or when objects are transformed in very unusual ways, then correct identification will be unlikely.

There are a number of implications in these principles for the design of instructional messages. It is obvious that the message designer needs to know what the important parts of items are, and to present them in such a way that they are not degraded. Less obvious is the need to make sure that the student has well-established schemata that will permit correct identification. The designer may have to insist that certain information be taught before the message is presented.

It should also be noted that, although these theories of object identification might superficially resemble theories of concept learning, parts should not be confused with critical attributes of concepts. There is a great deal of evidence that people do not classify things on the basis of their critical attributes anyway (Rosch, 1978; Lakoff, 1987), relying more on global similarity and prototypes. The theories of object recognition that we have examined can accommodate both approaches to concept classification. (See Chapter 5, Concept Learning.)

### 3.6. *The perception of objects' qualities, such as size, shape, or pitch, is facilitated when context provides standards against which comparisons can be made.*

The human perceptual system is not a scientific instrument, neither at the preattentive level nor at the level of attentive processing. We do not usually make absolute judgments of loudness, size, brightness, speed, and hue. Exceptions would involve people such as interior decorators who can match colors from memory, and musicians who have perfect pitch. Yet skills of this type are not the norm and cannot be counted on in the people for whom designers create messages.

While perception is poor at making absolute judgments, it is very good at making relative judgments about phenomena perceived simultaneously or in quick succession. When we listen to two notes in quick succession, we can easily tell which is the higher of the two. Likewise, we can tell the brighter of two lights, the larger of two figures, or the quicker of two images moving across a screen when these are viewed simultaneously. When one of the objects we perceive is a calibrated measuring device, such as a tuning fork or a ruler, we can even make absolute judgments of qualities such as musical pitch or length. But we have to perceive both the measuring device and the object we are measuring at the same time or in close temporal proximity to be able to do this. Differences in the degree and nature of stimulation are easy for the perceptual system to detect when all parts of the message can be processed simultaneously.

Messages whose interpretation depends on accurate judgments of some quality or other should therefore include a standard for comparison, especially when what is presented in the message is novel. Archaeologists always include a shovel or meter stick in photographs of artifacts made *in situ* in order to indicate the size of the objects. Map makers always include a scale so that accurate estimates of distances can be made. The paint-sample books used by interior decorators contain many colors on one page so that comparisons can be made. Musicians use pitch pipes or tuning forks to judge whether their instruments are in tune. Likewise, message designers must use similar devices to allow judgments to be made about the relative intensity and scale of the relevant qualities of what is perceived. The simplest and least obtrusive way of doing this is to provide some additional context in a picture that includes something with which the perceiver is familiar. Showing a person standing beside a strange new animal would be an example. Slightly more obtrusive and very effective is the use of analogy. Placing a picture of a Saturn V rocket beside a drawing of fifty upended buses, or showing a microchip next to the head of a match, are examples.

3.7. *The interpretation of what is perceived is determined to a large extent by what has already been perceived in the immediate spatial and temporal context. When this context is particularly strong, items and events that do not fit the context will be misperceived.*

Although existing knowledge and expectations do not influence preattentive perceptual organization, they have a marked influence on the interpretation of what is perceived. Studies of the interpretation of ambiguous text in contrasting contexts (Sulin & Dooling, 1974) have shown that totally different interpretations can be reliably predicted when readers are given different contexts for interpretation. The perception of ambiguous drawings is similarly affected by context (Owen, 1985a, 1985b). It is clear that context creates expectations in people that very heavily bias their interpretation of what they perceive, and that this is especially true when a message is ambiguous.

There are several theoretical explanations for why this occurs. What they have in common is the idea that cognitive acts, such as stimulated recall of items from memory, cause certain memory structures to become active. Whether these structures are thought of as schemata (Neisser, 1976; Rumelhart & Norman, 1981) or nodes in a network (Anderson, 1984; Rumelhart & McClelland, 1986) is immaterial to this discussion. What is important is the idea that memory is activated by the association of a percept with a memory structure, and that interpretation is an attempt to find a way in which the percept can be assimilated to the structure. Although this process is clearly a two-way street, with structures being activated bottom-up and attempts at interpretation being made top-down, and although it has the flexibility to accommodate memory structures to percepts that do not necessarily fit with what is recalled, once a structure is active every attempt will be made to associate the percept to that structure. Thus, either some sense will be made of the message, even if it results in an erroneous interpretation; or the person will return to the message for more information, this time seeking specific clues that confirm the relevance of the message to the active structure; or the amount of effort the person is willing to invest in the message will be exhausted and the person will give up. (Recall that matching perceived information to internal representations requires the investment of effort; Salomon, 1983.)

What all this means for the message designer is apparently simple: make sure a context is provided for interpretation by activating the right memory structure. However, the simplicity of this injunction may be deceptive. To begin with, so long as the person is awake and alert, memory structures will already be active. The message must therefore be sufficiently appealing to compete successfully with ongoing cognitive activity. Second, the relevant structure must be present in semantic memory, and the designer may have no way of determining this. It is not all of what a person has learned some time in the past that determines the context for perception. It is what is active when perception takes place that makes the difference. Simply determining current knowledge, through a pretest perhaps, is necessary but not sufficient for the creation of an appropriate context. The designer needs to go further and make sure that knowledge is activated before the message is presented to the perceptual system.

### 3.8.    The context in which a message is intended to be interpreted may be activated by means of an advance organizer.

This principle summarizes a great deal of what has been said in this section. Ausubel's (1963) idea of "advance organizer" is that learning will be more meaningful if information is presented to the student that sets up "cognitive scaffolding" on which to build the comprehension of new information. Overviews, outlines, statements of objectives and pre-instructional questions all serve this purpose well. The demonstrated effectiveness of this technique has meant that the use of advance organizers and allied strategies, such as Reigeluth's "epitome" (Reigeluth & Stein, 1983), have become standard practice in the design of instruction. As Mayer (1979) has pointed out, this is because the presence of an advance organizer makes it much easier to assimilate new information to what already exists in memory.

The advance organizer, of course, is itself a message. This means that it too needs to be designed with care. Whether in text or in graphic form (Jonassen & Hawk, 1984; Moore & Readance, 1984), the advance organizer needs to do two things. First, it should include all of the main points the ensuing messages convey. Organizers that are incomplete will fail to draw attention to all of the parts of the message the students need to consider. Second, the organizer should show how the parts of the message are related to each other, not just what they are. Thus, their purpose is to let the students anticipate structure as well as content.

With proper design and careful use, advance organizers can serve the message designer well. At the very least, they can help overcome the ambiguity that might characterize a message received out of context. Beyond that, they can serve to help students organize the information they have perceived and thus make it easier to understand what the message means.

# II.  Message Design Variables

The principles we have looked at so far have been derived primarily from research aimed at developing theory about perception and closely related aspects of cognition. They have been generally well-grounded empirically and theoretically. However, they have been quite general, and although useful to the message designer, perhaps not as specific as some would like. For that reason, we now turn to perceptual principles that are more closely tied to the items in the message designer's tool-kit, to the particular factors in a message over which there is a measure of control. As we shall see, these include the many variables that affect the way a message is presented, such as the use of detail and color in pictures, the use of different ways of presenting text with different type styles and layouts, and the use of narration. Clearly, this is a vast area to cover and must be constrained in some way. For that reason, the topics have been selected on the basis of two criteria: they epitomize a number of similar design principles, and they are consistent with the more general perceptual principles presented in the first part of this chapter.

A note of caution. Much of the research that leads to the principles presented below has been conducted to find out what works in instruction, not to build basic perceptual and cognitive theory. As a result, the studies err on the side of identifying the sufficient rather than the necessary conditions for learning. Clark (1983) has pointed out that discovering what works is not the same as determining *why* it works, or what psychological processes are necessary for learning to occur. This means that the principles that follow suggest design strategies that may not be the best (others may be better, but no one has experimented with them yet) and may not work in circumstances that differ to any extent from those in which the research that gave rise to them was conducted. In this respect, they stand in contrast to the principles we have already proposed, which hold across most circumstances. But that is the price you have to pay for guidelines that deal with the more specific aspects of message design.

# 4.  The Perception of Pictures

Any division of a discussion of instructional message components will be arbitrary. The organization we shall follow moves from pictures to diagrams, to charts and graphs, to text, to combinations of these, and finally to sounds. We begin with pictures.

### 4.1.   Pictures are usually more memorable than words, and are thus useful when information has to be remembered.

It is generally agreed that information presented in pictures is encoded twice, once as a picture and once as a verbal label that names the picture. The redundancy in memory that results from this "dual coding" (Paivio, 1971, 1983) or "conjoint retention"(Kulhavy, Lee, & Caterino, 1985; Schwartz, 1988), means that information can be retrieved either from the pictorial or from the verbal memory, doubling the chances that it will be recalled.

Independent of dual coding, there is evidence that human memory for pictures is nothing short of remarkable. A number of years ago, Shepard (1967) reported better than 98 percent accuracy on a recognition test involving more than 600 pictures. Standing (1973) reported recognition accuracy of more than 80 percent in a similar study in which subjects saw approximately 10,000 pictures over a five-day period! Doubtless, such high levels of performance derive ultimately from the excellent pattern-recognition capabilities of the human perceptual system. The message designer may exploit these capabilities to advantage.

### 4.2.   Pictures play many roles in instruction. It is therefore necessary to know precisely what a picture's function is intended to be before it is designed.

This principle is clearly cautionary rather than prescriptive. Yet it is necessary because even today there is a temptation to include illustrations in instructional materials for their own sake, where they can do more harm than good. Moreover, even the serious and well-intentioned use of instructional illustrations is misguided when the function it is to perform is not clearly understood (Brody, 1982). Pictures whose function is to motivate have to be designed in very different ways from those intended to explain something.

A number of writers have described the many different functions of illustrations (Duchastel & Waller, 1979; Levin, Anglin, & Carney, 1987; Sless, 1981). The five functions identified by Levin *et al.* serve our purpose well. They are: (1) Decoration, where illustrations have little if anything to do with the instructional content, but may serve to attract and hold attention; (2) Representation, where illustrations depict elements of the instructional content; (3) Organization, where illustrations show such things as steps in a process, spatial arrangements, and the like; (4) Interpretation, where illustrations present abstract and usually difficult material in a more concrete, sometimes analogical way; (5) Transformation, where the illustration serves as a device to facilitate certain cognitive processes rather than being directly concerned with instructional content. For example, Levin, Shriberg, & Berry (1983) use transformational pictures to bring together in one interactive image a whole host of objects and events that students are to remember. Some examples of these five functions are shown in Figure 2.13. It should be noted that functions 3 and 4 are often performed by charts and diagrams as well as by pictures.

(A)

SECOND EDITION

CLAUDE A. VILLEE
Harvard University

WARREN F. WALKER, JR.
Oberlin College

FREDERICK E. SMITH
University of Michigan

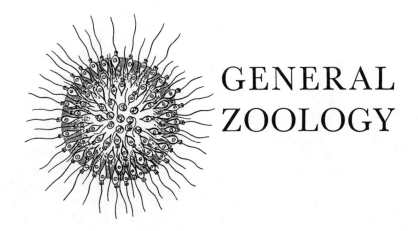

# GENERAL ZOOLOGY

W. B. SAUNDERS COMPANY

PHILADELPHIA AND LONDON  1963

**Figure 2.13.** Here we see Levin, Anglin, and Carney's (1987) five functions of illustrations: A. Decoration—the picture of the sperm invading the egg simply serves to make the title page of this textbook more appealing. B. Representation—the drawings show what

*(Continued)*

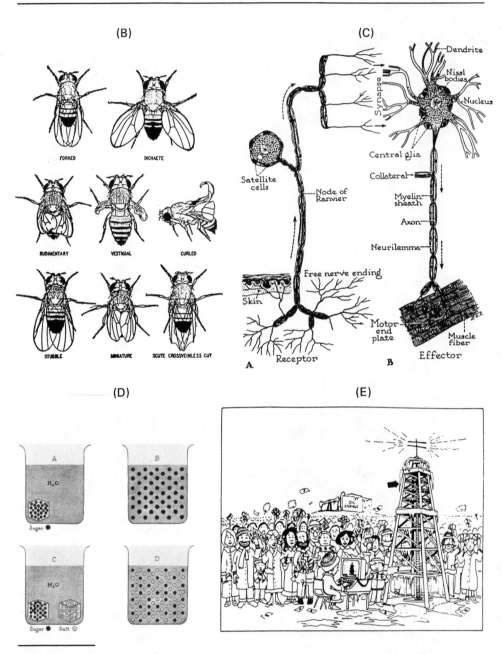

(B)

(C)

(D)

(E)

various mutant forms of the fruit fly look like. C. Organization—the spatial and some functional relationships among the parts of the two neurons are clearly shown in this illustration. D. Interpretation—diffusion is an abstract idea and a difficult one for beginning students to grasp; the illustration interprets the process in a concrete way. E. Transformation—this picture illustrates a number of characteristics of a town, such as a large population, high-technology industries, and a wealth of natural resources.

***4.3.*** *Students often need specific instructions as to how to look at and interpret a picture.*

Just as the perception and interpretation of messages are influenced by people's expectations, determined by the memory structures that are currently active, so their perception and interpretation of pictures are determined by what function *the viewer* thinks they are intended to fulfill. Without direction to the learner from the designer, there is no guarantee that the picture will play the role that was intended. Indeed, when pictures are used with other message forms, such as text, as they usually are, there is no guarantee that the student will even look at the picture, without instructions to do so (Anderson, 1970). Once the designer has determined which function the picture is to perform, directions on how to look at the picture can be written into the message. (Rigney, 1978, has referred to these as "detached strategies.") If the topic is oil refining, such directions for a descriptive picture might read, "Notice the large number of pipes and tanks that make up an oil refinery." For an organizational picture (possibly in a more schematic form) showing the refining process, "Notice that the lightest fraction (gasoline) is extracted first, and heavier fractions later." For an interpretative picture of the fractioning process, "Look carefully at the temperature graph in the corner of the picture. You will notice that the lighter fractions evaporate at lower boiling points and can therefore be separated, through pipe 'A' leaving the fractioning tower, from the other, heavier, fractions."

***4.4.*** *Purely decorative pictures should be used sparingly.*

Since the purpose of decorative pictures is not directly instructional, it is best not to overuse them. If they are used excessively, then one of two things could happen. Either students will cease to attend to *any* illustrations because they do not contain useful information. Or students will force themselves to see relevant information in decorative pictures where, in fact, there is none. In either case, the result is not what the designer desires.

***4.5a.*** *Representational pictures should be "true to life" with the proviso that what is depicted is within the realm of experience of the student and that the student's experience is close enough to that of the designer for there to be common ground for the identification of the features that are illustrated.*

This principle is the closest we dare get to realism theories! The two provisos, however, do quite a bit to bring this principle into line with the tenets of cognitive theory. If the function of a picture is to show what something looks like, then it stands to reason that it should resemble its referent in relevant ways. To teach identification successfully through pictures is to teach for transfer. It is expected that the student will be able to identify real objects, not more pictures of them. Since teaching for transfer requires a degree of similarity between the teaching and application phases (Butterfield & Nelson, 1989), representational pictures should contain much of the shape, detail, size, color, and context of the original.

However, as we saw above, what is perceived as real depends on the similarity of the message to the learner's internal representations, not to the domain of reference. This will pose problems if the student's knowledge of the world does not correspond sufficiently with the picture's domain of reference for identification to take place. When that happens, the "wrong" memory structure will become active, the features depicted by the picture will be misidentified, and the student will become confused. Before using a "realistic" picture, the designer needs to ascertain whether the learner has the memory structures in place to which the information in the picture can be assimilated in the way the designer intends.

> *4.5b. When a learner's internal representations are not compatible with the information presented in a message, pictures can be used to activate memory structures that are analogically similar to those to which the information in the picture should be assimilated.*

When the conditions specified by the provisos in the previous principle are not met, then the designer can use an analogy that is within the student's realm of experience. Although analogies involve memory structures that are not from the same content domain as what is being taught, they have certain formal properties that are very similar to those of that content domain (Gick & Holyoak, 1983; Royer & Cable, 1976). The flow of electricity through a wire is often explained by the analogy of water flowing through a hose: voltage is not unlike water pressure, amperage corresponds to rate of flow, switches are like faucets, resistance is like a kink in the hose. Since people usually have more experience with water flowing through hoses than with electricity flowing through wires, activating schemata associated with the former is a useful place to begin teaching about electricity. The notions of "pressure," "rate of flow," and so on, are common to the familiar and unfamiliar content domains, and serve as a temporary structure to which the new ideas can be assimilated.

As we have seen, visual perception is fundamentally concerned with spatial organization. This means that pictures, which are excellent at showing spatial relationships, are admirably suited for presenting certain analogies. They can show the formal properties upon which the analogy is built very well. Thus, the concepts of diastolic and systolic blood pressure might be explained by means of the analogy of a hand pump, as shown in Figure 2.14.

> *4.5c. When representational pictures are used either for literal or analogical illustration, the appropriate schemata must be activated before the picture is presented.*

Even if the learner's knowledge of the world is compatible with the intent of the picture in the message, or even if an appropriate analogy is found, the

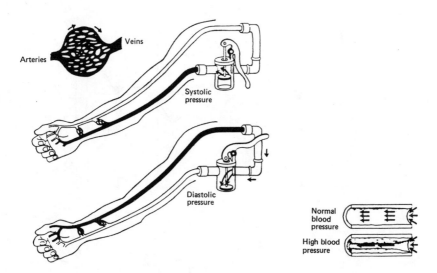

**Figure 2.14.** This analogical picture captures the formal properties of the circulatory system and explains diastolic and systolic blood pressure through the analogy of the hand pump. Once the connection is made that the pump represents the heart, then the picture is a lot easier to understand than a more representational picture would be (Eisenberg & Eisenberg, 1979).

designer must prepare the student to see the picture. As we have seen, people can see anything they want to in a picture, so it is usually necessary to indicate to them what to expect. Often, the context in which the picture is seen is sufficient. Presenting a picture of an elephant in a lesson on wild animals is not likely to lead to an interpretation concerning circuses or the Republican party. However, the context has to be set up initially at some time or other, and this the designer must be sure to do. It is also wise to emphasize the context immediately before the presentation of a picture, for example by stating, "This animal is the largest land animal in the world, it lives in India and Africa, . . . ."

### 4.6. *Organizational pictures should incorporate devices that stress temporal and spatial relationships.*

It should be noted that the principles we have just described for representational pictures can apply to any picture. Pictures whose purpose it is to help students organize content have the additional function of making relationships among items explicit. The clearest example of this is a picture illustrating content that requires students to master the steps in performing a task, such as is shown in Figure 2.15. The designer needs to show how each step is performed in the correct order. There are four types of devices that the designer can use in order to achieve this. First, the pictures can be presented in "cartoon strip" fashion, each successive panel lying to the right of or below the

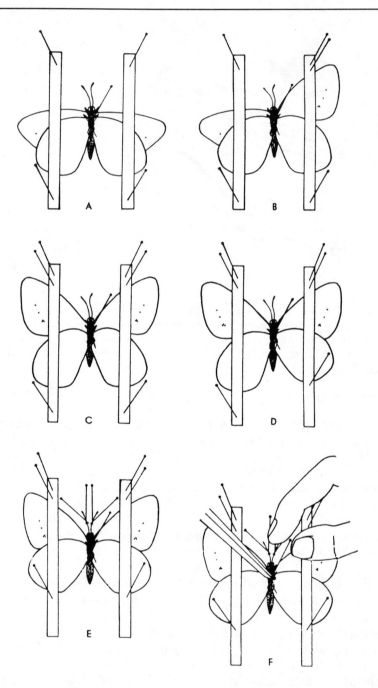

**Figure 2.15.** In this illustration, pictures succeed each other left-to-right, top-to-bottom. The sequence of steps in spreading a butterfly is shown clearly and no text is needed to explain what to do. The sequence is also indicated by the letter under each picture (Borror & White, 1970).

preceding one on the assumption that people will "read" them left to right and top to bottom. Second, the sequence of events within a picture or between panels can be emphasized by means of arrows, numbers, or labels. In this way, it will not be necessary to rely on the natural way we have of reading. Third, the pictures illustrating each strip can be shown one at a time in the correct sequence. Here the order in which students see the pictures is controlled by the device used to show them. Fourth, in many cases the same result can be achieved using a motion picture. Indeed, for many sequential tasks in which there are either no distinct break points between the individual tasks, or where the motion of an activity itself is important, film and videotape are the preferred ways to present content.

When the content requires the students to learn spatial organization, then a different set of devices can apply. Often, simply following the principles for designing representational pictures will be sufficient to show spatial relationships. A representational picture of a building is going to show the doors and windows in the correct relationships to each other. However, other enhancements might be necessary to make the spatial relationships among the features shown in pictures more obvious. One obvious example is the stereometric diagrams overlaid on works of art in order to show their composition and perspective. Other examples include the superimposition of features of maps over aerial photographs, the drawing of boundaries around features of a picture, and so on.

### 4.7. *Interpretative pictures should be simplified and labelled so that only those aspects having to do directly with what is being interpreted are immediately accessible to perception.*

Since the function of interpretive pictures is to explain often complex and difficult phenomena, it is imperative that they be made as simple as possible without oversimplifying the content of what they convey. Figure 2.16 shows an example. There is a tendency to use realistic pictures in an interpretive way; inevitably they do not work. Effective interpretative pictures are often line drawings or cut-aways. It is only once the irrelevant and distracting detail has been stripped away that students can see and understand the processes that are illustrated. Labels often contribute to this process. Examples would include a labelled drawing explaining how the water cycle works, or a simplified cut-away of a jet engine. In neither of these cases would a photograph, say, be capable of explaining the way these operate.

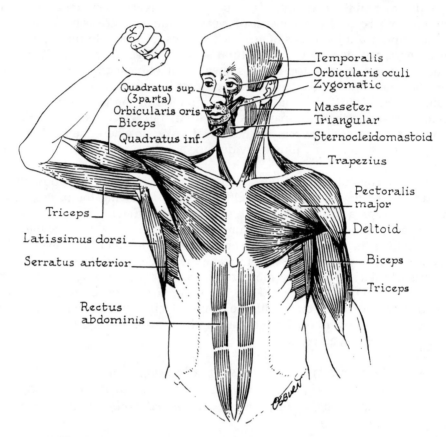

Labels in figure:
Quadratus sup. (3 parts)
Orbicularis oris
Biceps
Quadratus inf.
Temporalis
Orbicularis oculi
Zygomatic
Masseter
Triangular
Sternocleidomastoid
Trapezius
Pectoralis major
Deltoid
Biceps
Triceps
Triceps
Latissimus dorsi
Serratus anterior
Rectus abdominis

**Figure 2.16.** While this relatively simple cut-away line drawing has lost a great deal of the information that would have been conveyed by a more realistic picture, none of the essential information has been lost. The addition of labels is partly responsible for this (Villee *et al.*, 1963).

> **4.8.** *Transformational pictures should be sufficiently realistic to be memorable, and should integrate all of the elements that are to be learned in a sensible, if sometimes fanciful, way.*

Levin's work on transformational pictures is based on the assumption that the association within pictures of many items in interaction with each other makes them easier to recall. Typically, students are taught how to construct interactive mental images into which important things to remember are embedded. Figure 2.17 gives an example. Later, when it comes time to recall the items, the image is recalled and the items within it are retrieved. Usually, these items are associations, often acoustic, to other items that are not normally related and that are the real items the lesson is dealing with.

WOLFRAMITE (wolf)   SOFT Mineral (baby)
DARK Color (mean dark cat)
Used in HOME (living room)

**Figure 2.17.** This illustration from a study by Morrison and Levin (1987) helps students create an interactive image to remember characteristics of the mineral wolframite. The wolf serves as an acoustic mnemonic for the name "wolframite." The setting reminds us that it is used in the home. The black cat reminds us of its color, and the baby that it is a soft mineral.

Message designers have rarely set out to construct transformational pictures. To begin with, they are perhaps best constructed mentally by the students themselves. But the research of Levin and his associates has shown that presenting pictures such as these is sometimes a useful thing to do. It is important for the message designer who attempts to do this to be sure that the items to be remembered are clearly discernible and that interactions among them, however improbable, are clearly evident.

### 4.9. *Color can serve two purposes in messages: to illustrate the colors of things in the real world, and to draw attention to message features.*

The function of color in messages is treated in numerous places in this chapter, under topics where it has a particular role to play. However, color has traditionally been of considerable interest to message designers in its own right because it is something that can easily be manipulated in visual messages and because its indiscriminate use has obvious deleterious effects. A great many claims about the affective impact of color have been made, some of which have been investigated (for example, Winn & Everett, 1979), but few of which have been substatiated firmly enough to lead to design principles. What is more, most recent research on color has tended to address problems at a very basic psychophysiological level that is of little value to message designers (see Boynton, 1988, for a review). All of this points to the trickiness of color as a message design variable.

The most consistent and applicable information we have about the effectiveness of color comes from research into its role in illustration and in cueing. A great deal of this research has been conducted by Dwyer and his colleagues (Dwyer, 1972, 1978, 1987; Clark & Angert, 1985). This work has demonstrated that color can function as a useful aid in identification. Pileated woodpeckers are generally black with red crests on their heads. Therefore, an instructional picture of the bird that shows its plumage as black except for its red crest will improve the chances that a person will be able to identify one accurately in the field.

A second use for color in instructional messages exploits the fact that colors vary both in hue and brightness. This means that they can be used to create contrasts among different parts of a message such that attention is drawn to the parts that stand out because their color is bright or strident. Here, it is not necessary that the colors correspond to colors of things in the real world. Using bright red to color the forearm of an athlete throwing a javelin is not intended to mean that the arm is in fact red. It serves simply to draw attention to the position in which the arm is held to bring off a good throw.

## 5. The Perception of Diagrams, Charts, and Graphs

Pictures tend to be best for teaching about concrete objects and phenomena. Diagrams, charts, and graphs are useful when it comes to more abstract concepts and the relationships among them. While an interpretive picture can adequately teach about the water cycle, the procedure by means of which legislation passes through the American Congress requires some form of diagrammatic illustration. While the effects of climatic changes on agricultural land can be shown very well by representational pictures, only charts or graphs can show trends such as changes in annual rainfall or hours of sunshine which bring these effects about. In spite of this, many of the principles for the effective design of pictures also apply to the design of diagrams, graphs, and charts. This is particularly true in the case of organizational and interpretative illustrations. We now turn, therefore, to principles for the design of these formats that are unique to them and are over and above those principles we have just proposed for pictures. Reviews of the research from which the principles were derived have been provided by Winn (1987, 1989b) and by Winn and Holliday (1982).

*5.1. By and large, the structural conventions of diagrams, charts, and graphs may be used in metaphorical ways in order to make abstract ideas more concrete and easier to grasp.*

A great deal of the ability of diagrams, charts, and graphs to communicate derives from the way they show relationships among the elements that make them up. While these elements can represent concrete objects or abstract ideas (shown as small pictures, icons, symbols, or labels), the way relationships are conveyed is fairly conventional and consistent across instances. Some of these conventions arise from the manner in which preattentive processes organize what is perceived, while others are learned and bound up in the conventions of literacy and artistry of our culture. It is on these conventions that the principles concerning the design of diagrams, charts, and graphs are built.

*5.2. The efficiency and accuracy with which information in charts and diagrams is processed depend on the locations of the elements in relation to each other.*

One of the most complete accounts of how diagrams convey information is provided by Larkin and Simon (1987). This account describes a production-system model of information processing which supposes that processing is directed by the satisfaction of a series of ordered conditions that are prerequisite to the achievement of a goal. In order to solve a typical weight, rope, and pulley problem in physics, shown in Figure 2.18, the processing of the information in a

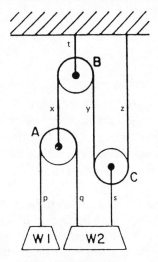

**Figure 2.18.** Diagram of the rope and pulley problem used by Larkin and Simon (1987) in their production-system model of how diagrams convey information.

diagram in which the problem is posed requires the inspection of various locations in the diagram in order to find information relevant to the solution of each step in the problem. Thus, if the student is to determine what the weights must be of two blocks, attached to pulleys in a pulley system, for the system to balance, the perusal of the diagram must proceed in a certain sequence. Departures from that sequence will lead to dead-ends and back-tracking, will require increased loads on working memory, and will increase the likelihood of error. In preparing the diagram, the message designer should therefore perform a careful task analysis of the processes leading to the correct solution, and should lay the diagram out so that the parts of the diagram that the student must view in sequence are indeed in sequence in the diagram. Another example: A chart listing the main agricultural products of the midwestern states could arrange the states alphabetically, geographically from east to west and north to south, by size, or by population. Task analysis would probably reveal that geography is a more important determinant of what crops grow best than size or population. Therefore, the designer would want to design the chart so that the states were listed according to some geographical criterion, running form north to south or east to west, rather than according to some other scheme.

These two examples illustrate how specific design principles are often derived from more fundamental perceptual principles. In this case, it is assumed that the early stages of perceptual organization will establish grouping and sequence relationships among elements in the diagram and chart on the basis of the physical proximity of the elements to each other. Thus, students will tend to see the pulleys, weights, and ropes in the physics diagram as forming a hierarchy of perceptual and conceptual units on the basis of their apparent relatedness. The student reading the agricultural products chart will associate the states to each other in ways determined by the order in which they are presented, or by where the lines marking rows and columns are drawn. The designer's failure to attend to likely organizations on the one hand, or creating poor organization in layout or in the thicknesses of the lines in the chart on the other, will lead to an ineffective message.

> ### 5.3. *Increasing the discriminability of elements in a chart or diagram can reduce the success with which students perceive the overall pattern of the relationships that are illustrated. Conversely, reducing the discriminability of the elements improves the chance that the relationships will be perceived and understood.*

There is evidence for a relationship between the distinctiveness of the elements in a diagram and the likelihood of its being processed as a whole or as a collection of unrelated elements (Sutherland & Winn, 1987; Winn, 1988b; see Figure 2.19). However, this relationship is not clear-cut and may be related to the familiarity of students with the material that is illustrated and with the strategies they use to learn the material (Winn & Sutherland, 1989). However, when considered in light of more basic perceptual research, it seems likely that increasing the detail in the elements in a diagram or chart, and thus the relative

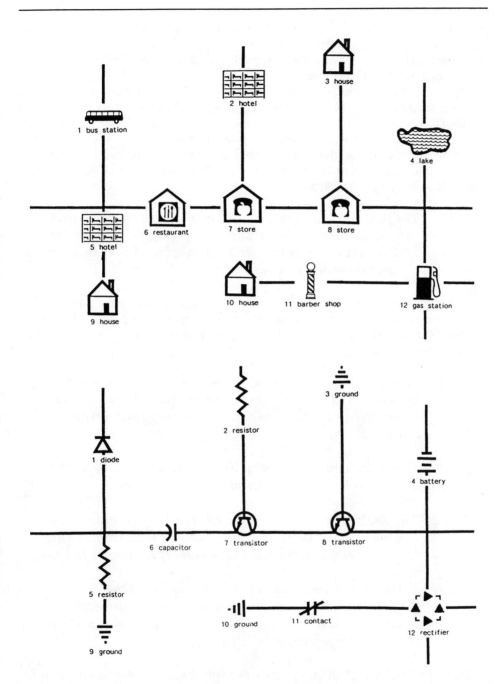

**Figure 2.19.** One of the maps and circuit diagrams used by Winn and Sutherland (1989) in their study of how the familiarity of material affects how people process patterns and sequences. The subjects who saw the unfamiliar circuit diagram could not use some of the strategies used by subjects who saw the map.

discriminability of the elements, draws students' attention to the elements and away from the overall pattern of the relationships among them. To use a phrase employed earlier, varying the discriminability of elements can affect the level at which students "enter the illustration."

The implications of this for the designer are simple. If the task is for the students to understand the relationships among the objects or ideas presented in the chart or diagram, the elements representing them should be presented in such a way that they look the same, say as labelled boxes. If, on the other hand, the intention is that the elements themselves should be studied individually, perhaps in a particular order, then they should be made distinctive by using a unique icon or symbol for each.

> **5.4.** *The perception and interpretation of diagrams and charts can be influenced by a variety of graphic techniques which serve to clarify and emphasize the nature of relationships among elements.*

This is something of a catch-all principle that draws the designer's attention to a myriad of techniques developed in the graphic arts for the design of graphics (Bertin, 1981, 1983; Rankin, 1986; Tufte, 1983). A number of subprinciples can be listed without comment.

> **5.4a.** *The strength of a relationship between two elements can be suggested by the thickness of the line or arrow connecting them. Thicker lines suggest stronger relationships.*

> **5.4b.** *Captions can effectively direct attention where the designer wishes it to be directed.*

> **5.4c.** *The relative size of elements is perceived as communicating their relative power or importance. The larger the element, the more important it is thought to be.*

> **5.4d.** *Estimates of magnitude are easier to make in one dimension, such as on linear scales representing quantities, than in two dimensions, such as circles that are used to represent quantities.*

These principles and others like them form the basis of much of graphic design. They are far too numerous to go into here. Most follow the principles of basic perceptual processing.

### 5.5. *The relative position of elements to each other in charts and diagrams is important in determining the nature of the perceived relationship among them.*

A number of the conventions affecting how diagrams and charts are perceived and interpreted appear to be derived from linguistic and cultural conventions. Research using essentially meaningless diagrams has shown that, nonetheless, people still interpret their meaning in consistent ways (Levin, 1987; Winn, 1989a; Winn & Solomon, 1990). For example, when two nonsense words are placed beside each other in boxes linked by a line, thus forming a very simple diagram like the one shown in Figure 2.20, even though no relationship between them can be determined semantically, people will usually state that the word on the left is the cause and the word to its right the effect. Other consistent conventions are that: the element on the left is seen to possess the element on its right as an attribute; the element above another is considered to cause or possess the one below; when the two elements are shown so that one includes the other within it, as in a Venn diagram, the included element is seen as the effect or the attribute of the other, as well as the subordinate category. In all of these cases, experimental

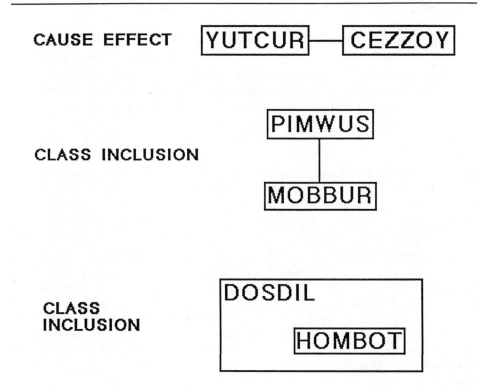

**Figure 2.20.** Even when the words have no meaning, causes are still seen to lie to the left of their effects, and subordinate categories below or inside superordinate ones.

results show not just statistically significant biases in interpretation, but that these biases are almost universal. Only a very few people give different interpretations.

> **5.6a.** *The interpretation of graphs is based on a number of mathematical conventions relating to the function of the* x *and* y *axes.*

Kosslyn, Simcox, Pinker, and Parkin (1983) have conducted an extensive survey of the variables that affect the perception and interpretation of graphs. Dozens of principles for graph design are implicit in what they say. Likewise, the work of Cleveland and McGill (1984, 1985) provides a number of suggestions for graph design. But the basic convention is almost always that points, or elements, placed higher on the page or screen are seen as having more of the attribute that the graph describes. This means that it is possible for the viewer to gain a general understanding of the way the variables or categories are related in the graph without even knowing what these are. The shape of the function line or the relative heights of the bars in the bar graph in Figure 2.21 are sufficient in themselves to convey a great deal of information even if the scales on the axes are not shown, or indeed if there are no labels anywhere to be seen.

> **5.6b.** *The interpretation of graphs depends on the successful application of a variety of perceptual and cognitive processes. The accuracy with which people carry out these processes varies. Therefore, graphs should contain features requiring processes that people are known to perform accurately.*

Cleveland and McGill (1984, 1985) and Simkin and Hastie (1987) have performed what amounts to task analyses of the perceptual processes needed to interpret graphs. More important to the message designer is that the accuracy with which perceivers perform these tasks has been rank-ordered. The implication is therefore that the graph should contain only those features that call on processes with which people are generally highly accurate in their judgments. These processes, ranked from most to least accurate, are: judging position along a common scale; judging positions along nonaligned scales; judging length, direction, and angle; judging area; judging volume and curvature; and judging the intensity of shading and color saturation. The designer is therefore well advised to use area, volume, color, and shading with care if the intent is to convey with any degree of accuracy the amount of something. However, these graphic devices can be useful when the intent is to show contrasts among quantities rather than actual amounts.

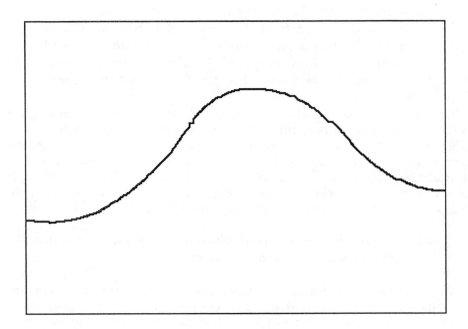

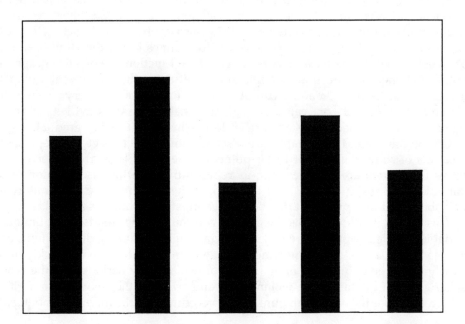

**Figure 2.21.** The *x* and *y* axes are not labeled in the line and bar graph. Yet the shape of the line is sufficient to tell us that something increased in value and then lost that value again. And the height of the bars tells us the relative values of the five variables without our having to know what they are.

> *5.6c.  Cartesian graphs (having an x and a y axis) are the best
> way to show particular amounts of something. Graphs
> that use other devices, such as area or volume, as in pie
> charts, are best confined to showing comparative
> amounts of something where precision is not important.*

It should be fairly obvious that Cleveland and McGill's ranking is due in part to the fact that human perceptual processes allow us to make only relative judgments of objects' qualities, which we discussed earlier. Thus, judgments along a line when a scale is present are more likely to be accurate than judgments of area. This is why cartesian graphs are good and pie charts are so bad at conveying accurate information about precise amounts of something, while the latter are fairly good at communicating *relative* quantities.

> *5.6d.  Line graphs are best at illustrating trends. Bar graphs are
> effective at showing comparisons.*

Another basic perceptual principle that relates to the interpretation of graphs is that the eye tends to follow lines as it moves over an illustration. We saw above that relationships among elements in illustrations can be expressed by joining them with lines or arrows in particular ways, thus controlling the sequence in which attention is paid to them. This phenomenon, which the Gestaltists referred to as "good continuation" (Wertheimer, 1938), also applies to the function lines of cartesian graphs. People are very sensitive to changes in the direction of lines. This means that it is easier for a person to read the function line of a line graph in terms of changes in direction than it is to read off the values at particular points against the scales on the $x$ and $y$ axes. As a result, line graphs are very effective at communicating trends; one can see at a glance whether the stock market has gone up or down, and whether the advance or decline has been rapid or gradual.

On the other hand, bar graphs are discontinuous. The bars clearly represent amounts of something at particular points on the scale. They are perceived in terms of discrete areas rather than as representing continuous variation of a variable. As a result, people tend to compare the length of one bar to its two neighbors, and interpret what they see as a contrast rather than as a trend.

This means that line graphs are good at communicating trends in continuous variables, while bar graphs are best at showing contrasts among discrete units on a scale. Thus, a line graph showing average monthly rainfall will quickly and clearly show the rising and falling pattern of wet and dry periods over the year. A bar graph of the same data will invite a comparison of the amount of rain that falls in each month with the amount in the preceding and the following months.

# 6. The Perception of Text

Over the last decade, a great deal of interest has been expressed in how to improve the comprehension of text by varying the way it is presented to the reader. Jonassen's (1982, 1985) two-volume book *The Technology of Text* has made a major contribution to this effort. Much of this interest has been inspired by the increasing capability of microcomputers to display different styles and sizes of type, while at the same time limiting the amount of text that can be shown to roughly 25 percent of what fits on a sheet of 8 1/2 by 11-inch paper.

> **6.1.** *Over and above the meaning in its words, text has properties in common with other forms of illustration. In this respect, the perception of text is no different from the perception of anything else.*

This principle is simply a reminder that text is looked at in two ways. Obviously, it is read for the meaning that is expressed in the words it contains. The vast literature on reading is concerned primarily with this aspect of text. However, text, like pictures, diagrams, or charts, communicates a great deal of information by its appearance on the page or screen that is independent from the information conveyed in its words. At the simplest level, the number of paragraph indentations conveys whether the text contains one idea or many, whether it is "chopped up" or not. The presence of a heading points to the start of a new set of ideas. Underlining or bold-faced type indicates that these are important words and phrases. All of this information is conveyed and understood even before the words are read for their meaning.

When text is considered at the level of its appearance, then all of the principles that we have encountered so far concerning the perception of any message are relevant. As examples, we shall look at the ways in which text can be organized and how its structure can control attention.

> **6.2.** *In text, attention is drawn to words or passages that stand in contrast to the rest of the body of the text.*

In text, as in anything that is perceived, attention is drawn to the novel, to what stands out. In text, this means type that is set differently from the bulk of the text. The variables that the message designer has to work with are type size, style, and, increasingly, color.

Size is difficult to deal with in type set solid on the page. This is obviously because the height of the letters is limited by the space on, and between, the lines. Thus, designers will probably only use larger type sizes in headings, where there is more room above and below for the larger letters.

Type style and color, on the other hand, do not face this constraint. Thus, setting a word or phrase in bold or italic type, underlining it, using a different font, using all capital letters, or changing color draws attention to the word or phrase. There are a number of things the designer must be cautious about, however. The first is not to overdo it. In any passage, it is sufficient to use just one variation of one factor to control where attention is placed. This means that changing the font while at the same time changing to bold is unnecessary and makes the page look messy or even confusing. A simple change to bold-faced type or to a different color is much more effective. Figure 2.22 gives examples of what to do and not to do.

---

## This is a  GOOD  example of getting attention in text.

## This is a **b□□** example of getting attention in text.

**Figure 2.22.** When highlighting text, it is only necessary to draw attention by altering one feature, such as type size, rather than two. The second sentence shows what not to do.

---

Second, large portions of text should not be highlighted. If emphasized text runs for a paragraph or two, then it becomes "normal" in the eyes of the reader, and the fact that there is something special about it is forgotten.

Third, the designer should avoid using ornate fonts simply to highlight text. It is in a sense unfortunate that many computer software packages come with extremely fancy, glitzy fonts. They look spectacular and certainly demonstrate the capabilities of the computer to use a great variety of type styles. However, many are so ornate as to be difficult to read. This is true of those that employ exotic letter forms, such as "Old English," and of those that use textured backgrounds for the individual letters. (The type designers often appear to have overlooked the importance of figure-ground distinctions in their eagerness to create a unique font.) These fonts are best left to headings and titles, and should not be used for emphasis in bodies of text.

> *6.3a. The way blocks of text are laid out on the page or screen serves as a way for the reader to organize the ideas that the text contains.*

A number of writers have proposed that text layout be treated far more seriously as a way to organize ideas. Hartley (1982, 1987) and Twyman (1981) have described how variations in text formatting affect comprehension. Horn's (1982) "Structured Writing" technique relates formatting concerns more formally with the structure of content derived from a careful content analysis. These endeavors pay particular attention to the clear subdivision of text into paragraphs and other units of various sizes, and to the use of headings, subheadings, and marginal annotation. As a result of the work of researchers such as these, there exists a considerable body of evidence linking text format to the comprehension of content. Of the many suggestions for design that emerge from this literature, the following are among the more important.

### *6.3b. Line breaks should be dictated by the sense of the text rather than by the amount of space available on a line.*

It is taken for granted that where new paragraphs occur is determined by where new ideas are introduced in the text. This principle extends that idea to lines in addition to paragraphs. Hartley (1987) offers a fine example in Figure 2.23. Here, the text format is determined by the syntax of the sentences and not by any requirement to justify the text or fill the line. This approach to layout is particularly useful in instructional or programmed text, where steps in a sequence or items in a list are presented. Obviously, it is not intended for use by novelists!

### *6.3c. The paragraph structure of text should be highlighted beyond simply indenting the first line of each paragraph.*

Again, this is intended for structured instructional text. It is useful to make the distinction between paragraphs, which is the same as the distinction between

---

Now the sons of Jacob were twelve. The sons of Leah; Reuben, Jacob's firstborn, and Simeon, and Levi, and Judah, and Issachar, and Zebulun. The sons of Rachel; Joseph, and Benjamin: And the sons of Bilhah, Rachel's handmaid; Dan, and Naphtali. And the sons of Zilpah, Leah's handmaid; Gad, and Asher. These are the sons of Jacob, which were born to him in Padan-aram.

Now the sons of Jacob were twelve;
The sons of Leah;
   Reuben, Jacob's firstborn,
   and Simeon, and Levi, and Judah,
   and Issachar, and Zebulun:
The sons of Rachel;
   Joseph, and Benjamin:
And the sons of Bilhah, Rachel's handmaid;
   Dan, and Naphtali:
And the sons of Zilpah, Leah's handmaid;
   Gad, and Asher:
These are the sons of Jacob, which were born to him in Padan-aram.

**Figure 2.23.** In the second version of this passage from the Old Testament, the text is organized on the basis of its sense, not just to fit the lines. Its structure is more apparent, and it is easier to understand (Hartley, 1987).

---

main ideas, as clear as possible. Simply indenting the first line of a paragraph is sometimes not sufficient. Leaving extra space between paragraphs, and even drawing horizontal lines between them, makes the structure of the text more apparent. The resulting appearance is that of blocks of text. These are perceived by the reader as units and are assumed to reflect the structure of the ideas the text contains. The structure of the text itself may then function as an organizer for the text's content.

### 6.3d. *The use of marginal headings and annotations can considerably improve students' organization of text material.*

Simply making syntactic distinctions clear by breaking lines according to sense rather than space, or making paragraphs clear by emphasizing their perceptual unity, is not always sufficient on its own to help students comprehend text. The use of headings or annotations, set off clearly in the margins rather than in the usual in-text position of paragraph headings, gives the learner an idea of what each block of text is about. Headings function as labels for paragraphs, naming the topic they deal with. Annotations are typically longer, more descriptive, and discursive. They are particularly effective for "skimming" the text or for quick review after the text has been read. Secondarily, they also make the perceptual distinctions themselves clearer, emphasizing breaks in the text.

### 6.4a. *The ease with which text is read is affected in complex ways by such factors as type size, line length, the amount of space between lines, type and background color, and level of illumination.*

Perhaps the most sustained program of research on typography was that carried out by Miles Tinker between 1922 and 1967, much of which was summarized in *The Legibility of Print* (Tinker, 1963). Recently, Sutherland (1989) has assessed the contribution of Tinker's work. Claiming that it is extremely relevant today now that desktop publishing (Misanchuk, 1992) has put the tools for designing text into the hands of anyone with a microcomputer, Sutherland has identified optimal conditions on most factors affecting the reading and processing of type from which guidelines for message designers can be developed. These include type size, line length, the amount of space between lines, type and background color, and level of illumination, as well as many others. The following principles are derived from Sutherland's work. They are by no means exhaustive. The interested reader can refer to Tinker or Sutherland for a more complete discussion.

*6.4b.  At normal reading distance (15 inches), 10 point type in
19 pica lines set with 2 to 4 point leading produces
optimal legibility.*

The technical terms need explanation. There are 12 points to a pica, six picas to an inch, and therefore 72 points to an inch. "Leading" refers to the space between lines of type. In layman's terms, this principle recommends fairly short lines of text set in type that is a little larger than that typically used in newspapers, with a small amount of space between the lines. Figure 2.24 shows what this looks like. Note that Tinker found that increasing as well as decreasing these values slowed reading down. Bigger type and more space do not mean easier reading. By way of comparison, the text you are now reading is set in 10 point type with a 30 pica line length and 2 point leading.

*6.4c.  Text set in lower case letters is easier to read than text
set in all capitals.*

Most text is set in lower case, with upper case letters at the beginnings of sentences, for names, and so on. A few computers still only allow upper case letters to be shown on the screen, and even a few computer printers are still bound by this limitation. Generally, though, there is no real reason for designers to use all capitals. Any temptation to do so should be resisted.

The reason that lower case letters are easier to read is that many of them vary in their height above and below the line (many have "ascenders" and "descenders"), as illustrated in Figure 2.25. All capital letters sit on the line and have the same height. The result is that many lower case words have a unique shape that helps distinguish them from other words. Thus, "word" has a different shape from "worm," because the ascender of the final "d" makes it tall at the end. "WORD" and "WORM" both form identical rectangles. The designer needs to be aware that some typefaces, particularly some used on computer screens and printers, do not have ascenders and descenders in their lower cases. This principle is obviously invalid here.

*6.4d.  Black type on a white background is optimal.*

This, of course, is normal practice for printed text. However, the norm for computer screens was traditionally white text on a black (or dark) background. The advent of the Macintosh computer, and the flexibility of many word processors to use different foreground and background colors, now means that designers can use black letters on a white background on computers too.

1. There was not a drop of ink in the house, for someone had broken the bottle we kept it in, so Mary decided to finish her letter with a pen. 2. Yesterday I went down town to buy some shoes and rubbers, but when I got home, I found I had forgotten to go to the flower-store to get them.

10 points, 19 picas, set "solid"

1. There was not a drop of ink in the house, for someone had broken the bottle we kept it in, so Mary decided to finish her letter with a pen. 2. Yesterday I went down town to buy some shoes and rubbers, but when I got home, I found I had forgotten to go to the flower-store to get them.

10 points, 19 picas, 1 point leading

1. There was not a drop of ink in the house, for someone had broken the bottle we kept it in, so Mary decided to finish her letter with a pen. 2. Yesterday I went down town to buy some shoes and rubbers, but when I got home, I found I had forgotten to go to the flower-store to get them.

10 points, 19 picas, 2 point leading

1. There was not a drop of ink in the house, for someone had broken the bottle we kept it in, so Mary decided to finish her letter with a pen. 2. Yesterday I went down town to buy some shoes and rubbers, but when I got home, I found I had forgotten to go to the flower-store to get them.

10 points, 19 picas, 4 point leading

**Figure 2.24.** This re-creation by Sutherland (1989) of some of the materials used by Tinker in his studies of typography shows the optimal combination of type size, line length, and leading. The best combinations are enclosed in the box.

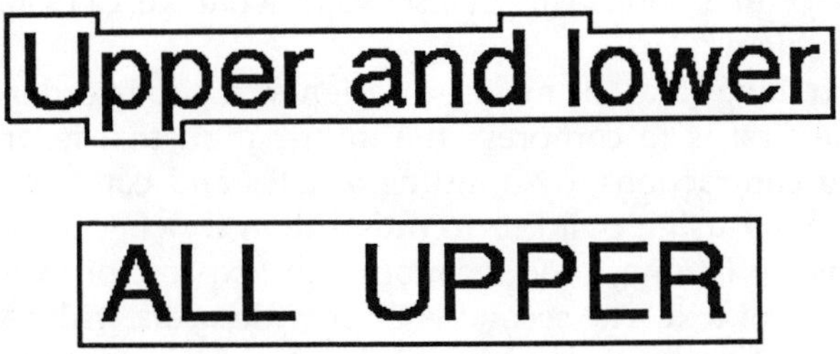

## Upper and lower

## ALL UPPER

**Figure 2.25.** The ascenders and descenders give words set in lower-case type a distinct shape. Words set in upper case are all rectangular and indistinguishable one from the other. Lower case is easier to read as a result (Sutherland, 1989).

6.4e. *Legibility of text depends on the contrast in luminance between the letters and the background rather than on any particular color combinations.*

Some colors are brighter than others. Yellows, light greens, and, of course, white tend to be the brightest, with blues and black being the darkest. The criterion for selecting colors for type and its background should be the contrast in brightness. It is difficult to prescribe color combinations in any absolute way. To begin with, what is blue to one person could be purple to someone else. What is more, the legibility on computer screens of type of different colors on different backgrounds will vary from one variety of machine to the next, and even within machines of the same class. The designer will just have to experiment with combinations that provide both the right amount of contrast and a pleasing appearance.

6.5. *Less text can be displayed on a computer screen than on a typical page. This means that the designer needs to condense text so that more information can be presented in each "screenful," and to provide effective ways of "paging" through electronic text.*

We have already made a number of observations concerning the special concerns that arise from displaying text on computer screens. Hartley (1987) has provided a useful review of many of the differences that exist between printed and electronic text. One of the most fundamental of these has to do with the amount of information that can be presented at once. Because an 80 column by 25 row screen can present only 25 percent of the information on an 8 1/2 by 11-inch printed page, many more computer "pages" will be necessary to present the same amount of information as printed pages. What is more, scrolling and paging through electronic text are far less conveniently carried out than thumbing through a book. It is much easier to get lost in electronic text than it is to lose your place in a book. This gives rise to what Kerr (1986) has called the "wayfinding problem."

There are two things that the message designer can do in order to reduce these difficulties. The first is to compress the information that is presented on the screen by using contractions, by omitting articles and conjunctions to create a telegraphic style, by using point form rather than flowing prose, and by using graphics, whose efficiency and economy of expression we have already discussed, instead of text. The second is to provide users with ways of knowing where they are in the text, and to furnish them with easy means of returning to where they have been. This is particularly important when the text has a hierarchical structure accessed through one or more levels of menu. Such text structures are increasingly common as hypermedia packages, database packages, and CD-ROM become available. Help facilities, menu bars, icons, and other devices can be used for this.

### 6.6.    Broad, shallow menu structures are more useful than narrow, multi-level structures.

This rather specific principle is included because it is related to the preceding one, and also because the design of computer menus is increasingly of concern to the casual programmer. A number of studies (Fenton, 1987; Seppala & Salvendy, 1985; Snowberry, Parkinson, & Sisson, 1983) have reported that working through menus is most successful when each menu has many items to choose from, meaning that users need to traverse fewer levels in a hierarchy of sub-menus in order to get to where they want to go. In the case of narrower, deeper menus, it might be easier for the user to find an item at each level, but the need to work through more levels of what is already on the screen will probably be overlaid and obscured by a new window, or perhaps be removed altogether, making it far more difficult to remember where you are (the wayfinding problem again) and to retrace your steps. The broad, shallow menu structure should be used whenever possible. A good example is the menu of the word processor I am using to write this chapter, Microsoft's "Word." Sixteen commands are written on two lines at the bottom of the screen, which is quite a lot. However, most have only one "layer" beneath them, meaning that I can get back to my typing very easily. The options that have an additional layer, like the one that allows me to set up for fancy printing, are not those that are used the most frequently.

# 7. Illustration and Text Together

Although a great deal of research has been conducted on the perception of illustrations and of text separately, they are more often than not used together in instructional materials. It is therefore useful for the message designer to know something about how they are perceived in interaction with each other, and how, together, they facilitate or impede the comprehension of messages. There is evidence that illustration and text interact in interesting ways that sometimes run counter to what one might expect. The whole is different from, if not greater than, the sum of the parts. Research into the interaction of text and illustration is quite prolific and is summarized by Levie and Lenz (1982), and in several of the chapters to be found in books by Willows and Houghton (1987) and Mandl and Levin (1989).

### 7.1. *When they help at all, illustrations help in reading to learn, not learning to read.*

Levin (1989) has stated that adding illustrations to text does not help children learn to read. Indeed, there is even a suggestion that illustrating text makes it harder for children to learn to read (Willows, 1978). When facilitation effects for illustrations are found, it is when the text is to be read for its content and not to develop reading skills. What is more, illustrations cannot compensate for poor reading skills (Levin, Anglin, & Carney, 1987). The following principles therefore have to do with the illustration of text to improve comprehension, not reading skills *per se.*

### 7.2. *Generally, for illustrations to facilitate the comprehension of text, they need to be closely related to the text's content.*

At first glance, this looks like a statement of the obvious, and in many respects it is. However, two particular points need to be made. The first concerns the functions that illustrations are expected to perform in relation to the text. You will recall that we described a number of functions of illustration in Section No. 4 above. These included decoration, representation, organization, interpretation, and transformation. Levin, Anglin, and Carney (1987) compared the average effect sizes for picture facilitation of text comprehension for each of these functions separately. They found that decorative illustrations did not improve text comprehension at all, and that the most effective type of illustration was the transformational. It is clear that one of the things that distinguishes these two types of illustration is the extent to which they are connected to the content of the text. A decorative picture will only have a loose connection to the text, and perhaps no connection at all. On the other hand, a transformational picture is by its very nature intimately entwined in the meaning of the text. Indeed, it may be the only way in which the student can make the text meaningful. So there is a degree of subtlety in what at first sight appears to be a rather obvious principle. *Of course* illustrations should be related to the text if they are to assist comprehension. But the degree to which comprehension is facilitated will depend on the function the picture has *vis à vis* the text, and thus the extent of its connection to the text.

The second point is the other side of the coin. Peeck (1985) has shown experimentally that deliberately using illustrations that have nothing to do with the meaning of the text can interfere with comprehension. In all fairness, no designer would deliberately use pictures that did not fit with the text. But the important point is that poorly chosen pictures can have a detrimental effect and not just a neutral one.

**7.3.** *The degree to which illustrations facilitate the comprehension of text is the result of the interactions among the type of illustration, the outcome it is intended to attain, and the characteristics of the student.*

Levin (1989) argues that global statements about the effectiveness of illustrations in text, which ignore differences in the types of illustrations, differences in what illustrations can accomplish, and differences in student characteristics, cannot be made. Different types of pictures enjoy different degrees of success with different types of learning tasks. For instance, it is likely that different illustration strategies will be optimal when the task is to *understand* a text than when the task is to *remember* the text. Still others will be most effective when the student is expected to be able to *apply* the information the text presents. When student characteristics are also taken into consideration, the interactions become even more complicated. Yet it is at this level of complexity, which permits what Levin calls "transfer-appropriate processing" to occur, that the message designer needs to make decisions concerning the combination of text and illustrations. Not all possible permutations of illustration type, learning outcome, and student characteristic have yet been studied, which makes the message designer's job particularly difficult because design principles are not available. Yet a lack of sensitivity to the fact that these factors interact to determine the extent of the facilitation of text comprehension by illustrations will only make matters worse.

**7.4.** *Illustrations bring about the greatest facilitation of text comprehension when they represent content that is in some respect spatial.*

While written text is very good at discursive expression and at describing events in time, it is relatively poor at describing spatial layout and structure. As we saw earlier, Larkin and Simon (1987) suggest this is because in many types of illustration, a lot of the information is "indexed" by its location in two-dimensional space, meaning that less effort is required in searching for relevant information and less load is placed on memory. The same is true when illustrations are used with text, which means that they are particularly effective when the text's content is spatial. Norman (1990) has even gone so far as to claim that processing writing pushes cognitive skills to their limit and that we should therefore try to find ways to do without it.

> **7.5.** *Illustrations are least useful when the text they accompany deals with highly concrete content from which students can readily create their own mental images.*

Designers must not conclude from what we have said so far that pictures should always be used with text. A great deal of the success of illustrations derives from their ability to generate more concrete and memorable mental images of the content. When students create such images anyway, without the presence of illustrations, then obviously the addition of illustrations will not improve recall or comprehension. In such circumstances, it is even likely that supplied illustrations will not correspond to the images the students create for themselves, and will interfere with them. The designer therefore needs to guard against using illustrations when text is likely to lead students to create appropriate mental images on their own.

# 8. The Perception of Sounds

This last section contains principles that have to do with the use of sounds in instructional messages. By and large this means spoken narration, although music and sound effects do have important roles to play.

> **8.1.** *Sounds are organized, in time, in ways analogous to the organization of illustrations and text in space.*

At various places in this chapter, we have already alluded to the perception of sounds. This principle simply reminds us that research in auditory perception (Deutsch, 1986; Hawkins & Presson, 1986) and speech perception in particular (Jusczyk, 1986; Nussbaum & Schwab, 1986) has shown that the perception of sounds operates in some ways that are similar to visual perception. This applies both to the way auditory information is organized, and to the way attention is directed to it.

Sounds form clusters just as sights do, only in this case the proximity of one perceptual unit to another that determines message structure is temporal rather than spatial. Sounds, notes, or words that follow rapidly one after another, followed by a pause, will be perceived as a unit and will be interpreted as having some feature or theme in common. The simplest example of this would be Morse code, where the pauses between the dots and dashes are shorter than those between the clusters of dots and dashes that form letters, and the pauses between letters are shorter than those between the clusters of letters that form words. The placement of pauses in speech likewise demarcates perceptual units. Auditory messages therefore have hierarchical structures not unlike those we have described for visual messages.

As with what we see, what we hear also varies in various qualities. Instead of size, color, and shape, sounds have amplitude, frequency, duration, and timbre (or loudness, pitch, length, and tone). As in the case of visual stimuli, these qualities can also form the basis for structure and organization. Thus, loud sounds tend to be grouped apart from soft sounds, high-pitched sounds distinguished from lower sounds, long sounds from short sounds, and strident sounds from mellow sounds.

The usefulness of varying these qualities *per se* is limited to those occasions where the sounds themselves are what students have to learn about. This would include, obviously, music classes where rhythm and pitch are studied for their own sake. Training students in auscultation of the heart would be another example. The rhythm and quality of the sounds made by a healthy heart are different from those made by a diseased one. When these qualities are varied in narration, however, their instructional usefulness is virtually unlimited, opening up for the message designer the whole range and expressive power of the human voice to inform, persuade, and move.

Variations in the loudness, pitch, length, and tone of sounds can also control where attention is directed. The principle that we offered when discussing visual attention, that attention is drawn to what stands in contrast to its surroundings, applies to auditory perception just as well. Thus, rapid changes in volume, switching from a high-pitched to a low-pitched voice in a narration, speeding up speech or slowing it down, or changing from a menacing tone of voice to a soothing one will all draw the listener's attention.

### 8.2.   Speech is effective in communicating ideas that have to be understood in a particular sequence.

One of the greatest advantages of using speech in an instructional message is that the designer can hold information back from the student. Even in text, which like speech uses an essentially linear symbol system, students can skim, read ahead, and generally jump about, taking ideas out of order. In speech, this is mostly very difficult to do, unless you keep fast-forwarding or rewinding a tape. Through speech, the designer can give information to students in precisely the order and at exactly the speed that is judged to be best. This is useful to do in those situations where learning something out of sequence, or moving on to the next step before the previous one has been properly mastered, does more harm than good. Examples include assembling or disassembling machinery where a false step could be dangerous to life and limb, or learning a computer language where trying to write "while" loops before learning about conditional branching could lead to confusion and misconception.

### 8.3.   Speech is ephemeral.

The most serious drawback to using speech (or any sounds for that matter) in instructional messages is that they lack the permanence of text or illustration. Once a word is uttered, it is gone. We know that a single exposure to a fleeting piece of information, especially when others follow rapidly after it, is rarely sufficient for comprehension and retention. This means that the designer needs to consider a variety of techniques to help the student learn from speech. Two of these involve redundancy. In the first instance, what is said can simply be repeated—probably in different words to keep it interesting. This is necessary when speech is the only way in which the message is conveyed, and is referred to as "within-channel" redundancy. On the other hand, the designer might use "between-channel" redundancy, where what is spoken is duplicated either in text or in some form of illustration. Indeed, nowadays speech is mostly used in narration that accompanies visual messages (unless one includes talks or lectures, but these are not usually "designed" by message designers). A third option the designer might use is to make it easy for the student to translate the ephemeral information in speech into something more permanent. This could require nothing more complicated than leaving time between utterances for students to take notes. Or it might involve specific directions on how students might "recode" (Salomon, 1979) or "elaborate" the information so that it becomes more permanently established in memory. Levin *et al.*'s (1987) strategies for creating mental images to help understand and recall text come to mind as examples.

### 8.4. Text is more effective than speech when the content is complex and when supplementary explanations in visual illustrations are not available.

This follows from the previous principle. It is safest not to use speech on its own when the material to be learned is relatively complex or difficult, and especially when no additional instructional support using less ephemeral modalities is available. If other message characteristics, such as discursiveness or abstraction, require that words rather than pictures or diagrams be used, then text is the appropriate format to use.

### 8.5. Human speech is the most powerful and expressive medium the designer has available for use in instructional messages.

Given the ephemeral nature of speech and the need to supplant it on most occasions, why would the designer choose to use it for instruction? The answer is that human speech is expressively very powerful. It is the easiest way for the message designer to create mood, to appeal to emotions, to lighten or make more serious the "tone" of a message, to amuse, to sadden, to persuade, to coax, to chide, or to cajole. Granted, the Bergmans and Spielbergs of this world can do the same with film. However, with a moderately experienced narrator, any message designer can achieve comparable effects with speech.

The success of speech derives from the almost infinite control the human voice has over those qualities of sound with which we began this section—loudness, pitch, pace, and tone. The effects of varying these cannot, of course, be illustrated in the written words of this chapter. You are encouraged to listen to the great voices of our century, such as Orson Welles, Winston Churchill, Dylan Thomas, Katherine Hepburn, and Martin Luther King, to discern the power of speech.

Then listen to any performance by lesser-known or even anonymous narrators, and you will realize that you do not have to hire a star of stage, screen or politics in order to create an effective narration. Speech is naturally expressive. Anyone who can speak is therefore a potential narrator.

> ### 8.6. *When narration accompanies a message in another modality, the relationships between the two messages must be strong and apparent.*

This is not much more than a way of saying that the principles we presented when discussing using text and illustration together pertain when speech is used instead of text. Again, the principle seems to be a statement of the obvious. No designer would have a narrator speaking about petunias to accompany a football training film.

However, there is a tendency, especially among novice designers, to try to create metaphors by using a narration that only relates to the visual part of the message in some symbolic or allegorical manner. Thus, in our example the viewer might interpret the film about football to mean that the apparent virility and vigor of football players is nothing but show, and that they are sensitive and delicate underneath. But to pull something like this off, the designer has to be far better than most! It is therefore best to stick with fairly literal relationships between narration and film or slide.

## Chapter Conclusion

We conclude this chapter not with an attempt to summarize any of what has been said, but with a few general comments. The principles and discussion must speak for themselves. Any attempt to summarize or recapitulate would therefore be redundant.

First, obviously, the principles are not exhaustive of the possible prescriptions that arise from the research on perception and related aspects of cognition. The literature is vast and, as we have seen from our sample of it, ranges from extremely fine-grained psycho-physiological work on preattentive processes to the more general study of the perception and interpretation of illustration, text, and speech. To create a set of prescriptions for the designer that would cover *all* of this research while at the same time anticipating *every* contingency that the designer is likely to face would be virtually impossible.

The selection of principles that arises from this constraint also deserves comment. Indeed, the reader might have detected a certain ambiguity in what has been presented. This stems from an ambiguity in the author's (and perhaps the reader's) mind about what is most useful for message designers. It would be nice, I suppose, if this chapter had presented nothing but a list of do's and don'ts with a sufficiently strong empirical basis to make the designer's task simply a matter of finding the right principle and doing what it said to do. This is not possible. The reason is, again, the enormity of the task. But over and above that, it is precluded by the fragmented nature of the research that deals with perceptual matters at a level of specificity that permits such prescriptions to be stated unequivocally. In short, we just do not know enough of the particulars of perceptual and related processes, and must therefore rely on more general principles to guide our design decisions. Nonetheless, some fairly precise prescriptions have been presented, particularly in the second part of the chapter, that serve as examples of what such principles might look like.

This brings us to the next point. Even if it were possible to develop an exhaustive list of principles to guide the message designer directly in a reliable and consistent manner, one might question whether this might not ultimately be self-defeating. Design well done is a dynamic and creative process, not a mechanically applied technique. All the principles in the world cannot guarantee that what is designed will be effective, attractive, motivating, or even acceptable. It is therefore more productive, I believe, to make the designer aware of the general issues that surround human perception and cognition, and to state guiding principles at a fairly general level, allowing designers to exercise judgment based upon experience and creativity as they work from these principles toward decisions for specific actions. Many principles offered in this chapter are of this kind.

This approach to identifying design principles and to message design itself will only succeed if designers come to grips with fundamental theory for themselves and do not rely solely on people like the authors of the chapters in this book to tell them what to do. The most important role for psychological research and theory in message design is to furnish analytical tools, not to provide cut-and-dried recipes for design. Any designer who finds any of the principles or comments in this chapter useful or simply interesting is therefore encouraged to dig deeper into the literature cited here, and particularly to keep up with the burgeoning research on perception and cognition, in order to cultivate an understanding of the processes by means of which people learn. Only then will the designer develop the solid basis for instructional decision-making toward which the principles presented in this chapter have pointed. There is simply no other way message designers can learn their business, or that message design can be done.

# References

Anderson, J. R. (1983). *The architecture of cognition.* Cambridge, MA: Harvard University Press.

Anderson, J. R. (1984). Spreading activation. In J. R. Anderson & S. M. Kosslyn (Eds.), *Tutorials in learning and memory: Essays in Honor of Gordon Bower.* San Francisco: Freeman.

Anderson, R. C. (1970). Control of student mediating processes during verbal learning and instruction. *Review of Educational Research, 40*, 349–369.

Antes, J. R., & Mann, S. W. (1984). Global-local precedence in picture processing. *Psychological Research, 46*, 247–259.

Ausubel, D. (1963). *The psychology of meaningful verbal learning.* New York: Grune and Stratton.

Belland, J. C., Taylor, W. D., Canelos, J., Dwyer, F., & Baker P. (1985). Is the self-paced instructional program, via microcomputer-based instruction, the most effective method of addressing individual learning differences? *Educational Communications and Technology Journal, 33,* 185–198.

Bellezza, F. W. (1986). A mnemonic based on arranging words in a visual pattern. *Journal of Educational Psychology, 78,* 217–224.

Bertin, J. (1981). *Graphics and graphic information processing.* New York: Walter de Gruyter.

Bertin, J. (1983). *Semiology of graphics.* Madison, WI: University of Wisconsin Press.

Biederman, I. (1987). Recognition by components: A theory of human image understanding. *Psychological Review, 94,* 115–147.

Biederman, I. (1990). Higher level vision. In D. N. Osherson, S. M. Kosslyn, & J. M. Hollerbach (Eds.), *Visual cognition and action.* Cambridge, MA: MIT Press, p. 49.

Boden, M. (1988). *Computer models of mind.* New York: Cambridge University Press.

Borror, D. J., & White, R. E. (1970). *A field guide to the insects.* Boston: Houghton Mifflin, p. 16.

Bovy, R. C. (1983). *Defining the psychologically active features of instructional treatments designed to facilitate cue attendance.* Presented at the meeting of the American Educational Research Association, Montreal, April.

Boynton, R. M. (1988). Color vision. *Annual Review of Psychology, 39,* 69–100.

Brody, P. (1982). In search of instructional utility: A function-based approach to pictorial research. *Instructional Science, 13,* 47–61.

Butterfield, E. C., & Nelson, G. D. (1989). Theory and practice of teaching for transfer. *Educational Communications and Technology Journal, 37*(3), 5–38.

Calis, G. J., Sterenborg, J., & Maarse, F. (1984). Initial microgenetic steps in single-glance recognition. *Acta Psychologica, 55,* 215–230.

Carpenter, C. R. (1953). A theoretical orientation for instructional film research. *AV Communication Review, 1,* 38–52.

Cecala, A. J., & Garner, W. R. (1986). Internal frame of reference as a determinant of the oblique effect. *Journal of Experimental Psychology: Human Perception and Performance, 12,* 314–323.

Clark, F., & Angert, J. (1985). *Synthesizing the research findings of Dwyer and his associates: A quantitative assessment.* Unpublished manuscript.

Clark, R. E. (1983). Reconsidering research on learning from media. *Review of Educational Research, 53,* 445–460.

Clark, R. E., & Salomon, G. (1985). Media in teaching. In M. C. Wittrock (Ed.), *Handbook of research on teaching, third edition.* New York: Macmillan, 464–478.

Cleveland, W. S., & McGill, R. (1984). Graphical perception: Theory, experimentation, and application to the development of graphical methods. *Journal of the American Statistical Association, 79,* 531–554.

Cleveland, W. S., & McGill, R. (1985). Graphical perception and graphical methods for analyzing scientific data. *Science, 229,* 828–833.

Dale, E. (1946). *Audio-visual methods in teaching.* New York: Dryden Press.

Deutsch, D. (1986). Auditory pattern recognition. In K. R. Boff, L. Kaufman, & J. P. Thomas (Eds.), *Handbook of perception and human performance, volume 2.* New York: John Wiley, 32-1–32-49.

Duchastel, P., & Waller, R. (1979). Pictorial illustration in instructional texts. *Educational Technology, 19*(11), 20–25.

Dwyer, F. M. (1972). *A guide for improving visualized instruction.* State College, PA: Learning Services.

Dwyer, F. M. (1978). *Strategies for improving visual learning.* State College, PA: Learning Services.

Dwyer, F. M. (1987). *Enhancing visualized instruction: Recommendations for practitioners.* State College, PA: Learning Services.

Eisenberg, A., & Eisenberg, H. (1979). *Alive and well: Decisions in health.* New York: McGraw-Hill.

Fenton, D. M. (1987). Computer menu design: An investigation of the interface between user characteristics and menu structures. *Australian Psychologist, 22,* 233–243.

Fleming, M., & Levie, W. H. (1978). *Instructional message design: Principles from the behavioral sciences.* Englewood Cliffs, NJ: Educational Technology Publications, p. 72.

Gibson, J. J. (1979). *The ecological approach to visual perception.* Boston: Houghton Mifflin.

Gick, M. L., & Holyoak, K. (1983). Schema induction and analogical transfer. *Cognitive Psychology, 15,* 1–38.

Hannafin, M. J. (1984). Guidelines for using locus of instructional control in the design of computer-assisted instruction. *Journal of Instructional Development, 7,* 6–10.

Hartley, J. (1982). Designing instructional text. In D. Jonassen (Ed.), *The technology of text, volume 1.* Englewood Cliffs, NJ: Educational Technology Publications, 193–214.

Hartley, J. (1987). Designing electronic text: The role of print-based research. *Educational Communications and Technology Journal, 35,* 3–17.

Hawkins, H., & Presson, J. (1986). Auditory information processing. In K. R. Boff, L. Kaufman, & J. P. Thomas (Eds.), *Handbook of perception and human performance, volume 2.* New York: John Wiley, 26-1–26-64.

Hoffman, D. D., & Richards, W. A. (1984). Parts of recognition. *Cognition, 18,* 65–96.

Holliday, W. G., Brunner, L., & Donais, E. (1977). *Journal of Research in Science Teaching, 14,* 129–138.

Horn, R.E. (1982). Structured writing and text design. In D. Jonassen (Ed.), *The technology of text, volume 1.* Englewood Cliffs, NJ: Educational Technology Publications, 341–368.

Jonassen, D. (1982, 1985). *The technology of text, volumes 1 and 2.* Englewood Cliffs, NJ: Educational Technology Publications.

Jonassen, D., & Hawk, P. (1984). Using graphic organizers in instruction. *Information Design Journal, 4,* 58–68.

Julesz, B. (1981). Textons, the elements of texture perception and their interactions. *Nature, 290,* 91–97.

Jusczyk, P. (1986). Speech perception. In K. R. Boff, L. Kaufman, & J. P. Thomas (Eds.), *Handbook of perception and human performance, volume 2.* New York: John Wiley, 27-1–27-57.

Kahn, J. I., & Foster, D. H. (1986). Horizontal-vertical structure in the comparison of rigidly transformed patterns. *Journal of Experimental Psychology: Human Perception and Performance, 12,* 422–433.

Kerr, S. T. (1986). Transition from page to screen. In S. Lambert & S. Ropiequet (Eds.), *CD ROM: The new papyrus.* Redmond, WA: Microsoft Press, 321–346.

Kinchla, R. A., & Wolfe, J. (1979). The order of visual processing: "Top-down," "bottom-up," or "middle-out"? *Perception and Psychophysics, 25,* 225–230.

Knowlton, J. Q. (1966). On the definition of "picture." *AV Communication Review, 14,* 157–183.

Kosslyn, S. M., Simcox, W. A., Pinker, S., & Parkin, L. P. (1983). *Understanding charts and graphs: A project in applied cognitive psychology.* ERIC Document Reproduction Service, ED 238 687.

Kulhavy, R. W., Lee, J. B., & Caterino, L. C. (1985). Conjoint retention of maps and related discourse. *Contemporary Educational Psychology, 10,* 28–37.

Lakoff, G. (1987). *Women, fire, and dangerous things.* Chicago: University of Chicago Press.

Larkin, J. H., & Simon, H. A. (1987). Why a diagram is (sometimes) worth ten thousand words. *Cognitive Science, 11,* 65–99.

Lesaga, M. I. (1989). Gestalts and their components: Nature of information precedence. In B. E. Shepp & S. Ballesteros (Eds.), *Object perception: Structure and process.* Hillsdale, NJ: Lawrence Erlbaum Associates, 165–202.

Levie, W. H., & Dickie, K. E. (1973). The analysis and application of media. In R. M. W. Travers (Ed.), *Second Handbook of Research on Teaching.* Chicago: Rand McNally, 858–882.

Levie, W. H., & Lentz, R. (1982). Effects of text illustrations: A review of research. *Educational Communications and Technology Journal, 30,* 195–232.

Levin, J. R. (1987). *Spatial metaphor and the syntax of graphics.* Unpublished paper, College of Education, University of Washington.

Levin, J. R. (1989). A transfer-appropriate-processing perspective of pictures in prose. In H. Mandl & J. R. Levin (Eds.), *Knowledge acquisition from text and pictures.* Amsterdam: North Holland, 83–100.

Levin, J. R., Anglin, G. J., & Carney, R. N. (1987). On empirically validating functions of pictures in prose. In D. H. Willows & H. A. Houghton (Eds.), *The psychology of illustration, volume 1.* New York: Springer, 51–85.

Levin, J. R., Shriberg, L. K., & Berry, J. K. (1983). A concrete strategy for remembering abstract prose. *American Educational Research Journal, 20,* 277–290.

Mandl, H., & Levin, J. R. (Eds.) (1989). *Knowledge acquisition from text and pictures.* Amsterdam: North Holland.

Marr, D. (1982). *Vision.* New York: Freeman.

Marr, D., & Nishihara H. K. (1978). Representation and recognition of the spatial organization of three-dimensional shapes. *Proceedings of the Royal Society of London, 200,* 269–294.

Marr, D., & Ullman, W. (1981). Directional selectivity and its use in early visual processing. *Proceedings of the Royal Society of London, 211*, 151–180.

Mayer, R. E. (1979). Twenty years of research on advance organizers: Assimilation theory is still the best predictor of results. *Review of Educational Research, 49*, 133–167.

McNamara, T. P. (1986). Mental representations of spatial relations. *Cognitive Psychology, 18*, 87–121.

Merrill, M. D., & Tennyson, R. D. (1977). *Teaching concepts: An instructional design guide.* Englewood Cliffs, NJ: Educational Technology Publications.

Miller, G. A. (1956). The magical number seven, plus or minus two: Some limits on our capacity for processing information. *Psychological Review, 63*, 81–97.

Misanchuk, E. R. (1992). *Preparing instructional text: Document design using desktop publishing.* Englewood Cliffs, NJ: Educational Technology Publications.

Moore, D. W., & Readance, J. E. (1984). A quantitative and qualitative review of graphic organizer research. *Journal of Educational Research, 78*, 11–17.

Morrison, C. R., & Levin, J. R. (1987). Degree of mnemonic support and students' acquisition of science facts. *Educational Communications and Technology Journal, 35*, p. 70.

Navon, D. (1977). Forest before trees: The precedence of global features in visual perception. *Cognitive Psychology, 9*, 353–383.

Neisser, J. (1976). *Cognition and reality.* San Francisco: Freeman.

Nicoletti, R., & Umilta, C. (1989). Splitting visual space with attention. *Journal of Experimental Psychology: Human Perception and Performance, 15*, 164–169.

Norman, D. A. (1990, March). *In the coming age of interactive media, who needs writing?* Invited lecture, University of Washington, Seattle, WA.

Nussbaum, H. C., & Schwab, E. C. (1986). The role of attention and active processing in speech perception. In E. C. Schwab & H. C. Nussbaum (Eds.), *Pattern recognition by humans and machines. Volume 1: Speech perception.* New York: Academic Press, 113–158.

Ogden, C. K., & Richards, I. A. (1946). *The meaning of meaning.* New York: Harcourt, Brace, and World.

Owen, L. A. (1985a). Dichoptic priming effects on ambiguous picture processing. *British Journal of Psychology, 76*, 437–447.

Owen, L. A. (1985b). The effect of masked pictures on the interpretation of ambiguous pictures. *Current Psychological Research and Reviews, 4*, 108–118.

Paivio, A. (1971). *Imagery and verbal processes.* New York: Holt, Rinehart and Winston.

Paivio, A. (1983). The empirical case for dual coding. In J. C. Yuille (Ed.), *Imagery, memory and cognition.* Hillsdale, NJ: Lawrence Erlbaum Associates, 310–332.

Peeck, J. (1985, March). *Effects of mismatched pictures on retention of illustrated prose.* Paper presented at the annual meeting of the American Educational Research Association, Chicago.

Pentland, A. P. (1986). Perceptual organization and the representation of natural form. *Artificial Intelligence, 28*, 293–331.

Pinker, S. (1985). *Visual cognition.* Cambridge, MA: MIT Press.

Pomerantz, J. R. (1981). Perceptual organization in information processing. In M. Kubovy & J. R. Pomerantz (Eds.), *Perceptual organization*. Hillsdale, NJ: Lawrence Erlbaum Associates.

Pomerantz, J. R. (1986). Visual form perception: An overview. In E. C. Schwab & H. C. Nussbaum (Eds.), *Pattern recognition by humans and machines. Volume 2: Visual perception*. New York: Academic Press.

Pomerantz, J. R., Pristach, E. A., & Carson, C. E. (1989). Attention and object perception. In B. E. Shepp & S. Ballesteros (Eds.), *Object perception: Structure and process*. Hillsdale, NJ: Lawrence Erlbaum Associates, 35–90.

Pomerantz, J. R., Sager, L. C., & Stover, R. J. (1977). Perception of wholes and their parts: Some configural superiority effects. *Journal of Experimental Psychology: Human Perception and Performance, 3*, 422–435.

Pomerantz, J. R., & Schwaitzberg, S. D. (1975). Grouping by proximity: Selective attention measures. *Perception and Psychophysics, 18*, 355–361.

Pylyshyn, Z. (1981). The imagery debate: Analogue media versus tacit knowledge. *Psychological Review, 88*, 16–45.

Pylyshyn, Z. (1984). *Computation and cognition: Toward a foundation for cognitive science*. Cambridge, MA: MIT Press.

Rankin, R. (1986). *Communicating science concepts through charts and diagrams*. Ph.D. Dissertation, Griffith University, Brisbane, Australia.

Reigeluth, C. M., & Stein, F. S. (1983). The elaboration theory of instruction. In C. M. Reigeluth (Ed.), *Instructional design theories and models*. Hillsdale, NJ: Lawrence Erlbaum Associates.

Rigney, J. W. (1978). Learning strategies: A theoretical perspective. In H. F. O'Neil (Ed.), *Learning strategies*. New York: Academic Press.

Rock, I. (1986). The description and analysis of object and event perception. In K. R. Boff, L. Kaufman, & J. P. Thomas (Eds.), *The handbook of perception and human performance, volume 2*. New York: John Wiley, 33-1–33-71.

Rosch, E. (1978). Principles of categorization. In E. Rosch & B. B. Lloyd (Eds.), *Cognition and categorization*. Hillsdale, NJ: Lawrence Erlbaum Associates, 27–48.

Royer, J. M., & Cable, G. W. (1976). Illustrations, analogies and facilitative transfer in prose learning. *Journal of Educational Psychology, 68*, 205–209.

Rumelhart, D. E., & McClelland, J. L. (1986). *Parallel distributed processing, volumes 1 and 2*. Cambridge, MA: MIT Press.

Rumelhart, D. E., & Norman, D. A. (1981). Analogical processes in learning. In J. R. Anderson (Ed.), *Cognitive skills and their acquisition*. Hillsdale, NJ: Lawrence Erlbaum Associates.

Salomon, G. (1974). Internalization of filmic schematic operations in interaction with learners' aptitudes. *Journal of Educational Psychology, 66*, 499–511.

Salomon, G. (1976). Cognitive skill learning across cultures. *Journal of Communication, 26*, 138–145.

Salomon, G. (1979). *Interaction of media, cognition and learning*. San Francisco: Jossey Bass.

Salomon, G. (1983). The differential investment of mental effort in different sources of learning material. *Educational Psychologist, 18*, 42–50.

Salomon, G. (1984). Television is "easy" and print is "hard": The differential investment of mental effort in learning as a function of perceptions and attributions. *Journal of Educational Psychology, 76,* 647–658.

Schwartz, N. H. (1988). Cognitive processing characteristics of maps: Implications for instruction. *Educational and Psychological Research, 7,* 113–128.

Seppala, P., & Salvendy, G. (1985). Impact of depth of menu hierarchy on performance effectiveness in a supervisory task: Computerized flexible manufacturing system. *Human Factors, 27,* 713–722.

Shepard, R. N. (1967). Recognition memory for words, sentences and pictures. *Journal of Verbal Learning and Verbal Behavior, 6,* 156–163.

Simkin, D., & Hastie, R. (1987). An information-processing analysis of graphic perception. *Journal of the American Statistical Association, 82,* 454–465.

Sless, D. (1981). *Learning and visual communication.* New York: John Wiley.

Snowberry, K., Parkinson, S. R., & Sisson, N. (1983). Computer display menus. *Ergonomics, 26,* 699–712.

Standing, L. (1973). Learning 10,000 pictures. *Quarterly Journal of Experimental Psychology, 25,* 207–222.

Sulin, R. A., & Dooling, D. J. (1974). Intrusions of a thematic idea in the retention of prose. *Journal of Experimental Psychology, 103,* 255–262.

Sutherland, S. W. (1989). *Miles Albert Tinker and the zone of optimal typography.* Doctoral dissertation, University of Washington.

Sutherland, S. W., & Winn, W. D. (1987, February). *The effect of the number and nature of features and of general ability on the simultaneous and successive processing of maps.* Paper presented at the annual conference of the Association for Educational Communications and Technology, Atlanta.

Tennyson, R. D. (1981). Use of adaptive information for advisement in learning concepts and rules using computer-assisted instruction. *American Educational Research Journal, 4,* 425–438.

Tinker, A. M. (1963). *The legibility of print.* Ames, IA: Iowa State University Press.

Treisman, A. (1986). Features and objects in visual perception. *Scientific American, 255*(5), 114–125.

Treisman, A. (1988). Features and objects: The fourteenth Bartlett Memorial Lecture. *Quarterly Journal of Experimental Psychology: Human Experimental Psychology, 40A,* 210–237.

Treisman, A., & Gelade, G. (1980). A feature integration theory of attention. *Cognitive Psychology, 12,* 97–136.

Tufte, E. R. (1983). *The visual display of quantitative information.* Cheshire, CT: Graphics Press.

Twyman, M. (1981). Typography without words. *Visible Language, 15,* 5–12.

Ullman, S. (1985). Visual routines. In S. Pinker (Ed.), *Visual cognition.* Cambridge, MA: MIT Press, 97–159.

Umilta, C. (1988). Orienting of attention. In F. Boller & J. Graufman (Eds.), *Handbook of neuropsychology.* Amsterdam: Elsevier, 175–193.

Uttal, W. R. (1988). *On seeing forms.* Hillsdale, NJ: Lawrence Erlbaum Associates.

Villee, C. A., Walker, W. F., & Smith, F. E. (1963). *General zoology.* Philadelphia: W. B. Saunders.

Weinstein, C. E. (1978). Elaboration skills as a learning strategy. In H. F. O'Neil (Ed.), *Learning strategies*. New York: Academic Press.

Wertheimer, M. (1938). *Laws of organization in perceptual forms in a source book for Gestalt psychology*. London: Routledge and Kegan Paul.

Weyer, S., & Borning, A. (1985). A prototype electronic encyclopedia. *ACM Transactions on Office Information Systems, 3,* 63–68.

Willows, D. M. (1978). A picture is not always worth a thousand words: Pictures as distractors in reading. *Journal of Educational Psychology, 70,* 255–262.

Willows, D. M., & Houghton, H. (1987). *The psychology of illustration, volumes 1 and 2.* New York: Springer.

Winn, W. D. (1982). Visualization in learning and instruction: A cognitive approach. *Educational Communications and Technology Journal, 30,* 3–25.

Winn, W. D. (1983). Perceptual strategies used with flow diagrams having normal and unanticipated formats. *Perceptual and Motor Skills, 57,* 751–762.

Winn, W. D. (1987). Using charts, graphs and diagrams in educational materials. In D. M. Willows & H. Houghton (Eds.), *The psychology of illustration. Vol. 1. Basic research.* New York: Springer, 152–198.

Winn, W. D. (1988a). Instructional design and intelligent systems: Shifts in the designer's decision-making role. *Instructional Science, 16,* 59–77.

Winn, W. D. (1988b). Recall of the pattern, sequence and names of concepts presented in instructional diagrams. *Journal of Research in Science Teaching, 25,* 375–386.

Winn, W. D. (1989a, April). *Evidence for bias in the interpretation of simple diagrams.* Paper presented at the annual meeting of the American Educational Research Association, San Francisco.

Winn, W. D. (1989b). The design and use of instructional graphics. In H. Mandl & J. R. Levin (Eds.), *Knowledge acquisition from text and pictures.* New York: Elsevier, 125–144.

Winn, W. D., & Everett, R. (1979). Affective rating of color and black-and-white pictures. *Educational Communications and Technology Journal, 27,* 148–156.

Winn, W. D., & Holliday, W. G. (1982). Design principles for diagrams and charts. In D. Jonassen (Ed.), *The technology of text, volume 1.* Englewood Cliffs, NJ: Educational Technology Publications, 277–299.

Winn, W. D., & Solomon, C. (1990). *Syntactic and semantic influences on the interpretation of simple diagrams.* Seattle, WA: College of Education, University of Washington, unpublished paper.

Winn, W. D., & Sutherland, S. W. (1989). Factors influencing the recall of elements in maps and diagrams and the strategies used to encode them. *Journal of Educational Psychology, 81,* 33–39.

Yarbus, A. (1967). *Eye movements and vision.* New York: Plenum Press.

# Chapter 3

# Psychomotor Principles

## Alexander J. Romiszowski

### Syracuse University

## Introduction

In this opening part of the chapter, some of the history of research in this domain is reviewed, putting current research themes into an appropriate perspective. Following, in Section 1, are some general organizing concepts for message design in the psychomotor domain. First, the interdependence of the psychomotor, cognitive, and affective domains is reviewed, and the interrelationships of the present chapter with others in this book are emphasized. Second, some basic definitions of terms used in this chapter are given, together with a schema for their conceptual organization. Third, a cyclical model of skilled activity is proposed, illustrating the range of abilities which may have an influence on the execution of a skill. Finally, some other factors which are currently gaining prominence in the study of the development and acquisition of psychomotor skills are mentioned and their importance discussed.

### Early Research on Psychomotor Skills Acquisition

A historical analysis of changing emphases on research in the field is given by Irion (1966) in the opening chapter of the book by Bilodeau (1966). He divides the early work into three periods. The first period, running from the turn of the century to the early 1930's, was characterized by intensive study of the question of distribution of practice (massed versus spaced) but without much in the way of theory-building to explain the observed effects.

The second period, stretching through the decade from the mid-1930's to the mid-1940's, is characterized by a plethora of theory-building to explain the practice distribution phenomena.

The third period, running from the mid-1940's through to the mid-1960's, was a very active one for research on motor skills acquisition. The impetus given to this field of study by the Second World War continued into peacetime and was further driven by the growth in popularity of behaviorist theories and their application. Nowhere is the application of different reinforcement schedules and the observation of their result on learning easier to set up and measure than in the motor skills area.

Yet another area of research that flourished in this period addressed the problem of retention of learning of a motor task. These studies often used specially designed apparatus that presented the learner with a standardized task that could be replicated across many experiments with many different groups. One example is the pursuit rotor, a device used by many different researchers to measure the one discrete ability of manually tracking a point moving in a circle (Figure 3.1). This device was used to measure retention of an acquired skill after intervals of one week (Jahnke, 1958), up to four weeks (Jahnke & Duncan, 1956), up to one year (Bell, 1950; Eysenck, 1960), and even two years (Koonce, Chambliss, & Irion, 1964).

**Rotary Pursuit**

**Figure 3.1.** Rotary pursuit: an adapted record player, used in many psychomotor skill learning experiments.

Similar studies, but with different tasks on different devices and with other variables (such as number of practice trials or degree of feedback during practice), were also performed during this period (e.g., Bilodeau *et al.*, 1962, 1963, 1964). One general result of this research was to demonstrate the overall higher levels of retention over time that are common in the case of physical tasks, as compared to intellectual tasks.

# 1. Basic Concepts, Principles, and Assumptions

*1.1.* *Skills can be usefully classified along a continuum, from simple, reflexive (or "reproductive") to complex, strategy-based (or "productive"). The position of a skill on this continuum is a major determinant of the training approach that should be adopted.*

Perhaps one of the weaknesses of much of the earlier work on skill acquisition was the concentration on single, simple movements or a sequence of simple repetitive steps. The realization that these are typically performed in real life as components of more complex activity only began to be fully appreciated in the late 1960's. Pioneering work at the Perkins factory in the U.K. concentrated on the importance of the "planning" element in the knitting together of combinations of previously mastered movements into the skilled performance of a complex industrial task. These more complex skills were referred to as "planning" or "strategy" skills (Wellens, 1974). They have also been referred to as "productive" skills in that they require the performer to produce a situation-specific response.

In the U.S.A. a similar (though not quite identical) distinction was made in the context of sports training between "closed" and "open" tasks, the former requiring a response to a stable environment (e.g., bowling), and the latter requiring continuous adjustment to an unpredictable, changing environment, as during a football game (Poulton, 1957). A closer parallel to the reflexive/strategy skills continuum was given by Knapp (1963) in suggesting a classification of psychomotor skills along a habitual/perceptual continuum. Knapp stresses that whereas the habitual skills depend on the mastery and perfection of a specific stimulus-response chain, at the perceptual end of the continuum the individual must not only master a set of component basic skills, but also must learn to apply them according to the situation, and this requires an element of cognitive decision making.

This writer has chosen elsewhere (Romiszowski, 1980, 1981) to refer to the two ends of this continuum as "reproductive/productive" skills to emphasize the key aspects of this distinction and the link to the usage of the term "productive learning" in the cognitive domain. In so doing, I hoped to emphasize the view that the position of a given task on this continuum may be of greater importance to decisions about appropriate instructional methods than the domain into which the task is most easily classified. Figure 3.2 presents a classification schema that combines a four-domain classification of skills with the reproductive/productive continuum. Whereas the domains may influence certain aspects of instructional design (e.g., media selection), the position of a task on the reproductive/productive continuum influences instructional decisions in much more fundamental ways, such as decisions between expository and discovery instructional methods, or the extent to which "deep processing" discussions are an essential part of the method (Romiszowski, 1981).

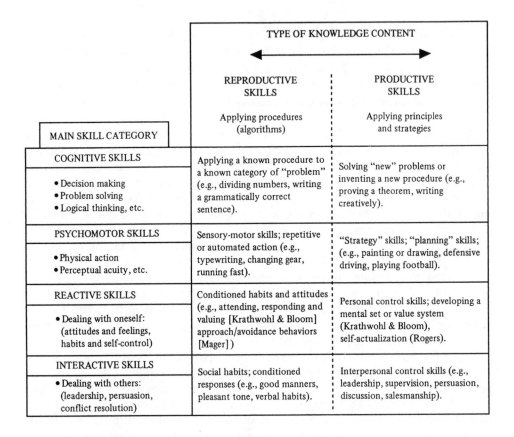

**Figure 3.2.** The skills schema (Romiszowski, 1981).

## 1.2.   *Psychomotor learning may involve the acquisition of skills or of knowledge or (most often) of both.*

Another point worth mentioning here is the confusion that seems to exist in the use of the term "psychomotor" as a definition of a domain of learning and its near (but apparently not exact) synonyms: sensory-motor skills; perceptual-motor skills; or just simply motor skills. All these, plus other variants, can be found in the literature, sometimes with the word "skills" attached and sometimes with alternatives such as "tasks" or "learning." It may be helpful to define how the terminology is being used in this chapter.

One should make an important distinction between "knowledge" and "skill." Knowledge is understood here to mean information stored in the performer's mind or available to the performer in some reference source. Skill is used here to refer to actions (intellectual as well as physical) which a performer executes in a competent manner in order to achieve a goal. You may use the knowledge available to you with more or less success in achievement of a goal. Generally, practice is essential to develop a higher level of skill (although we will see later that practice may be a necessary but not sufficient condition). In contrast, achieving knowledge may have an immediate and significant effect on performance, independent of practice.

### 1.3. *Skilled activity involves a complex cycle of information processing. The process is susceptible to improvement through training.*

Many authors have observed that skilled activity involves a cycle of stages, commencing with the reception of information from the environment and leading to some action on the environment. Wheatcroft (1973), for example, describes the physical skill cycle as commencing with the formation of an idea or purpose in the mind of the performer. This leads to:
— the reception of relevant information;
— its correct perception and interpretation;
— a decision on the appropriate action to take;
— and, finally, the action itself.
This is then followed by reception of further new information on the results of the action, perception, decision, further action, and so on. By incorporating in this model the aforementioned need to have previously gained knowledge of the procedure which is to be executed, the skill cycle can be represented as shown in Figure 3.3, (Romiszowski, 1981). This model enables one to distinguish between the automated, REPRODUCTIVE (reflexive, closed, etc.) skills and the more PRODUCTIVE (strategy, planning, open, etc.) skills. Indeed, three basic categories of skilled behavior are postulated;

- *Totally reflexive and automated skills* (like typing), in which the sensory information which is perceived directly triggers a physical action without any significant involvement of the brain. Such skills are characterized by the ability of the performer to be engaged in conversation on some other topic without any deterioration of performance of the physical activity being performed. The performance "loop" for such skills may be described as "S – 1 – 4 – R" in Figure 3.3.
- *Skills which depend on the recall of a possibly complex, but essentially algorithmic, procedure* and the execution of a series of linked actions in sequence. Many industrial and sports skills fall into this category. The performance "loop" for these skills can be described as "S – 1 – 2 – 4 – R" in Figure 3.3.
- *Skills which depend on the analysis of the incoming sensory information in order to formulate a plan of action that is appropriate to the situation* and, possibly, to evaluate alternative plans before deciding on the appropriate action. These are the strategy skills which distinguish the exemplary football player from many others who have equally (or even more) developed speed, strength, stamina, and ball-control skills. The performance loop for these skills is

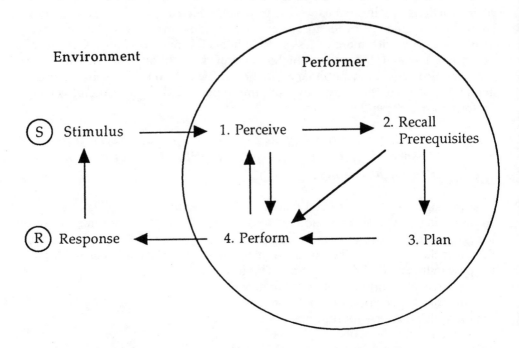

**Figure 3.3.** A four-stage performance cycle: extending the S–R model (Romiszowski, 1981).

"S – 1 – 2 – 3 – 4 – R." Actually, this is a simplification, for a lot of internal looping may take place as well. For example, as performance is about to commence, internal control processes may sense that the external situation has changed and the planned response is no longer adequate, so the internal loop (1 – 2 – 3 – 4) is repeated. Also, as the planning (information processing) is performed, new insights, rules, or relationships may be remembered for future use (2 – 3 – 2 – 3 – 2, etc.).

The skills-cycle draws our attention to the impossibility of instructional design for psychomotor training without taking into consideration the factors of perception, memory, intellectual skills, and cognitive strategies. Yet, much of what we might call "pure" motor skill research has focused on effects of fatigue, on reaction times, on manual dexterity, on the sequencing and spacing of practice sessions, and on strength and stamina. Much of this research leads to the formulation of principles for the planning of practice sessions and workout routines, rest periods and their frequency, even diets, but not, strictly speaking, to principles of "instructional message design."

We shall address some of these principles in the sections which follow, interpreting message design rather liberally as also including the design of practice schedules. After all, the learner must be informed of the recommended schedule, and it does form part of the overall instructional plan. We shall not restrict ourselves, then, to principles associated with the performance subsystem.

> **1.4.** *There are many subskills or abilities that influence the level of competence with which a psychomotor activity is executed. Some are generic abilities; others are task-specific subskills. They can be classified into the four sectors of the "skill execution cycle" (see Figure 3.4).*

In the three subsystems listed in addition to Effectors (performance), there are many instructional design principles which are particularly relevant for the psychomotor domain but which may not be adequately dealt with, from this viewpoint, in the other chapters in this volume. Some examples will follow.

In relation to the Receptors, much research has focused on the development of the ability of attention and concentration, so important in many physical activities. There has also been much research on the development of perceptual acuity and discrimination in psychomotor tasks.

In relation to the role of Store (memory), there has been an upsurge of recent research (e.g., Carroll & Bandura, 1982, 1987, 1990) which suggests that observation of actions, their mental rehearsal, and storage in memory may play a much greater role in psychomotor learning than was previously thought.

In relation to Processor (cognitive processing), there is a body of recent research, based largely on Schmidt's (1975) account of schema theory, directed specifically at problems of psychomotor skill development. We shall therefore, where appropriate, complement the principles already listed in other chapters of this book with those that are of particular relevance to message design for the psychomotor domain.

We can illustrate the integrated nature of psychomotor and cognitive (and affective) domains by reference to Figure 3.4, an "expanded" representation of the skill cycle (Romiszowski, 1981, 1986), which suggests twelve important areas of ability that play a part in the execution of a skilled activity. The twelve areas of ability shown in the outer circle of Figure 3.4 play a greater or lesser role in the execution of a given activity depending on where the activity lies on the "reproductive/productive" skill continuum (see Figure 3.2). Use of this model as an aid to the analysis of a skilled activity will enable the reader to identify the important areas of ability for a given skill and therefore the chapters in this book which might be most useful in the search for relevant message design principles.

> **1.5.** *The execution of skilled activities is strongly influenced by the "inner self."*

In the central part of Figure 3.4, it is suggested that the effectiveness of execution of the skill cycle, however well developed the individual abilities, is strongly dependent on aspects of the "inner self" of the performer, such as feelings, beliefs, personality traits, attitudes, etc. This brings to our attention the links between the psychomotor and the affective domains. Once more, some of the principles to be found in the chapters on motivation and on attitudes are also

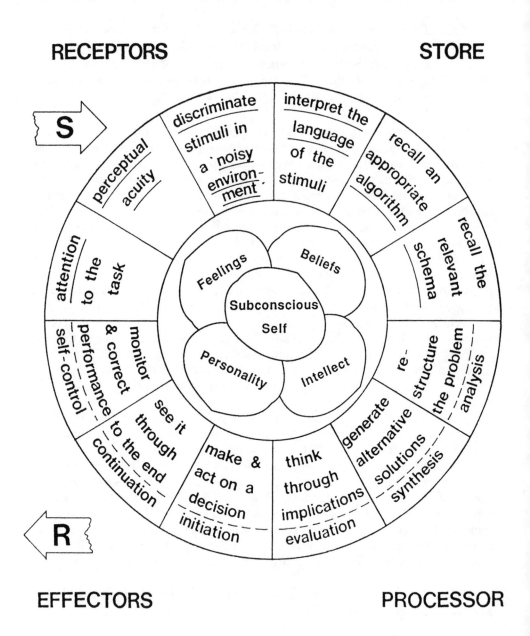

**RECEPTORS**                                                              **STORE**

**EFFECTORS**                                                              **PROCESSOR**

**Figure 3.4.** The skills cycle: extending the performance analysis model yet further (Romiszowski, 1981).

relevant to message design for psychomotor skills training. Once more, however, we will supplement the principles found there by some that have come from research specifically directed at physical skills. In particular, there is a growing amount of work on the development of a "winning attitude" in athletes and sportsmen. Many new techniques of achieving this, such as, for example, the use of relaxation exercises, or mental imagery, are being tried out. It is appropriate in the present chapter to look at these new developments and the message design principles that they suggest.

## 2. The Processes of Psychomotor Skill Learning and Psychomotor Skill Instruction

2.1. *Mastery of physical tasks progresses through a series of identifiable stages as skill develops. These stages are useful evaluation milestones that should be looked for as a guide to the progress of instruction.*

Much has been written on the classification of motor tasks and skills in an attempt to create some form of taxonomy or schema that would assist workers in the psychomotor domain in a way similar to the two well-known taxonomies in the cognitive and affective domains (Bloom *et al.*, 1956; Krathwohl *et al.*, 1964). An attempt to classify the models was made by Gilchrist and Gruber (1984), who created a four-category classification for no less than twelve different models encountered in the literature.

None of these various models, however, seem to serve the same function as the Bloom and Krathwohl taxonomies of indicating a sequence or hierarchy of stages through which mastery progresses. Such a hierarchical model of stages to mastery is useful for the planning of instructional sequences and the development of appropriate evaluation instruments and criteria for each stage in the sequence. It so happens that such a hierarchical description of skill development, based on very detailed experimental observation of industrial skills acquisition, has been in the literature for some time, but appears to have been largely overlooked by the majority of recent researchers. The stages through which the mastery of industrial skills progresses were described by Seymour soon after the Second World War and then were progressively refined and supported by more rigorous experiment (Seymour, 1954a, 1954b, 1955, 1956, 1959, 1966, 1968).

Similar descriptions have appeared more recently in the literature, apparently derived independently from observations in other domains of skilled activity. Examples are the account given by Adler (1981) based on observations in sports activities and theoretical ideas drawn from Poulton's (1957) analysis of open/closed skills and Schmidt's (1975) schema-theory model of motor skill learning, and another by Gentner (1984) based on observations of the development of expertise in typing.

The stages of development of psychomotor skills derived from the above research particularly that of Seymour, are:

**Stage 1:** *Acquiring knowledge* of what should be done, to what purpose, in what sequence, and by what means. Further knowledge is acquired as the learning process progresses. What is required up-front is the minimum knowledge necessary to start performing the task in a meaningful manner.

**Stage 2:** *Executing the actions in a step-by-step manner,* for each of the steps of the operation. The characteristics of this stage are: there is a conscious application of the knowledge, i.e., the "what and how" aspects of the operation are controlled by the conscious thinking-out of each step; the perceptual information necessary to initiate and control action—the "when-to-do and how-well-done" aspects—is almost exclusively visual (sometimes auditory). The observable result of these two characteristics is that execution of the task is erratic and jumpy. Time taken on a given step may vary considerably between attempts.

**Stage 3:** *Transfer of control* from the eyes to other senses or to kinesthetic control through muscular coordination. The release of the sense of vision (at least partially) from the direct control of each movement allows for more efficient "advance planning" of subsequent movements in the sequence. The subsequent actions flow on directly without any apparent break between one movement and the next.

**Stage 4:** *Automatization of the skill.* This stage is characterized by a reduction of the need for conscious attention and "thinking through" of the actions. Performance becomes a set of reflex actions, one triggering off the next, without direct conscious effort of the performer. The observable progress in this stage is that the performer may execute the task and at the same time be thinking or talking about other matters, even to some extent attending to other events in the environment, without this having any appreciable effect on the speed or quality of execution of the task.

**Stage 5:** *Generalization of the skill* to a continually greater range of application situations. This last stage applies to the productive/strategy/planning end of our skills continuum. In fact, most sports, most crafts, and most design skills are at least in some respects "productive." However well the basic physical skills involved are automatized, one can still differentiate football players on the basis of their gamesmanship, motorists on the basis of their "road sense," and lathe operators on the basis of how they strike the balance between speed and quality of work.

### 2.2. *Most early instruction in psychomotor skills can be planned as variations of a basic three-stage model: basic minimum knowledge–demonstration of actions– development of proficiency.*

The following general model is presented here as an overall framework upon which to hang the details of an instructional design that may be suggested by the more specific principles that follow in later sections of this chapter. Figure 3.5 presents a summary of the model. It is worded in most general terms, as it was developed to serve equally well as a framework for skill development in any domain, not exclusively the psychomotor domain (Romiszowski, 1981, 1984, 1986). Also, it is an idealistic model, suggesting discovery methods of learning whenever the knowledge content to be acquired is composed of general principles or complex conceptual schemata for decision-making. This is based on the general support in the literature for the increased power of these methods in terms of transfer/generalization and long-term retention. However, reality often dictates the use of expository methods due to the lack of time and facilities for discovery learning.

|  | REPRODUCTIVE SKILLS | PRODUCTIVE SKILLS |
|---|---|---|
| Imparting the knowledge content | Expository or discovery methods (dependent on the type of knowledge). | Discovery methods (principle learning is always involved). |
| Imparting the practical application | Expository methods (demonstration and prompted practice).<br><br>Note: Imparting the knowledge and skills content may be combined. | Expository methods (demonstration and prompted practice). |
| Developing proficiency | Supervised practice of whole task and/or special exercises.<br><br>Continuing feedback of results. | Discovery methods (guided problem-solving).<br><br>Continuing feedback of results. |

**Figure 3.5.** Instructional strategies for the development of skills (Romiszowski, 1981).

The model suggests three basic steps or stages in the overall instructional process:

**Stage 1:** *Imparting the knowledge content.* This refers to the minimum knowledge required to understand why, when, and how to perform the task. It relates to the first stage of skill development as outlined in the previous section. Generally speaking, this would take place by means of expository methods. However, in the case of productive skills, it may be desirable to teach the underlying basic concepts and principles by means of discovery techniques. This is in line with general principles for the cognitive domain.

**Stage 2:** *Imparting the practical application.* This refers to the initial demonstration and controlled practice of the task being taught. It relates to the second stage of skill development as outlined in the previous section. The rationale here is that if there is a "best" method of executing the task, it should be demonstrated, or modeled, for the trainee. Unlike the conceptual learning in the previous stage, where exposure to "right and wrong" may be beneficial in sharpening the trainee's powers of discrimination, there is no benefit for the trainee in practicing an incorrect movement.

In many cases, where the amount of basic knowledge to be imparted is small, it is possible to combine the two stages described above into one. This is one of the characteristics of the TWI (Training Within Industry) methodology, which was so successfully used to train inexperienced workers in the industrial skills required by factories during the Second World War (McCord, 1976). This method commences with a step-by-step demonstration, accompanied by an explanation of the "key points" (essential knowledge) by a skilled worker to the novice, followed by a repetition of this process by the novice to the skilled worker, who observes and corrects both the execution and the explanation aspects as necessary. This very simple procedure is effective and efficient when the task complexity is not too great and the amount of necessary basic knowledge is small.

**Stage 3:** *Developing proficiency.* This refers to the provision of appropriate conditions for further practice to mastery. It relates to the remaining three stages of skill development outlined in the previous section—transfer of control, automatization, and generalization. The first two of these are relevant in the case of skills that lie toward the closed, or reproductive, end of our skills continuum. The third relates to skills at the productive end. Typically, however, a complex skilled activity is composed of both reproductive and productive skill elements. Car-driving involves the smooth changing of gears, acceleration, automatized glancing in the rear-view mirror, and also the roadcraft skills of judging safe distances between vehicles, selection of the appropriate gear for each situation, prediction of possible acts by other road users, and the adoption of appropriate defensive-driving strategies.

In the next four sections of this chapter, we shall examine the more specific principles that may be used as guidance in the detailed design of instruction according to this basic model. Because of the quantity of research on specific aspects, and also because of the traditional divisions of the research in the field, we shall group the principles into four categories:
— information (explanation, demonstration, and guidance);
— practice (frequency, spacing, etc.);
— feedback (frequency, form, quality, etc.);
— transfer and generalization.
Then, we shall follow with some principles for special cases, such as: the pre-training of specific sub-skills by means of part-task trainers, or special exercises;

the mental and psychological preparation of the trainee for the training experience, through relaxation, mental imagery, and so on.

# 3. Principles for the Imparting of Information to the Trainee

### 3.1. Simple tasks with limited background knowledge may be demonstrated and explained simultaneously as an illustrated narrative.

This is probably the most common approach to imparting the information necessary to perform a physical task. It is typical, for example, of the TWI methodology noted above, which must be one of the most commonly used formal methodologies of industrial skills training. It is also the natural approach adopted by most sports coaches in demonstrating and explaining aspects of technique. Graham (1988) analyzed videotapes of a particularly effective volleyball teacher's instructional method. She found the combined demonstration/explanation to be the preferred communication method, rating it as "high" on counts of: gaining the student's attention; identification and organization of learning cues; and ensuring clarity of communication.

Much research of a more rigorous nature supports the value of both practical demonstration and supporting verbal cues. The series of experiments performed over the last decade by Carroll and Bandura (reported individually below) reinforce the importance of observational learning and its support by appropriate verbal coding or cues. Excessive verbal support of the demonstration, or purely verbal instructions unaccompanied by visual demonstrations, are generally found to be ineffective.

### 3.2. Tasks with little if any new knowledge to learn, apart from the movement pattern of the action, may be effectively learned without explanations, simply through observation of a model performance.

A series of recent experiments by Carroll and Bandura examine the role of visual demonstration (and feedback) on the mastery of a movement task (Carroll & Bandura, 1982, 1987, 1990). In this case, the task to be learned was a novel pattern of movement specially designed so that visual control could not naturally be applied. The movement consisted of a complex nine-step movement of the arm and wrist while holding a small paddle. The nine stages are illustrated in Figure 3.6. As the movement is carried out at the side and behind the body, visual control of the movement by directly observing it is very limited (and was totally eliminated in the experiments by the use of goggles to limit the learners' angle of vision).

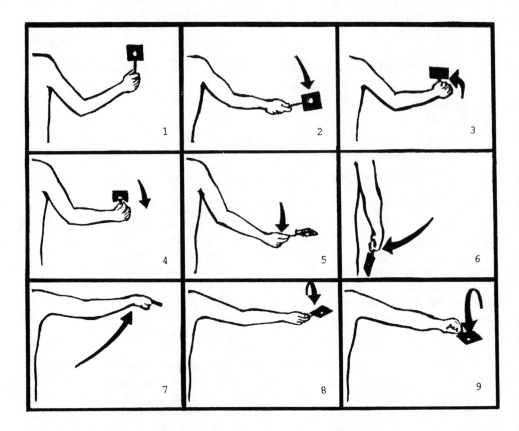

**Figure 3.6.** Complex sequence of paddle movements used for observational learning experiments (Carroll & Bandura, 1982, 1987, 1990).

In these experiments, it was found that the visual presentation of model enactment was the most influential single component of training design. Across the series of experiments, visual modeling of the intended movement, visual feedback of actual movements (by video cameras shooting from behind the subject), photographs of the nine stages to be arranged into correct sequence, and a variety of verbal cues were used in different combinations with different groups. The overall conclusions supported the importance of a clear and sufficiently repeated visual enactment of the task as the principal factor leading to effective learning. An important point from these experiments is that visual feedback is useless unless it can be compared to a model of the correct action. This comparison can be to a visual model, but is even more effective when the visual enactment has been transformed into a mental model in the mind of the performer.

### 3.3. Complex tasks, involving a large amount of new knowledge but little new skill, may be learned better through exploratory activity with outline notes or a physical model to follow.

Many complex physical tasks are difficult not because of the exceptional levels of physical skill and dexterity that they demand, but rather because of the way in which a large number of actions, depending on a variety of (largely pre-learned) skill components, are "put together" in the execution of the task. These are the characteristics of the "craft" skills, as opposed to, for example, the high-speed repetitive skills of the industrial operator. A "mechanically inclined person" seldom needs a practical, step-by-step demonstration of a task, such as the dismantling and assembly of a piece of kitchen equipment or an automobile engine, in order to succeed the first time in the physical aspects of repair. Is this a personal preference or learning style of the few "born mechanics," or is there a general advantage to learning by exploring in such tasks? A recent study by Baggett suggests that it may well be the latter case (Baggett, 1983). She compared the learning effectiveness of a number of alternative procedures for the learning of a model helicopter assembly task. Different combinations of exploratory practice using an assembled helicopter as a model guide, with or without procedural instruction supplied by a narrated film (screened either before or after practice sessions), were assigned to a total of 360 college students. The results showed that success on an immediate post-test assembly task, without a model guide, was proportional to the total amount of exploratory practice received and was not dependent on having viewed the film.

### 3.4. Retention of a complex task involving procedural knowledge is better if the task is learned through exploratory practice followed by expository review, rather than through expository demonstration followed by practice.

The same study (Baggett, 1983) followed up the students' abilities on the helicopter assembly task after an interval of one week. At this time, the most successful students were those who had the greatest amount of exploratory practice first and then viewed the film last. Those who viewed the film first were significantly inferior on the delayed test, and did not differ significantly from those who had not seen the film but only practiced. It would seem that the filmed demonstration was of more value as a synthesizer and reinforcer of learning that had occurred through practice first, than as an advanced demonstration of correct procedures.

Baggett explains these findings as arguing for a form of neo-Piagetian progression in physical procedure training, from the practical (concrete) experience, through the visual (iconic), to the linguistic (symbolic). Another possible explanation could be drawn from the general literature on expository versus discovery learning, which would suggest benefits in the practical "discovery" approach if there are some "general principles of model assembly" that can help across several phases of the assembly task when they are discovered and understood. The long-term effect of the film, seen after the building experience rather than before, may be seen as analogous to the de-briefing after an experiential exercise. Some deep processing and organization of the knowledge gained through practical experience may be encouraged even if the film script was not specifically designed to promote "reflection-in-action." Those who saw the film before practice had no relevant experience to reflect on; hence no deep processing was possible.

### 3.5.   *Observation of a sequential action pattern before attempting to execute it enhances learning.*

The research on tracking skills, springing from wartime gunnery and radar needs, paints a picture that contrasts with the findings just discussed. A series of experiments carried out by Poulton (1957) showed that observation of a pursuit-tracking activity before practicing it significantly improved the accuracy of performance. Similar results have been obtained by other researchers (Pew, 1974). Carroll and Bandura (1982) established the learning effectiveness of visual observation of the required movement sequence prior to its practice. Later Carroll and Bandura (1987) showed the importance in this process of the translation of the visually presented model into an internal cognitive representation of the movement, which was then used as the model with which to compare the monitoring information. Similar results and opinions were reported by Adams (1986).

Are these findings in opposition to those reported by Baggett? On the contrary, they can be seen to support each other at a higher level of generality. The discovery-learning-based explanation of Baggett's findings, proposed above, is based on the hypothesis that learning methods which involve deeper mental processing of sensory information are more effective. The suggestions and explanations offered by Carroll and Bandura are based on a similar general hypothesis. The difference between the two experimental situations lies in the type of learning task that is being studied. In one case, the critical learning is of visual patterns and relationships among components. In the other, it is the shape, sequence, and timing of a single, multi-stage movement. In the first case, practical exploration presents the visual relationships among parts in a manner that is more conducive to mental representation of the critical information than is a film sequence. In the second case, a film (video) presents the sequence of the task in a manner that is conducive to this mental representation.

### 3.6.   *The formation of a mental representation (memory) of an action pattern before practice enhances learning.*

Carroll and Bandura (1987) provide experimental evidence that the formation of a mental representation as an internal model for the later control of action is, indeed, an important aspect of the learning of new movements. They compared subjects' performance on the movement task and their use of feedback information before and after they had formed an internal representation, or model, of the activity. The presence and power of the internal representation were measured by the subjects' ability to distinguish between correct and incorrect pictorial representations of the steps in the movement activity and their sequence.

Subjects progressively improved their scores on these cognitive tests as the experiment progressed. Practice was under the conditions of visually monitoring a video of their movement pattern with a concurrently screened video of the correct movement pattern. All subjects would do well in matching their pattern to the concurrent video model. However, when the video model was removed at a time when they were still scoring poorly on the cognitive picture-matching tests, performance deteriorated at once. When, later on, they were demonstrating higher ability on the cognitive tests, removal of the concurrently playing video of model performance had little or no effect on the subjects' performance.

The experimenters suggest that at this later stage, the mental representations of the physical actions are sufficiently well developed to act as a standard for the comparison and control of physical action. They argue that cognition is an essential element in the acquisition of skill in motor tasks, a viewpoint previously expressed by Marteniuk (1976) and Newell (1978) and supported by earlier work, such as that of Adams (1984, 1986) and Bandura (1986). Connections can also be made in this respect to much earlier work on action feedback and learning feedback (Annett & Kay, 1957), which showed that for feedback to be effective in the promotion of learning, it must promote the formation of cause-effect relationships in the mind of the learner and not be used simply for the online monitoring and control of action. We shall come back to this in the section on feedback later in the chapter.

### 3.7. The mental rehearsal of an observed task enhances its initial learning and long-term retention.

If mental models are helpful (perhaps essential) to the mastery of complex new movement patterns, then thinking about, and with, these models either before or between practice sessions may be expected to have beneficial results on learning and retention. This is an easily observable effect in the area of intellectual skills, where, for example, the thinking through of the process of problem-solving in a particular domain is often found to be as useful a learning exercise as the actual application of the process to specific problem cases. Why should this not also be true in the psychomotor domain? The use of mental rehearsal as a skills training technique has a long history, for example in the thinking and talking through of football strategies during a pre-game briefing discussion. Often, these "think-throughs" are taken further, each strategy being given a code name by which it can be evoked during the game. Sometimes the steps or components of the strategy are likewise named, so the players may recall the sequence, pace, or nature of each step by means of an appropriate code word.

Bandura and Jeffery (1973), in an experimental situation similar to the one described earlier and involving the learning of an action pattern, found that the transformation by learners of the sequence of actions demonstrated into a sequence of symbolic codes, and the use of these codes as a means of mental rehearsal of the sequence, had a significant positive impact on learning and retention.

In a later experiment, Bandura and Jeffery (1973) found that verbal labels were particularly effective as symbolic codes in terms of long-term retention of the skill. Still later, Jeffery (1976) found that similar results were obtained on the learning and retention of physical assembly tasks. The more complex the task, the greater the value of mental rehearsal.

> *3.8.    Verbal coding, or cueing, of the steps in an action pattern, when accompanying a model demonstration, helps the learner to form a mental representation of the action and also enhances learning and retention.*

The research just mentioned lends support to this principle. Earlier research had already established its general truth (Gentile, 1972; Shea, 1977; Ho & Shea, 1978; Winther & Thomas, 1981). In their most recent experiments, Carroll and Bandura (1990) have added further evidence. Using the familiar paddle-waving task (Figure 3.6), referred to above, they supplied groups of subjects with different amounts of visual demonstration (amounts found in previous experiments to be respectively sufficient and insufficient for the formation of useful mental representations of the physical action). They accompanied the visual demonstrations with standard verbalized descriptions of each step in the movement using non-technical descriptions of the action involved. The results showed that the effects of verbal coding of the actions were insufficient to transform the ineffectiveness of only two demonstration/practice trials. However, the effect of the verbal coding during eight trials was significant in its effect both on learning the action pattern and on subjects' ability to perform a cognitive test designed to measure the strength and accuracy of their mental representation of the action pattern.

Findings of this nature suggest that some form of verbal cueing as an aid to the internalization of motor skills should in general be provided. These cues should be meaningful to the learners but as simple and non-technical as possible.

> *3.9.    Verbal coding and cues, by themselves, not accompanied by a visual demonstration, are not very effective.*

In a recent experiment, Carroll and Bandura (1990) showed that verbal coding or cueing was not in itself sufficient to overcome the defective instructional design of insufficient demonstration and practice opportunities. One might expect, therefore, that purely verbal instruction would in general be inadequate for the teaching of all but the simplest of physical tasks. This was indeed demonstrated experimentally by Reeve and Proctor (1983). These experimenters compared three groups: movement practice with a label; movement practice without a label; a label (description) of the movement but without practice. Whereas the label-only group did well in remembering the verbal names for the sequence of positions in a complex movement, they were inferior to the other groups in the task of replicating the movement correctly.

### 3.10. The demonstration of a task should be shown from the viewpoint of the performer.

Given that observational learning is so critical a part of the development of a motor skill, it would seem to be important to demonstrate the execution of a task as clearly and unambiguously as possible. One aspect of importance is to demonstrate the task from the viewpoint of the performer rather than from that of an observer standing to the side or in front of the performer. Often, instructors may demonstrate a sequence of movements while facing a group of students. The students must then "invert" the demonstration in their minds, imagining how it would appear to watch one's own hands performing the movements. It would be better to attempt to demonstrate exactly what the student will see when performing.

Experimental support for this principle can be found in many studies (Seymour, 1955, 1966; Roshal, 1961; Greenwald & Albert, 1968; Locatis & Atkinson, 1984). It is, however, sometimes difficult to arrange such "performer's viewpoint" demonstrations in practice. The students must stand alongside or behind the demonstrator (sometimes impossible) and only one or two at a time. The use of mediated demonstrations can often overcome such difficulties. The camera (film or video) is positioned behind the performer as close to the head as possible, thus giving a view of the task being performed which is as close as possible to the view the student will have when performing the task in later practice sessions (this is sometimes called "zero camera angle").

## 4. Principles for the Planning of Practice in Psychomotor Skills Learning

### 4.1. Closely integrated and coordinated activities are better learned by the "whole task" method.

One of the most researched questions in the psychomotor skills area is the question of part-versus-whole practice. Results have been sometimes conflicting, but a general pattern has emerged over the years. In general, the breaking up of complex activities, which involve the coordination of several actions carried out in unison, into separate practice sessions for each activity does not pay off. Learning is more effective when the task is practiced as a whole, allowing the separate movements to be coordinated in all the practice sessions (McGuigan & MacCaslin, 1955; Briggs & Waters, 1958; Crossman, 1959; Knapp, 1963; Naylor & Briggs, 1963). This finding seems to hold good in simplified laboratory practice tasks, in real-life industrial skills, and in sports.

### 4.2. Prerequisite subskills that are initially below "minimum threshold levels" should, however, be developed prior to the practice of the whole task.

There may, however, be benefits in the pre-training of certain basic skills of dexterity, speed, or accuracy when these are prerequisite components of the complex task and are known to be poorly developed in the trainees. Several examples of such pre-training exercises and their effectiveness in the industrial skills arena are given by Seymour (1954a, 1954b, 1955, 1966).

An illustration of a very effective training schedule for the highly coordinated skill of "panel-beating" is shown in Figures 3.7 and 3.8 (Romiszowski, 1968, 1974, 1988). Before engaging in the practice of real panel-beating tasks, trainees practice the accurate control of a hammer under conditions of enhanced feedback (Figure 3.7) until a predefined threshold level of accuracy is reached. Then they progress to the panel-beating simulator (Figure 3.8), where they practice coordinated two-handed activity as in the real task, but with enhanced feedback and task simplification in certain aspects. Only when certain threshold performance criteria are reached on the simulator exercise does normal whole-task practice commence. This training sequence was found to significantly reduce the mean time to mastery of this highly complex task, under real industrial conditions.

It is important to note that the pre-training of specific movement or perceptual skills before their integration into a more complex pattern of skilled activity is not the same as the division of the activity itself into separately practiced parts. The simplification of a complex task by enhanced feedback, as in this example, or by other means such as slowing down reality, reducing the degrees of freedom, etc., has been used with some success in many experiments and real-time training simulators (e.g., Briggs, 1961; Briggs & Naylor, 1962; Wheatcroft, 1973).

### 4.3. Tasks composed of a sequence of relatively independent actions are better learned by the "progressive parts" method.

The alternative to the whole-task practice approach is often referred to as the "parts" approach. However, this can be organized in a number of ways. Two particular sequences which have been used are the "pure" or "sequential" parts and the "cumulative" or "progressive" parts methods. In the sequential parts method, a four-step task (e.g., A-B-C-D) would be practiced in four stages, each concentrating on one of the parts, i.e., A alone, then B alone, and so on, until all parts have been practiced separately. Only then does practice of the whole task commence. In the progressive parts method, the stages of practice grow cumulatively, for example, A alone, then B, then A and B, then C alone, then A and B and C, then D, and finally the whole task A-B-C-D. Some research has shown both of these approaches to be equally effective (and better than the whole-task method) for some simple sequential tasks. However, the bulk of the research supports the superiority of the progressive-parts approach (Seymour, 1954b, 1955, 1956, 1959; Singleton, 1959; Naylor & Briggs, 1963; Welford, 1968).

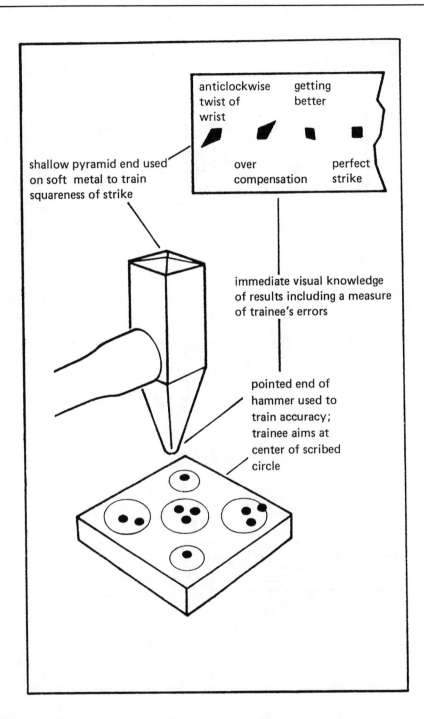

**Figure 3.7.** Special training hammer to enhance feedback during practice (Romiszowski, 1968, 1974, 1988).

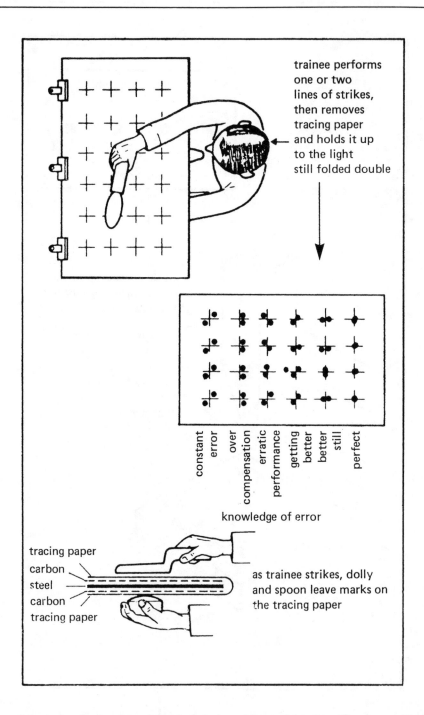

**Figure 3.8.** A simple simulator/part task trainer for panel beating (Romiszowski, 1968, 1974, 1988).

### 4.4. The progressive parts method may be successfully "forward chained" or "backward chained."

The more usual organization of parts practice is by "forward chaining" or progressing from the first to the last step in the sequence. An alternative approach is the "backward chaining" sequence in which the last step of the task is practiced first. Typically, the whole task would be demonstrated to the trainee. Then on the second demonstration the trainee would take over the execution of the last step in the task. In subsequent stages, the trainee would practice the last two steps, then the last three, and so on to finally practicing the whole task. This sequence grew out of animal conditioning experiments where the "shaping" of a multi-stage procedural task can best be achieved in this manner, as the last step is the one which leads to the reinforcing event (say, food). As training progresses, causal (S–R) links are automatically formed between earlier and later steps.

Some researchers (e.g., Mechner, 1965) have advocated this approach for human learning of sequential tasks. Gilbert (1961) demonstrated the superiority of this sequence over the forward chaining approach in teaching young children to tie their shoelaces. The theoretical advantage of this sequence is not related so much to the characteristics of the task as to the potentially greater motivation that it might generate in learners who are interested in achieving the end result of the task but are liable to lose interest if the earlier steps in the execution of the task are not seen to be clearly relevant to the end goal.

Luckily, in most cases of human learning of psychomotor tasks, it is quite easy by means of whole-task demonstration and explanation to establish the causal links between the steps and so ensure that interest and motivation are maintained even in the forward-chained progression. It may be for this reason that both the forward and backward chained progressive parts methods seem to be equally effective in the industrial and sports skills areas.

### 4.5. Spacing of practice sessions generally leads to more effective (but not necessarily more efficient) learning.

It was mentioned in the opening section of this chapter that the question of the spacing and duration of practice sessions was one of the first questions to generate a rich body of research in the psychomotor domain. Irion (1966) describes how the phenomena of massed-versus-spaced practice, observed and measured intensively in the early years of this century, underwent a series of different theoretical explanations. The general experimental findings, whatever their explanations, seem to indicate that for most tasks the spacing of practice sessions leads to more effective learning. Classical experiments like the one illustrated in Figure 3.9 (Kimble & Shatel, 1952) demonstrated the overall benefits of distributed over massed practice. In this experiment, the distributed practice groups rested briefly between each trial and then longer after 20 trials, while the massed practice group only rested after every 20 trials.

It is interesting to note the differential effects of the two treatments. While the massed practice groups did not regress during the long rest periods (as did the spaced practice groups), the progress during practice sessions of the spaced

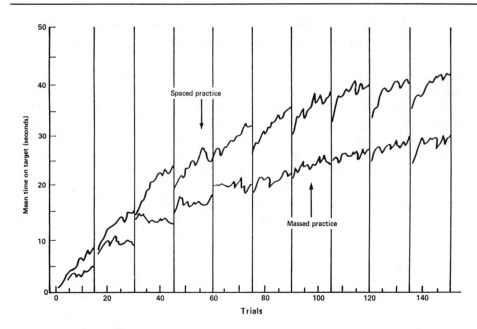

**Figure 3.9.** A comparison of learning curves for massed practice and spaced practice (Kimble & Shatel, 1952).

practice groups was so much better that they gained a clear advantage over a given number of trials. This type of result suggests that some further learning may be occurring during the rest periods between trials. We shall return to this point.

Many experiments, utilizing a variety of different tasks, have shown results similar to those of Kimble and Shatel, who used the classic pursuit rotor setup. Some have looked at the question of efficiency as well as effectiveness of learning. For example, Tsao (1948) found that while the amount of learning over a given number of trials was greater for the spaced practice condition, the amount of learning per unit time was greater for the massed practice group, that is, the greater learning achieved did not compensate the greater time taken due to the rest pauses between trials. Later experiments have not always born out this finding (Welford, 1987). Other recent work (reviewed later) relates both the effectiveness and the efficiency of learning to what takes place during the rest periods.

### 4.6.   Continuous practice may be more effective in the case of later proficiency, building on highly coordinated and "productive skill" tasks.

There are some studies that have not favored spaced over massed practice. These tend to suggest that for more complex tasks in which much decision-making is involved or where there is a high level of coordination or rhythmic activity, long and continuous practice sessions are more effective than spaced practice (Irion, 1966; Welford, 1968). Also, some studies, reviewed by Singer (1982), suggest that although spaced practice may show an advantage in short-term performance immediately after a series of trials, this is largely lost over time as the massed practice groups seem to regress less and sometimes even improve without practice in the long term.

Singer also draws our attention to some dangers or limitations of long, continuous practice sessions:

a. in the case of young children and adult beginners who may have relatively short attention spans and whose concentration tends to wander (hence the importance of the "attention" capability in the "expanded skill performance cycle"—see Figure 3.4);

b. in the case of dangerous or fatiguing tasks, errors increase as fatigue sets in, leading to the reinforcement of bad habits and possibly to accidents (hence the importance of the "continuation" capability in the skill cycle; see Figure 3.4).

In general, therefore, it would seem best to commence basic training of a complex skilled activity or of its component subskills under distributed practice conditions. Then, as competence increases and as simpler component skills are integrated into more complex "whole-task" practice, to gradually proceed to longer sessions of continuous practice.

### 4.7. Spacing of practice is more effective in repetitive, high-speed and, generally, "reproductive skill" tasks.

The research and viewpoints quoted above would suggest that spaced training sessions with short rest stops between every few trials (or every trial in multi-step tasks) may be a more effective method in the case of repetitive high-speed skills of a "reproductive/automated" nature. An extensive review and reassessment of previous research, performed by Lee and Genovese (1988) and published in a special issue focusing especially on the practice distribution issue in relation to sports training, seems to confirm this general finding.

An important body of recent research has focused on what happens during the rest periods in a spaced practice schedule. It had been observed in many experiments over the years that if other activities of a quite different nature were executed during these periods, the overall learning was less improved and most, or all, of the advantage of spacing the practice could be lost. It was initially believed that some form of neural development, a form of maturation process, was occurring but could be easily interrupted by other activities. Later, the view that mental rehearsal of the physical activities was taking place during the rest intervals became more prevalent (Adams, 1955; Knapp, 1963). (See also Principle 3.7 earlier in this chapter.)

> ***4.8.*** *Learning is enhanced when systematic mental rehearsal takes place during rest intervals. This rehearsal can be a planned element in the formal practice session and can be based on group activities.*

Whatever the theoretical explanations for the positive effects of mental rehearsal on practical execution of tasks, the benefits can be reaped by encouraging learners to think through the procedures of novel tasks in-between practice sessions and, in particular, in the intervals between the trials in a spaced-practice routine. As these are short and still part of the training session, it is generally possible to "orchestrate" this mental rehearsal by the provision of verbal labels that can be rehearsed overtly as a group. Such techniques are part of the practice of many sports coaches. Theoretical justification has been provided by many writers (Luria, 1961; Vygotsky, 1962; Meichenbaum & Goodman, 1971). Shasby (1984) reviews the research on this technique, finding it very effective with young children who have problems of motor control.

> ***4.9.*** *Novel tasks are better learned under conditions of guided and prompted practice.*

> ***4.10.*** *Tasks which are similar to previously mastered tasks are better learned under "problem-solving" conditions of free practice.*

Both the above principles are supported by research such as that of Singer and Gaines (1975). The subjects in this experiment learned a sequential manipulation task under one of two conditions: heavily guided and prompted practice that ensured error-free execution of the task in every practice trial, or trial-and-error practice in which the learners had to correct any wrong moves in the light of subsequent feedback (see Figure 3.10). Learning of the initial task was much more efficient under the error-free condition, but subsequent learning of a second similar (but somewhat different) task was more effective under the trial-and-error condition.

> ***4.11.*** *The pacing of high-speed tasks promotes more rapid progress to mastery.*

This principle is often overlooked in the design of instruction due to too much emphasis on the principles of self-paced learning. In tasks where speed is a criterion, the principle of allowing a student to progress "at his/her own pace" needs careful interpretation. Practical experience shows that when forced pacing is applied to the practice of high-speed industrial tasks (Agar, 1962; Romiszowski, 1968) or to typing skills (Pask, 1960; Sormunen, 1986), learning rates are very significantly enhanced, and ultimate performance levels achieved may be much higher than under self-paced practice conditions. The "RITT" methodology developed first at the SKF company in Sweden and later widely

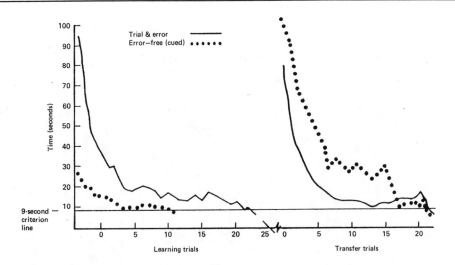

**Figure 3.10.** A comparison of the effects of cued learning and trial-and-error learning on acquisition and transfer (Singer & Gaines, 1975).

used for training in high-speed machine operation skills (see Figure 3.11) has been reported to produce reductions in average learning time to "experienced worker standards" of productivity of up to 90% (Agar, 1962; Romiszowski, 1968, 1974; Wellens, 1966, 1974). These reductions were achieved in field tests comparing a carefully planned training methodology, which incorporated tape-recorder-paced practice, with previous less well-planned methods; so it is possible that many factors contributed to the learning effectiveness and efficiency improvements. However, the pacing element is no doubt a very important contributing factor. Amswych (1967) found reductions in learning time in excess of 30% in a more controlled experiment in which the only element in an overall instructional design which was varied was the introduction of tape-recorder-pacing.

In the area of typing and keyboarding skills in general, the power of appropriate pacing is well understood, from early uses of music as a source of controlled rhythm to Pask's early "SAKI" computer controlled Self Adaptive Keyboard Instructor (Pask, 1960), the highly successful "Sight-and-Sound" tape-paced training systems used widely throughout the United Kingdom (Romiszowski, 1974, 1988), and the current crop of microcomputer-based typing tutors that use forced pacing (e.g., the very effective "Mavis Beacon" system—Software Toolworks, 1987).

It should be pointed out that in all such systems that give good learning results, there is, in addition to forced pacing, an element of self-pacing. Each exercise incorporates a device to force the pace to a given predetermined level, but the student has choice over the level of pacing to apply at a given time in the learning process. The student will work at a given pacing criterion until this is quite mastered and is then free to choose to progress to a slightly higher criterion.

**Figure 3.11.** Use of an audio-tape training program for paced practice of a task.

### 4.12. *The setting of goals can, in general, lead to more rapid mastery of a skilled activity.*

The phenomenon observed in the high-speed repetitive work skills discussed above is also well known to sports and games instructors, but in a more general sense of "goal setting." The goal may be speed related but may also employ any other relevant performance criteria. When practicing for a long distance race, pursuit of the goal may be paced, as in racing against a series of constantly fresh sprinters who change on every lap of the track. Alternatively, the goal may be just held in the mind, as in the case of a race target time.

Barnett and Stanicek (1979) found that the setting of personal goals in terms of scores in archery led to significant improvements as compared to students who did not set themselves such goals. Setting a specific "hard" goal for students on motor tasks leads to greater learning and performance improvement than just asking students to "do their best" (Locke & Bryan, 1966).

### 4.13. *The total time/effort required to achieve mastery of a task is a complex function of many factors and varies considerably from one individual to the next.*

Despite all the research effort over the years to establish clear cause-effect relationships between certain practice variables and the rate of learning of a skill, we are still no nearer to the numerical formula, hinted at by Gagné (1954), of a precise relationship of the amount of practice on an exercise or device that is necessary to establish a required level of operational skill. Broad bands of typical learning times can be obtained in given specific situations, but the exercise of predicting the learning times or numbers of trials required on a different (though similar) task is not an accurate science. One must just remember the research of Singer and Gaines (1975), quoted earlier, to see how complex the relationships are. Learning will depend on what has been previously learned by the individual, and on the means by which it was learned, as well as on a host of individual differences in learning skill and in relevant abilities like the ones listed in the expanded skill cycle (Figure 3.4). It is unrealistic to prescribe a fixed practice time or a fixed number of practice trials for a given skill learning activity. Rather, the exercise should be set up so that individuals can measure their progress toward specific goals and can therefore vary the amount of practice necessary to achieve the goal in relation to their own personal requirements.

### 4.14. *The mastery-learning model is a useful approach to the planning of practice schedules for the development of psychomotor skills.*

Given the above observations regarding goals and the variability of the necessary quantity of practice, it would seem appropriate to build psychomotor skills training schedules around some form of the mastery-learning model (Carroll, 1963; Bloom, 1968) in which learning time (and number of practice trials) are variable as required to achieve a given learning criterion. Many practical skills training schedules do indeed exhibit many of the characteristics of the classical mastery-learning model. In the industrial training sector, the TWI (Training Within Industry) instructional model, referred to earlier, which was developed in response to the need for rapid and effective job instruction during the Second World War and which is arguably the most extensively used formal model for the planning and execution of such training, incorporates the essential elements of mastery-learning.

Ashy and Lee (1984) review the research on the effectiveness of mastery-learning as an approach to the organization of sports psychomotor skills instruction. Their review is generally favorable to the use of this approach with young children. A study by Blakemore and Goldberger (1984) of college students learning racquetball found that those who practiced under a mastery-learning model generally learned more effectively during initial stages, but that over time both mastery and non-mastery groups performed equally. However, low aptitude students seemed to benefit more significantly under mastery-learning.

# 5. Principles for the Planning of Feedback in Psychomotor Skills Learning

**5.1.    *In general, learning feedback (results information) promotes learning, and action feedback (control information) does not.***

The distinction between so-called "learning feedback" and "action feedback" has been made by Annett (1959), Holding (1965), and several other researchers. Annett found that subjects pressing down on a spring balance device with their outstretched hand would not learn to exert a given pressure accurately despite many trials when they had the benefit of the scale supplying them with information. When the scale was covered while they made their attempt and then uncovered, so they could see the result of their attempt and the extent of any error, they did learn to exert a given pressure without the aid of the scale readings. Thus, continuous knowledge, supplied visually, of the pressure being applied (action feedback) guaranteed error-free practice but did not result in the learning of the "feel" of applying the correct pressure. Later knowledge (of results) did result in progressively more accurate attempts and led to effective learning of the "feel" of executing the task (hence the term "learning feedback").

**5.2.    *Enhanced action feedback may improve learning if it does not substitute an artificial control mechanism for a natural one.***

Many of the early experimental studies on the effects of feedback on psychomotor tasks did not make a clear distinction between action and learning feedback and so gave conflicting results. It is true, however, that some well-designed and controlled studies have given results that are not quite as categorical as Annett's. For example, Goldstein and Rittenhouse (1954) found that a buzzing noise which sounded all the time that performance was "on target" but switched off when performance wandered "off target" led to more effective learning than provision of a "score" as knowledge of results at the end of a practice trial.

One can note, however, a fundamental difference between the visual feedback of the balance scale in Annett's experiment and the audio feedback in this one. In controlling the pressure exerted on the balance by the continuous action feedback supplied by the scale reading, the subject is not required to transfer control to the kinesthetic feel of the muscles in the arm when the correct pressure is applied. Many trials can be executed, but no effort will be made to control the action in the manner that it must be controlled in later test situations when no scale is available to give visual action feedback. In the case of the buzzer, continuous action feedback is available to inform the subjects whether they are on or off target, but the correction of accuracy of performance must be effected by the senses and muscles that are naturally involved in the execution of the task. Thus, what is being encouraged rather than inhibited is the transfer of control to the psychomotor system which will have to be used once the buzzer feedback is withdrawn.

The spanner, or torque-wrench, simulator (Wheatcroft, 1973) shown in Figure 3.12 is, on the other hand, rather similar to the action-feedback condition in Annett's experiment. When the correct torque is being applied, the green light lights up. If the acceptable torque range is exceeded, the light changes to red. There is danger of relying on the appearance of the light as the principal source of control information for the task. Wheatcroft realizes this and recommends that the simulator be used initially for a few trials with the use of the visual action feedback, but that later practice should be performed with the eyes closed, only to be opened after the application of force to the spanner in order to verify the extent of error. In this way, the action feedback is transformed into learning feedback and, most likely, learning is enhanced.

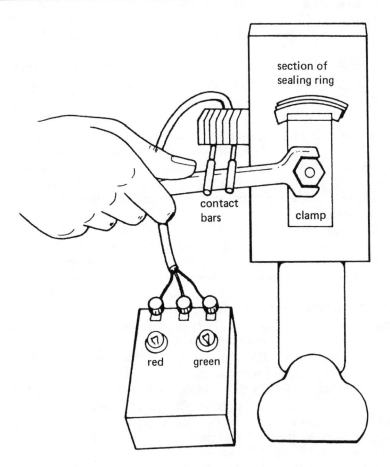

**Figure 3.12.** Torque wrench simulator (Wheatcroft, 1973).

### 5.3.   *Supplementary or enhanced feedback should not be intrusive in the process of task performance.*

The natural "action" feedback used in controlling a task is an integral part of the work environment. Artificially supplied feedback, whether automatically generated or supplied during practice by an instructor, is not always well integrated into the task environment. A flashing light signifying an error message may hinder rather than promote the development of a skill if it distracts the learner's attention from other significant aspects of the task in progress. When the eyes are actively in use tracking some naturally occurring action feedback, it is better to avoid the introduction of other visually perceived feedback. A bell or buzzer may be used to alert the learner of some off-target condition without drawing attention away from the principal control activities of the task.

Learning feedback is not usually as distracting as inappropriate action feedback because it is generally provided at the end of a practice trial when attention to the control aspects of the task is no longer required. However, if the learning feedback is difficult to interpret or is unduly full and complex, it may serve to confuse the performer rather than correct the performance (Katz, 1967).

### 5.4.   *Supplementary feedback (whether action or learning) should be designed to exercise the control systems that will ultimately be used in the execution of the task.*

The important point with respect to action feedback and learning feedback is that the feedback should encourage the learner to utilize the control systems that will be called into play when the task reaches the stage of automatization. If kinesthetic control is employed to a great degree by experts, then any enhanced feedback system used during initial training should encourage the development of kinesthetic control.

In the filing simulator shown in Figure 3.13, the correct horizontal motion of the "file" across the "workpiece" produces a filing-like rubbing sound. Any rocking of the file out of the horizontal as it moves (a common learner's error which produces poor work) breaks contact with one or other side of the "workpiece" and sets off an electrical buzzer (Romiszowski, 1968, 1974; Wheatcroft, 1973; Wellens, 1974). This knowledge of error must be interpreted and the file position brought back to the horizontal under the control of the same arm muscles that are used by a skilled craftsman.

In the welding simulator (Romiszowski, 1968, 1974, 1988) shown in Figure 3.14, there is a combination of action feedback and learning feedback. During one practice trial, the learner moves the welding torch from right to left in step with the slowly moving motor-driven pointer. This part of the motion is keeping the eyes busy. (In the real-life task, the eyes examine the condition of the pool of molten metal formed by the torch and use this information to control the speed of movement of the torch from right to left.)

At the same time the torch must be kept at a constant, unchanging distance from the workpiece. This is controlled in the simulator by the ring on the end of the torch threaded on the horizontal guide wire. Whenever the ring touches the

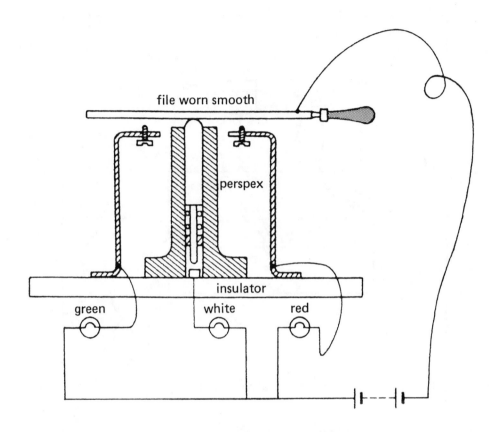

**Figure 3.13.** Filing simulator (Wheatcroft, 1973).

torch, supplementary action feedback is provided by the noise of the counter B clicking away. As the eyes are otherwise engaged, the equipment encourages the learner to correct this by the "feel" of the torch.

The mastery of this smooth control of the motion and position of the torch is complicated by the requirement to feed in the simulated "welding rod," held in the left hand, with a series of short, brisk movements. As learning progresses, this two-hand coordination skill is developed in a manner very similar to the way it will be practiced in the real task. At the end of a trial run, numerical values of the two counters A and B provide knowledge of results which can be compared against past performance or some personal goal. These readings have been taken for many welders and are correlated to skill on the real job so that the learning feedback can be graphed over time and compared to absolute criteria that have meaning in terms of job performance. However, neither the audible action feedback nor the numerical learning feedback is likely to develop inappropriate use of the senses on the job.

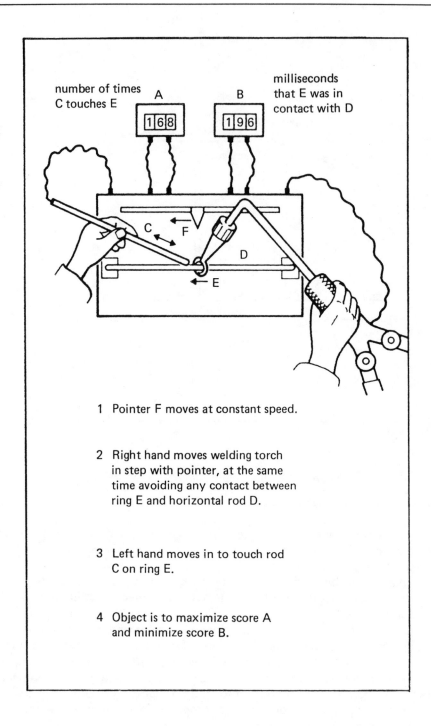

number of times
C touches E

milliseconds
that E was in
contact with D

1  Pointer F moves at constant speed.

2  Right hand moves welding torch
   in step with pointer, at the same
   time avoiding any contact between
   ring E and horizontal rod D.

3  Left hand moves in to touch rod
   C on ring E.

4  Object is to maximize score A
   and minimize score B.

**Figure 3.14.** Training simulator for gas welding (Romiszowski, 1968, 1974, 1988).

5.5. *Learning feedback can be further categorized as knowledge of results and knowledge about performance. In general, feedback is more effective in promoting learning when it transmits more complete information.*

The distinction between knowledge of the results of a practice trial and knowledge about how the results were achieved highlights two ways in which the instructional system may seek to correct the performance of a task. The first supplies information about the correctness of a response and possibly the direction and extent of an error. The second informs the performer how the response was executed and may comment or correct certain aspects of this execution.

The "panel-beating" exercises previously discussed (shown in Figures 3.7 and 3.8) illustrate this distinction. In the hammering exercise, when using the pointed end of the hammer to practice accurate strikes, the mark left on the target at a certain direction and distance off-center supplies quite precise knowledge of results but no knowledge about how or why the particular result was achieved. When using the pyramid-shaped end of the hammer to practice hitting the work squarely, the mark left on the target supplies knowledge of results (was the hit square to the workpiece) and also knowledge about the performance. A reference chart may be supplied to present an interpretation of each characteristic shape of the mark in terms of the probable performance errors that caused it. For example, a deformed diamond-shaped dent, with one corner somewhat longer than the others, is pointing in the direction in which excessive force or twist was applied (see the explanations shown in Figure 3.7). This aspect of the feedback in this exercise has been found to be particularly effective in rapidly correcting poor performance on the sub-skill of hammer control (Romiszowski, 1968, 1974, 1988).

5.6. *In general, knowledge of performance enhances the learning effectiveness of a practice exercise.*

In a classic experiment, Wallace and Hagler (1979) demonstrated the effectiveness of knowledge-of-performance, by comparing two training conditions for the development of basketball shooting skills. One supplied knowledge-of-results (KOR) and knowledge-of-performance (KOP), the other KOR and social reinforcement (encouragement, congratulations). The treatment group receiving the KOP performed significantly better during initial learning and improved by a larger margin during an interval without practice.

Cole (1981) performed a study of the instructional methods of expert golf instructors. She documented the extensive use of so-called "teacher-augmented feedback," which was principally composed of corrective and constructive comments that the instructors made to the students regarding the process of task execution, i.e., knowledge of performance (KOP).

### 5.7. In "productive" skills, knowledge of performance may be obtained through a process of debriefing or reflection-in-action.

In the case of "productive" skills involving a high level of strategy planning and decision making, the appropriate feedback not only may, but should, take the form of KOP. In these skills it is not sufficient to compare results with expectations, but it is necessary to engage in an analysis of the causes for an observed discrepancy, reflect on the plans that were implemented, and evaluate the reasons for their shortcomings; all this leading to the synthesis of new plans or strategies for the next practice trial. Such reflective debriefing, either instructor-led or spontaneous, is now recognized as an essential element of the development of productive skills in any domain. In the psychomotor domain, this is seen in the importance given to the before-and-after-the-game strategy discussions in the locker room. It is also apparent in the stress laid on the "reflection-in-action" approach to skill development in professions such as surgery (Schon, 1983).

The Metropolitan Police Driving School in London has for over thirty years used a methodology of intensive reflective analysis and strategy planning in the development of high levels of roadcraft skills in the police drivers. Many hours are spent in a variety of extreme driving conditions with an instructor listening to a continuous verbal explanation by the driver of the perception, interpretation, analysis, and decision-making processes going on in the driver's mind as new situations are encountered. Periodically, the car is stopped for a reflective analysis of the actions/decisions taken (Romiszowski, 1981).

Welford (1968) comments on the old adage of "practice makes perfect" by quoting Sir Frederick Bartlett as saying in relation to skill development. . . "it is not practice but practice *the results of which are known* that makes perfect." We could now add that in the productive skills arena. . . "practice the results of which are known *and the reasons for these results are understood through reflective analysis and are used in strategic planning,* makes perfect."

### 5.8. Knowledge of performance may be furnished by automated means such as video recordings. They must be used correctly.

Given the need to analyze information about the performance that led to the results of a skilled activity, it would seem natural to employ film or video recordings to capture the details of movement sequences or game strategies for later reflective analysis. The technique is not that new, having had adherents such as the legendary football coach "Bear" Bryant, who used it intensively (and at great cost) in the 16 mm film days prior to the advent of reusable videotapes (Gilbert & Gilbert, 1988). Many athletics coaches also used film to record their crack athletes' "westward rolls" or other specialist high jumps to act both as models for the younger generations and as feedback to the crack jumpers themselves. Much use was made of slow-motion sequences to enable a detailed analysis of the movement patterns to be made. With the appearance of the video camcorder, the technique has become almost an obsession.

Rothstein and Arnold (1977) performed an analysis of over 50 studies that used video feedback in the teaching of sports including 18 areas of sports activity. About 40% of these studies showed significant effects on learning from the use of video feedback, and 60% did not give significant differences. A more detailed analysis of differences between the studies led to the conclusion that significant effects tend to be obtained:

a.  when prolonged and regular use of video feedback is employed (five weeks is suggested as the minimum period);
b.  when the performers are already past the rank beginner stage in the skills area being developed and are able to perceive the key points in the movement patterns and interpret them correctly for themselves;
c.  or, if used with beginners, the instructor must assist in, or indeed lead, the process of reflective analysis, using the video information as only one part of a carefully planned training debriefing session.

Later studies tend to confirm that there is more to the effective use of video as feedback than the mere presentation of the video to the learners. For example, Sim and Stewart (1984) found that video feedback was not successful in improving the high-jumping skills of mildly and moderately retarded adults. This and other studies reinforce the view that video feedback can be a powerful component in a reflective debriefing strategy, but that the learners must develop the appropriate cognitive tools needed to interpret and use the information provided. The work on schema theory and its relation to the learning of psychomotor skills, described earlier, supports this view.

## 6. Principles for the Planning of Transfer

*6.1.*   *In general, variability of practice exercises enhances transfer and generalization of a motor skill, but this may depend on whether the skill is reproductive (closed) or productive (open).*

Since the beginning of the century the prevailing viewpoint was that the more similar two tasks are, the greater the transfer of learning from one to the execution of the other. The amount of transfer was deemed to be proportional to the "number of identical elements" in the two tasks (Thorndike, 1903). However, experimental evidence did not always support this viewpoint. Then in the latter half of the century, as schema theory became accepted, the alternative viewpoint emerged that the amount of transfer of learning to similar, yet different, tasks was related to the amount of practice on similar, yet different, examples. In the field of psychomotor learning, this viewpoint was clearly articulated by Schmidt (1975), who proposed that goal-directed movement leads to the storage in memory of information on the stimulus conditions, the response specifications, the performance feedback received, and the overall final result. These combine in memory to form a "motor schema" that enables the repetition of the movement, or indeed the performance of a new variation of it. As Gabbard (1984) summarized it, a major prediction of schema theory is that "increasing the variability of practice on a given task will result in increased transfer to a novel task of the same movement class."

Many studies have been performed to test and further refine Schmidt's propositions. Kerr and Booth (1977) compared groups of children learning to throw accurately without the usually available visual cues at targets set up a given distance away. (They could not see the target directly, nor their own hands.) One group had 16 trials at a target 3 feet away, receiving knowledge of results after each throw. They were then tested by computing the mean error of a further 8 trials at the same target (without knowledge of results). The other group had 8 trials at a target 2 feet away and a further 8 trials at a target 4 feet away (all with knowledge of results). They were then tested exactly as the first group, i.e., mean error of 8 trials at a target 3 feet away. The group who had varied practice was more accurate on the test, even though they had not practiced at all on a target set at the distance used in the test.

These experiments and others—Gabbard (1984) reviews several more—lend strong support to the schema-theory explanation of transfer. They also suggest approaches to the planning of skill learning for transfer, particularly in the early years of schooling, when basic psychomotor skills are being developed. A varied program of physical activities should develop more powerful motor schemata, which should facilitate the later learning of specific sports.

However, experience in some sports and in many high-speed, repetitive industrial skills has not supported the variability-of-practice principle. In diving, for instance, each specific dive has a procedure of its own. Practicing several styles of diving, rather than concentrating one's practice on one specific dive, does not lead to better performance on that particular dive. Furthermore, practicing variations of style on the one dive tends to reduce the accuracy of the diver. A similar situation has been reported in repetitive industrial skills; indeed Seymour (1966) has used the amount of variability of movement execution (or the lack of it) as a measure of the extent to which a skilled activity has been mastered.

One way to resolve these apparent differences is by means of the "skills continuum" (reproductive-productive, or closed-open), which was introduced earlier in this chapter. The further a skilled activity is toward the productive (or open-skills) end of this continuum, the more possible variability exists and the more important it becomes to practice across the range of variability in order to ensure effective transfer to yet different specific cases. The further the activity lies toward the reproductive (or closed-skills) end of the continuum, the less permissible is variability in execution, and so the less valuable is variability of practice (indeed it may be harmful).

6.2. *Near-transfer may possibly be enhanced by practice designed on the "identical elements" principle, but far-transfer is better enhanced by practice designed on the "variability" principle.*

Cronbach and Snow (1977) propose the concepts of "near-transfer" (between very similar tasks) and "far-transfer" (between somewhat different tasks) and suggest that near-transfer is enhanced through similarity of practice trials, while (the educationally more important) far-transfer is enhanced through variation of the practice trials across the full range of possible variability. They were not writing specifically in relation to psychomotor skill learning, but in a more general vein; indeed Clark and Voogel (1985) have suggested that the near and far transfer concept is most useful in the case of knowledge acquisition (near-transfer in the case of procedural knowledge and far-transfer in the case of declarative knowledge). In this case, "very similar" tasks would be, for example, different cases of a procedure with different data, but all to be executed by applying the same algorithm (e.g., a set of long-division tasks).

An analogous psychomotor situation might be a task that follows exactly the same set of steps but varies in some aspect such as size of the components (e.g., the assembly of different sizes of ball bearings, or tapping of a screw thread by hand in holes of different diameters). In such cases, practice on only one size may be expected to transfer effectively to other sizes (so long as the size differentials are not so large as to necessitate the use of different movements and muscle combinations to execute the task).

6.3. *In the case of planning for far-transfer, the variability of the practice exercises should be so designed as to define, or refine, "motor concepts" and "motor schemata" in the learner's mind.*

According to Schmidt's (1975) theory, a motor schema is a structure of interrelated "motor concepts" analogous to the structure of a cognitive schema. A concept in the cognitive domain is defined by a series of attributes that define its "boundary" more or less precisely. Just so, a motor concept, such as "throwing a ball accurately," is defined and bounded by certain attributes, such as: distance to throw, force to apply, angle of release of the ball, and arm speed at the moment of release. These attributes are not, of course, defined verbally or mathematically, but are nevertheless "known" and "interrelated" within the player, so that any required distance of throw, as stimulus, produces an appropriate combination of the other attributes as response.

The implication for instructional design is that practice should be designed to vary in terms of all the critical attributes of the motor concept. The above analysis, in terms of four attributes of throwing, is a simplified case. Consideration of throwing forward, backward, or to the side of the body; throwing while standing still, or on the move, and so on will increase the number of dimensions along which it may be desirable to vary the practice sessions.

*6.4.    In the case of near-transfer, the training and practice
should be so designed as to form an exact model, or
program, of ideal performance in the learner's mind.*

As near-transfer situations are most common in high-speed, repetitive tasks
that follow a set pattern of steps, effective transfer may be defined as moving to
the execution of slightly different variants of the task without appreciable loss of
speed and accuracy. The speed of execution of successive steps is often faster
than the time required to mentally process the eternal results of the step from
visual or auditory feedback information. The period of time required for mental
processing of sensory information is in the region of 200 milliseconds. A pianist
or a drummer may often be executing a pattern of movements where each step
(movement) follows the other at intervals of, say, 50 msec. There is no possibility
of control of rhythm or finger sequence by processing of external sensory
feedback data. High-speed typing or data entry (400 characters/minute or more)
is a similar example from the job skills context.

Such examples have led to the formulation of the concept of "motor
programs": a set of muscle commands that allows specific movements or
movement patterns to be performed without any peripheral (external) feedback
(Keele, 1968). The movement pattern may initially be learned with the aid of
external feedback, but speed development takes it to the point where control
must be internalized (to the kinesthetic feedback within the muscles) or further
performance improvement becomes impossible. The motor program may be
conceived as an internally stored "template" of the correct movement pattern
that is compared to the actual movement patterns as they are being executed.

Evidence of the existence of such "templates" has been furnished by various
experiments and observations of deafened or blinded organisms (birds and
monkeys as well as humans) who can continue to accurately execute complex
psychomotor activity patterns, learned earlier before the loss of sight or hearing,
without any additional special training. (See Kerr, 1982, pp. 266–271, for some
examples.) Seymour's (1954a, 1954b, 1966) observations of the stages of
development of high-speed industrial skills, from erratic step-by-step execution
under external feedback control to fluid execution under internal kinesthetic
control, would suggest that such internal models of psychomotor activity are an
essential part of high-speed repetitive skill development.

As motor skills are learned, initially with the presence and use of external
control, it is important for the instruction to ensure that the correct motor
program is internalized. Later unlearning of an ineffective or inefficient motor
program can be a very difficult process. Learning correct touch typing is much
more difficult if high proficiency in two-finger typing has already been
developed. Improving on a much practiced, but mediocre, tennis stroke is
tougher than learning a completely new stroke. The instructor or instructional
designer must therefore be certain of what constitutes an effective motor
program for a given skill. This requires careful task and skills analysis at a very
minute level of detail in order to identify the exact movement sequences that
should be taught.

**6.5. In the case of multi-step sequential tasks not regularly practiced, a "primacy-recency" effect may occur and may have to be counteracted by appropriate practice schedules.**

The "primacy-recency" effect has been known for some time in the area of verbal learning, dating back to the early days of research on short- and long-term memory by means of sequences of nonsense syllables. Subjects typically recalled the first and last few syllables in the sequence presented better than the ones in the middle of the sequence. In the psychomotor domain, a similar effect was noted by Magill and Dowell (1977) in a sequential task of moving a sliding handle to a series of predefined positions in a given sequence while blindfolded. When the number of sequential positions was low (say 3) errors were constant and quite small across the sequence. When the number of sequential positions to be found was higher (6 to 9), errors in positioning were generally higher after a similar amount of practice. However, the errors were especially high on locating the positions in the middle of the sequence. Errors increased significantly from position to position, falling again on the last one or two positions in the sequence.

A possible approach to overcoming this effect is to "chunk" a multi-step precision task into shorter training sequences during initial training. A nine-step task could be trained as three-step subtasks, which would later be chained together once proficiency has been developed on each "chunk" separately. This approach should ensure more effective transfer to the real-life execution of the whole task.

**6.6. Transfer and retention of motor skills are improved by "over learning" or "over practice."**

As early as 1954, Robert Gagné observed that trainers at that time were still enamored of Thorndike's (1903) "hallowed principle," which suggests that the amount of transfer of learning is proportional to the number of identical elements in the two tasks, when both practical observation and some experimental evidence suggests that more probably "the amount of transfer of learning is proportional to the amount of initial practice" (Gagné, 1954). Singer (1982) makes the further point that there is much evidence that "over-learning" or "over-practice" is beneficial in terms of long-term retention, although there is a law of diminishing returns in force which may establish limits beyond which formally organized "over-practice" would not be cost-effective. However, psychomotor skills are usually learned in order to be used fairly regularly. Thus a naturally occurring over-learning phenomenon is present. When the practice situation is well designed, in terms of variety of practice situations or careful motor programming, whichever is appropriate to the skill in question, over-practice may also be expected to enhance transfer.

6.7.   *As learning and practice progress, care must be taken to*
       *avoid too fast a progression to more difficult tasks.*
       *Information overload generally results in a deterioration*
       *of task execution.*

Information overload is one source of stress on a task performer. Just as there
are physical limits on the rate of information processing, so too the performer has
a problem if information rate or quantity is such that effective processing cannot
keep up. Typically, one (or a combination) of three things occurs:
   a. accuracy is traded for speed—the performer works faster but makes more
      errors, as in the case of forced-pace typing training;
   b. speed is traded for accuracy—the incoming information is processed as
      before, at the rate which ensures low errors, but this causes a queuing
      problem of incoming information, and if the situation involves working
      with a fixed-speed machine or playing a sport against competition, the
      slowing down of reactions to new information is bound to lead to
      problems, errors, danger, or defeat;
   c. speed is maintained by selecting some of the incoming information and
      acting on it while disregarding other information—if this is done
      arbitrarily, errors will inevitably result; but if the performer has some
      experience-based strategy upon which to select/reject incoming
      information, this can be an effective way of coping with the stress of the
      situation.
Instructional designers should keep the phenomenon of information overload
in mind when planning psychomotor training, particularly for high-speed
industrial skills. Several approaches have been found to be helpful in avoiding or
staving off the onset of information overload. Welford (1976) mentions the
following:
   a. devising ways of "chunking" the incoming information so that more can
      be handled by the performer without creating stress;
   b. devising ways of helping the performer predict what may come up next
      and thus be selective in the information attended to and processed;
   c. devising ways of pacing the performance of the task so that both
      information overload is avoided and the task is performed at an acceptable
      level of proficiency;
   d. establishing realistic "threshold levels" for the performer and working
      within them.
These suggestions are most difficult to implement in competitive sports, where
little control can be exercised over the information that will be received by the
performer. In the case of industrial skills, however, much can be done by a
process of systems engineering where man and machine are considered together.
Ergonomics and more recently computer system interface design are examples of
approaches that may have to come to the assistance of the instructional designer
in such cases.

*6.8. The practice of complex motor skills may benefit from part-task trainers or simulators. By constructing a sequence of simple-to-complex practice situations, the dangers of information overload can be avoided.*

Information overload is not always related to some absolute physiological limit. Often it is caused by a psychological limit of a temporary nature due to the pace or complexity of the training exercise. When complexity, rather than high speed, is the potential cause, much can be done through the progressive structuring of training from relatively simple to more complex practice situations. Methods for the planning of such progressions have often appeared in the literature (e.g., Miller, 1974; Rucker, 1986; Alessi, 1988). The paper by Rucker is particularly interesting, as it deals with a case study of a complex psychomotor skill in dental surgery. The following progression of training and practice exercises was found to be most effective in terms of both basic learning and transfer to the job:

a. Dental students are acquainted with the postural and positional parameters of balanced psychomotor performances (imparting the basic minimum knowledge).

b. Students learn the basic psychomotor skills in a setting that simulates an optimal operational setting as regards spatial dimensions, tissues, and perceptual features (sight, sound, smell); but each component skill is separately demonstrated and practiced before being integrated into the whole performance. (The setting is first used as a part-task trainer to implement an expository instructional design, and later as a full simulation environment to integrate the separate subskills into a total performance through student directed and paced practice).

c. Students apply the basic skills in an optimal clinical setting where complexity and difficulty of cases presented are carefully monitored and graded (real-life practice under carefully controlled difficulty/complexity conditions).

d. Students apply their knowledge of postural and positional parameters, together with their already developed basic skills, to an ever-widening range of non-ideal operational settings, so they can learn to adapt equipment and methods to their needs as human operators (progressive transfer to the full range of real-life situations under a student-driven, largely experiential, instructional strategy).

Similar progressions, from conventional instruction, to part-task trainers, to relatively high-fidelity full simulators, and finally to transfer to further on-job training, can be found in many other contexts (for example, in current Air Force pilot training, many military skills training contexts, and some complex industrial skills areas). The above-mentioned example is particularly interesting, however, because not only does it follow this now-common progression of training environments, but also it follows quite closely the general psychomotor skills training model presented at the beginning of this chapter (see Figure 3.5).

In the next section, we shall look more closely at the principles that might guide the design and use of psychomotor skills training simulators and part-task trainers, focusing especially on the question of simulation fidelity.

# 7. Principles for the Design of Simulators and Part-task Trainers: The Question of Fidelity

**7.1.**   *The prevalent practice of putting emphasis on high fidelity to the real task in all respects is not a very cost-effective approach to training device design and may not even be the most effective approach irrespective of costs.*

The practice of training device and simulator design, which extends back into the last century (Hays & Singer, 1989) but which became big business since the Second World War, has tended to aim for near-total "fidelity" of the training device to the real task. Some psychologists have questioned this approach, arguing that not only is the pursuit of full simulation very costly but also it may sometimes be detrimental to training effectiveness (e.g., Gagné, 1954). However, the field was largely driven by engineering and work study rather than psychology or learning theory, and this tended to maintain the push for high levels of fidelity in simulators.

High-fidelity training devices abound in the military arena, for example, the many generations of flight simulators, which range from the relatively simple (yet quite high fidelity) Link trainers of wartime to recent NASA astronaut training environments. As recently as 1974, a review of United States Air Force experience with simulators, while admitting that the pursuit of high levels of fidelity added much to the cost, claimed that studies have never shown that high fidelity is associated with poor training (Miller, 1974). However, this was not an accurate statement, for much earlier research had been inconclusive on this point, and some (e.g., Cox *et al.*, 1965) had strongly suggested the opposite view. Martin and Waag (1978), working on U.S. Air Force projects, then demonstrated that flight simulators with very high fidelity could provide *too much* information to the novice trainee and could significantly reduce the effectiveness of training.

The question of fidelity in training device design is therefore important, both from a training effectiveness viewpoint and for sheer economic reasons.

**7.2.**   *Current viewpoints give training effectiveness precedence over fidelity. Effectiveness may often be enhanced by adopting lower levels of fidelity.*

Gagné (1954) argued that training effectiveness as a guiding principle should replace the "identical elements" principle first suggested by Thorndike (1903) in the design of training devices and simulators. The idea has taken a long time to catch on, but there is evidence that at last this has become the official orientation.

Recent U.S. Government contracts for complex training simulations bind the contractors to designing, developing, installing, and demonstrating the training effectiveness of the system. This is quite a departure from previous practice, which expected simply the delivery of a simulated system that "looked and behaved like the real thing."

Given the mounting body of research showing that high fidelity does not necessarily pay off in terms of higher training effectiveness, designers of simulation systems are beginning to take more notice of the instructional design principles at play. Recently, an attempt was made by Singer and Perez (1986) to collect and organize the principles of training device design as part of a federally funded project that aimed to develop an expert system that might improve the effectiveness of the design process in this now multi-billion dollar a year business. One outcome of this work was the identification of the multiple factors that influence the optimal levels of fidelity that should be built into training devices. Some of these factors as well as the multiple aspects of the concept of fidelity are discussed at length by Hays and Singer (1989). The following principles are based largely on this work.

> 7.3.  *It is important to distinguish between physical fidelity and functional fidelity. Training effectiveness in a given project may require different levels of physical and functional fidelity.*

Physical fidelity is "how much the training device looks and feels like the real thing." Functional fidelity is "how closely does the device behave like the real thing." It is reasonable to suppose that the optimal levels of fidelity for a given training device may be different for physical and functional aspects. This led Hays (1980) to suggest a $3 \times 3$ matrix experimental design to investigate optimal fidelity levels. Experimental versions of a training device could incorporate high, medium, and low levels of physical fidelity crossed with high, medium, and low levels of functional fidelity to give a total of nine different versions.

This experimental approach was used to investigate the relative effectiveness of different fidelity combinations on the learning of bicycle wheel truing, a task that involves a high level of psychomotor skill and eye-hand coordination (Baum *et al.*, 1982). Results showed that higher levels of physical fidelity improved training effectiveness and efficiency, but that functional fidelity was not an important factor.

Allen, Hays, and Buffardi (1986) performed a similar experiment on an electromechanical troubleshooting task. The task characteristics in this case were substantially different from the previously described experiment. In addition to the psychomotor aspects involved in manipulating and dismantling the device, a considerable amount of cognitive knowledge and skill are involved. Actually, the cognitive skills constitute the major part of the learning necessary to perform troubleshooting skills.

This experiment did not yield significant results in terms of training effectiveness (all groups learned to troubleshoot the equipment correctly), but did show marked differences in training efficiency (time and number of trials necessary to achieve mastery). Higher levels of fidelity, both physical and functional, resulted in higher levels of training efficiency. However, the overall importance of high functional fidelity was greater than high physical fidelity. This is just the opposite of the result in the previously described experiment.

These experiments suggest that instructional designers should plan appropriate levels of fidelity into psychomotor skill practice exercises, and that the optimal levels of physical and functional fidelity may be different for different categories of skill. It would seem that physical fidelity is more important in the case of reproductive skills, which involve little or no cognitive effort in their execution, while functional fidelity may be more important in the case of productive skills, that do depend on deeper cognitive processing of task information.

> **7.4.** *It is also important to distinguish "technical fidelity" as defined by an expert, from "perceived fidelity" as experienced by a trainee. For effective training it is the perceived fidelity that counts.*

Technical fidelity is the extent to which the training device replicates the working of the real system. Perceived fidelity is the extent to which the device appears to do so to the trainee. As pointed out by Smode (1971, 1972), this is an important distinction to make; "the real goal in training device design should be to base fidelity decisions on the trainee's perceptual requirements, for example, perceptual equivalence to the operational environment." Engineers and experts tend to pursue the technical equivalence of the mechanisms in the training device to the environment being simulated. However, if the reality is difficult for the novice trainee to interpret, or is too "information-rich," leading to information overload, then the pursuit of technical fidelity will tend to reproduce these impediments to learning in the training device.

The pursuit of perceptual fidelity focuses the designer's attention on the trainee and allows for the implementation of less expensive and possibly more effective solutions by seeking to provide the sensory information required by the trainee in order to learn in the simplest and easiest-to-interpret technical manner. This approach, according to Smode (1972), also encourages the designer to deliberately depart from high levels of fidelity and realism in the interests of enhanced training effectiveness (for example, by exaggerating the feedback information during initial stages of training).

> **7.5.** *Simulators are often used principally for the measurement of task performance rather than its improvement. Technical fidelity to the real task is important for performance measurement but less so for performance improvement (training).*

This point was made very emphatically by Gagné (1954) in observing that, at that time, military use of simulators was oriented much more to certifying competence than to this development. This emphasis may well have changed somewhat in the intervening years, but simulators are still often used as testing rather than training devices. The simple gas welding part-task trainer, shown in Figure 3.14 earlier in this chapter, was designed by the present author specifically with training in mind and was indeed demonstrated to be an effective training device. Over the years, however, the company where the device was developed used it much more systematically as a selection device than as a training device.

Gagné (1954) pointed out that the design approach should be different for testing and for training devices. In the former case, score validity and reliability are the issues, and in the latter, it is transfer of learning. In general, higher levels of technical fidelity may be required to ensure that performance test scores obtained on a simulator device are valid and reliable predictors of future on-the-job performance. On the other hand, we have already seen earlier that very high levels of technical fidelity in a simulator may reduce training effectiveness by introducing too much information or by rendering it impossible to incorporate sound instructional design principles in the training exercises.

> 7.6. *Exact simulation of a task is often in conflict with effective training, since it precludes the implementation of effective instructional design principles. Part-task training devices often overcome this problem, allowing sound design to be incorporated into simulated practice exercises.*

This point was in fact made as early as 1945 in research which demonstrated that the sacrificing of exact simulation can be necessary in order to enhance performance improvement (Lindahl, 1945). One approach suggested by Lindahl was the use of part-task trainers, devices that simulate key aspects of the total task in isolation from the other aspects and allow systematic development of certain key subskills required for effective task performance. This approach was also strongly advocated by Gagné (1954), who favored component practice over total simulation and expressed doubts whether any skills were ever effectively learned "all at once" exclusively through practice on-the-job or on fully realistic simulators.

The separate development of key subskills, often by means of specially developed training devices, was a key aspect of the "Skills Analysis Training" approach mentioned earlier (Seymour, 1954a, 1966, 1968), which became the most widely adopted approach to operator job skills training in Britain during the 1960's. Many examples of extremely effective training programs were implemented. One such program, in which the present author was involved, concerned the "ding men," who where a highly skilled group of sheet metal panel beaters employed at the end of a motor car body production line in order to repair any minute dents (or "dings") that the body panels may have suffered during transport or assembly. The "ding men" first have to discover undulations or dings, often fractions of a millimeter in depth, on the rough metal of the as yet unpainted car body, and then have to remove the dings by hammering them out. The tradition of the industry maintained that you have to serve an apprenticeship of some seven years alongside a skilled ding man to become a competent ding man yourself. Such was the implied level of required job skill.

When new automobile factories were established in Britain during the 1960's in regions without an experienced workforce, the problem of rapidly training teams of ding men led to the development of a system of part-task training exercises and devices for initial off-the-job training. Figures 3.7 and 3.8 earlier in the chapter show two of some half dozen part-task training devices developed for this project. Others addressed the subskills involved in actually locating the dings by a combination of sight and touch, and so on. Initial off-the-job development of the six subskills to predetermined criterion levels, followed by progressive transfer to on-the-job training, succeeded in producing teams of fully competent ding men in about seven weeks rather than the predicted seven years. No full-scale simulators were used on this project, but each subskill was separately practiced under partially simulated job conditions.

### 7.7. *Progress to "full" (higher fidelity) simulation appears to be governed by several interacting factors: the context of the training, the task content, the learners, and the stage of learning.*

The progress from part-task training exercises to the complete job, or to a more complete simulation of the job, is another aspect of instructional design that requires close scrutiny. In overall terms, progress from simplified part-task exercises to more complete simulations and finally to on-job training has been recommended by many authors and is to be seen in many military and business training systems. Just exactly when and how to make the transitions has not been all that well defined, however. Overall approaches, such as the progressive parts sequence of training, are recommended. Aspects of the design of the parts themselves have been rather neglected in the literature. It seems to be assumed that the designer knows how to design the partial training exercises.

Hays and Singer (1989) review the literature on the design of such progressive sequences of exercises from the viewpoint of fidelity. How should fidelity increase as trainees proceed to more complete practice of a task? Should the part-task training exercises themselves aim toward high or low levels of fidelity? Are the principles of design the same or different for different task categories or in different training contexts? Their review of existing research suggests that at least four factors are particularly important to take into consideration when designing progressions of exercises for the training of complex psychomotor tasks: the training context, type of task, the trainees, and the sequence of progression to mastery. The research base on these factors is not very extensive or conclusive, but there seem to be certain tendencies at least hinted at by available data. On the basis of this, Hays and Singer (1989) propose a series of relationships, more in the form of hypotheses requiring further research than fully researched and proven principles. The remainder of the principles listed in this section are those proposed by Hays and Singer.

**7.8.** *Context of training: it is more important to plan how the training device is used (the overall instructional design) than the exact design specifications of the device itself.*

This principle almost has the flavor of an axiom. It is found in Gagné's (1954) influential paper on training device design. Micheli (1972) demonstrated that the way that a training device is incorporated into the overall training program and how it is used within that program may be more of a factor influencing ultimate training effectiveness than the exact design specifications of the device itself (macro-design taking precedence over micro-design). In a similar vein, Montemerlo (1977) argued that the training effectiveness of a full-scale simulator is a function of the total training design and not just the design characteristics of the simulator. The whole debate has some similarity to the "media as mere vehicles" debate that has been raging for some time in the instructional design literature (Clark, 1983).

**7.9.** *Content of training: "reproductive" psychomotor skills seem to benefit from relatively high levels of physical fidelity but may require relatively moderate levels of functional fidelity; in contrast, "productive" skills that rely on cognitive decision-making strategies seem to benefit from high levels of functional fidelity but require only moderate levels of physical fidelity.*

This principle has been addressed above in the discussion of the two experiments utilizing a 9-cell matrix to define and compare different combinations of functional and physical fidelity (Baum *et al.*, 1982; Allen, Hays, & Buffardi, 1986). Other work supporting this principle has been reported by Fink and Shriver (1978), who found that the fidelity levels necessary for decision-making (e.g., in equipment maintenance) were quite different from those necessary for operating the controls of the same equipment. Also, Miller (1980) observed that the importance of fidelity was not so much a question of physical or functional congruence as the provision in the simulator of appropriate cues to guide the trainee's behavior in performing the task. These authors tend to use classifications of tasks into equipment maintenance and equipment operation, or cognitive and psychomotor, or closed and open. We are suggesting here that the more generic classification along a reproductive skills/productive skills continuum, presented at the beginning of this chapter, may be a more useful classification schema to adopt.

> **7.10.** *The trainees: on physical skills involving machines, trainees with lower levels of mechanical comprehension or prior mechanical experience may benefit from higher levels of both functional and physical fidelity.*

There is quite a body of research, extending over many decades that compares the instructional effectiveness of real objects, three-dimensional models, two-dimensional pictures or photos, and schematic diagrams for the teaching of the structure, the functioning, or the operation of complex systems. In general, there are two somewhat opposed sets of findings. On the one hand, the simplification of reality has been shown to enhance learning effectiveness, particularly in relation to the understanding of structure and functional process. On the other hand, learning to operate, dismantle, or fix complex machinery may require higher levels of physical fidelity, this being particularly so for trainees who are new to the context of mechanical work or who are below average in terms of mechanical comprehension or spatial reasoning test scores. In relation more specifically to training simulators, Grimsley (1969), Blaauw (1982), and Allen, Hays, and Buffardi (1986) have found rather similar effects. It is believed that the mechanically more competent or experienced trainees can more readily transfer from a low fidelity part-task training exercise to the real task.

> **7.11.** *Stages of training: in general, low levels of (both physical and functional) fidelity are more appropriate during initial training, and higher levels are appropriate during advanced practice and training for transfer.*

The above-mentioned research also supports the position that, in general, the level of fidelity may be rather low in initial training, but at some point it must be increased in order to reach levels equivalent to the real task. It may often be too big a jump for trainees to progress directly from relatively low fidelity part-task training exercises to the real-life task with all its complexities. Hays and Singer (1989) suggest a four-step process, from quite low levels of fidelity in initial (they call it "indoctrination") training, to somewhat higher levels in practical "familiarization" training, then to even higher levels in the stage of skill-development practice (part-task trainers or a medium-fidelity simulator), and high levels of fidelity on the final stages of "transition training" to the real job. They also suggest that functional fidelity should in general approach real-task levels more quickly than physical fidelity.

# 8. Principles for the Development of the "Inner Self"

In this section we shall review some of the principles that are being applied with increasing frequency, particularly in the training of athletes and sports teams, to prepare the players psychologically for maximum performance and to develop greater levels of self-control over the "inner self," the feelings and beliefs that influence peak performance. Whereas the area of growth in application of these principles is in sports, we are beginning to see them applied also in the industrial skills arena, where the practice of engaging in relaxation exercises and mental imagery prior to work is beginning to become popular. Questions may be posed as to whether these popular developments are just a passing fashion, or whether there is a sound research basis for the underlying principles of these new techniques. It is true that many of the self-analysis and self-control training programs are not strictly research based. Much of the experimental data that is available are from case studies, not always rigorously controlled. The proponents of the techniques often argue that they are not subject to the classical methods of research, as they are influencing internal states rather than specific externally measurable outcomes. Whatever the merits of such arguments, it is appropriate to review the main principles upon which this movement is based, for there is a growing amount of evidence that whatever the more detailed (and as yet not fully understood) reasons may be, the overall effects of programs of psychological preparation of athletes do have beneficial effects on their performance.

### 8.1. Relaxation exercises, prior to engaging in skilled activities, tend to enhance performance levels.

The practice of relaxation exercises is not entirely new in athletics and sports training circles. What is rather new, however, is the orientation that tends to be given to these exercises in many contemporary training programs. Relaxation was in the past seen to be part of the warmup process, i.e., light exercise and physical relaxation in order to prepare the body for the effort that is about to be demanded of it. Now it tends to be seen as having an even more important role in preparing the mind of the athlete. The objective is to clear the mind of negative or irrelevant thoughts and prepare it to be particularly receptive to positive thinking about the physical activity that is about to commence. Relaxation routines are now often seen as the first step in a process of mental rehearsal, often bordering on auto-suggestion. We will review the rest of this process later on.

The relaxation routines most often described in the literature (e.g., Jacobson, 1957, 1964; McAuley & Rotella, 1982; Rose, 1985) involve initial breathing exercises, sometimes with a musical background or with a planned effort to concentrate on the process of breathing itself. The objective is to give the mind something to focus on while the exercise is being conducted and to lead to a feeling of general well-being and receptiveness. The breathing exercises are generally followed by some body exercises, especially of the shoulder and neck but sometimes extending to a more comprehensive set that involves all the limbs of the body. It is only after these initial exercises are complete that the main relaxation routines commence. These are most often performed in a sitting position, less often lying flat on one's back. Usually, there is an element of meditation involved in this stage. It can be induced by appropriate music, by some object on which to focus attention (e.g., a lighted candle), by another person (or a tape recording) conversing in soothing tones, or by some mental image or word on which the subject focuses attention (a mantra).

This stage of mental relaxation should be maintained for some minutes until, as Rose (1985) puts it, quoting Wordsworth, the subject attains "a happy stillness of mind." Somewhat more quantitative measures of the immediate effects of such meditative relaxation sometimes include a drop in body temperature and a slowing of the rate of heartbeat (Jacobson, 1957; Rose, 1985). The extent to which such changes in physiological processes affect later physical action is more difficult to determine, though Niddefer & Deckner (1970) documented some case studies that showed a positive effect on performance, and some medical studies (quoted in Rose, 1985) show that top-notch sports performers do tend to differ from their less competent colleagues in respect of such measures as heartbeat rates immediately prior to action.

Whether the effects on performance of deep mental relaxation are as significant as claimed by the proponents of the techniques, and whether the techniques work for all or just for some, there is no question that the techniques themselves can be learned by a willing and motivated student. Whereas a novice may take twenty or thirty minutes to reach the low-heartbeat deep relaxation states described above, regular practitioners can "get there" in a minute or two.

## 8.2. Mental rehearsal of impending activity, which concentrates on imagining success, tends to improve performance.

The deep mental relaxation described above is preparation for the mental rehearsal of the impending activity. Unlike the use of imagery as described earlier, which rehearses the pattern of movement involved in a task, the imagery suggested in relation to the preparation of the "inner self" is often referred to as "positive thinking." Most writers suggest that subjects should recall successful instances from past performance or imagine new successes. McAuley & Rotella (1982) contrasts the use of such "mastery imagery," as he calls it, with "coping imagery" in which a subject imagines a possible mistake or a successful move by an opponent and reflects on how to deal with the situation in order to recover. He concludes that coping imagery is useful some time (weeks or days) before a competition (e.g., debriefing after a previous competition), but that only mastery imagery should be encouraged immediately prior to competition in order to "maximize the performer's self-confidence and positive expectancies." This viewpoint gives one a particularly clear idea of the different manner in which a coach should design a pre-game briefing session, as compared to a post-game debriefing.

Proponents of such "positive thinking" approaches tend to teach their trainees to use specific techniques for the promotion of positive thoughts and the blocking of negative thoughts.

### 8.3. Thinking oneself into the role of a known expert performer and identifying as completely as possible with that "role model" tend to improve performance.

This principle has been suggested by the work of Lozanov (1978) and others who have contributed to the methodologies variously termed "suggestology," "suggestopaedia," or "accelerated learning." These methodologies, based on a body of empirical work originally carried out in Eastern European countries during the 1960's, propose that imagining you will be successful in what you are about to attempt is good, but imagining yourself to BE someone who habitually is successful in that activity is even better.

In the psychomotor skills arena, this methodology is used by encouraging the trainees to select and study a role model and then, just prior to competition, to actually become this role model in one's imagination. Typically, film or video material of exemplary performances will be studied earlier in the training program. This serves two functions: the conventionally accepted one of demonstrating the finer points of technique as part of the basic instructional process, and the suggestopaedia-based function of making the trainee intimately familiar with a particular exemplary performer's style so that during pre-practice mental rehearsal sessions the trainee can as-it-were step into the shoes of the role model and "become" that exemplary performer.

This methodology is not restricted to establishing mindsets for competitive sports. Sir John Whitmore, former European saloon car racing champion and now sports psychologist and management training consultant, has adopted what he learned in competitive motoring to a number of more mundane skilled activities. In his book *Superdriver: Discover the Joys of Driving*, which was commissioned by the Royal Automobile Club in Great Britain to promote safe and responsible driving on the roads, he outlines an approach to driving for the everyday motorist that embodies all the principles discussed so far in this section: pre-practice "awareness relaxation," mental imagery of "responsible driving situations" and, particularly, the imaging of an "ideal driver," whether real or imaginary, followed by conscious "role playing" of that ideal driver both in mental rehearsal sessions and actually at the driving wheel (Whitmore, 1988).

### 8.4. Engaging in appropriate "self-talk" with oneself (a form of "inner game") can have significant positive effects on performance.

The final principle we highlight is the one perhaps first formulated by Timothy Gallwey as the "inner game" (Gallwey, 1974). As a professional tennis player and later coach, Gallwey devoted himself to studying" the problem of how human beings interfere with their own ability to achieve and learn." His search for practical ways to overcome the mental obstacles that prevent maximum performance led him to postulate that every game is really composed of two parts: the outer game "which is played against an external opponent to overcome external obstacles and to reach an external goal," and the inner game "that takes place in the mind of the player and is played against such obstacles as lapses of concentration, nervousness, self-doubts, and self-condemnation." The player of the inner game "comes to value the art of relaxed concentration above all other skills . . . discovers a true basis for self-confidence . . . and learns that the secret to winning any games lies in not trying too hard."

Gallwey bases his methodology on the metaphor of an internal conversation with oneself, and since a conversation usually requires two participants, he postulates two "selves": Self 1 and Self 2. When I talk to myself, the "I" and the "myself" are two separate entities. The "I" seems to give instructions and the "myself" seems to perform the action. Gallwey's approach concentrates on "improving the relationship between the conscious 'teller' (Self 1) and the unconscious automatic 'doer' (Self 2)." Self 1 is the producer of a dialogue that attempts to direct, criticize, question, correct, and remind the body prior to, during, and after an attempt at movement. This, according to Gallwey, interferes with natural learning and occurs too slowly in fact to be able to effectively control physical action (see our earlier discussion of reaction and processing times). Therefore, if any competent skilled activity is carried out, it must be despite Self 1 rather than because of it. Self 2, the automatic "doer," must be capable of controlling movement activity without the interference of Self 1.

The "inner game" methodology concentrates on techniques for reducing the conscious interference of Self 1 in the process of execution of the task by Self 2. Players are instructed to attend to aspects other than the technical execution of the appropriate actions. In tennis, the player may be told to watch the ball (of course) but to consciously attend to the color of the ball or the beauty of its motion, letting the body and the sensory system automatically take care of the execution of the appropriate tennis stroke. Other tactics for occupying Self 1 include giving the player a song to sing or hum, asking the player to engage in predictions about aspects of the game that are not directly related to the control of movement, in short, anything that might help the player act automatically and unconsciously in the execution of the skilled activity.

This principle would, in many respects, appear to run counter to some of the other principles presented earlier in this chapter. The present situation is that while many of those other principles have been put to rigorous experimental verification, the inner game approach has little research data to support it. On the other hand, the methodology has now been applied to a wide variety of sports (e.g., Gallwey, 1976; Gallwey and Kriegel, 1977; Niddefer, 1976; Austin & Pargman, 1981; Unestahl, 1983), apparently with immense practical success.

Perhaps the apparent conflict between principles is not real if we remember some of the observations from the very first section of this chapter on the stages through which the mastery of a psychomotor skill progresses. Perhaps the automatization and increased fluidity of high-speed industrial skills, noted by Seymour (1954a, 1954b, 1966), and the observed ability of highly skilled typists to engage in conversations with neighboring typists without any noticeable deterioration in either speed or accuracy of their typing are analogous to the tennis player in the state of "relaxed concentration" described by Gallwey. By analogy to proven training practices in these other fields, we may see that there is a stage of early training when verbalizing, conscious self-analysis of performance, and self-evaluation are important tactics; but there comes a stage in the development of exemplary levels of skill when these early learning aids become a hindrance to further progress. That is the stage when the inner game approach may well come into its own.

# Chapter Summary

The first two sections of this chapter set the scene for our analysis of the principles that may be used to guide message (and overall instructional system) design in the psychomotor domain. Some of the long history of research in this field was reviewed, some of the similarities and differences between the psychomotor and the other recognized domains of learning were highlighted. Then, in the second section, some conceptual models for classifying psychomotor skills and their instructional requirements were reviewed. Also the conceptual model of skilled activity was proposed as a cycle of internal processes that may be involved to a greater or lesser extent in the execution of a given task.

In the next three sections of the chapter, we reviewed the principles of instructional design that seem appropriate in the psychomotor domain, taking as our organizing framework the classical "presentation–practice–feedback" model of the instructional process that has been one of the main legacies of the behaviorist traditions of the earlier part of this century. Then, in section six, we tempered this approach by reviewing principles that are based more on information processing theories and, in particular, on the particular version of schema theory that Schmidt (1975) proposed for the psychomotor domain. These two sets of principles, drawn from two different and sometimes opposed psychological camps, were seen to be compatible and indeed complementary when the psychomotor domain (or indeed all of the so-called domains of learning) are viewed from the perspective of the reproductive/productive continuum skills classification model (Romiszowski, 1981).

In section seven, we made a digression into the topic of the design of simulators and part-task trainers, as this is a particular growth area of activity and one which often figures strongly in the instructional design equation, both on the cost and the effectiveness side.

Lastly, in section eight, we examined a few of the most commonly encountered principles that underpin the many existing approaches to preparing the "inner self" of the skilled performer so as to maximize the probability of exemplary performance. Some of these principles are less supported by research than might be desired and, in the eyes of some researchers, some of the methodologies based on these principles are questionable. However, the growing popularity of these approaches among trainers whose very survival depends on the competitive success of the people they train suggests that far from ostracizing this area of developments, researchers should work toward the creation of a more systematic program of investigations into the underlying principles. In the meantime, practical psychomotor skill trainers may benefit by attempting to judiciously build this set of principles into some of their advanced training programs. Much of the research in this area will have to be based on case studies, and it is the practical trainer who has the conditions to set up such case situations for study.

# References

Adams, J. A. (1955). A source of decrement in psychomotor performance. *Journal of Experimental Psychology, 49*, 390–394.

Adams, J. A. (1984). Learning of movement sequences. *Psychological Bulletin, 96*, 2–28.

Adams, J. A. (1986). Use of the model's knowledge of results to increase the observer's performance. *Journal of Human Movement Studies, 12*, 269–281.

Adler, J. D. (1981). Stages of skill acquisition: A guide for teachers. *Motor Skills: Theory into Practice, 5*(2), 75–80.

Agar, A. (1962). Instruction of industrial workers by tape recorder. *Affarsekonomi, 10*. Original in Swedish.

Alessi, S. M. (1988). Fidelity in the design of instructional simulations. *Journal of Computer-Based Instruction, 15*(2), 40–47.

Allen, J. A., Hays, R. T., & Buffardi, L. C. (1986). Maintenance training simulator fidelity and individual differences in transfer of training. *Human Factors, 28*(5), 497–509.

Amswych, R. J. (1967). An investigation into the use of tape recorded programmes for craft training. *Programmed Learning and Educational Technology.* London, UK, July.

Annett, J. (1959). Learning a pressure under conditions of immediate and delayed knowledge of results. *Quarterly Journal of Experimental Psychology, 11*, 3–15.

Annett, J., & Kay, H. (1957). Knowledge of results and "skilled performance." *Occupational Psychology, 31*, 69–79.

Ashy, M. H., & Lee, A. M. (1984). Applying the mastery learning model to motor skill instruction for children. *The Physical Educator, 4*(2), 60–63.

Austin, J. S., & Pargman, D. (1981). The inner game approach to performance and skill acquisition. *Motor Skills: Theory into Practice, 5*(1), 3–12.

Baggett, P. (1983). *Learning a procedure from multimedia instructions: The effects of film and practice.* Boulder: Colorado University, Institute of Cognitive Science. 46 pages. ERIC No. ED239598.

Bandura, A. (1986). *Social foundations of thought and action: A social cognitive theory.* Englewood Cliffs, NJ: Prentice-Hall.

Bandura, A., & Jeffery, R. W. (1973). Role of symbolic coding and rehearsal processes in observational learning. *Journal of Personality and Social Psychology, 26*, 122–130.

Bandura, A., Jeffery, R. W., & Bachica, D. L. (1974). Analysis of memory codes and cumulative rehearsal in observational learning. *Journal of Research in Personality, 7*, 295–305.

Barnett, M. L., & Stanicek, J. A. (1979). Effects of goal setting on achievement in archery. *Research Quarterly, 50*, 328–332.

Baum, D. R., Riedel, S., Hays, R. T., & Mirabella, A. (1982). *Training effectiveness as a function of training device fidelity.* ARI Technical Report 593. Alexandria, VA: U.S. Army Research Institute.

Beasley, W. F. (1985). Improving student laboratory performance: How much practice makes perfect? *Science Education, 69*(4), 567–576.

Bell, H. M. (1950). Retention of pursuit rotor skill after one year. *Journal of Experimental Psychology, 40,* 648–649.

Bilodeau, E. A. (Ed.) (1966a). *Acquisition of skill.* New York: Academic Press.

Bilodeau, E. A. (1966b). Retention. In E. A. Bilodeau (Ed.), *Acquisition of skill.* New York: Academic Press.

Bilodeau, E. A., Jones, M. B., & Levy, C. M. (1964). Long-term memory as a function of retention time and repeated recalling. *Journal of Experimental Psychology, 67,* 303–309.

Bilodeau, E. A., Levy, C. M., & Sulzer, J. L. (1963). Long-term retention under conditions of artificially induced recall of related events. *Perceptual Motor Skills, 16,* 859–919.

Bilodeau, E. A., Sulzer, J. L., & Levy, C. M. (1962). Theory and data on the relationships of three factors of memory. *Psychological Monographs, 79*(20), whole issue.

Bilodeau, I. McD. (1966). Information feedback. In E. A. Bilodeau (Ed.), *Acquisition of skill.* New York: Academic Press.

Blaauw, G. (1982). Driving experience and task demands in simulator and instrumented car: A validation study. *Human Factors, 24*(4), 473–486.

Blakemore, C. L., & Goldberger, M. (1984). *The effects of mastery learning on the acquisition of psychomotor skills.* ERIC No. ED261987.

Bloom, B. S. (1968). Learning for mastery. *Evaluation Comment, 1*(2), Los Angeles, CA: U.C.L.A.

Bloom, B. S., Engelhart, M. D., Hill, W. H., Furst, E. J., & Krathwohl, D. R. (1956). *Taxonomy of educational objectives, Handbook 1: The cognitive domain.* New York: David McKay.

Briggs, G. E. (1961). *On the scheduling of training conditions for the acquisition and transfer of perceptual-motor skills.* NAVTRADEVCEN Technical Report No. 836-1

Briggs, G. E., & Naylor, J. C. (1962). The relative efficiency of several training methods as a function of transfer task complexity. *Journal of Experimental Psychology, 6*(4), 505–512.

Briggs, G. E., & Waters, L. K. (1958). Training and transfer as a function of component interaction. *Journal of Experimental Psychology, 56,* 492–500.

Carroll, J. B. (1963). A model of school learning. *Teachers College Record, 64.*

Carroll, W. R., & Bandura, A. (1982). The role of visual monitoring in observational learning of action patterns: Making the unobservable observable. *Journal of Motor Behavior, 14*(2), 153–167.

Carroll, W. R., & Bandura, A. (1985). Role of timing of visual monitoring and motor rehearsal in observational learning of action patterns. *Journal of Motor Behavior, 17*(3), 269–281.

Carroll, W. R., & Bandura, A. (1987). Translating cognition into action: The role of visual guidance in observational learning. *Journal of Motor Behavior, 19*(3), 385–398.

Carroll, W. R., & Bandura, A. (1990). Representational guidance of action production in observational learning: A causal analysis. *Journal of Motor Behavior, 22*(1), 85–97.

Clark, R. E. (1983). Reconsidering research on learning from media. *Review of Educational Research, 53*(4).

Clark, R. E., & Voogel, A. (1985). Transfer of training principles for instructional design. *Educational Communications and Technology Journal, 33*(2), 113–123.

Cole, J. L. (1981). Teacher-augmented feedback: Shortening the "fairway" between theory and instruction. *Motor Skills: Theory into Practice, 5*(2), 81–87.

Cox, J. A., Wood, R., Boren, L., & Thorne, H. W. (1965). *Functional and appearance fidelity of training devices for fixed procedures tasks.* HumRRO Technical Report 65-4. Alexandria, VA: Human Resources Research Organization.

Cronbach, L. J., & Snow, R. E. (1977). *Aptitudes and instructional methods: A handbook of research on interactions.* New York: Irvington Publishers.

Crossman, E. R. F. W. (1959). A theory of the acquisition of speed skill. *Ergonomics, 2*, 153–166.

Eysenck, S. B. J. (1960). Retention of a well developed motor skill after one year. *Journal of Psychology, 63*, 267–273.

Fink, C. D., & Shriver, E. L. (1978). *Simulators for maintenance training: Some issues, problems and areas for future research.* Technical Report AFHRL-TR-78-27. Lowry Air Force Base, Colorado: Air Force Human Resources Laboratory.

Fleishman, E. A. (1966). Human abilities and the acquisition of skill. In E. A. Bilodeau (Ed.), *Acquisition of skill.* New York: Academic Press.

Fleishman, E. A. (1972). The structure and measurement of psychomotor abilities: Some educational implications. *The psychomotor domain: Resource book for media specialists.* Published for the National Special Media Institutes. Washington, DC: Gryphon House.

Gabbard, C. P. (1984). *Motor skill learning in children.* ERIC No. ED293645.

Gagné, R. M. (1954). Training devices and simulators: Some research issues. *American Psychologist, 9*(7), 95–107.

Gallwey, W. T. (1974). *The inner game of tennis.* New York: Random House.

Gallwey, W. T. (1976). *Inner tennis: Playing the game.* New York: Random House.

Gallwey, W. T., & Kriegel, R. (1977). *Inner skiing.* New York: Random House.

Gentile, A. M. (1972). A working model of skill acquisition with application to teaching. *Quest, 17*, 3–23.

Gentner, D. R. (1984). *Expertise in typewriting.* CHIP Report, 121. La Jolla, University of California, San Diego: Center for Human Information Processing. ERIC No. ED248320.

Gilbert, T. F. (1961). Mathetics: The technology of education. *Journal of Mathetics, 1 & 2.* (Two complete issues.)

Gilbert, T. F., & Gilbert, M. B. (1988). The science of winning. *Training,* August, 33–40.

Gilchrist, J. R., & Gruber, J. J. (1984). Psychomotor domains. *Motor Skills: Theory into Practice, 7*(1/2), 57–70.

Goldstein, M., & Rittenhouse, C. H. (1954). Knowledge of results in the acquisition and transfer of a gunnery skill. *Journal of Experimental Psychology, 48*, 187–196.

Graham, K. D. (1988). A qualitative analysis of an effective teacher's movement task presentations during a unit of instruction. *Physical Educator, 45*(4).

Greenwald, A. G., & Albert, S. M. (1968). Observational learning: A technique for elucidating S–R mediation processes. *Journal of Experimental Psychology, 76*, 267–272.

Grimsley, D. L. (1969). *Acquisition, retention and retraining: The effects of high and low fidelity in training devices.* HumRRO Technical Report 69-1. Alexandria, VA: Human Resources Research Organization.

Hays, R. T. (1980). *Simulator fidelity: A concept paper.* ARI Technical Report 490. Alexandria, VA: U.S. Army Research Institute.

Hays, R. T., & Singer, M. J. (1989). *Simulation fidelity in training system design.* New York: Springer-Verlag.

Ho, L., & Shea, J. B. (1978). Levels of processing and the coding of position cues in motor short-term memory. *Journal of Motor Behavior, 10*, 113–121.

Holding, D. H. (1965). *Principles of training.* Oxford, UK: Pergamon Press.

Holding, D. H., & MacRae, A. W. (1964). Guidance restriction and knowledge of results. *Ergonomics, 7*, 289–295.

Holding, D. H., & MacRae, A. W. (1966). Rate and force of guidance in perceptual-motor tasks with reversed or random spatial correspondence. *Ergonomics, 9*, 289–296.

Hunt, D. P. (1964). Effects of nonlinear and discrete transformations of feedback information on human tracking performance. *Journal of Experimental Psychology, 67*, 486–494.

Irion, A. L. (1966). A brief history of research on the acquisition of skill. In E. A. Bilodeau (Ed.), *Acquisition of skill.* New York: Academic Press.

Jacobson, E. (1957). *You must relax: A practical method of reducing the strains of modern living.* New York: McGraw-Hill.

Jacobson, E. (1964). *Anxiety and tension control.* Philadelphia, PA: Lippincott.

Jahnke, J. C. (1958). Retention in motor learning as a function of amount of practice and rest. *Journal of Experimental Psychology, 55*, 270–273.

Jahnke, J. C., & Duncan, C. P. (1956). Reminiscence and forgetting in motor learning after extended rest intervals. *Journal of Experimental Psychology, 52*, 273–282.

Jeffery, R. W. (1976). The influence of symbolic and motor rehearsal in observational learning. *Journal of Research in Personality, 10*, 116–127.

Jones, M. B. (1966). Individual differences. In E. A. Bilodeau (Ed.), *Acquisition of skill.* New York: Academic Press.

Katz, M. S. (1967). Feedback and accuracy of target positioning in a homogeneous visual field. *American Journal of Psychology, 80*, 405–410.

Keele, S. W. (1968). Movement control in skilled motor performance. *Psychological Bulletin, 70*, 387–403.

Kerr, R. (1978). Schema theory applied to skill acquisition. *Motor Skills: Theory into Practice, 3*(1), 15–20.

Kerr, R. (1982). *Psychomotor learning.* New York: Saunders College Publishing.

Kerr, R., & Booth, B. (1977). Skill acquisition in elementary school children and schema theory. In D. M. Landers and R. W. Christina (Eds.), *Psychology of motor behavior and sport (Vol. 2)*. Champaign, IL: Human Kinetics Publishers.

Kimble, G. A., & Shatel, R. B. (1952). The relationship between two kinds of inhibition and the amount of practice. *Journal of Experimental Psychology, 44*.

Knapp, B. N. (1963). *Skill in sport: The attainment of proficiency*. London: Routledge and Kegan Paul.

Koonce, J. M., Chambliss, D. J., & Irion, A. L. (1964). Supplementary report: Long-term reminiscence in the pursuit-rotor habit. *Journal of Experimental Psychology, 67*, 498–500.

Krathwohl, D. R., Bloom, B. S., & Masia, B. B. (1964). *Taxonomy of educational objectives, Handbook 2: The affective domain*. New York: Longman.

Lee, T. D., & Genovese, E. D. (1988). Distribution of practice in motor skill acquisition: Learning and performance effects reconsidered. *Research Quarterly for Exercise and Sport, 58*(4).

Lee, T. D., Magill, R. A., & Weeks, D. J. (1985). Influence of practice schedule on testing schema theory predictions in adults. *Journal of Motor Behavior, 17*(3), 277–287.

Lindahl, L. G. (1945). Movement analysis as an industrial training method. *Journal of Applied Psychology, 29*, 420–436.

Locatis, C. N., & Atkinson, F. D. (1984). *Media and technology for education and training*. Columbus, OH: Charles Merrill.

Locke, E. A., & Bryan, J. F. (1966). Cognitive aspects of psychomotor performance: The effects of performance goals on levels of performance. *Journal of Applied Psychology, 50*, 286–291.

Lozanov, G. (1978). *Suggestology and outlines of suggestopaedia*. New York: Gordon and Breach.

Luria, A. R. (1961). *The role of speech in the regulation of normal and abnormal behavior*. New York: Liveright.

Mager, R. E. (1968). *Developing attitude toward learning*. Belmont, CA: Fearon Publishers.

Magill, R. A., & Dowell, M. N. (1977). Serial-position effects in motor short term memory. *Journal of Motor Behavior, 9*, 319–323.

Marteniuk, R. G. (1976). *Information processing in motor skills*. New York: Holt, Rinehart, and Winston.

Martin, E. L., & Waag, W. L. (1978). *Contributions of platform motion to simulator training effectiveness: Study 1-basic contact*. Technical Report AFHRL-TR-78-15. Brooks Air Force Base, TX: Air Force Human Resources Laboratory.

McAuley, E., & Rotella, R. (1982). A cognitive-behavioral approach to enhancing gymnastic performance. *Motor Skills: Theory into Practice, 6*(2), 67–75.

McCord, B. (1976). Job instruction. In R. L. Craig (Ed.), *Training and development handbook*. New York: McGraw-Hill.

McGuigan, F. J. (1959). The effect of precision, delay and schedule of knowledge of results on performance. *Journal of Experimental Psychology, 57*, 79–84.

McGuigan, F. J., & MacCaslin, E. F. (1955). Whole and part methods in learning a perceptual motor skill. *American Journal of Psychology, 68*, 658–661.

Mechner, F. (1965). Science educational and behavioral technology. In R. Glaser (Ed.), *Teaching machines and programmed learning II: Data and directions.* Washington, DC: National Educational Association, Department of Audiovisual Instruction.

Meichenbaum, D., & Goodman, J. (1971). Training impulsive children to talk to themselves: A means of developing self control. *Journal of Abnormal Psychology, 77,* 115–126.

Micheli, C. S. (1972). *Analysis of the transfer of training, substitution and fidelity of simulation of training equipment.* TAEG Report 2. Orlando, FL: Training Analysis and Evaluation Group.

Miller, G. A. (1956). The magical number seven, plus or minus two. *Psychological Review, 63,* 81–97.

Miller, G. G. (1974). *Some considerations in the design and utilization of simulators for technical training.* Report AFHRL-TR-74-65. Brooks Air Force Base, TX: Air Force Human Resources Laboratory.

Miller, K. E. (1980). *Simulation in maintenance training.* Naval Training Equipment Center, Orlando, FL.

Montemerlo, M. D. (1977). *Training device design: The simulators versus simulation controversy.* Naval Training Equipment Center, Orlando, FL.

Naylor, J. C., & Briggs, G. E. (1963). Effects of task complexity and task organization on the relative efficiency of part and whole training methods. *Journal of Experimental Psychology, 65,* 217–224.

Newell, K. M. (1978). Some issues on action plans. In A. E. Stelmach (Ed.), *Information processing in motor control and learning.* New York: Academic Press.

Niddefer, R. M. (1976). *The inner athlete.* New York: Crowell.

Niddefer, R. M., & Deckner, C. M. (1970). A case-study of improved athletic performance following the use of relaxation procedures. *Perceptual and Motor Skills, 30,* 821–822.

Pask, G. (1960). Electronic keyboard teaching machines. In R. Glaser and A. Lumsdaine (Eds.), *Teaching machines and programmed learning, Vol. 1.* Washington, DC: National Education Association of the United States.

Pew, R. W. (1974). Human perceptual-motor performance. In B. H. Kantowitz (Ed.), *Human information processing: Tutorials in performance and cognition.* Hillsdale, NJ: Lawrence Erlbaum Associates.

Poulton, E. C. (1957). On prediction in skilled movement. *Psychological Bulletin, 54,* 467–478.

Poulton, E. C. (1966). Tracking behavior. In E. A. Bilodeau (Ed.), *Acquisition of skill.* New York: Academic Press.

Reeve, T. G., & Proctor, R. W. (1983). An empirical note on the role of verbal labels in motor short-term memory tasks. *Journal of Motor Behavior, 15*(4), 386–393.

Rogers, C. R. (1969). *Freedom to learn.* New York: Merrill.

Romiszowski, A. J. (1968). *The selection and use of teaching aids.* London: Kogan Page.

Romiszowski, A. J. (1974). *Selection and use of instructional media: A systems approach.* London: Kogan Page.

Romiszowski, A. J. (1980). A new approach to the analysis of knowledge and skills. *Aspects of Educational Technology, XIV*. London: Kogan Page.

Romiszowski, A. J. (1981). *Designing instructional systems*. London: Kogan Page.

Romiszowski, A. J. (1984). *Producing instructional systems*. London: Kogan Page.

Romiszowski, A. J. (1986). *Developing auto-instructional materials*. London: Kogan Page.

Romiszowski, A. J. (1988). *Selection and use of instructional media—Second edition*. London: Kogan Page.

Rose, C. (1985). *Accelerated learning*. Grat Missenden, UK: Accelerated Learning Systems, Ltd.

Roshal, S. M. (1961). Film mediated learning with varying representation of the task: Viewing angle portrayal of demonstration, motion and student participation. In A. A. Lumsdaine (Ed.), *Student response in programmed instruction*. Washington, DC: National Academy of Sciences, National Research Council.

Rothstein, A. L., & Arnold, R. K. (1977). Bridging the gap: Application of research on videotape feedback and bowling. *Motor Skills: Theory into Practice, 1*(1), 35–62.

Rucker, L. M. (1986). *Performance simulation: The method*. Paper presented at the Annual Meeting of the American Educational Research Association, San Francisco, April. ERIC No. ED276350.

Schmidt, R. A. (1975). A schema theory of discrete motor skill learning. *Psychological Review, 82*, 225–260.

Schon, D. A. (1983). *The reflective practitioner*. New York: Basic Books.

Schon, D. A. (1987). *Educating the reflective practitioner*. San Francisco: Jossey-Bass.

Scott, M. G. (1955). Measurement of kinesthesis. *Research Quarterly, 26*, 324–351.

Seymour, W. D. (1954a). *Industrial training for manual operations*. London: Pitman.

Seymour, W. D. (1954b). Experiments on the acquisition of industrial skills. *Occupational Psychology, 28*, 77–89.

Seymour, W. D. (1955). Experiments on the acquisition of industrial skills—part 2. *Occupational Psychology, 29*, 82–98.

Seymour, W. D. (1956). Experiments on the acquisition of industrial skills—part 3. *Occupational Psychology, 30*, 94–104.

Seymour, W. D. (1959). Experiments on the acquisition of industrial skills—part 4. *Occupational Psychology, 33*, 18–35.

Seymour, W. D. (1966). *Industrial skills*. London: Pitman.

Seymour, W. D. (1968). *Skills analysis training*. London: Pitman.

Shasby, G. (1984). Improving movement skills through language. *Motor Skills: Theory into Practice, 7*(1/2), 91–96.

Shea, J. B. (1977). Effects of labeling on motor short-term memory. *Journal of Experimental Psychology (Human Learning and Memory), 3*, 92–99.

Sim, L. J., & Stewart, C. (1984). The effects of videotape feedback on the standing broad jump performances of mildly and moderately mentally retarded adults. *Physical Educator, 4*(1), 21–29.

Singer, M. J., & Perez, R. S. (1986). A demonstration of an expert system for training device design. *Journal of Computer-Based Instruction, 13*(2).

Singer, R. N. (1982). *The learning of motor skills*. New York: Macmillan.

Singer, R. N., & Gaines, L. (1975). Effects of prompted and problem-solving approaches on learning and transfer of motor skills. *American Educational Research Journal, 12,* 395–404.

Singleton, W. T. (1959). The training of shoe machinists. *Ergonomics, 2,* 148–152.

Smith, K. U. (1966). Cybernetic theory and analysis of learning. In E. A. Bilodeau (Ed.), *Acquisition of skill.* New York: Academic Press.

Smode, A. F. (1971). *Human factors inputs to the training device design process.* Orlando, FL: Naval Training Equipment Center.

Smode, A. F. (1972), *Training device design: Human factors requirements in the technical approach.* Orlando, FL: Naval Training Equipment Center.

Software Toolworks. (1987). *Mavis Beacon teaches typing.* A typing training software package. Sherman Oaks, CA: The Software Toolworks.

Sormunen, C. (1986). A comparison of two methods for teaching keyboarding on the microcomputer to elementary grade students. *Delta Pi Epsilon Journal, 28*(2), 67–77.

Thorndike, E. L. (1903). *Educational psychology.* New York: Lemcke and Buschner.

Thorndike, E. L. (1927). The law of effect. *American Journal of Psychology, 39,* 212–222.

Thorndike, E. L. (1931). *Human learning.* New York: Appleton Century.

Tsao, J. C. (1948). Studies in spaced and massed learning: Time period and amount of practice. *Quarterly Journal of Experimental Psychology, 1,* 29–36.

Turpin, B. A. M. (1982). Enhancing skill acquisition through application of information processing. *Motor Skills: Theory into Practice, 6*(2), 77–83.

Unestahl, L. E. (1983). *The mental aspects of gymnastics.* Oregro, Sweden: VEJE Publishing.

Vygotsky, L. S. (1962). *Thought and language.* Cambridge, MA: The M.I.T. Press.

Wallace, S. A., & Hagler, R. W. (1979). Knowledge of performance and the learning of a closed motor skill. *Research Quarterly, 50,* 265–271.

Welford, A. T. (1968). *Fundamentals of skill.* London: Methuen and Company.

Welford, A. T. (1976). *Skilled performance: Perceptual and motor skills.* Glenview, IL: Scott Foresman.

Welford, A. T. (1987). On rates of improvement with practice. *Journal of Motor Behavior, 19*(3), 401–415.

Wellens, J. (1966). Swedish training system breaks the language barrier. *Industrial training international.* London, UK.

Wellens, J. (1974). *Training in physical skills.* London: Business Books.

Wheatcroft, E. (1973). *Simulators for skill.* London: McGraw-Hill.

Whitmore, J. (1988). *Superdriver: Discover the joy of driving.* Hove, UK: Fernhurst Books, for the Royal Automobile Club.

Winters, L., & Reisberg, D. (1985). *Does imagined practice help in learning a motor skill?* Paper presented at the Meeting of the Eastern Psychological Association, Boston, MA, March 21–24. ERIC No. ED261059.

Winther, K. T., & Thomas, J. R. (1981). Developmental differences in childrens' labeling of movement. *Journal of Motor Behavior, 13.*

# Chapter 4

# Learning Principles

## Michael J. Hannafin

Florida State University

and

## Simon R. Hooper

University of Minnesota

## Introduction

During the past two decades, cognitive psychology has dominated the research in learning and instruction. Many developments have significant implications for designing instructional messages. Yet, despite these advances, behavioral psychology continues to dominate the design of instructional strategies. Both behavioral and cognitive psychologies offer significant potential for instructional improvement; both require thoughtful consideration.

Although both assume an active participant, behaviorism and cognitivism presume fundamentally different roles for the learner during instruction; consequently, each implies somewhat different approaches to message design. From a behavioral perspective, the learner responds to stimuli during instruction. Through reinforcement, successive approximations of the response are transformed into the desired behavior. However, other than an overt response, learner thought is virtually ignored. Learning is assumed to be the product of causal links between instructional stimuli and student responses, which are strengthened or weakened through reinforcement. Different responses to the same stimulus are attributed to complex stimulus–response–reinforcement networks that establish conditional associations, and not to student mediation. Behavioral approaches to instruction, such as programmed instruction, are outcome-based and emphasize small step size, overt responses, and frequent reinforcement of responses.

Cognitive approaches, on the other hand, emphasize learning as a process, and the role of the student in mediating learning. The learner organizes knowledge and meaning by modifying mental representations. The metaphor of the information processing system is often used to illustrate this process. Essentially, information is selected from the environment and placed in a temporary buffer called working (or short-term) memory. Once selected, the information is subsequently either discarded or processed more completely. Encoding occurs when new and existing information is integrated in working memory and transferred into long-term (permanent) memory.

Long-term memory comprises schemata, which are organized networks of related knowledge. Each schema provides slots into which new knowledge is placed. The degree to which slots are instantiated, or filled, mediates comprehension. Furthermore, schemata provide a framework within which related, but unfamiliar, knowledge may be subsumed. Consequently, schemata are constantly refreshed and restructured through new knowledge, while additional connections among related schemata are made. Retrieval, for both responding and restructuring with new knowledge, requires activation among various related schemata which are cued based upon ongoing cognitive demands. Cognitive approaches emphasize strategies that foster meaningful learning and regulate the flow of information among the environment, working memory, and long-term memory (Hannafin & Rieber, 1989).

Many principles cut across this text, and will not be repeated here. Rather, this chapter focuses on overarching learning principles. Instead of deriving superficially distinct principles based on a particular psychological bias, we have integrated both the principles and the supporting foundations, and cited research from varied psychological orientations. The purpose of this chapter is to identify learning principles, based in various psychological paradigms, with significant potential for instructional message design.

# 1. General Principles

### 1.1. *Learning is more correctly attributable to well-orchestrated design strategies than to the inherent superiority of various media.*

The debate over the effectiveness of instructional media has escalated during the past decade. Clark (1983) suggested that little research evidence of inherent superiority of one medium over another exists. Where differences have been found they may be attributable to factors such as non-equivalence of instructional versions, novelty effects, and greater emphasis on instructional design rather than on inherent properties of the medium. These are important distinctions. Effective instruction, independent of particular media, is based upon the selection and organization of instructional strategies, and not simply the medium per se. In effect, Clark argued that the critical features of effective delivery systems are pedagogical and not technological in nature.

Consider the popular arguments in support of emerging technologies such as interactive videodisc. Advantages are often described in terms of image fidelity, speed of lesson segment access, and the capacity to let learners control their instructional sequence. All are formidable technological capabilities, yet the strengths lie not with the technological capability per se, but with the manner in which messages and strategies are invoked. Capability defines what can be, but pedagogy defines how best to utilize capabilities. It makes little sense, for example, to permit a computer to speed through difficult video segments simply because they can be accessed instantaneously. We would, as a matter of design, control access rates and lesson activities to optimize both human and technological capabilities. The manner in which capabilities are exploited is a question of pedagogy, not simply technological capacity.

Yet, considerable technological differences do exist. We cannot design messages using technological capabilities that are unavailable. Some media, for example, permit interactive control of presentation stimuli, various levels of user access, or the instantaneous storage, analysis, and retrieval of performance data; others do not. So, while similar learning effects are theoretically possible given extraordinary adaptations, it is often simply not feasible to replicate capabilities across media. The advantages of different delivery systems are often based on efficiency, logistical superiority, and availability versus the elusive best medium.

### 1.2.   The more frequent the $S{\to}R{\to}S^R$ association, the stronger the learning; the more valued the reinforcer, the stronger the stimulus control.

Thorndike's (1911) Law of Exercise states that the probability that a given stimulus (S) will elicit a particular response (R) increases in proportion to the amount of practice. Repeated pairings of foreign vocabulary terms and corresponding pictures followed by praise ($S^R$) , for example, are more likely to strengthen the association than infrequent pairings.

Craik and Lockhart (1972) distinguished between two types of repetition: maintenance and elaboration. Maintenance involves the repetition of an event without attempting to process the event at a deeper level. Activities such as drills for basic arithmetic facts or foreign language vocabulary terms typically emphasize maintenance repetition. Elaboration repetition, on the other hand, attempts to promote deeper processing by providing redundant information. Familiar, related information is typically added during instruction to enhance, extend, or modify propositions in short-term memory in order to link with knowledge already successfully encoded. For example, elaboration through face–name mnemonics, which require the learner to associate to–be–learned names with familiar objects, improved student's ability to associate artist's names with their paintings (Carney, Levin, & Morrison, 1988). Presumably, such methods transform unfamiliar stimuli into familiar cues which help to restrict the retrieval path to relevant and related propositions stored in long-term memory.

Of special significance for instruction, however, is the perceived value of the reinforcer. Students are likely to engage instruction more purposefully when the associated reinforcing stimuli are perceived as valuable. Many teenagers, for example, might perceive teacher praise as relatively worthless, but view use of the family automobile as quite valuable. The strength of the S–>R association, therefore, is mediated by the individually perceived value of the reinforcing stimulus (Gagné, 1985). Further, students will tend to seek those reinforcers thought to be most rewarding, occasionally creating problems resulting from competing stimuli. Though certain reinforcement value patterns emerge within subgroups, such as economic rewards for money–oriented learners or praise for many young learners, value is largely idiosyncratic.

Consider the following example. As designers of a mathematics unit to teach seventh graders how to divide fractions, you face an interesting dilemma. If you accept the premise that correct answers will be strengthened via reinforcement, then you must determine which reinforcers will be valued. For a few students, simply obtaining the correct answers will be intrinsically rewarding. However, many students will not find division of fractions to be inherently rewarding. Indeed, you might anticipate the need to identify rewards that are sufficiently powerful that competing responses (e.g., writing letters to friends, doodling on notepads, etc.) are offset. Determining reinforcers of sufficient value to strengthen desired performance across a group as diverse as seventh graders is no small task.

### 1.3.  *Learners with significant organized prior knowledge related to lesson content demonstrate better strategic behavior, make better lesson judgments, and assimilate new instruction more completely than learners with limited prior knowledge.*

David Ausubel (1960) was among the most prominent cognitive theorists to describe the role of prior knowledge in mediating learning. Prior knowledge is often characterized metaphorically as schemata—organized networks of prior knowledge. The availability and sophistication of various schemata enable learners to compare and contrast to-be-learned information with existing knowledge, to assimilate new information meaningfully within existing knowledge, and to continually restructure knowledge accordingly.

Likewise, the availability of related schemata improves metacognition, that is, the individual's knowledge and regulation of cognitive processes (Flavell, 1979). Metacognitive knowledge includes awareness of person, task, and strategy variables affecting cognitive processes; regulation refers to the purposeful manipulation of cognitive processes. Increases in related prior knowledge expand the foundation requisite to effective monitoring, thereby improving the individual's ability to identify and select appropriate strategies, to detect and repair unsuccessful strategies, and to otherwise make judgments as to both information needs and strategy requirements (Wagoner, 1983).

We can use the plight of the novice small business person in an advanced workshop in cost-accounting to illustrate the influence of prior knowledge. Even if we assume that no participants were familiar with the specifics of cost-accounting, experienced participants would possess considerable related prior knowledge (e.g., maintaining ledgers, reconciling quarterly statements, etc.).

Those with an accounting schema would likely be well-equipped to request specific clarification, provide conditional circumstances to test the sensitivity of cost-accounting procedures, and otherwise sort through instruction based upon their own metacognitive dictates. However, the novice would have only limited knowledge upon which to base strategic learning activities, rendering him or her much more dependent on the basic lesson structure than the other participants.

Although attempts have been made to train cognitive monitoring, programs that teach collections of learning strategies but disregard regulation are likely to prove unsuccessful. Effective training programs focus attention on the tactics of learning and promote identification of instructional goals, permit the student to experience the effects of cognitive strategies, and develop the student's metacognitive knowledge of specific learning strategies (Derry & Murphy, 1986).

### 1.4. Learning improves as the quality of cognitive engagement increases and declines as the quality of engagement decreases.

Contemporary cognitive theorists differentiate between superficial responding and deepened cognitive processing. The goal is to elevate the yield of instructional transactions by actively manipulating lesson content and concepts, and not merely responding to them. Such approaches stress qualitative over quantitative aspects of instructional transactions.

Cognitive engagement refers to "... the intentional and purposeful processing of lesson content" (Hannafin, 1989). Engagement, in effect, requires strategies that promote manipulation rather than memorization, as the means through which learners acquire both lesson knowledge and deeper conceptual insight. Engagement can be elevated through a variety of activities such as inducing cognitive dissonance, posing argumentative questions requiring the development of a supportable position, and causing learners to generate a prediction and rationale during a lesson.

Engagement methods, good and bad, can be easily illustrated through a typical introductory social studies unit on the Second World War. During typical information-intensive lectures, teachers deliver factually accurate, chrono-logically correct lectures. Some students listen, others may take notes, and a few particularly motivated students venture a question or two to clarify the lecture. Students, even the motivated ones, fail to engage the content deeply; instead, they assume a largely passive role.

In contrast, engagement can be promoted in a variety of ways. The unit might be introduced by having students discuss the circumstances leading to their most recent personal argument. Later in the unit, students might be asked to describe how the causes of World War II were like their own arguments, and how both they (individually) and nations might avoid or reconcile conflicts. Finally, students might assume roles as world leaders, and respond to the circumstances leading up to World War II by underscoring an adolescent's perspective on global conflict. In effect, students engage lesson content actively by relating it to individual experiences, thereby increasing the likelihood that knowledge will be meaningfully integrated.

### 1.5.   *Learning via multi-modal instruction improves when there is significant conceptual and temporal overlap between the information presented in each modality.*

Technological advances have increased the potential for presenting information in multiple modalities. For example, the computer is capable of the single or combined presentation of information via text, graphics, animation, video, or sound. Furthermore, there is compelling evidence to suggest that recall can be improved when information is presented simultaneously in both text and graphics rather than by either method alone.

Paivio (1979) suggested that the effectiveness of dual coding, the process of integrating existing information with new information from multiple sources, is due to the additive effect of the coding mechanisms. For example, written instruction routinely employs both textual and visual components that employ separate, but potentially complementary, coding mechanisms. Text employs a linguistic coding mechanism that encodes information in serial form; graphics employ an imagery system that may be used to encode spatial information.

It is important, however, to identify the conditions that influence the effectiveness of multiple presentations. First, information depicted in each modality must be congruent. Dual coding of text and graphics, for example, is affected by the degree to which the graphics and text reflect redundant information. Non-redundant information increases the processing requirements of the task and may hinder encoding. Second, effective multiple coding is limited to presentations employing different coding mechanisms. Dual coding is ineffective when both sources of information employ identical coding mechanisms. Identical presentation of words in sound and text, for example, should be avoided.

Figure 4.1 illustrates the complementary effects of congruent, as well as the negative effects of conflicting, text and graphics. In the first frame, the narrative identifies both important terms and functions, while the graphic identifies both the position of the key terms and the manner in which air flow is influenced by the aerodynamics of the rocket. The second frame, using the same "good" graphic, presents text which is only incidentally supported in the visual. In fact, the narrative requires illustration not provided; in this case, the graphic will likely interfere with, rather than complement, the text.

### 1.6.   *Meaningfully learned knowledge is more retrievable, durable, and generalizable than knowledge that is not meaningful.*

Cognitive researchers generally agree that learners store the meaning rather than the exact content of information. Yet designers rarely make learning meaningful by organizing information to support integration within the learner's unique cognitive structures. Instead instruction often focuses on low-level manipulations, characterized by the designer's judgments of the structure of lesson content.

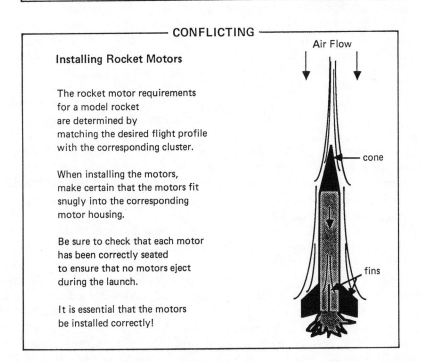

**CONGRUENT**

Air Flow

**Drag and Rockets:**
**Functional Resistance**

The flow of air across
a solid object creates drag—
a type of resistance or friction.

The aerodynamic properties
of the rocket not
only reduce drag,
but use some of the resistance
to stabilize the flight.

The cone causes drag to be
distributed evenly throughout
the body of the rocket. The fins
then direct the air equally around
the base to create identical resistance,
thereby stabilizing the flight.

cone

fins

**CONFLICTING**

Air Flow

**Installing Rocket Motors**

The rocket motor requirements
for a model rocket
are determined by
matching the desired flight profile
with the corresponding cluster.

When installing the motors,
make certain that the motors fit
snugly into the corresponding
motor housing.

Be sure to check that each motor
has been correctly seated
to ensure that no motors eject
during the launch.

It is essential that the motors
be installed correctly!

cone

fins

**Figure 4.1.** Congruent versus conflicting use of text and graphics.

Mayer (1984) described three methods through which lesson information may be meaningfully learned: selection, organization, and integration. For learning to take place, information must initially be perceived or selected. Perceived information must then be organized in working memory before it is stored in long-term memory. The nature of the organization in working memory determines the meaningfulness of the learning. When a lesson offers little guidance as to the organization of the content, and the individual is unable to organize the content successfully, then only rote learning will likely occur. If the learner organizes the information by identifying logical relationships within the content, then deeper and more meaningful learning may ensue. For learning to be completely meaningful, however, organization must involve integration of organized information within existing, familiar knowledge.

Consider an example of meaningful learning of a simple economics concept: competition. At the simplest level, selection, a student might be taught the definition of competition, and the concepts of market share and profit motive. Selection activities might center principally around identification of relevant features; only nominal meaning has been assigned. Subsequent activities might then be designed to aid in organizing various aspects of the lesson. For example, the effects of increases and decreases in market share on net profits might be illustrated. The illustration should help to clarify the internal connectedness among various aspects of the lesson content. Finally, competition might be likened to other concepts already familiar to the student. Market share might be described metaphorically as economic politics, where success depends on attaining the support of the highest percentage of the voting public. Alternatively, profit motive might be equated with Darwin's "survival of the fittest" thesis. At this level, competition concepts are integrated with existing knowledge, resulting in learning that is most meaningful.

Recently, Mayer (1989) described a series of experiments that increased the meaningfulness of instruction. Conceptual models, like metaphors, are essentially simplified representations of relationships among more complex lesson concepts. For students with low related prior knowledge, conceptual models were found to improve conceptual retention and problem solving. Models help the learner to build a mental framework which focuses attention on relevant lesson content and provides an "engine" which can be used to generate solutions to unfamiliar problems.

Hannafin and Hughes (1986) demonstrated how a visual model, an aggregate time-thrust curve (a graph depicting the thrust produced by each of a series of model rocket motors), could be used to vary the flight profile of a rocket (see Figure 4.2). The curve illustrates the interrelationship among several concepts central to model-rocketry: thrust, burn duration, and flight profile. The model depicts visually the flight profile resulting from clusters of rockets of varied properties with a verbal statement suggesting that aggregate time/thrust curves essentially represent the overall flight profile resulting from various rocket clusters. This model provides an accurate and concise, yet relatively complete, representation of complex interactive relationships described by Mayer.

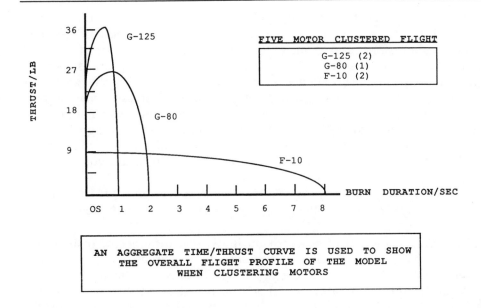

**Figure 4.2.** Conceptual model illustrating complex interrelationships among related factors (Hannafin & Hughes, 1986).

### 1.7. *Learning improves as depth of processing increases; learning further improves as the nature of the processing becomes increasingly relevant to the instructional task.*

Craik and Lockhart (1972) proposed that information is processed at different levels, or depths, and results in memory traces of different strength. Semantic processing, which focuses on the meaning of a task, is assumed to be encoded more deeply than processing that focuses only on the verbatim or literal aspects of a task. Information which is processed deeply is subsequently more retrievable than information processed shallowly.

Anderson and Reder (1979) suggested that the effects of depth of processing can be explained in terms of elaboration. Effective processing is a function of the number of elaborations generated during learning, not semantic encoding. Information is most retrievable when the learner generates many meaningful elaborations, since elaborations provide redundancy: as redundancy increases, recall increases.

To facilitate recall, elaborations should be concrete and based on the learner's prior experience. In the model rocketry lesson, elaborations can be provided to increase the meaningful integration of the concepts. For example, the relationship between thrust and burn duration might be likened to the effects of fast and slow methods of air discharge on the flight of a balloon. Whether released rapidly or slowly, the same amount of air escapes. Differences will be observed in the initial speed of the balloon and the duration of the balloon's flight. This elaboration is concrete and relevant to virtually all students' experiences, while being a reasonable characterization of the relationship between thrust and burn duration.

Morris, Bransford, and Franks (1977) described the concept of "transfer appropriate processing" to characterize optimum processing levels. Transfer appropriate processing matches processing activities with the goals and objectives of a learning task. Thus, although semantic processing may improve recall, at times non-semantic processing may be more appropriate. For example, there is little sense to testing vocabulary meaning after a foreign language pronunciation lesson. Clearly, the semantic meaning of the vocabulary words would have little to do with the ability to correctly pronounce the words.

### 1.8.  Instructional "power" often compensates both for learner differences and the influence of adjunct lesson strategies.

Through the myriad of research on individual differences, instructional designers have sought reliable, time-tested principles for how best to accommodate individual differences. Though intuitively attractive, however, much of the aptitude-treatment and achievement-treatment interaction (ATI) research is largely inconclusive (Tobias, 1976). Indeed, the quest has yielded few reliable guidelines regarding how to accommodate individual differences such as learner preference. On the contrary, there is evidence that students often learn best from instruction they prefer the least (Clark, 1982).

Why have there been so few reliable guidelines? Often the research on learner aptitudes and adjunct lesson strategies is conducted under controlled laboratory conditions. These conditions often do not represent, nor can they be replicated in, real-life settings, where the myriad of factors influencing learning is apparent. Controlled research studies typically isolate the effects of particular aptitudes or strategies rather than examine the effects interactively and collectively with other typical methods.

Finally, many strategies simply lack the singular power to influence learning significantly in typical lesson designs. The effects of individual strategies are rarely additive—they do not individually account for significant performance variance when used in combinations. Mental imagery, for example, may yield significant laboratory differences that, when combined with other strategies typically employed in practice, are partially or completely obscured. In practice, their contributions to learning are often nominal.

### 1.8a.  The contribution of adjunct instructional strategies increases as lesson organization decreases.

Mayer (1984) provided perhaps a realistic assessment of the contribution of adjunct instructional strategies. Adjunct strategies tend to supply organization not inherent within the lesson or otherwise obvious to learners. In doing so, they may be especially useful in helping the student to select and organize relevant lesson content not yet apparent.

The relationship between lesson organization and the value of adjunct activities is shown in Figure 4.3. Where lesson organization and activities are

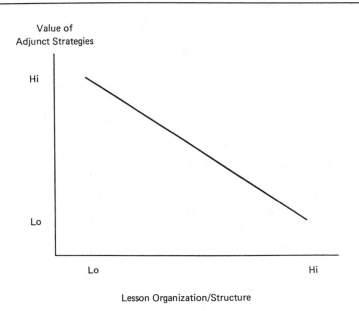

**Figure 4.3.** Relationship between lesson structure and the value of adjunct strategies.

cogent, the necessity for many adjunct activities decreases (though will not likely interfere if well designed); where lesson organization is weak, however, the activities are likely to support learning.

Another way to view adjunct activities is that they provide methods to extend or alter how lesson content is processed. In poorly designed lessons, such activities may guide the learner to form correct or desirable associations. Even in well-designed instruction, activities can be used to introduce related information not embedded within the lesson, to provide metaphors and examples likely to solidify lesson concepts, to prompt learners to engage in metacognitive activities, or to elicit learner-based elaborations related to the lesson.

It is possible, for example, to supply prequestions that cause learners to direct greater attention to activity-relevant knowledge than normally allocated. Activities can also be designed to prompt the student to predict what will occur next in a passage or experiment, thereby causing the student to generate an individually relevant perspective which serves to elaborate subsequent instruction. In each case, the activity can alter how, and what, information is selected by the student without altering basic lesson information.

> ***1.8b.*** *The influence of many individual differences decreases as the availability of generally powerful strategies increases.*

The search for truly individualized instruction has typically ventured into dynamic assessments of learner preferences, cognitive states, and cognitive styles. To many, especially those interested in artificial intelligence-based (AI) applications of computer-based instruction, the capability to alter lesson strategies dynamically seems the most essential manifestation of truly individualized instruction.

Yet, apart from extreme individual differences, such as blindness, psychomotor impairments, and deafness, many learner differences and preferences are of substantially less consequence in practice than in theory (cf. Cronbach & Snow, 1977). This may be caused by an inability to accurately identify truly important differences, limited understanding of the contextual conditions affecting such differences, poorly conceived adaptations based upon such differences, or the comparative impotence of many individual differences in the presence of generally powerful strategies. In fact, some have argued that research on aptitude-treatment interactions (ATI) may be most fruitful in identifying how best to mitigate, rather than adapt to, learner differences (Jonassen, 1982).

### 1.9.  Learning improves as the amount of mental effort invested by learners increases.

Although research supporting the differential learning effectiveness of media per se may be suspect, evidence suggests that different media may influence the amount of effort a student is willing to invest. Salomon (1984) reported that the amount of invested mental effort (AIME) in a task varies interactively with the perceived demand characteristics of a task (PDC) and student's perceived self-efficacy (PSE). Children with high PSE invest greater effort when tasks are perceived more as challenging than simple, while children with low PSE invest greater effort when goals are perceived as less challenging but attainable. Learning from a book, for example, is generally high in PDC, while learning from television has low PDC. Children with high PSE, therefore, may invest more effort and achieve greater success learning from a book (high PDC) than from television (low PDC), while the pattern may be reversed for children with low PSE.

The relationship among AIME, PDC, and PSE is shown in Figure 4.4. A typical lesson focusing on the circulatory system must be completed by students of vastly different PSEs. Materials are needed to depict the flow of blood from the arteries, through the chambers and valves of the heart, and back throughout the body. Three candidate media systems might include a videotape lesson, a computer-animated depiction, or a paper-and-pencil workbook. Apart from differences in availability and the cost to design, develop, and install each option, the varied student perceptions of each system warrant consideration. High PSE students might perceive video as low in cognitive demand, and invest relatively little mental effort; conversely, they might consider both the computer and workbook lessons as more difficult, and invest more effort. Low PSE students, on the other hand, are more likely to view the *task* of learning about the circulatory system as difficult rather than the media used to depict it. They need to perceive the task as attainable irrespective of specific media.

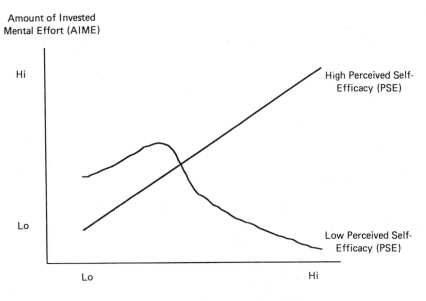

**Figure 4.4.** Relationship among AIME, PSE, and PDC.

# 2. Learner Attributes, Characteristics, and Strategies

### 2.1. *Meaningful learning can be facilitated by generative activities that help the learner to process and encode lesson content uniquely.*

Despite recent advances in cognitive psychology, most instruction still focuses principally on designer-centered strategies. Typical is the emphasis on mathemagenic strategies which supply considerable external structure to support the attainment of specific learning objectives (Rothkopf, 1970). Mathemagenic activities include embedded questions related to lesson objectives, practice activities designed to promote proficiency, and adjunct strategies such as mnemonics designed to improve memory for key lesson concepts. Though such approaches are most certainly successful in imparting a lesson designer's view of lesson structure and priorities, they do little inherently to optimize the unique processing and encoding capabilities of learners.

Generative strategies, on the other hand, assume that meaning is constructed uniquely by the learner (Wittrock, 1974). Generative approaches attempt to draw existing knowledge into short-term memory to aid in the processing of new information. For example, students might be asked to provide an example from their own experience to illustrate problems dealing with sales agents, or to draw upon personal beliefs to characterize the merits and problems of a free enterprise system. In effect, generative approaches rely on the learner to individually mediate meaning rather than to assume that supplied meaningfulness can be transmitted to all learners.

### 2.1a. *Learner-centered instructional activities, such as notetaking, can improve the acquisition, retention, and meaningfulness of learning.*

Many activities, including those invoked spontaneously by learners as well as those prompted externally during a lesson, rely on the individual to identify which strategies to apply, as well as how and when to apply them. These activities represent a philosophical shift in the locus of responsibility for assigning meaning to knowledge. Such strategies differ fundamentally from imposed, structured lesson activities in that the learner dictates the nature of the activity as well as the lesson content to be manipulated.

Notetaking, for example, permits the student to determine which information is to be selected and how it is to be processed. Notetaking research can be classified into two related categories: those concerned with the external storage functions of notes and those concerned with the encoding functions of notetaking (Rickards & Friedman, 1978). Essentially, the external storage function provides a vehicle to review important information that the student is unable to encode successfully during instruction. The information may be subsequently reviewed in order to reconstruct meaning. For example, lectures in first-year medical school courses tend to be very dense informationally, and proceed at an unusually rapid rate. All information cannot be effectively assimilated during the lecture, so students are often advised to record rudimentary notes during lectures, and to subsequently complete and review notes after the lecture. The notes, in effect, serve as an external buffer where information is stored in order to reduce ongoing cognitive load.

The encoding functions presumably aid the student in meeting identified knowledge requirements (Barnett, DiVesta, & Rogozinski, 1981) and in enhancing depth of processing of selected information (Bretzing & Kulhavy, 1981). Rickards and Friedman (1978) suggested that generative notetaking increases the amount and nature of information encoded during learning. Students appear more likely to recall important information selected in their notes, and are able to evaluate the meaning of information with the fuller context available after instruction. This also tends to reduce the ongoing cognitive demands to a degree, while permitting non-linear reconstruction of facts and events presented initially in linear form.

Generative notetaking may also promote the integration of information within existing knowledge structures in long-term memory (Peper & Mayer, 1978). Presumably, students identify and select information based upon a schema-driven need to know. The selected information is subsequently elaborated and used to restructure related knowledge, thereby improving integration with existing knowledge.

**2.1b. *Elaborating on lesson content improves both the meaningfulness of learning and the retrievability of knowledge.***

A compelling body of research supports the value of elaboration for the acquisition and recall of information (e.g., Gagné, 1978). Techniques to promote elaboration include asking learners to summarize information in their own words and relate information to their prior experiences. Information is presumably stored as propositions in interconnected networks. When information is encoded, new propositions are added to the network. The greater the number of elaborations associated with a specific proposition, the easier it is to recall that proposition from LTM. Elaboration facilitates retrieval by establishing alternate retrieval pathways, thus improving the spread of activation. Additionally, it provides information from which an answer can be constructed (Gagné, 1985).

The precision of an elaboration has an important effect on recall. Effective elaborations interconnect the information to be recalled. Such structures, termed precise elaborations, are more effective than global elaborations for improving near-transfer recall (Gagné, 1985). Suppose, for example, one wanted to remember the sentence: "The strong man won the prize." One elaboration is: "The strong man won the first prize"; a more precise elaboration is: "The strong man won the weightlifting prize." The second elaboration is more precise in that it connects an attribute of the man (strong) with the ramification of the attribute (weightlifting prize). In effect, precise elaborations restrict the spread of activation to closely related propositional networks—those most relevant to recall under known or immediately related retrieval contexts (Stein *et al.*, 1982).

# 3. Organization

**3.1. *Concrete information is more easily depicted, more imagable by learners, better remembered, and more consistently interpreted than abstract information.***

Generally, concrete information is more readily represented and less susceptible to misinterpretation than abstract lesson content (Hannafin, 1988). To the degree lesson concepts permit, instruction intent is generally less ambiguous using concrete versus abstract images.

Several researchers have documented differences in memorability and imagability. Paivio, Yuille, and Madigan (1968), for example, studied the concreteness and mental imagery of several hundred nouns. They concluded that a strong correlation existed: as concreteness increases, imagability likewise increases; as concreteness decreases, imagability decreases.

The concrete term "house," as shown in Figure 4.5, can be readily and unambiguously depicted. Others may draw a somewhat different house or include different details, but the basic structure will be virtually unanimously

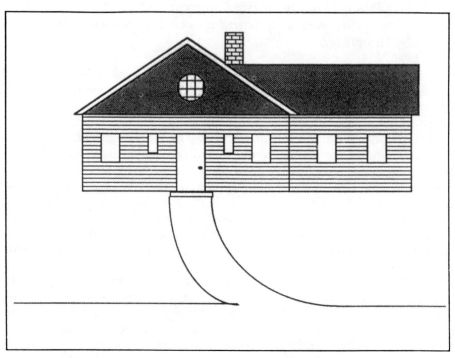

**Figure 4.5.** Picturability of concrete "House" and abstract "Magic."

interpreted as a house. On the other hand, the more abstract term "magic" is more difficult to represent unambiguously. Some might interpret the illustration as "surprise," which might parallel certain attributes of the intended term, or "genie," which may only reflect concrete properties of the illustration. The problem is not simply limited to imagability, but with the potential for enduring misinterpretations as well (Hannafin, 1988).

### 3.2. Generally, lesson-centered strategies should be employed for unfamiliar content; as familiarity increases, strategies should become more learner-centered.

Lesson-centered strategies, like mathemagenic strategies, are designed to promote mastery of lesson content. When lesson content is unfamiliar, few supporting cognitive structures are available to support the induction of new knowledge. Lesson strategies typically focus on acquiring essential information, attaining basic competence, and avoiding enduring misconceptions (Spiro, Feltovich, & Coulson, 1990).

Once familiarity has been attained, however, learners possess the knowledge and competence needed to gain deeper and more uniquely assigned meaning. Schemata are available to aid in the selection and processing of appropriate lesson elements. Consequently, learners are better able to supply the needed cognitive support and to integrate new knowledge meaningfully. Strategies at this stage should capitalize on unique processing potential.

Consider what happens when an entry-level airline mechanic trainee begins initial training. There are many highly standardized methods for jet-engine maintenance which must be learned and demonstrated. These methods are typically taught fairly explicitly, and are highly structured. This is due to the assumption that the content will be unfamiliar, and trainees are unlikely to generate appropriate strategies on their own. In addition, there are obvious risks involved with inadequate quality control. Proven methods are likely to be vastly superior to the hit-or-miss methods of student-centered, trial-and-error learning.

On the other hand, as the trainee acquires experience and high degrees of proficiency, related content becomes much more familiar. As subsequent training is provided, he or she can draw upon experiences that parallel new information, thereby improving the potential meaningfulness of the knowledge. The trainee can draw on both content closely related to new training and individual experiences that can be applied to make effective choices in strategy selection and use.

### 3.3. The amount of information that can be presented simultaneously increases as ability, maturity, motivation, and related prior knowledge increase.

Processing ability is believed to be limited, in part, by the capacity of working memory. The capacity of working memory is limited to approximately seven discrete pieces of information (Miller, 1956), each of which may represent a single idea or may be a cue which activates a complex set of organized information.

Further, encoding has temporal requirements that vary according to both familiarity and task complexity. Consequently, working memory acts like a narrow funnel to broker the flow of information between the environment and long-term memory: if the flow is moderate, then more information can be processed; if overfilled, then only part can be processed and the rest of the information overflows and is lost. It is vital, therefore, to regulate the flow of information during instruction and to ensure that important information is processed appropriately.

Several factors influence the probability that lessons will be processed appropriately. Though age and maturity are often identified, global factors such as ability and prior knowledge exert significant control. Capable learners have evolved more refined strategies for coping with learning, and are generally better than less able learners at distinguishing important from unimportant information. Given extensive prior knowledge, learners are better able to assimilate new information readily while integrating new knowledge within rich, intact schemata. Cognitive load is minimized by the familiarity of the new content (Hannafin & Rieber, 1989) and the establishment of implicit schema-driven knowledge needs that aid in both selection and integration (Pichert & Anderson, 1977).

### 3.4. Logically organized text is better remembered than poorly organized text.

Researchers have manipulated numerous presentation variables to improve learning efficiency and effectiveness. Typical is research that attempts to increase reading speed during instruction. However, improvements in reading speed are often unrelated to learning per se. Instead, effectively designed text helps the learner to organize and locate information, and to facilitate the flow of information between short- and long-term memory.

Two presentation strategies that may have important effects on learning are text segmentation and conceptual chunking (see Figure 4.6). Text segmentation refers to the manner in which lesson text is displayed. Segmented text is broken up into meaningful, coherent phrases. Non-segmented text appears as a continuous flow of information across a page or screen, with line endings determined arbitrarily by the space available. Effectively segmented text improves encoding and retrieving and is more easily integrated than poorly segmented text (Frase & Schwartz, 1979).

Chunking is the organization of conceptually related blocks of information. Effective conceptual chunking reflects the optimal amount of related information that can be presented before working memory is overtaxed. Typically, chunks of related content are organized based upon the conceptual overlap of the available content, the familiarity of the lesson content, and an estimate of the complexity of the content. As conceptual overlap and lesson familiarity increase, the size of the chunk increases; as complexity increases, the size of the chunk is generally reduced. Activities are then routinely designed to facilitate the encoding of lesson chunks. Instruction that has been organized, or chunked, helps to control the flow of information into working memory. In addition, it promotes effective

---

┌─────────────── Segmented and Continuous Text ───────────────┐

This is segmented text.
In segmentation,
text is broken up into meaningful phrases.


This is not segmented because there is no evidence of
meaningful phrases, and no attention to the con-
tiguity of related idea units is evident.

└─────────────────────────────────────────────────────────────┘

┌─────────────────────── Chunked Text 1 ───────────────────────┐


Chunking refers to the amount of related information
that can be readily encoded
before working memory becomes overtaxed.


Each idea unit corresponds to a lesson chunk.


└─────────────────────────────────────────────────────────────┘

┌─────────────────────── Chunked Text 2 ───────────────────────┐

Chunking is affected
by the conceptual density of the lesson content
as well as the familiarity of lesson content.



As familiarity increases, chunks can increase.


As familiarity decreases, chunks are generally smaller.

└─────────────────────────────────────────────────────────────┘

**Figure 4.6.** Examples of segmentation and chunking.

encoding by simplifying the selection task while reducing extraneous or potentially distracting elements.

# 4. Sequence of Instruction

### 4.1.   *From an instructional perspective, the nature of learner control is of substantially greater consequence than whether or not control of lesson features is provided.*

Though considerable interest has been evident in providing learners with control over instruction—especially in computer-based instruction (CBI)— research in learner control has generally proven equivocal (Steinberg, 1977). Presumably, given control over their instruction, learners should be able to work at their own pace, seek additional help as and when needed, and otherwise maneuver through instruction in ways that uniquely match their individual learning needs and styles.

Unfortunately, learners frequently make poor instructional choices. Students who chronically fail in mathematics are unlikely to make good math instruction decisions. They are unlikely to estimate correctly whether practice is needed, the number and difficulty of the problems to be attempted, and when sufficient mastery has been attained to end the lesson. They simply lack the requisite knowledge needed to make successful metacognitive judgments related to mathematics learning and instruction (Garhart & Hannafin, 1986). Interestingly, even successful learners often make poor choices, tending to spend more time on practice and review than needed (cf. Tennyson, 1984).

Much of the attention to learner control has been misguided. Typically, learner control has been viewed as a singular entity without regard for important differences in *what* is controlled. Some aspects of control affect instructional sequence, others permit access to lesson support information, and still others support learner-centered activities.

Control of sequence-altering options, such as to quit a lesson, skip instructional segments, or alter the sequence of instruction, are of substantial potential consequence to intended learning outcomes. Ineffective learners can compound the task difficulty by making unwise or ill-conceived choices. Learner control of access to non-sequence features such as help segments, however, seems unlikely to hinder learning. To the contrary, such options offer considerable potential with only modest associated costs and risks.

### 4.2.   *Both task and learner attributes influence the locus of instructional control.*

Lesson control exists along a continuum from lesson-imposed (or external) to learner (internal) controlled. Complete lesson control involves the regulation of all execution or sequence decisions. This can simply be a linear design, but often it is manifested through rigid, imposed performance standards. Learner controlled instruction allows potential control of lesson features, options, and attributes such as lesson sequence, pace, and the number of questions to complete during instruction (Hannafin, 1984).

Most instruction is neither completely learner nor lesson controlled, but includes features of both. Adaptive CBI control strategies, for example, prescribe learning sequences that are continuously updated to accommodate the learner's changing needs, ongoing performance, and unique background (Ross & Morrison, 1988). Advisement is similar to adaptive control. However, instead of imposing control decisions, the learner is advised as to the best options given his or her current status (Tennyson, 1984). Thus, the independence of the learner is maintained while simultaneously providing information to guide effective decision making. The task for the designer, therefore, is to match lesson control options with the demands of the lesson content and the academic history of the learner.

> *4.2a. Generally, imposed lesson control is appropriate when learners are immature and lack requisite prior knowledge, or when eternally imposed performance sequences are required.*

In general, imposed lesson control becomes more necessary as learners are less familiar with lesson content. Students who are unfamiliar with lesson content have little capacity to identify the implicit structure of learning tasks and are often poor judges of ongoing comprehension. Consequently, they select ineffective learning strategies and make poor sequencing decisions (Gay, 1987). It is difficult, for example, for trainees in electronics to select which among a series of instructional segments are needed prior to assembling a circuit board; they have little experience with the required task and little related knowledge to support the decision.

Likewise, imposed control may be warranted when highly explicit procedures must be learned due to the requirement for exactness. In the previous example, electronics trainees needed to know not only what information was required but also the order in which assembly steps must be taken. While it may be of some interest to determine the steps through discovery, it is often unwise and inefficient to have students stumble through unspecified activities. Indeed it is likely to be a source of considerable frustration to the student.

> *4.2b. Learner control is generally appropriate when learners are more able, possess significant related knowledge, or when the learning task has no rigid hierarchical or procedural requirements.*

In many cases, learners possess sufficiently refined skills, knowledge, and abilities that they can successfully assume a significant degree of control over lesson activities and sequence. Able learners often apply highly evolved strategies during lessons. These strategies enable them to identify unique information needs as well as the appropriate methods for addressing the identified needs. By placing more control in their hands, they are able to acquire needed knowledge more meaningfully and efficiently without the structure imposed by a lesson designer (Hannafin, 1984).

Likewise, many learning tasks do not have rigid hierarchical or procedural requirements. It is unnecessary, in many cases, to enforce a particular sequence since it is not an integral part of either the performance requirements or the instructional sequence.

Take, for example, the teaching of early Roman history. It may make sense to employ a chronological strategy, or perhaps a lesson might be organized according to the reigns of various Caesars. However, it is unlikely that a single, absolute sequence is essential. It might be best to permit students to determine their own "best way" to organize and sequence the lesson content.

On the other hand, externally imposed requirements may dictate lesson sequence, or the task itself may be inherently hierarchical or procedural. Some assembly tasks, for example, require that skills be developed in a prescribed order; many intellectual skills require that enabling knowledge, fundamental to comprehending higher level skills, be acquired beforehand.

### 4.2c. *Adaptive lesson control may be used to accommodate individual differences and variations in acquisition rate.*

Adaptive designs essentially adjust features such as the amount, pace, and difficulty of instruction based upon unique learner needs (Carrier & Jonassen, 1988; Tennyson, 1984). Though recent developments emphasize computer-based instruction, adaptive environments have been designed for non-computer media as well. Early programmed texts, interrupted video, and print instructional materials, for example, employed lesson-prompted, learner-implemented directions. Such lessons might direct students with poor test scores to review materials, or might recommend different follow-up activities based upon ongoing performance, interests, or backgrounds.

Substantial heterogeneity in target populations can be accommodated by adapting to criterion-based individual differences. One common strategy is to adjust for entry differences by assessing pre-lesson knowledge and adapting starting points accordingly. Pretests or skill inventories, for example, are often administered in order to determine which lesson segments are unnecessary, and where to begin lesson activities. The premise is that adaptations can be made by identifying existing lesson-relevant knowledge in advance, and providing instruction only as needed.

Differences in acquisition rate can also be accommodated via adaptation. Adaptive control attempts to optimize the time spent on instruction, as well as the amount of instruction provided. Successful learners, for example, might require fewer examples and practice items, comprehend denser instructional chunks, or require less explanation and guidance than unsuccessful learners. Adaptive designs permit such variations to be identified dynamically, and appropriate instructional adaptations to be made accordingly.

Ross and Morrison (1988) described a series of contextual adaptations designed to promote meaningful learning during computer-based instruction. Background information is obtained from each student, and is subsequently integrated within the lesson for individual students. For instance, individual students might be queried as to birthdate, favorite song, preferred music, and so on. The information could then be introduced into a lesson shell, which customizes the context of the lesson with the information provided by each student.

> **4.2d. *Advisement strategies should be used to provide students with the information needed to make informed lesson control choices.***

Whereas learner control promotes independent learning, it does so with the risk of ineffective learner choices; adaptive instruction promotes control of content, but does little to cultivate individual responsibility or accommodate learner choices. Advisement helps to promote learner independence without relinquishing the benefits associated with adaptive control. Advisement provides the supporting information needed to make effective lesson choices while permitting control over lesson sequence decisions. Interestingly, when given suggestions during computer-based instruction, students virtually always heed the advice (Hannafin & Colamaio, 1987).

Several types of advice can be provided. Tennyson and Christensen (1988) provided feedback of current versus required performance requirements with advice as to the best choice for the next section. Advice can also assist the learner to select examples or practice problems of varied difficulty, to recommend to repeat or skip lesson segments based upon ongoing performance, or to identify strategies to remember lesson content.

# 5. Instructional Strategies

## 5.1. *Orienting activities influence intended as well as incidental learning.*

Orienting activities are "... mediator(s) through which new information is presented to the learner" (Hannafin & Hughes, 1986, p. 239). As such, learner perceptions are shaped by the perspective induced by the orienting activity. Orienting activities can be either affective or content-based, depending on the degree to which lesson content, per se, is manipulated during the activity. In addition, the degree to which the orienting perspective is either broadened or limited affects how subsequent information is selected and organized.

### *5.1a. Affective orienting activities heighten generalized arousal, which increases the probability that subsequent attention will be improved.*

One common goal of instruction is to increase the sense of importance, relevance, or urgency of forthcoming instruction. Motivation theorists as well as everyday teachers have long cautioned about the importance of ensuring that learners are in the "right frame of mind" prior to starting lesson activities. Affective orienting activities emphasize techniques that promote generalized, rather than content-specific, orienting perspectives (Hannafin, 1987). They attempt to prime the learner affectively, to cause the student to engage the lesson willingly, and to establish the motivational conditions of learning prior to instruction.

On the other hand, though arousal is necessary, it is an insufficient condition for effective learning. Simply becoming more excited prior to instruction will not ensure that the subsequent instruction will be engaged appropriately. The activity must promote interest without distracting from the instruction that follows. Affective orienting activities can either enhance or hamper learning, depending upon the degree to which the resulting arousal induces the student to engage the subsequent task.

Consider, for example, affective methods for orienting students to a home economics lesson on kitchen safety. Students might view a videotape featuring an interview with a child who recently injured an arm as the result of parental oversight. This might be accompanied by narrative on the incidence of serious injuries in the home and the responsibility of adults to prevent such accidents. The goal is obviously to increase the student's willingness to engage instruction by heightening arousal relative to the lesson.

On the other hand, students may become aroused by a clever animation sequence, featuring music and humor, that is contextually unrelated to the lesson. To the tune of a popular hard-rock tune, a familiar cartoon character races across the television screen and is struck in the face with a cream pie. Students might find this introduction quite amusing, but it is unlikely that they will be aroused productively for the kitchen safety lesson. Their arousal has resulted in elevated expectations unrelated to, even inconsistent with, the lesson. Expectancies may be set for highly visual, music-intensive instruction whereas the topic, kitchen safety, is completely incompatible. Simply elevating arousal, in the absence of an appropriate orienting perspective, is unlikely to improve, and may actually hamper, learning (Hannafin, 1987).

### *5.1b. Explicit, content-based activities tend to promote intended but limit incidental learning while more integrative, contextual activities can support both intended and incidental learning.*

Content-based orienting activities influence how and what a learner perceives and processes. Highly explicit activities, such as pre-instructional objectives, influence the perceived importance attributed to related information in very specific ways. Learners tend to use the explicit framework to identify objective-relevant content and to reject lesson content not required to address the objective. The more specific the orienting objective, the more focused the learner can become in selecting the intended information. However, as specificity increases, it becomes less likely that the student will retain incidental, but potentially objective-relevant, information (Hannafin & Hughes, 1986).

Cognitive orienting activities, such as advance organizers, attempt to stimulate, induce, or provide a framework to facilitate subsumption of lesson information. Cognitive orienting activities provide a more abstract and non-specific perspective than behavioral activities. They rely more on individual learners to create an anticipatory perspective than on the specific organization and content of the lesson. Presumably, schemata will be instantiated that are relevant to the activity. The resulting knowledge will be integrated within more inclusive schemata than through simple memorization.

Integrative orienting activities often promote learning of both higher level learning and supporting information. Such activities may, for instance, pose a broadly defined problem, but cue the learner to the types of information required to resolve the problem.

In a simulated economics lesson, for example, many content-based methods for orienting students can be developed. The student could be given very explicit prequestions to be answered during the lesson, such as: "Which three nations have the largest annual Gross National Product (GNP)?" Students would likely find this activity useful in sorting through subsequent instruction to locate intended information, but might be less likely to remember important related lesson content such as the similarities and differences among the economies of the nations. On the other hand, a cognitive orienting activity, such as describing the experience of purchasing an identical item for significantly less money at one store versus another, could be used to induce individual perspectives related to the role of competition on pricing.

An integrative orienting activity might prompt the student to observe the effects of various increases and decreases in supply and demand factors on cost, and to subsequently hypothesize a relationship between supply and demand of given commodities. The broad problem (generating and supporting the hypothesis) requires attention to particular mediating factors, in this case those related to variations in supply and demand.

### 5.2. *The acquisition of unfamiliar content can be improved via familiar examples, analogies, and metaphors, while such strategies are less essential for familiar content.*

Often, learners possess organized knowledge that supports learning in ways not possible through imposed strategies. Students assimilate new knowledge within highly evolved supporting schemata, knowledge that provides a powerful, fertile framework for assigning meaning to new lesson content (Rumelhart & Norman, 1981). In such cases, learners are able to associate meaning more or less instantaneously within existing knowledge, and do not require extensive assistance to comprehend.

In other cases, however, lesson content is sufficiently unrelated to existing knowledge, or the relationships are not readily apparent, that existing cognitive structures are of limited help. Learners are unable to retrieve relevant knowledge, or to integrate new knowledge effectively within existing schemata. Unfamiliar lesson content benefits from strategies that concretize and organize lesson content. Strategies such as metaphors allow the mapping of parallel properties of familiar, but unrelated, concepts to new knowledge (Becker & Carrier, 1985).

The metaphors of the heart as a pump and the electrical system of a house as the nerve network of the body have been used widely. In essence, the metaphor serves as a conceptual model which maps the features of a known concept to one not yet known. Obviously, one who already knows about the heart or the nerves does not need the familiarizing function of the metaphor. One who is not acquainted with them, however, will receive familiar, albeit simplified, models to both instantiate relevant schemata and revise and restructure knowledge about the heart and nerves.

### 5.3. The type and location of embedded questions influence both what information is selected and how it is processed.

Questions have the potential to mediate subsequent instruction, to organize previous instruction, or to restructure existing knowledge depending upon position and processing requirements (Hamilton, 1985). Different types of questions pose unique processing requirements, ranging from recall of simple verbatim responses for incomplete sentences to deeper analytical processing for response to compare and contrast questions. Further, question placement (i.e., prior to versus after corresponding instruction) can influence both which information is selected and how the information is subsequently processed.

### 5.3a. Prequestions tend to focus students toward question-relevant content, while postquestions tend to aid in organizing and reconstructing lesson events.

Prequestions both establish expectancy and aid in selection. Very specific, content-based prequestions limit the relevance of lesson content to those elements required to answer the question. Likewise, prequestions of a more integrative nature, those requiring that subordinate detail be comprehended in order to provide higher-order answers, aid the student in organizing incoming information around established themes or perspectives (Reynolds & Anderson, 1982).

Postquestions also promote organization, but they do so by causing the learner to establish relatedness not immediately apparent among lesson elements (Rickards, 1979). Inferences, for example, are often formed when a learner is prompted to answer a question based upon two or more propositions encoded without established retrieval pathways. Once the relationship has been prompted through the question, lesson knowledge can be reorganized, schemata can be restructured, and new meaning can be reconstructed.

### 5.3b. Question structure influences both the response requirements and depth of comprehension.

Early research emphasized recall versus recognition questions and the corresponding differences in required processing and responding. Forced-choice questions inherently limit and define the domain of possible answers. In doing so they require that discriminations be made among plausible alternative answers. In many cases, though, forced-choice questions provide a very satisfactory method; responses can usually be completed with a minimum of complexity. In others, however, the task dictates different requirements (cf. Sullivan & Higgins, 1983).

Recall involves the uncued production of a response or retrieval of relevant knowledge under nominal cuing. Recall questions expand the domain of possible answers but introduce significant procedural and management complications. While no discrimination among plausible distractors is required, significant organization of knowledge is typically assumed.

Correspondingly, comprehension requirements vary with different question types. Forced-choice questions permit inferences to be drawn about the learner's ability to compare among given alternatives and select the best answer, but cannot be used to verify unprompted or nominally prompted responses. The reverse is true for recall questions: We can safely draw conclusions about the response itself, but cannot infer much about the ability of the learner to make selective discriminations. Effective questioning requires a match between the response and corresponding processing requirements.

The constructed-response question, shown in Figure 4.7, relies on the student's ability to recall relevant knowledge, to organize related knowledge logically, and to prepare a coherent written response. Criterion knowledge must be demonstrated with a minimum of prompting. However, such formats are often likely to yield conservative estimates of knowledge due to the potential confounding response requirement: It is conceivable that students have acquired the requisite information, but are unable to write well enough to convey their knowledge.

The forced-choice version of the question minimizes the problem of response complexity, but alters the performance requirement appreciably. The student is required only to identify the correct answer among a limited number of given options. Yet, such questions can add a level of conceptual difficulty not possible with open-ended questions The forced-choice question requires that important conceptual discriminations be made among similar emotions as well as among the causes. Contrasted with the constructed-response version, greater distinction among potentially misinterpreted or confused points in the lesson can be assessed.

Describe how Devon felt
after his conversation with Ginger.

_____

_____

_____

_____

_____

Which of the following best describes
how Devon felt after his encounter with Ginger?

a) sad to hear of the cancellation

b) sad that Ginger would not go

c) angry to hear of the cancellation

d) angry that Ginger broke the date

**Figure 4.7.** Sample constructed-response and multiple-choice questions.

### 5.4. The consequences of a response may either strengthen or weaken desired behavior.

One goal of teaching is to encourage appropriate behavior while discouraging undesired responses. Two methods of influencing behavior are reinforcement and punishment. Although the importance of reinforcement and punishment has been generally acknowledged, their functions are debatable.

From a behavioral perspective, reinforcement and punishment are explained in terms of satisfaction. Thorndike's (1911) Law of Effect states that behavior followed by satisfying events will be more strongly connected than behavior followed by punishment. Satisfying events include both positive and negative reinforcers that *increase* the likelihood of a response. Without reinforcement, responses will eventually extinguish. Positive reinforcement occurs when an individual responds appropriately in order to receive a stimulus; negative reinforcement occurs when an individual responds appropriately in order to avoid an undesirable stimulus.

Punishment, on the other hand, *decreases* the likelihood of repeating a response. Punishment occurs when an individual ceases to respond undesirably in order to avoid a stimulus. Thus, a student who receives a failing grade for plagiarism has been punished if he or she ceases to plagiarize after the aversive stimulus.

In contrast, cognitivists view feedback as information which can be used to restructure knowledge and support the metacognitive regulation of ongoing performance. For example, positive and negative feedback may inform the student of progress toward a goal: Positive feedback may indicate the student is achieving mastery; negative feedback may warn the student of sub-par performance. Feedback may also provide a kind of elaboration, where additional information is paired with existing knowledge to strengthen encoding and promote retrievability. In each case, the student restructures knowledge based upon the information provided, makes appropriate metacognitive adjustments, and proceeds based upon the additional information provided.

### 5.5. Feedback strategies vary in complexity, effectiveness, and function.

Schimmel (1988) outlined four levels of feedback: confirmation, correction, explanation, and diagnosis. Confirmation, also referred to as knowledge of results (KR), informs the learner of the accuracy of a response. It is generally effective for reinforcing correct answers. However, for incorrect answers confirmation provides little information from which the student can deduce the correct answer.

Corrective feedback supplements incorrect answers with knowledge of the desired or correct response (KCR). Corrective feedback helps to identify faulty reasoning contributing to errors. Typically, corrective feedback might provide statements such as "The correct answer is . . ." to supplement the knowledge of results given through confirmation feedback.

Explanatory feedback generally identifies relevant information and outlines the progression of events central to the desired response. The rationale for such feedback is that many responses are based upon flawed knowledge and beliefs, beliefs that can be very durable and create considerable learning inhibition. In such cases, it is not simply an inaccurate response, but the entire system of beliefs and misconceptions that requires attention. Faulty logic can be addressed directly by explaining lesson concepts in order to restructure inaccurate knowledge and beliefs (Spiro, Feltovich, & Coulson, 1990).

Diagnostic feedback attempts to identify the source of misconceptions by comparison with common errors. The comparisons may be accomplished technologically, such as computer matching against common misconceptions, or can be done by having learners compare responses to prototype answers. If detected, diagnostic feedback typically highlights the error and attempts to prescribe a solution.

An additional level, elaborative feedback, provides additional related information designed to supplement or extend the knowledge assessed in the corresponding question. Elaborative feedback is based upon the same cognitive premise of elaboration in general, that is, the attempt to promote meaning by establishing connections between new content and the learner's prior knowledge.

Figure 4.8 illustrates some of the functional differences among feedback options to the same question. Confirmation simply recognizes the accuracy or inaccuracy of a student's answer. When contrasted with corrective, explanatory, and diagnostic feedback, the progressive differences in both the amount and nature of the information provided become apparent. Feedback requirements are influenced by the degree of competence required and the relative stage in promoting competence: Feedback during initial acquisition tends to be more elaborate; feedback during later stages tends to be more concise. Salisbury (1988), for example, noted that many skills must become more or less automatic. Initial activities must be highly supported in order to solidify the necessary knowledge. Subsequent activities, however, are designed to promote fluency and efficiency. Assuming the requisite knowledge has been encoded, the goal of automaticity training is to produce appropriate responses with a minimum of conscious thought. Simplified feedback is likely to be most appropriate at this point. In cases of sub-standard performance, students might require increased basic instruction prior to high production automaticity training.

### 5.5a. The value of corrective feedback is mediated, to a significant degree, by the response confidence of learners.

During lessons, students answer questions with confidence varying from absolute certainty to a wild guess. The effectiveness of corrective feedback varies accordingly, but it is generally most effective when response confidence is high (Kulhavy, Yekovich, & Dyer, 1976).

Figure 4.9 illustrates the relationship among response accuracy, response confidence, and the value of corrective feedback. When confidence is low, little supporting knowledge likely contributed to the response. As a result, whether correct or incorrect, little restructuring is possible. Though feedback is of

```
┌─────────────────── CONFIRMATION ───────────────────┐
│                                                     │
│              Your answer was incorrect.             │
│                                                     │
└─────────────────────────────────────────────────────┘
```

```
┌──────────────────── CORRECTIVE ────────────────────┐
│                                                     │
│              Your answer was incorrect.             │
│          The correct answer was "Jefferson."        │
│                                                     │
└─────────────────────────────────────────────────────┘
```

```
┌──────────────────── EXPLANATORY ───────────────────┐
│                                                     │
│        Your answer was incorrect because Carter was from │
│          Georgia. Of all those listed, only Jefferson called │
│                   Virginia "home."                  │
│                                                     │
└─────────────────────────────────────────────────────┘
```

```
┌──────────────────── DIAGNOSTIC ────────────────────┐
│                                                     │
│              Your answer was incorrect.             │
│            Your choice of Carter suggests           │
│              that some extra instruction            │
│          on the home-states of past presidents      │
│                 might be helpful.                   │
│                                                     │
└─────────────────────────────────────────────────────┘
```

```
┌──────────────────── ELABORATIVE ───────────────────┐
│                                                     │
│         Your answer, Jefferson, was correct.        │
│                                                     │
│              The University of Virginia,            │
│   a campus rich with Jeffersonian architecture and writings, │
│     is sometimes referred to as Thomas Jefferson's school. │
│                                                     │
└─────────────────────────────────────────────────────┘
```

**Figure 4.8.** Examples of feedback strategies.

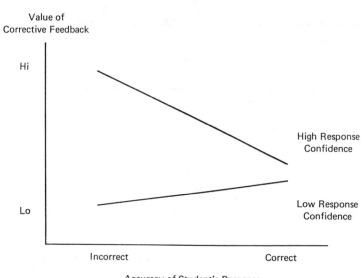

Value of
Corrective Feedback

Hi

High Response
Confidence

Low Response
Confidence

Lo

Incorrect                                    Correct

Accuracy of Student's Response

**Figure 4.9.** Relationship among response confidence, accuracy, and the value of corrective feedback.

relatively little consequence for high-confidence correct responses, it can be of significant value for incorrect responses. High confidence responses are the product of evaluating considerable related knowledge. Students study feedback longer following an incorrect response than a correct response, attempt to reconcile the feedback relative to supporting knowledge, and restructure their knowledge and beliefs accordingly (Anderson, Kulhavy, & Andre, 1971).

> *5.5b. During initial acquisition, feedback may be most successful if administered immediately and continuously following responses; during subsequent instruction, feedback should be intermittent and delayed.*

Feedback may be delivered on continuous or intermittent schedules. Continuous feedback requires every response to be reinforced; intermittent feedback requires that some be reinforced. Intermittent schedules comprise a variety of feedback options. They may be either fixed or variable, and may be based upon response rate or interval (Hannafin & Rieber, 1989).

In general, continuous feedback is effective for rapid acquisition of new knowledge, but resulting behavior can be readily extinguished. When feedback stops, the associated behavior soon fades. Conversely, stimulus control can be difficult to establish via intermittent feedback but it is more resistant to extinction. Continuous feedback should be used to establish effective responses while responses should be strengthened and maintained through intermittent feedback (Anderson & Faust, 1973).

Feedback timing, immediate or postponed, has also been studied with mixed results (Kulik & Kulik, 1988). Though immediate feedback has long been viewed as a basic premise of effective instruction, proponents of the delayed retention effect (DRE) suggest counter-intuitive methods. Postponing feedback, rather than administering feedback immediately following responses, often proves successful (Kulhavy, 1977).

Kulhavy and Anderson (1972) explained the effectiveness of delayed feedback in terms of the interference–perseveration theory: Immediate feedback causes incorrect answers to interfere with corrective feedback. However, when the response and feedback are separated temporally, incorrect answers fade from memory and are more easily replaced by correct answers. Delayed feedback thus creates a second learning trial as opposed to the single trial associated with immediate feedback. The effectiveness of delayed feedback may therefore be attributed to increased learning trials. When the delay is insufficient to create a separate learning trial, however, immediate feedback is generally more effective than delayed feedback.

### 5.6. Cognitive dissonance improves learning by inducing a need to know, or by establishing propositions that are inconsistent with the learner's belief or knowledge system.

Cognitive dissonance involves the introduction of an apparent inconsistency in what the learner believes to be true, or the creation of a learner-defined "need to know." By inducing cognitive dissonance, schemata are instantiated that increase both the relevant prior knowledge available during instruction and the nodes with which new knowledge can be linked. Dissonance-inducing activities heighten cognitive engagement by establishing implicit propositions to be refuted or proved through careful evaluation of new with existing knowledge. Significant restructuring is required in order to reconcile the apparent inconsistency.

Consider, for example, the statement, "The weight of this rock always changes." If such a statement were made to third graders during an introductory lesson on space, it would contradict an apparent truth. Yet, within the context of the lesson, weight as a measured phenomenon might be presented relative to gravitational influences (i.e., weight on earth, theoretical weightlessness in space, weight as measured on the moon versus the planet Saturn, etc.). The apparent contradiction could be reconciled during the lesson through the induction of relevant knowledge, and knowledge restructured accordingly.

# 6. Transfer and Generalization

### 6.1.  *Transfer and generalization are influenced, in part, by the psychological orientation manifested in instruction.*

Though distinctions between transfer and generalization are often unclear, an operational difference may be useful: Transfer is primarily a retrieval and production phenomenon; generalization is primarily an encoding phenomenon. Transfer refers to the application of knowledge in situations with varying similarity to the setting in which the knowledge was initially acquired (Gagné, 1985). Transfer requires that relevant knowledge be retrieved and subsequently applied in contexts different from those initially encoded. When learning to fly a single-engine aircraft, for example, a student might be able to transfer existing related knowledge, such as knowledge of hang-gliding, to comparable aerodynamic tasks such as turning, climbing, and stalling.

Generalization occurs during encoding, and is influenced by the degree to which common attributed properties and other features of the instruction are apparent to the learner. Generalization can involve "likeness" among either stimuli or responses, or both. Likeness may be supplied in the form of examples and analogies, or by explicit directions to compare and contrast current concepts with others that share related properties. For instance, the functional similarities between the metaphoric heart and the pump enable learners to identify conceptual parallels which are subsequently used to support the learning of heart functions. Likewise, the simile ". . . the foreigner was like a 'fish out of water' " connotes to the learner a sense of discomfort and alienation. Methods can be imposed to make obvious particular properties or attributes that are shared, thereby allowing the student to generalize among familiar and to-be-learned concepts.

In contrast, students may individually increase the generalizability of knowledge by integrating current knowledge within existing knowledge. During a lesson on gravitational attraction, for example, a student may recall knowledge pertaining to an astronaut's walk on the moon and the proportional reduction of the influence of gravity. The student may, apart from explicit instruction, generalize that gravitation attraction is influenced by mass.

### 6.1a.  *Transfer is affected by the degree of similarity between the conditions affecting acquisition and those regulating retrieval and performance.*

Several factors affect the ability to apply knowledge to similar (near transfer) and different (far transfer) settings. The degree of similarity (or difference) between the initial encoding context and the retrieving context influences the transferability of knowledge. Near transfer tasks require restricted spread of activation among propositions closely related to the initial encoding context; far transfer involves spread of activation among related propositions during retrieval.

Clark and Voogel (1985) suggested that behavioral methods promote near transfer but limit far transfer, while cognitive methods promote far transfer to the detriment of near transfer. In part, transfer is influenced by the strategies generated through each orientation. Behavioral methods tend to emphasize strict control of known response-mediating stimuli. Target stimuli, such as oral reading vocabulary, are associated with desired responses that are consequently reinforced. Practice typically focuses on mastery of defined objectives and specified performance. In effect, breadth of comprehension is mediated by the specificity of the lesson objectives, and the corresponding range of associations conditioned during instruction. Consequently, behavioral methods tend to provide very efficient methods for near-transfer training and other circumstances where knowledge or performance is largely context-bound.

Cognitive methods, on the other hand, often attempt to decontextualize instruction and to elicit learner-supplied meaning rather than to impose focusing lesson structure. Analogies and metaphors are provided in lieu of rules and procedures, and examples tend to reflect varied applications versus those specifically isolated as a performance outcome. The goal is typically to promote complete integration with existing knowledge; strategies employed emphasize divergent rather than convergent processing.

Figure 4.10 illustrates the ways in which behavioral and cognitive methods influence how students might select, organize, and integrate the information in a lesson on literary style. The focus is on imagery as a vehicle for expressing emotion. In the behavioral example, the learning of specific, discrete elements of imagery in the writing of Steven King is emphasized. In the cognitive example, imagery is presented as a literary phenomenon with varied methods that are manifested in different ways in the writing of familiar authors. Whereas the behavioral method is most likely to ensure that specific aspects of King's imagery are learned, the cognitive method is more likely to promote transfer of the concepts of imagery in literature.

Obviously, both cognitive and behavioral methods provide important methods for influencing transfer. The methods are potentially complementary, but they are not interchangeable. Few strategies promote both far and near transfer successfully, so the task is to match transfer requirements and instructional methods accordingly.

> ### 6.1b. *Stimulus generalization can be improved by varying the range of presentation stimuli for which a similar response is to be made; response generalization can be improved by expanding the range of responses made conditionally under similar stimulus control.*

Generalization can occur at either the stimulus or response side of an instructional transaction. On the stimulus side, the family or class of stimuli for which a similar response is to be made is increased (Gropper, 1983). The development of many mathematical concepts, for example, is often dependent on

---

┌─────────────────── Behavioral Lesson Strategy ───────────────────┐

Now that we have completed reading Hemingway's "Snows of
Kilimanjaro" and London's "To Build a Fire," we will read
Steven King's popular novella, "The Body."

Before starting this unit, let's identify what to focus on.

By the end of this unit, you will:

    identify at least two examples of King's use
      of verbal metaphor in the introduction;

    list the two most important methods used
      to induce images of the antagonist and the protagonist;

    identify two instances where vivid images were
      employed for the main character, and list two key terms
      used by King to invoke character imagery.

└──────────────────────────────────────────────────────────────────┘

┌──────────────────── Cognitive Lesson Strategy ────────────────────┐

Imagery is perhaps the most powerful tool available
to an author. There are many different ways that
imagery can be used. Hemingway, for example, used
exceptionally vivid and colorful characterizations.
Jack London, in "To Build a Fire," developed a strong
sense of identification to conjure images of conflict
and despair.

Today we explore imagery in the writing of a
contemporary author, Steven King. However, the piece
we will consider, *The Body,* is unusual for King.
Unlike the horror images so vivid in his other works,
King introduces softer, more personal images. In fact,
for those of you who have seen it, the acclaimed movie,
"Stand By Me," was inspired by this story.

As you read his novella, see how King moves you
with his subtle uses of imagery.
Consider how the methods differ from his more popular
novels, and how his methods of characterization
draw from the styles of London, Hemingway, and others.

└──────────────────────────────────────────────────────────────────┘

**Figure 4.10.** Behavioral and cognitive strategies.

---

the applicability of identical operations to apparently diverse problems. Simple decimal subtraction skills must be generalized to money management as well as a host of additional related tasks. The response remains essentially unchanged, but the range of events for which the response is appropriate increases.

On the response side, the association between stimulus and response is not singular, but is varied and often multi-dimensional. Whereas stimulus generalization allows learners to know the varied circumstances requiring the same action, response generalization supports the conditional nature of responding. It is commonplace for varied responses to be elicited by the same stimulus. Take, for example, the class of conditionally appropriate responses to red lights while driving. In response to a red light indicator on a dashboard, at times the correct response is to fasten seat belts, while at others it is to release the parking brake. In still other cases, a red light indicates that the driver must stop an automobile. In each case, the same basic stimulus elicits different responses based upon the complex networks of S–>R chains.

# Chapter Summary

Obviously, the foregoing are not, nor were they intended to be, an exhaustive set of learning principles. The goal of this text, and this chapter in particular, is to identify powerful guidelines and heuristics for which a high degree of consensus exists. This necessarily excludes ongoing research—research with considerable potential to restructure instructional messages. Much of the promising research in artificial intelligence and cognitive psychology, for example, is still too formative in nature to generate principles likely to meet with widespread endorsement. Perhaps future revisions will indicate how much of the promise of cognitive psychology for instruction has been realized.

This chapter represents a distillation of sorts, where the volumes of research on teaching, thinking, and learning are condensed to yield a limited number of time-tested, reliable message design principles. The principles are intentionally media-independent, and are designed to provide an overall working framework for the selection and design of instructional messages across media. Clearly, we do not advocate one medium over another, nor does such an endorsement seem prudent or justifiable given the power of various media to operationalize the principles in this chapter. Instead, this chapter focuses on generalizable principles and supporting rationale with application across a range of instructional problems and media. It is a perspective that is central, but frequently overlooked, in instructional message design.

# References

Anderson, J. R., & Reder, L. M. (1979). An elaborative processing explanation of depth processing. In L. S. Cermak and F. I. M. Craik (Eds.), *Levels of processing in human memory* (pp. 385–403). Hillsdale, NJ: Lawrence Erlbaum Associates.

Anderson, R. C., & Faust, G. W. (1973). *Educational psychology: The science of instruction and learning.* New York: Dodd, Mead, and Co.

Anderson, R. C., Kulhavy, R. W., & Andre, T. (1971). Feedback procedures in programmed instruction. *Journal of Educational Psychology, 62,* 148–156.

Ausubel, D. (1960). The use of advance organizers in the learning and retention of meaningful verbal material. *Journal of Educational Psychology, 51,* 267–272.

Barnett, J. E., DiVesta, F., & Rogozinski, J. T. (1981). What is learned in notetaking? *Journal of Educational Psychology, 73,* 181–192.

Becker, C. B., & Carrier, C. A. (1985). Use of metaphor as an instructional medium. *International Journal of Instructional Media, 12,* 42–52.

Bretzing, B., & Kulhavy, R. (1981). Notetaking and passage style. *Journal of Educational Psychology, 73,* 242–250.

Carney, R. N., Levin, J. R., & Morrison, C. R. (1988). Mnemonic learning of artists and their paintings. *American Educational Research Journal, 25,* 107–125.

Carrier, C. A., & Jonassen, D. (1988). Adapting courseware to accommodate individual differences. In D. Jonassen (Ed.), *Instructional designs for microcomputer courseware* (pp. 203–226). Hillsdale, NJ: Lawrence Erlbaum Associates.

Clark, R. E. (1982). Antagonism between achievement and enjoyment in ATI studies. *Educational Psychologist, 17,* 92–101.

Clark, R. E. (1983). Reconsidering research on learning from media. *Review of Educational Research, 53,* 445–459.

Clark, R. E., & Voogel, A. (1985). Transfer of training principles for instructional design. *Educational Communications and Technology Journal, 33,* 113–125.

Craik, F. I. M., & Lockhart, R. S. (1972). Levels of processing: A framework for memory research. *Journal of Verbal Learning and Verbal Behavior, 11,* 671–684.

Cronbach, L., & Snow, R. (1977). *Aptitudes and instructional methods: A handbook for research on interactions.* New York: Irvington.

Derry, S. J., & Murphy, D. A. (1986). Designing systems that train learning ability: From theory to practice. *Review of Educational Research, 56,* 1–39.

Flavell, J. H. (1979). Metacognition and cognitive monitoring. *American Psychologist, 34,* 906–911.

Frase, L. T., & Schwartz, B. J. (1979). Typographical cues that facilitate comprehension. *Journal of Educational Psychology, 71,* 197–206.

Gagné, E. D. (1978). Long-term retention of information following learning from prose. *Review of Educational Research, 48,* 629–665.

Gagné, E. D. (1985). *The cognitive psychology of school learning.* Boston: Little, Brown, and Co.

Garhart, C., & Hannafin, M. J. (1986). The accuracy of comprehension monitoring during computer-based instruction. *Journal of Computer-Based Instruction, 13,* 88–93.

Gay, G. (1987). Interaction of learner control and prior understanding in computer-assisted video instruction. *Journal of Educational Psychology, 78,* 225–227.

Gropper, G. (1983). A behavioral approach to instructional prescription. In C. Reigeluth (Ed.), *Instructional-design theories and models* (pp. 106–161). Hillsdale, NJ: Lawrence Erlbaum Associates.

Hamilton, R. (1985). A framework for the evaluation of the effectiveness of adjunct questions and objectives. *Review of Educational Research, 55,* 47–85.

Hannafin, M. J. (1984). Guidelines for determining instructional locus of control in the design of computer-assisted instruction. *Journal of Instructional Development, 7*(3), 6–10.

Hannafin, M. J. (1987, April). *Motivational aspects of lesson orientation during CBI.* Presented at the annual meeting of the American Educational Research Association, Washington, DC.

Hannafin, M. J. (1988). The effects of instructional explicitness on learning and error persistence. *Contemporary Educational Psychology, 13,* 126–132.

Hannafin, M. J. (1989). Interaction strategies and emerging instructional technologies: Psychological perspectives. *Canadian Journal of Educational Communication, 18,* 167–179.

Hannafin, M. J., & Colamaio, M. (1987). The effects of variations in lesson control and practice on learning from interactive video. *Educational Communications and Technology Journal, 35,* 203–212.

Hannafin, M. J., & Hughes, C. (1986). A framework for incorporating orienting activities in computer-based interactive video. *Instructional Science, 15,* 239–255.

Hannafin, M. J., & Rieber, L. P. (1989). Psychological foundations of instructional design for emerging computer-based instructional technologies: Part I. *Educational Technology Research and Development, 37,* 91–101.

Jonassen, D. (1982). Aptitude- versus content-treatment interactions: Implications for instructional design. *Journal of Instructional Development, 5*(4), 15–27.

Kulhavy, R. (1977). Feedback in written instruction. *Review of Educational Research, 47,* 211–232.

Kulhavy, R. W., & Anderson, R. C. (1972). Delayed-retention effect with multiple-choice tests. *Journal of Educational Psychology, 63,* 505–512.

Kulhavy, R. W., Yekovich, F. R., & Dyer, J. W. (1976). Feedback and response confidence. *Journal of Educational Psychology, 68,* 522–528.

Kulik, J. A., & Kulik, C. L. (1988). Timing of feedback and verbal learning. *Review of Educational Research, 58,* 59–97.

Mayer, R. E. (1984). Aids to text comprehension. *Educational Psychologist, 19,* 30–42.

Mayer, R. E. (1989). Models for understanding. *Review of Educational Research, 59,* 43–64.

Miller, G. A. (1956). The magical number seven, plus or minus two: Some limits on our capacity for processing information. *Psychological Review, 63,* 81–97.

Morris, C. D., Bransford, J. D., & Franks, J. J. (1977). Levels of processing versus transfer-appropriate processing. *Journal of Verbal Learning and Verbal Behavior, 16,* 519–533.

Paivio, A. (1979). *Imagery and verbal processes.* Hillsdale, NJ: Lawrence Erlbaum Associates.

Paivio, A., Yuille, J., & Madigan, S. (1968). Concreteness, imagery, and meaningfulness values for 925 nouns. *Journal of Experimental Psychology Monographs, 76*(1 Pt. 2).

Peper, R. J., & Mayer, R. E. (1978). Notetaking as a generative activity. *Journal of Educational Psychology, 70,* 514–522.

Pichert, J., & Anderson, R. (1977). Taking different perspectives on a story. *Journal of Educational Psychology, 69,* 309–315.

Reynolds, R., & Anderson, R. (1982). Influence of questions on the allocation of attention during reading. *Journal of Educational Psychology, 74,* 623–632.

Rickards, J. (1979). Adjunct postquestions in text: A critical review of methods and processes. *Review of Educational Research, 49,* 181–196.

Rickards, J., & Friedman, F. (1978). The encoding versus the external storage hypothesis in notetaking. *Contemporary Educational Psychology, 3,* 136–143.

Ross, S., & Morrison, G. (1988). Adapting instruction to learner performance and background variables. In D. Jonassen (Ed.), *Instructional designs for microcomputer courseware* (pp. 227–246). Hillsdale, NJ: Lawrence Erlbaum Associates.

Rothkopf, E. (1970). The concept of mathemagenic activities. *Review of Educational Research, 40,* 325–336.

Rumelhart, D., & Norman, D. (1981). Analogical processes in learning. In J. R. Anderson (Ed.), *Cognitive skills and their acquisition* (pp. 335–339). Hillsdale, NJ: Lawrence Erlbaum Associates.

Salisbury, D. (1988). Effective drill and practice strategies. In D. Jonassen (Ed.), *Instructional designs for microcomputer courseware* (pp. 103–124). Hillsdale, NJ: Lawrence Erlbaum Associates.

Salomon, G. (1984). Television is "easy" and print is "tough": The differential investment of mental effort in learning as a function of perceptions and attributions. *Journal of Educational Psychology, 76,* 647–658.

Schimmel, B. J. (1988). Providing meaningful feedback in courseware. In D. Jonassen (Ed.), *Instructional designs for microcomputer courseware* (pp. 183–196). Hillsdale, NJ: Lawrence Erlbaum Associates.

Spiro, R., Feltovich, P., & Coulson, R. (1990). Multiple analogies for complex concepts: Antidotes for analogy-induced misconception in advanced knowledge acquisition. In S. Vosniadou & A. Ortony (Eds.), *Similarity and analogical reasoning.* Cambridge: Cambridge University Press.

Stein, B. S., Bransford, J. D., Franks, J. J., Owings, R. A., Vye, N. J., & McGraw, W. (1982). Differences in the precision of self-generated elaborations. *Journal of Experimental Psychology: General, 111,* 399–405.

Steinberg, E. (1977). Review of student control in computer-assisted instruction. *Journal of Computer-Based Instruction, 3,* 84–90.

Sullivan, H., & Higgins, N. (1983). *Teaching for competence.* New York: Teachers College Press.

Tennyson, R. (1984). Artificial intelligence methods in computer-based instructional design: The Minnesota Adaptive Instructional System. *Journal of Instructional Development, 7*(3), 17–22.

Tennyson, R., & Christensen, D. (1988). MAIS: An intelligent learning system. In D. Jonassen (Ed.), *Instructional designs for microcomputer courseware* (pp. 247–274). Hillsdale, NJ: Lawrence Erlbaum Associates.

Thorndike, E. L. (1911). *Animal intelligence, experimental studies.* New York: Macmillan.

Tobias, S. (1976). Achievement treatment interactions. *Review of Educational Research, 46,* 61–74.

Wagoner, S. A. (1983). Comprehension monitoring: What it is and what we know about it. *Reading Research Quarterly, 18,* 328–346.

Wittrock, M. (1974). Learning as a generative process. *Educational Psychologist, 11,* 87–95.

# Chapter 5

# Concept-Learning Principles

## Malcolm Fleming

### Indiana University

#### Revised & Updated by

## Anne Bednar

### Eastern Michigan University

## Introduction

Concepts are an essential part of learning to cope with our world. Without the ability to group objects, events, or ideas by common characteristics, we would be forced to learn about and deal with each separate object, event, or idea as altogether unique. The memory load would be impossible. Concepts enable us to simplify, categorize, and thus better cope with the diversity surrounding us. Of course, this action of simplification and categorization is arbitrary rather than absolute. As we use concepts in daily life we find that the boundaries separating them are fuzzy and ill-defined and that they change with the context in which they are embedded. So, such grouping together of different things, such attention to selected similarities while overlooking apparent differences, can get us into trouble. We misidentify and we stereotype. We mistake poisonous mushrooms for edible ones, and we ascribe erroneous characteristics to groups of people differentiated by color, sex, nationality, etc. That is, we can learn erroneous, stereotypic, non-functional concepts as well as functional concepts.

"Concept" has been variously defined. Some definitions have emerged related to the measurement of concept acquisition. At the introductory level in a given content, the common measure of concept acquisition is the common response (typically the name for the concept) given to a group of discriminably different objects.* For example, where a learner says "square" with reference to appropriate geometric figures, but not with reference to inappropriate figures, s/he may be said to have the concept, particularly if some of the individual figures are new to him/her. There are two critical aspects of this test. First, the same response must be made to a variety of different examples, e.g., small and large squares; red, green, and black squares, etc. Second, the test should involve objects not seen before, e.g., a large, orange square. This definition points up a fundamental distinction between memorization and conceptualization. Memory processes may include the recognition of a particular object, or the association of a particular word label with that one object, while concept formation involves a common label for a diverse group of objects. A concept can be applied whether or not the learner has ever before encountered certain examples of it or had occasion to associate them with the name.

At the level of advanced knowledge in a given content area, the measure of concept acquisition is the ability to appropriately apply the concept across contexts. For example, where an instructional design student applies the concepts of validity and reliability appropriately in test construction, in formulating interview questions for a needs assessment, and in dealing with observational data related to product evaluation, the student can be said to have the concepts of validity and reliability.

While useful for testing, such response-oriented definitions do not reveal much about designing instruction to teach concepts. Models which attempt to explain how we acquire concepts rather than measure their attainment yield definitions which are more helpful in terms of design guidelines.

The definition of "concept" in the classical view of concept learning has emphasized stimulus characteristics, i.e., the common characteristics of all examples of the concept, those which are individually necessary and collectively sufficient for category definition. These are called the critical (or criterial) attributes, while other characteristics that are not shared by all members of the class are variable attributes. For example, "square" can be defined by its critical attributes as "a closed geometric figure which has four equal sides and four equal angles." Its main variable attribute is size. Using this definition of concept, a learner can be said to know the concept when s/he can state the definition or recognize and identify correctly any geometric figure that exhibits the critical attributes. This definition of concept is functional for the designer because it indicates that the learner must attend to the critical attributes that distinguish examples from non-examples† of the concept. Thus, these are the very stimulus

---

* It should be clear that while the verbal label is a very important response, there are many others, e.g., pointing to examples, drawing examples, or otherwise behaving consistently toward them. For example, where a driver consistently stops at all red traffic lights, s/he can be said to have the concept "stop" whether or not s/he can say, write, or understand the verbal label.

† Some writers refer to positive examples and negative examples. We have chosen the simpler designation: examples and non-examples. Also, the words "instance" and "exemplar" are frequently used instead of the more common "example," which we will use.

attributes that the designer must emphasize, and it is on this basis that early instructional design models for concept teaching were built.

This classical view of concept has been criticized, however, in light of research claims that extensive effort has failed to produce critical attributes for most concrete (object) concepts let alone more abstract concepts. Instead, most real-world concepts have fuzzy boundaries, and not all objects, events, or ideas which might be considered part of the category are equally good examples of the concept, e.g., a robin has been found to be a more typical example of the concept "bird" than a penguin or an ostrich. In addition, the characteristics which might be listed as critical attributes are not common to all of the objects, events, or ideas that are part of the category, e.g., not all birds fly; and attributes, whether critical or variable, occur in clusters rather than being independent of each other.

Meaning is also context-dependent. For example, consider the concepts of art or justice. Objects which are considered art in one culture, during a specific historical period or even by a subset of individuals, are not necessarily considered art by others. Actions deemed just in one context are judged to be gross injustices in other circumstances.

In addition to the difficulty and artificiality of identifying critical attributes, their utility is in question. It has been demonstrated that we do not determine whether an object, event, or idea is representative of a concept by sorting through a list of critical attributes. Instead, we attend to both the critical and variable characteristics of the object, event, or idea, using them to form a "prototype," a mental model of the concept. When encountering a new example, we compare it to the prototype in order to decide whether it is a member of the concept class. Reciprocally, each encounter with an example can result in a revision or adjustment of the prototype and of the complex knowledge structure of which the prototype is part. Since the prototype is developed by each individual through his/her experience with members of the concept class, it is constantly evolving. In this view, concepts are seen as dynamic and context-dependent. This view of concepts is represented by a cluster of models called "prototype" models for concept acquisition.

As with the classical model of concepts, this prototype model is functional for the designer because it suggests what the learner must attend to, i.e., "best" examples of the concept, the rich contexts in which examples of the concept are embedded, linkages between the concept and other concepts, and clusters of attributes which are typical of but not critical to the concept definition.

Because of the centrality of examples, contexts, relationships among concepts, and attributes in these models of concept acquisition and in the design principles to follow, it is essential that the designer analyze concepts prior to designing messages to teach them. The analysis should yield both knowledge of the attributes of the concept and of the knowledge structure of which the concept is part. Specifically, analysis helpful for the designer would reveal the following: the "best" examples (as judged by experts in the field to be most typical); the attribute clusters (including both critical and variable attributes) which are common to the most typical examples of the concept; prerequisite and associative knowledge; the production systems (if/then statements) which guide expert use of the concept in decision making; and the relationships (superordinate, subordinate, and coordinate) between the concept and other concepts (Tennyson & Cocchiarella, 1986). While there are many types of analysis which identify some or all of these, one useful type of analysis is a schematic analysis.* Rather than being based on the hierarchical structure of attributes, a schematic analysis is based on the use of the concept in context and reflects the way in which the knowledge must be stored in memory for easy retrieval to be used in decision making in real contexts.

Implied in the prototype model is the fact that a learner's first contact with a concept will not result in deep, expert-level understanding; that concepts must evolve across experiences with members of the concept class. Concepts should be taught relative to the local context in which the learner will apply them. As the learner progresses in the application of the concept, the context will become more complex and the need to emphasize the variability of the concept will increase. We might then distinguish, while designing instruction, between introductory level concept learning and advanced knowledge, where introductory learning places more emphasis on best examples and attributes and advanced knowledge emphasizes the fuzziness of the concept boundaries and the dependence of the concept on context for definition. Caution must be exercised in applying this model, however, because there is evidence that the simplification involved in introductory experiences with concepts can lead to the development of misconceptions which interfere with development of advanced knowledge. Research on misconceptions indicates that single misconceptions are seldom held in isolation. Instead, as they are integrated into the knowledge structure held by the learners, they become part of elaborately constructed theories of how the world operates. Those theories are composed of clusters of correct concepts and misconceptions. Perhaps because of the complex structure they support, they are extremely resistant to change. And so, even introductory concepts should be taught in context rather than isolated from decision making situations.

The concept analysis phase, briefly noted above, is largely comprised of logical procedures. There follows the synthesis phase, largely comprised of the application of empirically derived principles for instructional design. The designer has analyzed learners and content structure (knowledge base/concepts and experiential base/contexts) and is now ready to consider how s/he will answer the design question: What instructional conditions will lead to the desired effect?

Predictably, there are concepts by which we simplify and systematize our dealing with the concept of concept. Several of these follow.

*Groupings according to the structure of attribute relationships:*

- Conjunctive concepts—defined by "and," by this attribute and that one and another one, i.e., the attributes which all examples have in common. For example, "apple" can be defined by such attributes as: edible fruit and from rosaceous tree and roundish and usually reddish.

---

* See other sources, such as Hayes, 1978; Norman & Rumelhart, 1975; Simon, 1979; Tennyson & Breuer, 1984; Underwood, 1983.

- Disjunctive concepts—defined by "or," i.e., examples having either one attribute (or set) or another attribute (or set). For example, "strike" in baseball can be defined as: batter swings or umpire calls or batter hits outside baselines.
- Relational concepts—defined by a relation between attributes rather than by their presence or absence. For example, "mountain" can be defined as an elevation of the earth's surface that is greater than a hill and less uniform than a plateau.

*Groupings by perceptibility of the examples:*

- Concrete concepts—those which have perceptible examples. For example, physical objects such as "truck" or "dog," sounds such as "squeak," and things that are perceptible to the sense of touch such as "hard" or "cold" are generally considered concrete.
- Abstract concepts—those which do not have perceptible examples. For example, feelings and attitudes such as "loyalty," ideologies such as "democracy," and concepts such as "infinity" are generally considered abstract.

*Groupings by ease of definition:*

- Well-defined concepts—those which have easily articulated critical and variable attributes. For example, geometric figures such as "square" and "circle," and science concepts such as "absolute zero" are defined in terms of lines and angles, points, and molecular movement (or kinetic energy), respectively.
- Fuzzy concepts—those which cannot be defined easily with a list of critical and variable attributes. For example, what are the critical attributes of "love"?

Some scholars would argue that even well-defined concepts cannot be absolutely defined in critical and variable attributes. For example, to what degree do the critical attributes associated with a geometric definition of a circle apply when a pre-school teacher asks her students to "form a circle"? Or, to what degree does our understanding of a concept simply reflect the current best interpretation of data? For example, the advent of quantum mechanics significantly changed scientists' definition of absolute zero.

*Groupings by relationships to other concepts in a hierarchical sense:*

Within a concept hierarchy, concepts are defined by their position relative to each other. A concept that has other concepts branching from it in the hierarchy is superordinate to those concepts and they are subordinate to it. Concepts that are on the same level of the hierarchy and share a common superordinate concept are coordinate to each other.

- Superordinate concept—Mammals, birds, and insects are all types of animals; animals is the superordinate concept.
- Coordinate concept—Mammals, birds, and insects are all examples of types of animals. They are coordinate concepts to each other.
- Subordinate concept—Cats, dogs, elephants, whales, prairie dogs, etc., are all types of mammals. They are subordinate to the concept mammal.

In what follows, principles of concept learning are discussed with reference to: types of concepts; prerequisites for concept learning; selecting examples and non-examples; presenting and sequencing instruction; and consolidating conceptual learning.

# 1. Types of Concepts

### 1.1. *Ease of concept attainment generally decreases as the overall complexity of the concept increases.*

A variety of dimensions contributes to the complexity of a concept, including the structure of its attributes (conjunctive, relational, or disjunctive—in order of increasing complexity), the degree to which its examples are perceptible (concrete vs. abstract), and the degree to which its definition changes from context to context. Generally a movement toward the complex end of any of these continua increases the difficulty of attaining the concept (Tennyson & Cocchiarella, 1986).

### 1.2. *Ease of concept attainment generally decreases as the overall number of both critical and non-critical properties increases.*

This principle is a variant of Principle 1.1, implying that concepts with fewer attributes are easier to learn than more complex concepts. Early instructional design models for concept teaching based on the teaching of critical attributes suggested that the designer further reduce the complexity of a concept teaching unit by using simplified representation to reduce the number of variable attributes apparent to the learner. More recent research suggests the opposite—presentation of rich examples (including both critical and variable attributes in context) contribute to a better consolidated prototype (Bransford *et al.*, in press; Spiro, 1988). Over-simplification and over-regularization of a concept frequently result in development of inert knowledge. The learner knows the concept in that s/he can correctly distinguish examples from non-examples in a controlled environment, but the same learner fails to recognize and apply the concept when it is dressed in the clothing which it wears in its real-world contexts, much of which may seem non-functional in distinguishing examples from non-examples in a controlled situation.

The key to simplification seems to lie in the use of successively more complex application contexts. Each context used is rich and full in its own right rather than over-simplified and over-regularized. But each successive context presents a slightly more complex application.

# 2. Selection of Examples and Non-Examples

## 2.1. Select "best" examples to facilitate development of a prototype.

Essentially, the "best" examples demonstrate what the concept is. There is evidence that, by studying the best examples closely, the learner forms an initial prototype of the concept. The prototype is thought to be a mental abstraction, a pattern, formed from the most frequently encountered attributes across a number of examples (Rosch, 1975; Medin & Smith, 1984). For example, given the concept "bird," the mental model is not specifically a robin, but rather is composed of the common attributes of all the birds which have been encountered as examples of the concept.

In analysis, the best examples are selected by asking content experts to rate the typicality of a range of examples. Those which are rated as most typical are the "best" examples.

## 2.2. Choose a wide variety of examples for instruction.

A correct classification of a concept avoids the errors of overgeneralization, undergeneralization, and misconception (see Figure 5.1). Using a wide variety of examples of the concept has the effect of showing the breadth of the concept, and thus prevents undergeneralization (Tennyson & Cocchiarella, 1986). For example, presenting the example "human" as the only example of the concept "mammal" could lead to undergeneralization, for the learner may extend the concept to include only upright animals such as monkeys. The concept "mammal" could be considerably broadened by adding dog, elephant, mouse, kangaroo, and whale to the initial example of human. Such broadening and diversifying of concept examples have the effect of not only demonstrating the extent of the concept, but also of clarifying the concept definition, i.e., showing that such features as size, uprightness, etc., are irrelevant because they vary across examples.

## 2.3. Choose both examples and non-examples when teaching coordinate concepts; choose only examples when teaching well-defined concepts.

Presenting examples gives the learner the opportunity to generalize from a single example across a class of examples. When a concept is well-defined, generalization skill may be sufficient to permit accurate classification. If a range

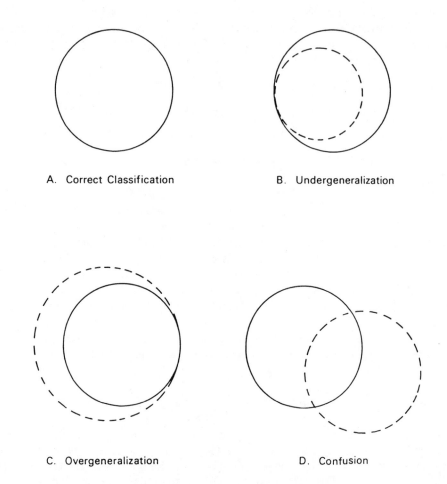

A.  Correct Classification                    B.  Undergeneralization

C.  Overgeneralization                         D.  Confusion

**Figure 5.1.** Graphic depictions of how a learner's concept (dotted lines) may differ from the correct concept (solid lines). The area in each circle represents the extent of the concept, i.e., the number and kinds of examples included. (After Sheppard, 1971.) An example of B (Undergeneralization) would be the use of "dog" to refer to only one kind, e.g., spaniel, or only dogs with long hair or brown color. An example of C (Overgeneralization) would be to use "dog" to refer to cats or to wolves as well.

of examples demonstrates what the concept is, however, non-examples show what it is not. Both are apt to be important to the learners' understanding where concepts are closely related, sharing attributes as coordinate members of a concept hierarchy. Presenting non-examples gives the learner the opportunity to discriminate, to prevent overgeneralization (Tennyson & Cocchiarella, 1986). For example, including "whale" in a set of examples used to teach the concept "mammal" might lead to overgeneralization to all fish. Presenting "fish" as a non-example could prevent overgeneralization to other aquatic animals.

**2.4.** *Choose close-in (little variety) non-examples, i.e., that have numerous attributes similar to the examples, and that differ from them only with respect to one (or two or three) criterial attributes.*

Note that the characteristics of non-examples here are just the opposite of those for examples. The effect is to clarify the boundaries between the concept and the others similar to it and thus prevent confusion and overgeneralization. Notice in Figure 5.2 that the non-examples $b^1$ to $d^1$ are similar to examples b to d, differing, in fact, on only one attribute apiece. For instance, d differs from $d^1$ only on being a closed figure. Matching examples with non-examples on the basis of variable attributes facilitates learning (Tennyson & Cocchiarella, 1986).

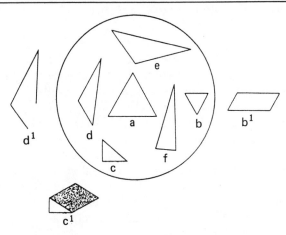

**Figure 5.2.** Possible examples and non-examples for teaching the concept of "triangle," examples inside the circle and non-examples outside. Choosing a variety of examples a–f instead of only one, typically "a," prevents undergeneralization. Choosing close-in non-examples $b^1$–$d^1$ accentuates the criterial attributes and prevents overgeneralization by showing the concept boundaries. What criterial attributes do $c^1$ and $b^1$ show?

Contrariwise, using an altogether different non-example does little for understanding. For example, a drawing of a face would be such an obvious (divergent) non-example of a triangle that it would serve no purpose. Similarly, using car or daffodil as a non-example of mammal contributes little, whereas using fish as a non-example delimits the concept relative to whales, as noted earlier.

This principle assumes that there are potentially confusing non-examples in the context, i.e., there are other concepts which have many attributes in common with examples (perhaps all attributes but one). As noted in Principle 2.3, this is usually the case when teaching coordinate concepts where use of non-examples is necessary to avoid overgeneralization to closely related concepts.

As a practical matter, experienced teachers will typically be well aware of close-in non-examples, for these will have been troublesome to learners, and hence to teachers, in previous classes.

# 3. Prerequisites

There may be some important prerequisites to learning a concept.

> **3.1.**  *Prior learning of relevant words, e.g., names of attributes, of examples, or of concepts, can facilitate concept learning. The same would hold for prior encounter with relevant objects, events, or relations.*

For example, observing and learning differences between certain attributes (large–small, red–green, 3–4, etc.) are obviously necessary before the learner can cope with concepts whose attributes (criterial or variable) are of that kind.

Similarly, knowing prerequisite or constituent skills or concepts may be essential. As is well accepted in instructional design theory (Gagné & Briggs, 1979; Reigeluth & Stein, 1983; Romiszowski, 1981), certain skills or other forms of knowledge may be prerequisite to later learning. For example, learning the concept "balanced chemical equation" may require math skills as well as knowledge of the valences of constituent chemical elements. Similarly, where a definition includes other concepts, those constituent concepts must be understood before the definition can be. For example, the definition of city, "large or important town," is of little value unless the learner understands three other concepts: large, important, town.

In addition, the number of examples a learner will need to acquire a concept is more closely related to prior knowledge than to intelligence or other individual differences. Such considerations can be pertinent to the pre-testing of learner's prior knowledge and to the careful sequencing of instruction both to activate the learners' recall of prior knowledge and to make such knowledge accessible to the learner during instruction on the new concept.

To flip the coin, in the same way that appropriate prior knowledge can facilitate learning new concepts, misconceptions or alternative frameworks can interfere with learning them (Stevens, Collins, & Goldin, 1979; Karplus & Stage, 1981). Because misconceptions become part of a learner's internal knowledge structure, they are especially resistant to change. Much of the misconceptions research is in the sciences, especially in teaching physics, but similar problems occur across contents.

> **3.2.** *Providing the learner with appropriate instructions can facilitate concept learning, including information about the concept (attributes, etc.), the desired response (concept identification, etc.), and a strategy to apply (drawing a picture to represent the concept, etc.).*

Thus, the designer cannot only take account of the learner's prior learning, but also s/he can add to it in preparation for concept instruction. For example, instructing learners to consider an analogy for abstract concepts can facilitate prototype formation by attributing to the abstract concept a set of attributes which belong to a more concrete concept (Newby & Stepich, 1987). The concept "justice" might be taught through its analogous relationship to the concept "scale": "Justice is like a scale in that it involves weighing both sides of an argument against one another and finding the balance point between them" (Newby & Stepich, 1987, p. 23).

# 4. Presenting Concept Instruction

Acquisition of the concept is hypothesized to occur in two phases, development of conceptual knowledge (the prototype and the knowledge structure in which it is embedded—including both critical and variable attributes, context, and connections to other concepts and prior knowledge) followed by the development of procedural knowledge (ability to solve domain specific problems, e.g., correctly classify examples and non-examples in context and apply that knowledge in problem solving) (Tennyson & Cocchiarella, 1986). While the development of conceptual knowledge seems a necessary prerequisite for procedural knowledge, the retention over time of procedural knowledge is what determines whether a learner can continue to use the concept correctly after instruction. Declarative knowledge, knowledge of the definition, context, and attributes, decreases even while ability to correctly classify examples increases.

The designer has a variety of instructional components to manipulate in the instruction initially to develop conceptual knowledge and later to develop procedural knowledge: (1) definitions and/or lists of attributes; (2) exposure to the context in which the concept is embedded; (3) examples and/or non-examples; (4) learner strategies; and (5) practice in classification. Ways of effective presentation of the components together with the relative emphasis to be given each and the sequencing of each will be considered here.

Initially the principles considered deal with presenting labels, definitions, and attributes.

### 4.1.  Use of the concept name in contiguity with presentation of each example facilitates concept learning.

Apparently, the concept name (e.g., the word "corpuscle") serves as a mediator for the concept learning process. At a minimum it indicates to the learner that all the pictures of different blood cells presented have something in common which s/he is to detect.

While concepts can certainly be formed from examples alone without the use of the concept name, it is generally highly desirable that a concept name be acquired so that the learner can thereafter readily and efficiently refer to the concept by means of a single word.*

### 4.2.  Use attributes as aids in finding meaning, not as algorithmic definitions or rules for classification of concepts.

There is a significant body of research which demonstrates that we do not classify concepts by working through a list of attributes and applying a rule (Rosch, 1975; Medin & Smith, 1984). Knowledge of attributes, however, can be helpful in identifying the distinguishing characteristics which separate coordinate concepts (Tennyson & Cocchiarella, 1986; Wilson, 1986).

There follow several principles dealing with use of context and ways of presenting examples.

### 4.3.  The presentation of visually richer and more realistic best examples leads to a richer and better consolidated prototype resulting in increased transfer.

Initial presentation of best examples should present those examples embedded in context, where learners can pay attention to the contextual attributes as well as to the critical, defining characteristics. Over-simplification and over-regularization can lead to the development of inert knowledge, knowledge which the learner can only use in a classroom context where prompted to apply it (Resnick, 1987; Spiro, 1988; Brown, Collins, & Duguid, 1989; Bransford *et al.*, in press). Learners fail to recognize concepts which were taught devoid of context when they encounter them outside of the introductory concept lesson. Where possible, having the learners actually use the new concept to solve problems in the context in which they will later be asked to use the concept will facilitate transfer to that environment. A case study approach may be especially effective.

---

* We should be careful to distinguish the concept label from what it refers to, i.e., the prototype. Both are important to instruction, but while a concept can be useful without a label, a label without knowledge of what it refers to is empty. Hence, the insistence by instructional designers on testing concept acquisition, not through recitation of a definition or recall of a label, but through performance that indicates functional knowledge of the concept.

**4.4.** *At the level of advanced knowledge, use examples which emphasize the differences and degree of variability of the concept within and across contexts.*

At the advanced level of knowledge, the learner is striving to use the concept in complex decision-making across a variety of contexts. Instruction which emphasizes the complexity of the concept rather than simplifying and regularizing it allows the learner to make the subtle judgments necessary at a practitioner level.

At this level of knowledge, the complexity of a concept can be communicated through use of multiple representations of that concept. For example, using more than one analogy or more than one model to illustrate a concept presents multiple perspectives from which the concept can be viewed (Spiro, 1988). Presenting multiple cases in which the concept applies is also important. When using multiple representations, analogies, or cases, instruction should establish direct links and comparisons to interconnect the instructional experiences.

**4.5.** *Presenting examples in close succession or simultaneously in small groups, and keeping previous examples in view while others are added facilitates concept acquisition.*

These procedures facilitate comparisons so that similarities and distinctions become apparent (Tennyson & Cocchiarella, 1986). Leaving examples in view further facilitates learning by reducing memory load. In contrast, where examples are presented one-at-a-time and not left in view, the learner must keep in mind all previous examples for comparison with each new one.

Note that this principle also relates to the interconnecting of cases and analogies as discussed in Principle 4.4 (Spiro, 1988).

# 5. Sequencing of Concept Instruction

A long-debated issue in instruction is that of induction vs. deduction; or, in our terms, presenting examples first and deriving the rule from them (called egrule) vs. presenting the rule first and illustrating with examples (called ruleg).

Mechner (1967) resolves the issue with reference to the initial difficulty of the concept for the particular learners. If it is relatively easy for the learners and they can understand it in its most abstract and general form (verbal definition), then use the rule-first or ruleg approach. This assumes the learners understand the words (other concepts) included in the definition. However, if the concept is difficult and the learners are not likely to understand initially the verbal definition, then use the example-first or egrule approach. The prototype model insists on early exposure to "best" examples. In the egrule approach, the prototype of the concept is built through exposure to the examples; and, only later, if at all, is the concept stated abstractly as a definition.

Other authors (Englemann, 1969; Hickey and Newton, 1964) recommend a combined approach called egruleg, i.e., give examples first, derive from them the rule (definition or set of attributes), and then apply it to further examples. Adding Mechner's view to this would yield a plausible strategy as follows:

A. Where the concept is difficult (too abstract) for the learner, use egruleg.

B. Where the concept would be understood in abstract form, use ruleg.

In applying this, the designer would, after choice of A or B, organize instruction accordingly and apply the preceding principles relative to examples and definitions as needed.

More recent debate in concept learning is paying less attention to whether examples or the rule should be presented first to learners and more to whether this general structure for a concept lesson is appropriate outside of a laboratory situation. As mentioned before, concepts taught in isolation from a context tend to become school learning that is not applied outside of the school context. If transfer of the concept for use in real-world contexts is the goal, then it is essential to teach the concept in a rich problem-solving context in which the new concept is knowledge used in solving the problem (Resnick, 1987; Spiro, 1988; Brown, Collins, & Duguid, 1989; Bransford *et al.*, in press). Then, whether the learner is exposed to the example or a definition first emerges during the process of using the knowledge, perhaps as an expert models problem solving in that particular context to the apprentice learner.

Whether in a more traditional concept learning lesson or a problem-solving context, there remains an important issue in concept instruction: Does one provide the attributes, i.e., list them or point them out in examples (exposition), or does one encourage the learner to find them (discovery)?

> *5.1.   Where concepts are especially complex (see Principle 1.1), or where coordinate concepts are especially close, or where attributes are not immediately apparent in examples, elaborating on the attributes increases concept attainment over expecting the learner to discover them.*

This is not to disparage the discovery method except where the criterion is learning efficiency. Discovery may well have the edge when it comes to arousing student interest and to constructing a learner's own interpretation of the problem situation. Pointing out the attributes in examples or describing the attributes as in a definition yields more rapid concept learning where discrimination between examples and non-examples is the criterion (Tennyson & Cocchiarella, 1986). It does not, however, necessarily facilitate transfer to use of the concept in contexts.

On the other hand, presenting the definition or a list of the attributes may be necessary for many concepts because one or more of the attributes critical for effective use of the concept is not readily observable in examples. This holds not only for obviously abstract concepts (democracy, power, brotherhood, catalyst, intelligence) but also for some apparently concrete concepts. For example, a vertebrate animal is characterized by a backbone, which is not directly observable in examples. Also, numerous objects are partly defined by their use, i.e., a hat by being worn on the head, a hammer being used to pound things. Just showing the physical attributes of these objects is not enough to define them; their physical function must also be shown or described for the learner to develop an understanding of the concept.

A caution in using Principle 5.1 is that the words (actually, other concepts) used in the definition must already be familiar to the learner or must be specially taught before the definition can be used in instruction (see Principle 3.1).

> 5.2. *Presenting the superordinate concept prior to introduction of the new concept allows learners to connect the new information to prior knowledge and reduces the time needed to acquire the new concept.*

Where efficiency is the goal, allowing the learner to activate the schema of which the new concept will become part allows the learner to assimilate the new information more rapidly.

> 5.3. *The initial examples presented should be the "best examples" (most typical in expert judgment) possible. Initial presentations should include only examples (no non-examples).*

Exposing the student to a best example or series of best examples facilitates development of the prototype. Good examples are learned before less typical examples (Tennyson & Cocchiarella, 1986).

> 5.4. *With coordinate concepts, subsequent presentations should be a mixture of examples and non-examples. Examples and non-examples should be shown simultaneously. Both should gradually increase in difficulty, i.e., examples becoming less typical of the concept class and non-examples becoming closer-in (increasingly similar to examples).*

This and Principle 5.3 reiterate a basic rule of instruction: begin with the familiar and simple and move toward the unfamiliar and complex. Also note, matching of examples to non-examples on variable attributes facilitates learning (Tennyson & Cocchiarella, 1986).

# 6. Confirmation of Concept Learning

**6.1.    *Transfer to new examples is facilitated by increases in the number of examples in the original instruction.***

**6.2.    *Where learners put newly-formed concepts to use, the concepts will be better learned.***

The opportunity to practice identifying examples and non-examples builds procedural knowledge. This practice may continue long beyond the concept lesson as learners apply the concept to real-world problems (Tennyson & Cocchiarella, 1986; Spiro, 1988).

Computer-based instruction is especially effective for practicing concept classification. It can be self-paced, provide adaptive feedback, and provide only the number of examples and non-examples the student needs. Using simulations, computers and interactive technologies can present realistic cases as examples.

Presenting even introductory concepts within the context of a case study or problem-solving situation facilitates transfer of those concepts to real-world situations (Spiro, 1988).

**6.3.    *Verify the learner's concept by presenting additional examples and non-examples not used during instruction and having learners identify them, or by requiring learners to use the concept in a problem-solving context.***

# Chapter Summary

In sum, a workable expository presentation method for concepts would be the following:

A.  Present one clear example in context.
    1.  Label it.
B.  Present the rule (definition).
C.  Present other examples of greater complexity and diversity (also in context).
    1.  Repeat labeling and point out attributes to draw connections between examples.
    2.  Get learners to label the examples.
    3.  Have all examples in view.
D.  If the concept is a coordinate concept, begin to introduce close-in (matching) non-examples showing the matched examples and non-examples simultaneously.
    1.  Use different labels for non-examples.

2. Point out differences in attributes.
E. Give learners practice in differentiating examples and non-examples and in applying examples.

Such a lesson to teach the concept "democracy" might begin with a discussion of governing to set a context for the concept. It would probably emphasize the different levels of formal and informal governance. Depending on the age level and experience of the learners, a prototype for democracy might be the federal government of the Untied States or a school governing body such as the Student Council. The characteristic (attribute) of rule by the majority might be articulated. The concept might be approached as a disjunctive concept since the rule may be either direct or through representation. Consequently, both of those concepts might be introduced, thereby leading to such variable attributes as free elections being described.

Additional examples of democracies would be introduced, varying the level of government and the characteristics of direct and indirect representation. Some would include other national governments, other state and local bodies, other clubs and organizations.

Since coordinate concepts such as dictatorship and monarchy exist (to mention only two of the concepts which might be considered coordinate to democracy), non-examples would also be introduced. These would be presented as matched pairs (for example two national governments similar except for the specific characteristics which comprise democracy). The non-examples would move from those which are more obviously not representatives of the class democracy toward those which might be more easily confused. As with the presentation of examples, care would be taken to represent governments at all levels rather than only national governments.

As a test of concept attainment, students might be given characteristics of several governments not used in the lesson and asked to indicate whether they were or were not democracies.

This description presumes a rather straightforward approach; that does not mean to indicate that such a lesson could not be treated very creatively and still follow the basic lines of a traditional concept learning lesson.

A contrasting problem-solving approach for a concept might be as follows:
A. Involve students in a real-world problem which focuses learner attention on the concept to be learned; label it.
B. Charge the learners to resolve the issue or to defend alternative points of view on the issue.
C. Model expert thinking on the issue; where possible allow learners to analyze the approaches, models, and thoughts of more than one expert.
D. Guide the learners to find evidence to support resolution of the problem in a certain direction or defense of a point of view. Such evidence might include the definition, attributes, examples, or non-examples of the concept.

In such a lesson, the teacher might start with a collection of papers or news articles dealing with the formation of various groups and the developing governments of those groups, e.g., a nation facing revolution, a new civic group, and an organization within the school. An open discussion might ensue about how people form organizations and decide how to govern themselves. Small groups might be formed to examine governance at different levels with the end goal of making recommendations to the national government, the civic group and the school club concerning their form of governance.

To ensure a variety of approaches, the teacher might create several groups at the same levels (i.e., three groups dealing with the problem at the level of a nation, three at the city level, and three at the school level). Depending on the age of the students, the teacher might expose them to modeling of experts in the field, i.e., individuals in government, news reporters, professors in organizational theory or political science, etc. S/He might further guide the process by requiring that each group outline two or three alternatives and then defend one, that they describe the distribution of power within the alternatives, etc.

At the end of the exercise the teacher might assess learning by providing a novel situation and having students apply the knowledge they have acquired and defend their thoughts. This teacher would not be looking for a right answer to a classification task, but rather for clear thinking spanning the issues.

Finally, the lesson might require each group to present their thinking about the issues and to challenge each others' thinking. At the end or in the middle of the exercise, they might try to classify their ideas into classical definitions of government, including democracy, monarchy, dictatorship, etc.

# References

Bransford, J. D., Sherwood, R. D., Hasselbring, T. S., Kinzer, C. K., & Williams, S. M. (in press). Anchored instruction: Why we need it and how technology can help. In D. Nix & R. Spiro (Eds.), *Advances in computers and instruction.* Hillsdale, NJ: Lawrence Erlbaum Associates.

Brown, J. S., Collins, A., & Duguid, P. (1989). Situated cognition and the culture of learning. *Educational Researcher, 18,* 32–42.

Collins, A., Brown, J. S., & Newman, S. E. (1988). Cognitive apprenticeship: Teaching the craft of reading, writing, and mathematics. In L. B. Resnick (Ed.), *Cognition and instruction: Issues and agendas.* Hillsdale, NJ: Lawrence Erlbaum Associates.

Engelmann, S. (1969). *Conceptual learning.* San Rafael, CA: Dimensions Publishing Co.

Gagné, R. M., & Briggs, L. J. (1979). *Principles of instructional design.* New York: Holt, Rinehart, & Winston.

Hampton, J. A. (1981). An investigation of the nature of abstract concepts. *Memory and Cognition, 9,* 149–156.

Hayes, J. R. (1978). *Cognitive psychology.* Homewood, IL: Dorsey Press.

Hickey, A. E., & Newton, J. M. (1964). *The logical basis of teaching: 1. The effect of subconcept sequence on learning. Final Report,* Office of Naval Research, Contract Non+ 4215(00).

Karplus, R., & Stage, E. K. (1981). *Misconceptions in science: Past work and present approaches.* Group in Science and Mathematics Education, University of California, Berkeley, California.

Klausmeier, H. J., Ghatala, E. S., & Frayer, D. A. (1974). *Conceptual learning and development: A cognitive view.* New York: Academic Press.

Mechner, F. (1967). Behavioral analyses and instructional sequencing. In P. C. Lange (Ed.), *Programmed instruction (Vol. 66), NSSE Yearbook Pt. 2,* Chicago: University of Chicago Press.

Medin, M. D., & Smith, E. E. (1984). Concepts and concept formation. *Annual Review of Psychology, 35,* 113–138.

Merrill, D. M., Tennyson, R. D., & Posey, L. O. (1992). *Teaching concepts: An instructional design guide* (2nd ed.). Englewood Cliffs, NJ: Educational Technology Publications.

Newby, T. J., & Stepich, D. A. (1987). Learning abstract concepts: The use of analogies as a mediational strategy. *Journal of Instructional Development, 10,* 20–26.

Norman, D. A., & Rumelhart, D. E. (1975). *Explorations in cognition.* San Francisco: Freeman.

Oden, G. C. (1987). Concept, knowledge, and thought. *Annual Review of Psychology, 38,* 203–227.

Reigeluth, C. M., & Stein, F. S. (1983). The elaboration theory of instruction. In C. Reigeluth (Ed.), *Instructional design theories and models: An overview of their current status.* Hillsdale, NJ: Lawrence Erlbaum Associates.

Resnick, L. (1987). Learning in school and out. *Educational Researcher, 16,* 13–20.

Romiszowski, A. J. (1981). *Designing instructional systems.* New York: Nichols Publishing.

Rosch, E. (1975). Cognitive representations of semantic categories. *Journal of Experimental Psychology: General, 104,* 192–233.

Rosch, E. (1978). Principles of categorization. In E. Rosch & B. B. Lloyd (Eds.), *Cognition and categorization.* Hillsdale, NJ: Lawrence Erlbaum Associates.

Rosch, E. H., & Mervis, C. B. (1975). Family resemblances: Studies in the internal structure of categories. *Cognitive Psychology, 7,* 573–605.

Sheppard, A. N. (1971). *Changing learner conceptual behavior through the selective use of positive and negative examples,* Ed. D. Thesis, Indiana University.

Simon, H. A. (1979). Information processing models of cognition. *Annual Review of Psychology, 30,* 383–396.

Spiro, R. (1988). *Cognitive flexibility theory: Advanced knowledge acquisition in ill-structured domains.* Technical Rep. No.441. Champaign, IL: Center for the Study of Reading.

Stanley, W. B., & Mathews, R. C. (1985). Recent research on concept learning: Implications for social education. *Theory and Research in Social Education, 12,* 57–74.

Stevens, A. L., Collins, A., & Goldin, S. (1979). Misconceptions in students' understanding. *International Journal of Man-Machine Studies, 11,* 145–156.

Tennyson, R. D., & Breuer, K. (1984). Cognitive-based design guidelines for using video and computer technology in course development. In O. Zuber-Skerritt (Ed.), *Video in higher education* (pp. 25–63). London: Kogan Page.

Tennyson, R. D., & Cocchiarella, M. J. (1986). An empirically based instructional design theory for teaching concepts. *Review of Educational Research, 56*, 40–71.

Underwood, B. J. (1983). *Attributes of memory.* Glenview, IL: Scott, Foresman.

Wilson, B. G. (1986). What is a concept? Concept teaching and cognitive psychology. *Performance and Instruction, 25*, 16–18.

# Chapter 6

# Problem-Solving Principles

## Richard E. Mayer

### University of California, Santa Barbara

## Introduction

Suppose we asked a student to read a passage about how a bicycle tire pump works and then we asked the student to suggest ways to make a pump more efficient. This is an example of transfer of conceptual knowledge, that is, of applying conceptual information from one domain to a novel situation; this is also an example of qualitative problem solving because the student must reason logically but without numerical quantities. I refer to this kind of thinking as *scientific problem solving*.

In contrast, suppose we taught a student the basic procedure for solving time-rate-distance equations, and then tested the student on a word problem that required using that equation. This is an example of transfer of a cognitive skill, applying a cognitive skill learned in one context to a more complex context; this is also an example of quantitative problem solving because the student must reason logically about numerical quantities. I refer to this kind of thinking as *mathematical problem solving.*

This chapter examines instructional design principles for teaching about conceptual information and cognitive skills in ways that enable students to engage in problem-solving transfer. The first section focuses on instructional design for scientific problem solving: a basic instructional theory is presented, followed by specific principles for fostering scientific problem solving. The second section focuses on mathematical problem solving: it begins with a basic instructional theory and then lays out the specific principles for fostering mathematical problem solving.

# I.  Instructional Principles for Scientific Problem Solving

How can we design instructional text so that students will be able to creatively use what they have learned to solve problems? To answer this question, this section presents principles for the design of instructional text when the goal of instruction is to enhance students' performance on tests of problem solving within a domain. The section begins by examining three theoretical questions—concerning the what, when, and how of instructional design for problem solving; then, the section focuses on principles—suggested by research but warranting further study—for how to help learners to direct their attention to conceptual information (i.e., how to acquire relevant information), to organize the information into coherent structures (i.e, how to build internal connections), and to integrate the information with their existing knowledge (i.e., how to build external connections).

## Theory: Cognition and Instruction in Scientific Problem Solving

*What is instructional design that promotes scientific problem solving?* Previous analyses (Mayer, 1984, 1987a, 1989) have shown that student learning can be evaluated in many ways including:

*verbatim retention*—in which the goal is to remember information exactly as presented in the text;

*non-conceptual retention*—in which the goal is to remember individual pieces of information that are not needed to support concepts;

*conceptual retention*—in which the goal is to remember information that is part of a system of conceptual knowledge needed for problem solving;

*problem-solving transfer*—in which the goal is to be able to solve problems that go beyond specific information presented in the text.

For example, Figure 6.1 presents a portion of an instructional text from the *World Book Encyclopedia* on how pumping systems work, with italics indicating the conceptual information about the cause-and-effect chain of events inside a pump; and Figure 6.2 presents some questions that evaluate verbatim retention, non-conceptual retention, conceptual retention, and problem-solving transfer. As can be seen, the definition of "conceptual knowledge" in this chapter goes beyond the definition of "concept" presented in Chapter 5 (Concept Learning Principles) to include explanative models which contain systems of interacting concepts.

Figure 6.3 summarizes three possible learning outcomes for a student who reads a text like the one in Figure 6.1 and answers questions like those in Figure 6.2. A student who performs poorly on all four types of questions could be called a *non-learner*. A student who excels on verbatim retention and non-conceptual retention could be called a *rote learner*. A student who excels on conceptual retention and problem-solving transfer could be called a *meaningful learner*. Problem-solving principles are defined as those intended to foster problem-

...It is theoretically possible for a lift pump to raise water 34 feet (10.4 meters). However, because of leakage and resistance, it cannot raise water that is deeper than about 25 feet (7.6 meters).

Bicycle tire pumps vary in the number and location of the valves they have and in the way air enters the cylinder. Some simple bicycle tire pumps have the inlet valve on the piston and the outlet valve at the closed end of the cylinder. A bicycle tire pump has a piston that moves up and down. Air enters the pump near the point where the connecting rod passes through the cylinder. *As the rod is pulled out, air passes through the piston and fills the areas between the piston and the outlet valve. As the rod is pushed in, the inlet valve closes and the piston forces air through the outlet valve.*

Pumping devices have been an important means of moving fluid for thousands of years. The ancient Egyptians used water wheels with buckets mounted on them to move water for irrigation. The buckets scooped water from wells and streams and deposited it in ditches that carried it to fields. In the 200's B.C., Ctesibius, a Greek inventor, made a reciprocating pump for pumping water...

**Figure 6.1.** Portion of a passage on pumps (*World Book Encyclopedia*, 1990).

| Type of test | Example |
|---|---|
| Verbatim retention | When asked to fill in the blank for "It is theoretically possible for a lift pump to raise water _____ feet" a student says: "25." |
| Non-conceptual retention | When asked to recall the information a student says: "In 200 B.C., the first reciprocating pump was invented." |
| Conceptual retention | When asked to recall the information a student says: "When the rod is pushed down, air is pushed out." |
| Problem-solving transfer | When asked, "How could you make a pump more efficient?" a student says: "Increase the size of the cylinder." |

**Figure 6.2.** Examples of four types of test questions.

Type of test

| Type of learner | Verbatim retention | Non-conceptual retention | Conceptual retention | Problem-solving transfer |
|---|---|---|---|---|
| Non-learner | - | - | - | - |
| Rote learner | + | + | - | - |
| Meaningful learner | - | - | + | + |

Note.   + indicates relatively good performance, - indicates relatively poor performance.

**Figure 6.3.** Three kinds of learning outcomes.

solving transfer and conceptual retention rather than other measures of learning (Mayer, 1984). This section, therefore, is concerned with text design principles that support meaningful learning—as measured by improved retention of conceptual information and improved problem-solving performance on transfer tests.

*When can instructional design promote scientific problem solving?* In order to successfully adapt instructional design principles for problem solving to a specific learning situation, an instructional designer should consider four elements: the instructional material (including both words and pictures), the student, the test, and the instructional manipulation (Mayer & Gallini, 1990). These four elements for successful instructional design interventions are summarized in Figure 6.4. First, the text must be potentially meaningful, that is, the text should convey information that can be used to solve problems, such as an explanation of how something works. If the text simply is a collection of random facts or descriptions, the potential for meaningful learning is lacking. Second, the student must be in need of high-quality instruction, that is, the student must not normally use productive learning strategies for processing expository text. If the student possesses learning skills and knowledge that allow him or her to productively process the text, then instructional design manipulations intended to elicit this processing are not needed. Third, the evaluation of the learning outcome must be sensitive to the goal of instruction, namely to promote conceptual retention and problem-solving transfer. If the test simply measures overall amount retained, there will be no way to document the effects of the instructional design manipulations. Finally, the instructional manipulations must

1. INSTRUCTIONAL MATERIAL IS POTENTIALLY MEANINGFUL:
Use explanative text and illustrations rather than collection of facts.

2. LEARNER WILL NOT NATURALLY ENGAGE APPROPRIATE COGNITIVE PROCESSING:
Teach low-prior knowledge or low-skill student.

3. TEST MEASURES LEARNER UNDERSTANDING:
Evaluate problem-solving transfer and conceptual retention.

4. INSTRUCTIONAL DESIGN FOSTERS APPROPRIATE COGNITIVE PROCESSING:
Use design principles to foster selective attention and building connections.

**Figure 6.4.** Four elements of successful instructional design for scientific problem solving.

be adapted in a way that is appropriate for the text, the learner, and the test. The next section summarizes techniques for accomplishing this goal.

*How can instructional design promote scientific problem solving?* A basic tenet of cognitive theories of learning is that meaningful learning occurs when a person *assimilates presented* information to his or her existing knowledge and/or *accommodates* his or her knowledge to fit new incoming information (Mayer, 1987a). Figure 6.5 presents a model of memory stores and cognitive processes involved in meaningful learning. As you can see, the model includes three memory stores (indicated by boxes):

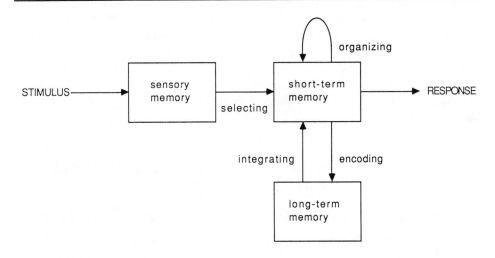

**Figure 6.5.** A model of the human information processing system.

*sensory memory*—sensory information from the eyes enters this rapidly fading, temporary store;

*short-term memory*—a limited amount of information transferred from sensory memory may be held and actively manipulated in this limited capacity store; and

*long-term memory*—this storehouse is where knowledge is permanently stored.

As you can see, the model includes four cognitive processes (indicated by arrows):

*selecting*—the learner pays attention to certain pieces of incoming information in sensory memory and transfers them to short-term memory for additional processing;

*organizing*—the learner builds connections among pieces of incoming information in short-term memory;

*integrating*—the learner transfers relevant information from long-term memory to short-term memory and connects it with incoming information; and

*encoding*—the learner transfers the constructed learning outcome from short-term memory to long-term memory for permanent storage.

The cognitive model of learning presented in Figure 6.5 suggests three cognitive conditions for meaningful learning: paying attention to relevant information, building internal connections, and building external connections (Mayer, 1984, 1987a). These three conditions are summarized in Figure 6.6, and examples from the pump text are given in Figure 6.7. (See also graphics in Figure 6.11.) First, the learner must select the conceptual information from the text, such as the cause-and-effect events that are italicized in Figure 6.1. Second, the learner must organize the information into a coherent structure, such as a chain of causes and effects in which one event serves as the cause of the next. Third, the learner must integrate this information within a familiar context, such as relating it to a concrete model of a pump or to some physical principles of air pressure. These three cognitive conditions represent special cases of cognitive processes that were discussed in Chapter 2 (Perception Principles) and Chapter 4 (Learning Principles). When the three conditions are met, students will build a learning outcome containing conceptual information that supports problem-solving transfer; when the first condition is not met, the result is no learning, and when the first condition is met but the second and/or third conditions are not met, the result is rote learning. The remainder of this section presents instructional design principles for fostering each of these three cognitive conditions for meaningful learning.

# 1. Principles for Acquiring Relevant Information

### 1.1.   Use text manipulations that guide attention to relevant information.

The first cognitive prerequisite for meaningful learning is that the learner pay attention to the relevant information. To accomplish this goal, the text must actually contain potentially relevant information; the instructional designer must

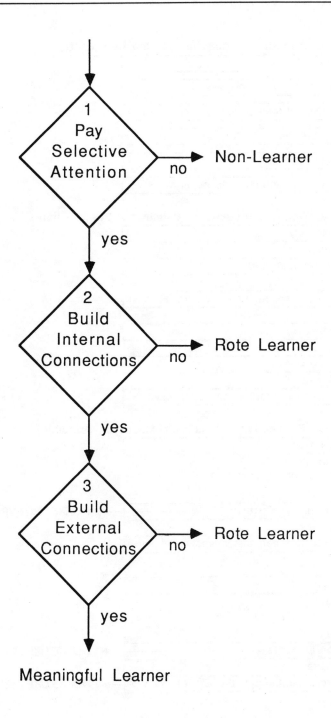

**Figure 6.6.** Three conditions for meaningful learning of scientific problem solving.

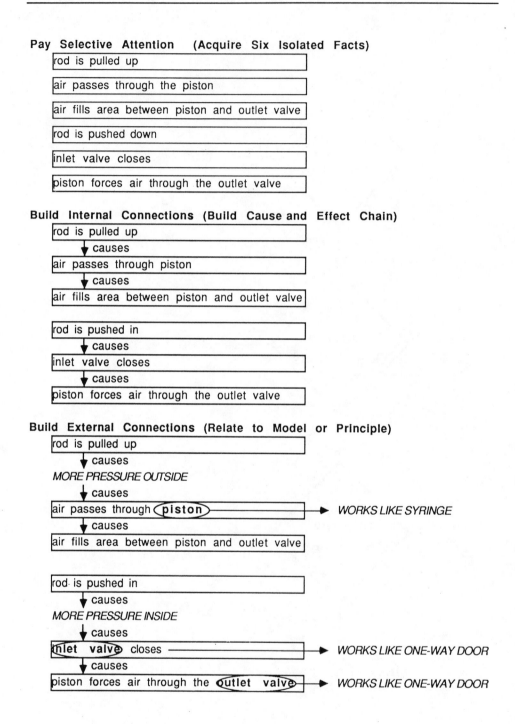

**Figure 6.7.** Examples of three conditions for meaningful learning.

successfully employ a procedure for identifying the relevant information; and the instructional designer must effectively draw the learner's attention to the relevant information (Mayer, 1984). For example, in Figure 6.1 the conceptually relevant information consists of "cause-and-effect" statements about how a change in the status of one component affects a change in the status of another component; this relevant information is italicized in Figure 6.1. The goal of attention-guiding manipulations in the text is to tell the reader how he/she should control his/her attentional processing. Instead of fostering a default strategy of viewing the text as a list of equally important facts, attention-guiding manipulations help the reader to allocate more of his or her attention to conceptually important information (Bromage & Mayer, 1981). Several specific recommendations for how to guide attention are given in the following three principles.

### *1.1a. Use headings, italics, boldface, larger font, bullets, arrows, icons, underlining, margin notes, repetition, and/or white space to highlight the relevant information.*

Readers may view an expository text as a list of facts, and therefore pay equal attention to each piece of information. The purpose of highlighting manipulations is to draw the reader's attention to specific relevant information in the text (Mayer, 1987a). For example, Figure 6.8 shows how white space can be used to highlight the "cause-and-effect" statements in the pumps text.

### *1.1b. Use adjunct questions to emphasize relevant information.*

Students may normally expect to answer non-conceptual retention questions such as those listed in Figure 6.2 and therefore attend to non-conceptual information in the text. In contrast, adjunct questions can be used to guide the reader's attention toward the conceptually relevant information in the text (McConkie, Rayner, & Wilson, 1973; Watts & Anderson, 1971). For example, Figure 6.8 includes several adjunct questions that focus on conceptually relevant information. These questions can have both a "backwards effect" of drawing the reader's attention back to relevant information in the current text, and a "forward effect" of drawing the reader's attention to conceptual type information in subsequent passages (Mayer, 1975). A related technique is to ask the reader to underline or highlight the conceptually relevant information in the passage.

### *1.1c. Use statements of instructional objectives to emphasize relevant information.*

Figure 6.8 also provides an example of how instructional objectives can be used to emphasize the conceptual information in the text, similar to the use of adjunct questions. It should be noted, however, that statements of instructional objectives could also be used to direct the reader's attention toward isolated facts rather than conceptual information (Mayer, 1984).

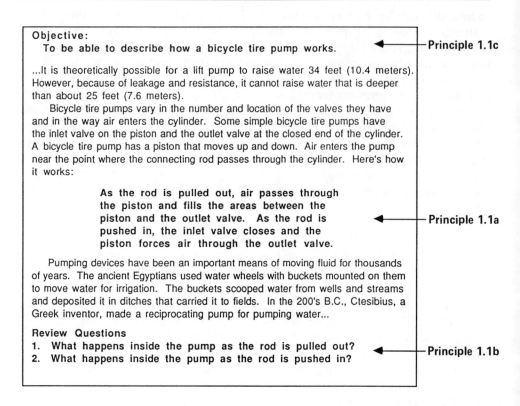

**Figure 6.8.** Examples of principles for acquiring relevant information.

# 2. Principles for Building Internal Connections

## 2.1. Use text manipulations that foster the building of internal connections.

Selectively paying attention to the relevant information is just the first step in meaningful learning. The second cognitive prerequisite for meaningful learning is that the learner organize the selected pieces of information into a coherent structure. The instructional materials should signal to the reader how to build internal connections that organize the material into the appropriate structure (Chambliss & Calfee, 1989; Cook & Mayer, 1988: Meyer, 1975; Meyer, Brandt, & Bluth, 1980), as described in the following seven principles.

### 2.1a. Use a coherent top-level structure for chapters.

We begin with the straightforward premise that students cannot discover the structure of a chapter if the chapter structure is incoherent. Therefore, the chapter should have an unambiguous underlying structure, corresponding to a basic expository text structure (Britton & Black, 1985; Calfee & Chambliss, 1987; Chambliss & Calfee, 1989; Cook & Mayer, 1988; Meyer, 1975; Meyer, Brandt, & Bluth, 1980). Figure 6.9 summarizes five basic top-level structures that are frequently used in expository text: cause-and-effect, compare-and-contrast, categorization, enumeration, and generalization. For example, in Figure 6.10 the top-level structure is enumeration because three types of positive displacement pumps are presented.

| Type of structure | Definition | Example |
|---|---|---|
| cause-and-effect | Describes a logically connected series of events or steps in a process, in which one event or step enables or causes the next. | Hearing involves five stages. First, sound waves are captured and focused by the external portion of the ear. Second, the sound waves travel down the auditory canal and strike the eardrum. In the third stage, the vibrations on the eardrum cause a series of similar vibrations in several small bones. Fourth, when these vibrations reach the cochlea in the inner ear they are translated into neural impulses. Finally, the brain interprets the neural impulses. |
| compare-and-contrast | Examines the similarities and differences between two or more things along one or more dimensions. | Empiricism and nativism offer two contrasting views of the origins of human knowledge and of human language learning. On the one hand, empiricism holds that all knowledge comes from experience and that language learning is the most heavily influenced by the environment. In contrast, nativism holds that knowledge is innate and we are born with the language concepts. |
| categorization | Presents a classification system for grouping items into classes or categories. | There are two major kinds of pumps: reciprocating pumps and rotary pumps. Examples of reciprocating pumps include a bicycle tire pump and a lift pump used for water wells. Examples of rotary pumps include the vane pump and the gear pump. |
| enumeration | Lists items that all belong to same topic. | Solids have four general characteristics. (1) Tenacity represents the solid's resistance to being pulled apart. (2) Hardness is a measure of a substance's ability to scratch another substance. (3) Malleability refers to a solid's ability to be hammered or rolled into thin sheets. (4) Ductility is the ability to stretch a solid into the form of wires. |
| generalization | Provides an assertion along with statements that clarify, extend, exemplify or support the assertion. | International comparisons indicate that American students lag behind their international counterparts in mathematics achievement. For example, in a recent study 50% of the elementary school children in the U.S. gave the correct answers for basic computation problems whereas 85% of Japanese children of comparable age computed correctly. One reason cited for the differences is that students in Japan spend approximately 50% more time in school studying mathematics than students in the U.S. |

**Figure 6.9.** Five types of text structure.

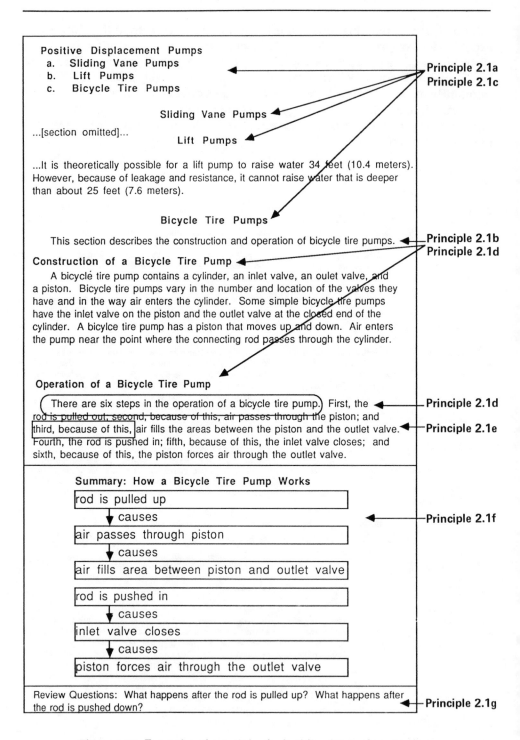

**Figure 6.10.** Examples of principles for building internal connections.

### 2.1b. Use a coherent structure for each subordinate topic.

The premise underlying Principle 2.1a should also be applied to chapter sections and subsections. Each section or subsection should have a clear structure. For example, in Figure 6.10 each section consists of two subsections, one describing the construction of a type of pump and one describing the pump's operation.

### 2.1c. Use preview chapter outlines matched to section headings.

A straightforward way to clarify the top-level organization at the beginning of a chapter is to state the section topics and their relations to one another, either in outline form or as an introductory paragraph. To help readers monitor their location in the outline, as they read the text, section headings should be used that correspond to the wording of the preview outline. An example is given in Figure 6.10. If possible, all section headings should be expressed in the same format and should hold the same relation to the chapter; for example, in Figure 6.10 the headings are all written as names of pumps and hold the "type-of" (or "example of") relation to the chapter topic. Other common relations between chapters and sections (or sections and subsections) include part of, characteristic of, evidence for, or leads to (Dansereau *et al.*, 1979).

### 2.1d. Use preview section outlines matched to the paragraph or sentence structure of the section.

Consistent with Principle 2.1c concerning the organization of sections into a chapter, each section should have a clearly articulated structure. The section should begin with a preview of the subsections, and subheadings should correspond to the wording used in the section preview. Wherever possible, use parallel subsection structures in all sections of a chapter. For example, in Figure 6.10 each of the three sections contains the same two subsections in adherence with Principle 2.1d.

### 2.1e. Use signals to clarify the text structure.

Signals are words or short phrases inserted in the text that clarify structural organization (Loman & Mayer, 1983; Meyer, 1975). For example, in a cause-and-effect passage, signals such as "first," "second," and "third" indicate the order of events; and signals such as "because of this," "this causes," or "the result is" indicate the causal structure of events. For example in Figure 6.10, signal words are used to indicate the order of steps in the operation of the bicycle tire pump.

### 2.1f. Use summaries to clarify text structure.

Just as preview outlines can be used at the beginning of a text to highlight its structure, summaries can be used at the end of a text to serve the same purpose

(Wittrock, 1974). Summaries may be presented in the form of tables, figures, or words. For example, Figure 6.10 includes a flowchart to summarize the cause-and-effect structure presented in the subsection on how a pump works. In addition, a matrix could be used for compare-and-contrast structure, a tree for classification, a hierarchy for enumeration, and a network for generalization.

### 2.1g.  Use summary questions to emphasize text structure.

Another way to foster the active building of internal connections is to ask the reader to summarize the passage by writing a short organized summary, an outline, or specific questions about the organization of elements in the text. Examples are given at the bottom of Figure 6.10.

# 3.  Principles for Building External Connections

### 3.1.  Use text manipulations that foster building of external connections.

The third cognitive prerequisite for meaningful learning is that the learner build external connections between the new incoming information and appropriate existing knowledge that is already in his or her memory. To accomplish this goal, the learner must have carried out the first two steps—paying attention to and coherently organizing the new information—and must have available appropriate existing knowledge into which the new information can be assimilated. In cases where the learner possesses appropriate existing knowledge, the text should include cues for how to integrate the presented information with existing knowledge; in cases where the learner does not possess relevant existing knowledge, the text should provide familiar background information as well as cues for how to assimilate new information to it. The following four principles provide specific examples of how to implement this general principle.

### 3.1a.  Use conceptual advance organizers to provide context.

A conceptual advance organizer presents the conceptual principles that underlie the to-be-read material, either in verbal or pictorial form (Ausubel, 1968; Mayer, 1979, 1989). The purpose is to provide an assimilative context for interpreting the information in the text. For example, in Figure 6.11 the conceptual advance organizer introduces the principle that gases flow from space with higher pressure (or density) to space with lower pressure (or density). This principle extends a similar principle in Chapter 4 (Learning Principles) by focusing on organizing new information in a way that will support problem solving rather than solely on the acquisition of new information.

### Introduction     ◄━ **Principle 3.1a**

Pumps operate on the following principle: Air moves from a space with more pressure to a space of less pressure. If there is a vacuum (low pressure), air will move in; if air is compressed from a larger space into a smaller space (high pressure) it will move out.

### Bicycle Tire Pumps
This section describes the construction and operation of bicycle tire pumps.

#### Construction of a Bicycle Tire Pump
A bicycle tire pump contains a cylinder, an inlet valve, an oulet valve, and a piston. Bicycle tire pumps vary in the number and location of the valves they have and in the way air enters the cylinder. Some simple bicycle tire pumps have the inlet valve on the piston and the outlet valve at the closed end of the cylinder. A bicycle tire pump has a piston that moves up and down. Air enters the pump near the point where the connecting rod passes through the cylinder.

#### Operation of a Bicycle Tire Pump
There are six steps in the operation of a bicycle tire pump. First, the rod is pulled out; second, because of this, air passes through the piston; and third, because of this, air fills the areas between the piston and the outlet valve. Fourth, the rod is pushed in; fifth, because of this, the inlet valve closes; and sixth, because of this, the piston forces air through the outlet valve.

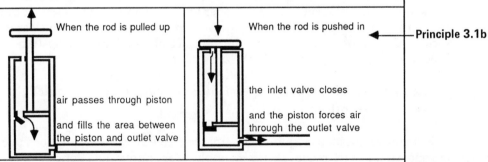

When the rod is pulled up     When the rod is pushed in ◄━ **Principle 3.1b**

air passes through piston and fills the area between the piston and outlet valve

the inlet valve closes and the piston forces air through the outlet valve

### Sarah's Answer to a Question About Pumps   ◄━ **Principle 3.1c**

Question: Suppose you pull up and push down on the handle of a bicycle tire pump but no air comes out. What could be wrong?
Answer: First, I thought of things that prevent the formation of a vacuum (or lower pressure) inside the cylinder when I pull up: if the valve is stuck open or the seal leaks, air would be sucked in from the hose into the cylinder. So one possibility is the outlet valve is stuck open. Second, I thought of things that prevent the formation of compression inside the cylinder when I press down: if the inlet valve is stuck open then the air would just escape upward through the inlet valve when I pushed down; another way this could happen is if there were a hole in the cylinder or piston.

Review Questions: How is the piston like a syringe? How is the inlet valve like ◄━ **Principle 3.1d**
a one-way door. What is the principle for air entering and exiting the pump?

**Figure 6.11.** Examples of principles for building external connections.

### 3.1b.  Use analogical models or pictures to provide context.

An analogical model (or concrete advance organizer) is a familiar visual or verbal representation of some system; the model contains elements, states, and actions (or operating rules) that map onto the elements, states, and actions of the real system. Seven characteristics of effective models include: *complete*—the essential elements, states, and actions of the system are represented; *concise*—the level of detail is minimal; *coherent*—the operation of the system is intuitively transparent; *concrete*—the level of familiarity and visualization is high; *conceptual*—the system is potentially understandable; *correct*—the elements, states, and actions correspond to the actual system; and *considerate*—the presentation style and vocabulary are appropriate for the learner (Levin & Mayer, in press). Figure 6.11 includes a model of a pump, showing its main parts, states, and actions. Possible analogies include the idea that a piston in a cylinder is like a syringe, and a valve is like a one-way door.

### 3.1c.  Show worked-out examples for procedures with annotations.

When the goal of instruction is to foster effective problem-solving performance, the text may include conceptual problems, along with worked-out solutions, showing each step in the solution process. The purpose of presenting worked-out examples is to help the reader to understand the process that can be used to approach the problem. In short, worked-out examples help the learner to focus on the process rather than the product of problem solving (Bloom & Broder, 1950). An example is summarized as part of Figure 6.11.

### 3.1d.  Use elaborative questions to encourage knowledge integration.

Elaborative questions require the learner to create answers to questions that go beyond simple fact retrieval; for example, elaborative questions require the learner to apply information in the text to a new context, to expand on certain aspects of the text, or to relate aspects of the text to some existing knowledge. Elaborative questions are intended to foster active learning strategies, epitomized by the building of external connections (Mayer, 1980). Figure 6.11 includes examples of elaborative questions for the pumps text.

# II.  Instructional Principles for Mathematical Problem Solving

In the foregoing section, we explored principles for improving instructional text, when the goal of instructon is to help students engage in qualitative reasoning about scientific concepts. In this section, we explore principles for improving students' mathematical problem-solving skills, that is, for helping students successfully apply quantitative reasoning skills to novel problems.

## Theory: Cognition and Instruction in Mathematical Problem Solving

*What is instructional design that supports mathematical problem solving?* Traditionally, instruction focuses on teaching students to perform specific skills that are identical to those that will be required on a test. For example, in teaching students to solve time-rate-distance problems, a common approach might be to have students learn to use the formula,

distance = rate × time

During instruction, students might be asked to answer questions such as: "If the rate is 5 miles per hour and the time is 2 hours, what is the distance?" Thus, the instruction focuses on substituting values for variables and on carrying out arithmetic operations. A direct test of *retention* of these skills would be to ask questions like those given during instruction, such as: "If the rate is 2 miles per hour and the time is 5 hours, what is the distance?"

However, when the goal of instruction is problem-solving transfer, instruction should focus on skills that will enable a student to apply what has been learned to new problems. For example, we might want our students to learn about time-rate-distance problems in a way that enables them to solve problems that go beyond what they were taught. As a *near transfer* problem, we might present the following problem: "John leaves his house at 1:00 and walks at a constant rate of 2 miles per hour. At 3:00, how far will he have walked?" As a *far transfer* problem, we might give this problem: "Two hikers start at the same time from towns 27 miles apart. They walk toward each other and meet in 3 hours. One hiker is going twice as fast as the other. What is the rate of each hiker?" In conclusion, this section is concerned with instructional design principles that promote problem-solving transfer of quantitative reasoning skills.

*When can instructional design promote mathematical problem solving?* Figure 6.12 lists four elements that may be related to instruction for mathematical problem solving: the material, the learner, the instruction, and the test. First, the to-be-learned material must be potentially meaningful; many components of the mathematics curriculum can be learned either as blind procedures or as meaningful concepts (Hiebert, 1986). Second, the learner must possess appropriate executing skills that are automatized, such as how to compute, but must lack some appropriate skills in how to represent problems and devise plans for solution. Third, the appropriate test of meaningful learning is transfer rather than retention. Fourth, instruction must foster transfer by teaching appropriate cognitive skills rather than focusing solely on getting the right answer.

*How can instructional design promote mathematical problem solving?* What do students need to be able to do in order to become productive problem solvers? Figure 6.13 summarizes four component processes that are involved in solving mathematical word problems: translating, integrating, planning, and executing (Mayer, 1983, 1985; Mayer, Larkin, & Kadane, 1984). Translating involves converting each sentence or phrase into internal representations. Integrating

| 1. TO-BE-LEARNED MATERIAL IS POTENTIALLY MEANINGFUL:<br>Emphasize meaningful concepts rather than blind procedures. |
|---|

| 2. LEARNER HAS COMPUTATIONAL SKILLS BUT LACKS PROBLEM-SOLVING SKILLS:<br>Teach less successful problem-solvers who have well-learned basic skills. |
|---|

| 3. TEST MEASURES LEARNER UNDERSTANDING:<br>Evaluate problem-solving transfer rather than rote retention. |
|---|

| 4. INSTRUCTIONAL DESIGN EMPHASIZES APPROPRIATE PROBLEM-SOLVING SKILLS:<br>Use design principles to foster problem representation and planning processes. |
|---|

**Figure 6.12.** Four elements of successful instructional design for mathematical problem solving.

**Example problem**
At ARCO gas sells for $1.13 per gallon.
This is 5 cents less per gallon than gas at Chevron.
How much do 5 gallons of gas cost at Chevron?

| Component Process | Type of knowledge | Example |
|---|---|---|
| Translating | Linguistic | ARCO = 1.13<br>ARCO + .05 = Chevron<br>Unknown = 5 x Chevron |
| Integrating | Schematic | Unknown = 5 x [1.13 + .05] |
| Planning & monitoring | Strategic | Add .05 to 1.13<br>Multiply result by 5 |
| Executing | Procedural | .05 + 1.13 = 1.18<br>5 x 1.18 = 5.90 |

**Figure 6.13.** Four components for meaningful learning of mathematical problem solving.

involves combining the relevant information into a single coherent representation of the problem. Planning involves devising and monitoring a strategy for how to solve the problem. Executing involves carrying out the solution plan. Together, translating and integrating constitute the problem representation phase of problem solving, whereas planning and executing constitute the problem solution phase of problem solving. In the remainder of this section, techniques for improving students' translating, integrating, and planning skills are described.

# 4. Principles for Translating Problem Sentences

## 4.1. *Provide guidance and practice in understanding sentences in the problem.*

The first step in solving a word problem is to translate each sentence into an internal mental representation (Kintsch & Greeno, 1985). Previous research has demonstrated that students have difficulty in understanding the sentences in word problems, particularly relational statements—i.e., statements that express a quantitative relation between two variables—such as the second sentence in the gasoline problem as presented in Figure 6.13 (Lewis & Mayer, 1987; Lewis, 1989; Riley, Greeno, & Heller, 1983). Instructional text should provide opportunities for students to acquire skill in the translation process—what could be called *translation training*. Specific examples of translation training are provided in the following two principles.

### 4.1a. *Provide guidance and practice in converting difficult problem sentences into equations, other words, procedures, pictures, or concrete models.*

A straightforward instructional design recommendation is to provide many opportunities for students to acquire proficiency in translating difficult sentences into equations, other words, procedures, pictures, or concrete models. The purpose of translation training is to help students develop cognitive skills for encoding quantitative statements. For example, a textbook might include the following problem as an example:

John has 5 marbles.

This is 3 more marbles than Sue has.

How many marbles does Sue have?

However, rather than focusing only on producing the correct answer, we could include translation training by asking the student to convert the second sentence into an equation involving "John's marbles" and "Sue's marbles" (such as "John's marbles = 3 + Sue's marbles"), asking the student to restate the second sentence in his/her own words with Sue as the subject (such as: "Sue has 3 less marbles than John"), asking students to restate the second sentence as a procedure for how to find Sue's marbles (such as: "Take the number of marbles that John has and subtract 3 from that number"), or asking students to draw a picture or move concrete objects to correspond to the second sentence. Figure 6.14 provides examples of multiple-choice items for translation training based on the gasoline problem. Students need to receive specific feedback and guidance concerning their answers and to practice on a wide variety of problems (Mayer, 1987b).

---

**Restating a problem sentence as an equation**

At ARCO gas sells for $1.13 per gallon.
This is 5 cents less than gas at Chevron.
Which of the following equations corresponds to this information?
(a)  ARCO - .05 = Chevron
(b)  ARCO + .05 = Chevron
(c)  None of the above

---

**Restating a problem sentence in other words**

At ARCO gas sells for $1.13 per gallon.
This is 5 cents less than gas at Chevron.
Based on this information, which of the following statements is true?
(a) Gas costs more at ARCO than Chevron
(b) Gas costs more at Chevron than ARCO
(c) None of the above

---

**Restating a problem sentence as a procedure**

At ARCO gas sells for $1.13 per gallon.
This is 5 cents less than gas at Chevron.
To find cost of gas at Chevron:
(a) Add 5 cents to the cost of gas at ARCO
(b) Subtract 5 cents from the cost of gas at ARCO
(c) None of the above

---

**Figure 6.14.** Translation training exercises.

---

### 4.1b. *Provide step-by-step instruction in how to represent difficult sentences.*

A straightforward method for providing translation training is to clearly specify a step-by-step procedure for converting sentences into diagrams, and then ask students to translate various sentences using this procedure. For example, Figure 6.15 provides a four-step worksheet developed by Lewis (1989) to help students represent relational statements in arithmetic word problems. The first step involves placing the value of the first variable on a number line; the second step involves placing the second variable either to the right of the first

### Example Problem
At ARCO gas sells for $1.13 per gallon.
This is 5 cents less per gallon than gas at Chevron.
How much do 5 gallons of gas cost at Chevron?

### Step 1
Draw a number line and place the variable and value from
the assignment statement at the middle of the line.

### Step 2
Tentatively place the unknown value (Chevron) on one side
of the middle.

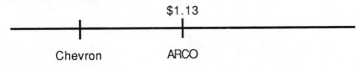

### Step 3
Compare your representation with the information in the
relation statement, checking to see if your representation
agrees with the meaning of the relation statement. If it does,
then you can continue. If not, then try again with the other side.

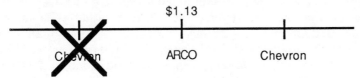

### Step 4
Translate your representation into an arithmetic operation.
If the unknown variable is to the right of the center, then
the operation is an increase, such as addition or multiplication.
If the unknown variable is to the left of the center, then the
operation is a decrease, such as subtraction or division.

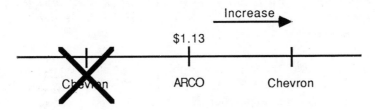

**Figure 6.15.** Translation training worksheet.

variable (signifying that it is greater than the first variable) or to the left (signifying that it is less than the first variable); the third step is compare the diagram with the sentence in the problem; and the fourth step is to determine the appropriate arithmetic operation. (This final step goes beyond translating.) After receiving instruction on how to use the worksheet, students actively apply this procedure to a wide range of problems. The purpose of training in understanding and using this worksheet is to provide students with a systematic procedure for translating sentences into meaningful representations.

# 5. Principles for Integrating Problem Information

### 5.1. *Provide guidance and practice in how to integrate problem information into a coherent representation of the problem.*

The second step in solving a word problem is to integrate each relevant piece of information into a coherent representation of the problem. Previous research has demonstrated that good problem solvers are able to sort problems into categories based on their mathematical properties, whereas less experienced problem solvers are more likely to misclassify a problem in a way that leads to an incorrect solution procedure (Hinsley, Hayes, & Simon, 1977; Mayer, 1981, 1982; Riley, Greeno, & Heller, 1983; Silver, 1979). Instructional text should provide opportunities for students to acquire skill in the integration process—what could be called *schema training.* However, it is important that schema training emphasize the mathematical properties of problems rather than focus on superficial aspects of problems such as keywords (Briars & Larkin, 1984). For example, a student using the *keyword approach* would add numbers if the problem contains the word "more" and subtract if it contains the word "less." This superficial way of categorizing problems can lead to errors when the required operation differs from the keyword; for example, in the marbles problem given above, the keyword is "more" but to solve the problem you must subtract 3 from 5. The next two principles provide specific examples of schema training.

### 5.1a. *Provide guidance and practice in selecting necessary numbers from a problem statement or in distinguishing relevant versus irrelevant information in a problem statement.*

As an example, consider the following problem: Karin's home is 8 blocks from her school. School starts at 8:00. She left home at 7:42 and arrived at school at 7:54. How long did it take her to get there?

Instead of asking only for the student to produce the correct answer, we could engage the student in schema training by asking, "Which numbers are needed to solve this problem?" (The correct answer, of course, is to select 7:42 and 7:54 but not to select 8 or 8:00.) In order to distinguish relevant from irrelevant information, the student needs to build a coherent understanding of the entire problem. Figure 6.16 provides multiple choice examples based on the gasoline problem.

---

**Selecting necessary numbers from a problem statement**

At the ARCO station on Maple Street, regular gas sells for $1.13 per gallon and super sells for $1.33 per gallon. This regular gas is 5 cents less than regular gas at the Chevron station on Oak street. How much do 5 gallons of gas cost at Chevron?
Which numbers are needed to solve this problem?
(a)  1.13, 1.33, 5, 5
(b)  1.33, 5, 5
(c)  1.13, 5, 5
(d)  None of the above

**Distinguishing relevant from irrelevant information**

At the ARCO station on Maple Street, regular gas sells for $1.13 per gallon and super sells for $1.33 per gallon. This regular gas is 5 cents less than regular gas at the Chevron station on Oak street. How much do 5 gallons of gas cost at Chevron?
Which of the following pieces of information is needed to solve this problem?
(a)  ARCO is on Maple Street
(b)  Chevron is on Oak Street
(c)  Super costs 20 cents more than regular at ARCO
(d)  Regular costs 5 cents less at ARCO than at Chevron

**Figure 6.16.** Schema training exercises.

---

### 5.1b. *Provide step-by-step instruction in how to recognize problem types.*

A straightforward method for providing schema training is to clearly define and exemplify each category of problem, and then ask students to sort a collection of problems into categories. For example, Figure 6.17 provides definitions and examples of three types of motion problems (Berger & Wilde, 1987; Mayer, 1981; Reed, 1987, 1989; Reed, Dempster, & Ettinger, 1985). The purpose of this first phase of training is to help students to differentiate their

| Type | Definition | Example |
|------|------------|---------|
| Round trip | A traveler (or vehicle) moves from point A to point B and returns. | George rode out of town on a bus at an average speed of 20 miles per hour and walked back at an average speed of 3 miles per hour. How far did he go if the entire trip took six hours? |
| Speed change | A traveler (or vehicle) travels at a certain speed for the first leg of a trip and then changes to another rate for the remainder of the trip. | Mary jogs and walks to school each day. She averages 4 km/h walking and 8 km/h jogging. The distance from home to school is 6 km and she makes the trip in 1 hour. How far does she jog in a trip? |
| Same direction | Two travelers (or vehicles) leave the same point at the same time traveling in the same direction at different rates. | Two bicyclists start from Lone Ridge at the same time and ride north on highway 50. The first bicyclist averages 12 miles per hour and the second averages 6 miles per hour. How long will it take for the riders to be 12 miles apart? |

*Schema instruction*

Sort the following problems into "round-trip", "speed change", "same direction", or "other" category:

Joe travels from Greenville to Ripley at an average speed of 200 mph while Sam drives from Greenville to Ripley at an average speed of 50 mph. How far from Ripley is Sam when Joe's plane lands there?

Joe travels from Greenville to Ripley at an average speed of 200 mph. He gets a ride back in Sam's car at an average speed of 50 mph. If the trip to and from Ripley takes a total of 10 hours, how far is it from Greenville to Ripley?

Joe travels from Greenville to Ripley part of the way by airplane and part of the way by automobile. The airplane travels at an average speed of 200 mph while the automobile averages 50 mph. If it takes Joe 10 hours to get from Greenville to Ripley, how far apart are they?

Joe leaves Greenville at 8:00 traveling at 50 mph towards Ripley. Sam leaves Ripley at 8:00 traveling at 200 mph towards Ripley. If they meet in 10 hours how far apart are the two towns?

*Sorting exercise*

**Figure 6.17.** Schema training worksheet.

schema for "motion problems" into more refined sub-schemas such as "round-trip" (in which a problem solver must equate two distances), "speed-change" (in which a problem solver must add two distances), and "same-direction" (in which a problem solver must subtract one distance from another). Following this direct instruction about problem types, students need practice sorting problems by type, such as shown in Figure 6.17. The purpose of this second phase of instruction is to help students develop skills for recognizing problem types.

# 6. Principles for Creating and Monitoring Solution Plans

## 6.1. *Provide guidance and practice in specifying and monitoring solution plans.*

Translation training and schema training provide the student with skills for representing problems. Once the problem is at least partially represented, the next step is to develop a plan for solving the problem. Students often do not generate the most efficient plan and often fail to recognize when a plan is not working or has not been carried out properly (Hiebert, 1986; McLeod & Adams, 1989; Schoenfeld, 1985). Traditionally, problem-solving instruction focuses on product, i.e., getting the right answer, rather than on process, i.e., specifying the method or strategy to be used in solving the problem. This is why students need guidance and practice in how to develop and monitor solution plans—*strategy training.* Two specific examples are given in the following two principles.

### 6.1a.  *Provide guidance and practice in establishing subgoals.*

A basic strategy in solving problems is to break a problem into smaller parts or subgoals (Mayer, 1983; Polya, 1945; Schoenfeld, 1985). To provide practice in establishing subgoals, students may be asked to list the needed variables or to identify the necessary operations required by various problems. Figure 6.18

---

**Establishing subgoals**

At the ARCO station on Maple Street, regular gas sells for $1.13 per gallon and super sells for $1.33 per gallon.  This regular gas is 5 cents less than regular gas at the Chevron station on Oak street. How much do 5 gallons of gas cost at Chevron?
What do you need to find in order to solve this problem?
(a) difference between regular and super at ARCO
(b) cost of regular gas per gallon at Chevron
(c) difference between cost of 5 gallons of regular gas at ARCO
     and  Chevron
(d) None of the above

**Identifying  necessary  operations**

At the ARCO station on Maple Street, regular gas sells for $1.13 per gallon and super sells for $1.33 per gallon.  This regular gas is 5 cents less than regular gas at the Chevron station on Oak street. How much do 5 gallons of gas cost at Chevron?
In order to solve this problem, which computations should be carried out?
(a) subtract,  then  multiply
(b) add,  then  multiply
(c) subtract,  subtract  again,  then  multiply
(d) None of the above

**Figure 6.18.** Strategy training exercises.

---

provides examples of multiple-choice exercises that focus on subgoals for the gasoline problem. Students need feedback and guidance concerning each problem.

### 6.1b. *Provide worked-out examples and ask students to compare them to their own step-by-step solutions.*

Figure 6.19 provides a worksheet for the gasoline problem in which the student is asked first to show each step in solving the problem, and then is asked to compare his/her steps to those given in a worked-out example for the problem. In this training, students learn how to describe their problem-solving process and to recognize ways in which their strategies can be improved. This procedure is consistent with successful thinking-skills programs that focus on helping students to compare their problem-solving strategies with strategies used by expert models (Mayer, 1983; Nickerson, Perkins, & Smith, 1985; Segal, Chipman, & Glaser, 1985). In particular, successful thinking-skills programs focus on the process of problem solving rather than solely on the product of problem solving, and teach specific strategies within subject matter domains rather than general strategies independent of subject matter.

---

**Example problem**
At ARCO gas sells for $1.13 per gallon.
This is 5 cents less per gallon than gas at Chevron.
How much do 5 gallons of gas cost at Chevron?

1. How many computations do you need to carry out? ___*2*___

2. What are you trying find in the first step? *cost of gallon at Chevron*

3. What are you trying to find in the second step? *cost of 5 gallons at Chevron*

**Worked-out answer:**

| | |
|---|---|
| 1.13 + .05 = 1.18 | Step 1: Find the cost of a gallon of gas at Chevron. |
| 1.18 x 5 = 5.90 | Step 2: Find the cost of 5 gallons of gas at Chevron. |

**Figure 6.19.** Strategy training worksheet.

# Chapter Summary

The top portion of Figure 6.20 summarizes three types of instructional design principles intended to promote scientific problem-solving performance. First, to encourage learners to pay attention to relevant information, text designers should consider using highlighting, adjunct questions, or statements of objectives. Second, to encourage learners to build internal connections, text designers should consider using preview outlines with headings, signal words, summaries, and summary questions. Third, to encourage learners to build external connections, text designers should consider using conceptual advance organizers, analogical models, worked-out examples, and elaborative questions. The goal of these design manipulations is to help the reader to control his or her cognitive processes during learning.

| | Type of principle | Type of cognitive process | Examples of principles |
|---|---|---|---|
| **Scientific problem solving** | Acquiring relevant information | Attentional processing | Highlighting<br>Adjunct questions<br>Statements of objectives |
| | Building internal connections | Organization processing | Preview outlines with headings<br>Signal words<br>Summaries<br>Summary questions |
| | Building external connections | Integration processing | Conceptual advance organizers<br>Analogical models<br>Worked-out examples<br>Elaborative questions |
| **Mathematical problem solving** | Translation training | Translating problem sentences | Training in how to convert sentences into equations, words or pictures |
| | Schema training | Integrating problem information | Training in how to distinguish relevant versus irrelevant information and how to recognize problem types |
| | Strategy training | Creating and monitoring solution plans | Training in how to establish and describe subgoals |

**Figure 6.20.** Summary of recommended principles.

The bottom portion of Figure 6.20 presents three types of instructional design principles intended to promote mathematical problem-solving performance. First, translation training is needed to help students understand each sentence in the problem. Second, schema training is needed to help students recognize problem types. Third, strategy training is needed to help students develop and monitor solution plans.

The goal of these training programs is to focus on the process of problem solving in a way that will enable students to transfer what they have learned to novel problems.

## Author Note

I appreciate the helpful comments provided by Malcolm Fleming and William Winn.

# References

Ausubel, D. P. (1968). *Educational psychology: A cognitive view.* New York: Holt, Rinehart, & Winston.

Berger, D. E., & Wilde, J. M. (1987). A task analysis of algebra word problems. In D. E. Berger, K. Pezdek, & W. P. Banks (Eds.), *Applications of cognitive psychology: Problem solving, education, and computing.* Hillsdale, NJ: Lawrence Erlbaum Associates, 123–137.

Bloom, B. S., & Broder, L. J. (1950). *Problem-solving processes of college students.* Chicago: University of Chicago Press.

Briars, D. J., & Larkin, J. G. (1984). An integrated model of skills in solving elementary word problems. *Cognition and Instruction, 1,* 245–296.

Britton, B. K., & Black, J. B. (Eds.) (1985). *Understanding expository text.* Hillsdale, NJ: Lawrence Erlbaum Associates.

Bromage, B. K., & Mayer, R. E. (1981). Relationship between what is remembered and creative problem solving in science learning. *Journal of Educational Psychology, 73,* 451–461.

Calfee, R. C., & Chambliss, M. J. (1987). The structural design features of large texts. *Educational Psychologist, 22,* 357–378.

Chambliss, M. J., & Calfee, R. C. (1989). Designing science textbooks to enhance student understanding. *Educational Psychologist, 24,* 307–322.

Cook, L. K., & Mayer, R. E. (1988). Teaching readers about the structure of scientific text. *Journal of Educational Psychology, 80,* 448–456.

Dansereau, D. F., Collins, K. W., McDonald, B. A., Holley, C. D., Garland, J. C., Diekhoff, G., & Evans, S. H. (1979). Development and evaluation of an effective learning strategy program. *Journal of Educational Psychology, 71,* 64–73.

Hiebert, J. (Ed.) (1986). *Conceptual and procedural knowledge: The case of mathematics.* Hillsdale, NJ: Lawrence Erlbaum Associates.

Hinsley, D. A., Hayes, J. R., & Simon, H. A. (1977). From words to equations: Meaning and representation in algebra word problems. In P. A. Carpenter & M. A. Just (Eds.), *Cognitive processes in comprehension.* Hillsdale, NJ: Lawrence Erlbaum Associates, 89–106.

Kintsch, W., & Greeno, J. G. (1985). Understanding and solving word arithmetic problems. *Psychological Review, 92,* 109–129.

Levin, J. R., & Mayer, R. E. (in press). Understanding illustrations in text. In M. Binkley & A. Woodward (Eds.), *Learning from textbooks: Theory and practice.* Hillsdale, NJ: Lawrence Erlbaum Associates.

Lewis, A. B. (1989). Training students to represent arithmetic word problems. *Journal of Educational Psychology, 81,* 521–531.

Lewis, A. B., & Mayer, R. E. (1987). Students' miscomprehension of relational statements on arithmetic word problems. *Journal of Educational Psychology, 79,* 363–371.

Loman, N. J., & Mayer, R. E. (1983). Signaling techniques that increase the understandability of expository prose. *Journal of Educational Psychology, 75,* 402–412.

Mayer, R. E. (1975). Forward transfer of different reading strategies evoked by test-like events in mathematics text. *Journal of Educational Psychology, 67,* 165–167.

Mayer, R. E. (1979). Can advance organizers influence meaningful learning? *Review of Educational Research, 49,* 371–383.

Mayer, R. E. (1980). Elaboration techniques that increase the meaningfulness of technical text: An experimental test of the learning strategy hypothesis. *Journal of Educational Psychology, 72,* 770–784.

Mayer, R. E. (1981). Frequency norms and structural analyses of algebra story problems into families, categories, and templates. *Instructional Science, 10,* 133–175.

Mayer R. E. (1982). Memory for algebra story problems. *Journal of Educational Psychology, 74,* 199–216.

Mayer, R. E. (1983). *Thinking, problem solving, cognition.* New York: Freeman.

Mayer, R. E. (1984). Aids to prose comprehension. *Educational Psychologist, 19,* 30–42.

Mayer, R. E. (1985). Mathematical ability. In R. J. Sternberg (Ed.), *Human ability: An information processing approach.* New York: Freeman, 127–150.

Mayer, R. E. (1987a). *Educational psychology: A cognitive approach.* Boston: Little, Brown.

Mayer, R. E. (1987b). Learnable aspects of problem solving: Some examples. In D. E. Berger, K. Pezdek, & W. P. Banks (Eds.), *Applications of cognitive psychology: Problem solving, education, and computing.* Hillsdale, NJ: Lawrence Erlbaum Associates, 109–122.

Mayer, R. E. (1989). Models for understanding. *Review of Educational Research, 59,* 43–64.

Mayer, R. E., & Gallini, J. (1990). When is a picture worth ten thousand words? *Journal of Educational Psychology, 82,* 715–727.

Mayer, R. E., Larkin, J. H., & Kadane, J. (1984). A cognitive analysis of mathematical problem-solving ability. In R. J. Sternberg (Ed.), *Advances in the psychology of human intelligence, Volume 2.* Hillsdale, NJ: Lawrence Erlbaum Associates, 231–273.

McConkie, G. W., Rayner, K., & Wilson, S. J. (1973). Experimental manipulation of reading strategies. *Journal of Educational Psychology, 65,* 1–8.

McLeod, D. B., & Adams, V. M. (Eds.) (1989). *Affect and mathematical problem solving.* New York: Springer-Verlag.

Meyer, B. J. F. (1975). *The organization of prose and its effect on memory.* Amsterdam: North-Holland.

Meyer, B. J. F., Brandt, D. H., & Bluth, G. J. (1980). Use of top-level structure in text: Key for reading comprehension of ninth-grade students. *Reading Research Quarterly, 16,* 72–103.

Nickerson, R. S., Perkins, D. N., & Smith, E. E. (1985). *The teaching of thinking.* Hillsdale, NJ: Lawrence Erlbaum Associates.

Polya, G. (1945). *How to solve it.* Princeton, NJ: Princeton University Press.

Reed, S. K. (1987). A structure-mapping model for word problems. *Journal of Experimental Psychology: Learning, Memory, & Cognition, 13,* 124–139.

Reed, S. K. (1989). Constraints on the abstraction of solutions. *Journal of Educational Psychology, 81,* 531–540.

Reed, S. K., Dempster, A., & Ettinger, M. (1985). Usefulness of analogous solutions for solving algebra word problems. *Journal of Experimental Psychology: Learning, Memory, & Cognition, 11,* 106–125.

Riley, M. S., Greeno, J. G., & Heller, J. I. (1983). Development of children's problem-solving ability. In H. P. Ginsberg (Ed.), *The development of mathematical thinking.* New York: Academic Press, 153–196.

Schoenfeld, A. H. (1985). *Mathematical problem solving.* Orlando, FL: Academic Press.

Segal, J. W., Chipman, S. F., & Glaser, R. (Eds.) (1985). *Thinking and learning skills, Volume 1: Relating instruction to research.* Hillsdale, NJ: Lawrence Erlbaum Associates.

Silver, E. A. (1979). Student perceptions of relatedness among mathematical verbal problems. *Journal for Research in Mathematics Education, 10,* 195–210.

Watts, G. H., & Anderson, R. C. (1971). Effects of three types of inserted questions on learning from prose. *Journal of Educational Psychology, 62,* 387–394.

Wittrock, M. C. (1974). Learning as a generative activity. *Educational Psychologist, 11,* 87–95.

# Chapter 7
# Attitude-Change Principles

## Anne Bednar

### Eastern Michigan University

and

## W. Howard Levie

### Indiana University

## Introduction

Traditionally the world of education has divided instructional outcomes into three domains—cognitive, affective, and psychomotor—with the cognitive domain dealing with thinking, the affective domain with feelings, and the psychomotor domain with physical movement. Originally the purpose of the division was to facilitate research (Martin & Briggs, 1986) while recognizing that the domains interact in actual teaching/learning situations. The practical effect of the separate research agendas, however, has been the development of separate theory and models of instruction for each of the domains. Further, within each domain, there have been extensive efforts to develop taxonomies of outcomes (Bloom, 1956; Krathwohl, Bloom, and Masia, 1964). Strategies for teaching many of the elements within the taxonomies have become further separated through research. Earlier chapters in this book, other than Chapter 1, dealing with Motivation Principles, have focused on outcomes which fall into the cognitive and psychomotor domains. The focus of this chapter is to be the affective domain.

Interestingly enough, one of the most pressing points in current research into instructional design for affective outcomes is whether the division of outcomes into the three previously-mentioned domains is valid. First, there is little agreement as to what exactly constitutes the affective domain. Martin and Briggs (1986) found that all of the following terms have been associated with affect by one author or another, but with little consistency: "self-concept, motivation, interests, attitudes, beliefs, values, self-esteem, morality, ego development, feelings, need achievement, locus of control, curiosity, creativity, independence, mental health, personal growth, group dynamics, mental imagery, and personality." Of these concepts, attitudes (including attitudes, beliefs, and values), self-development (including self-concept, self-esteem, ego development, locus of control, personal growth), and motivation are three of the concepts most consistently associated with the affective domain. All of these outcomes have strong cognitive and behavioral components as well as an affective component. Additionally, it is also argued that outcomes in both the cognitive and psychomotor domains contain affective components, that learning in the cognitive and psychomotor domains is influenced by attitude, self-concept, and motivation. At the core is the question whether the distinction between domains is valid and useful or dysfunctional, that is, whether the domains as identified are appropriate (Romiszowski, 1989).

Other issues inhibit research and application in the affective domain: If it is accepted as appropriate for educators to teach affective outcomes (rather than, or in collaboration with, the home and religious institution), how are the appropriate set of attitudes, values, etc., to be determined? Are affective goals ends in themselves, or are they means to other ends; that is, do attitudes, motivation, self-esteem, etc., influence a learner's ability to learn, or can they be desired outcomes of learning, or both? Will lessons targeting affective objectives be viewed as "brainwashing"? Will the methods associated with changing attitudes and beliefs be viewed as ethical?

Generally, then, recent research in the affective domain has been calling for the integration of the domains and for application of an instructional design process as well as of principles of design in creating lessons which include attention to the affective domain as an element of all learning (Martin & Briggs, 1986; Kamradt & Kamradt, manuscript in preparation). Across affective outcomes, collaborative learning activities, which (1) put control in the hands of the learners, (2) provide ample opportunity for modeling by accomplished learners, and (3) provide for success seem to facilitate achievement of affective goals (Martin, 1989). At the more micro design level, principles of design to achieve affective outcomes relate to the specific type of learning which is to take place, e.g., attitude change, enhancement of motivation, development of self-concept, etc.

Since motivation is dealt with in the opening chapter of this book, this chapter will deal with attitude change, one of the outcomes most consistently represented as part of the affective domain. It will look first at *principles* for design of instruction to change attitudes, and second at some of the *processes* being proposed for designing and structuring lessons which target affective goals.

## Instructional Design Principles for Attitude Change

As with the definition of the affective domain itself, there is little agreement as to a definition of attitude. It has long been one of the central concepts of social psychology, and considerable debate has appeared concerning its most useful conceptual and operational definition. Someone can be found who disagrees with almost any statement about the concept. McGuire (1985) noted that even the most accepted conceptual definitions of attitude vary across a number of dimensions. However, a few of the more generally agreed upon characteristics of the concept are:

**Attitude is a latent variable.** Attitudes, like many other constructs in psychology, are not directly observable but are *inferred* from behavior. In real life, these behaviors are usually people's verbal statements or their observable actions. The attitude itself, then, is usually conceived of as the readiness to respond in a certain way to a psychological object.

**Attitudes have objects.** People have attitudes toward specific referents (particular individuals, works of art, etc.), and toward events or behaviors (being arrested, painting with oils, etc.).

**Attitudes have an affective component.** Probably the most fundamental aspect of the concept is the emotional approach-avoidance tendency. An individual's affective evaluation of an object can vary in direction, either positive or negative; in degree, the amount of positiveness-negativeness, from strongly positive to mildly positive through neutral to mildly negative and strongly negative; and in intensity, the amount of commitment or involvement with which a particular position (direction and degree) is held. These affective reactions serve as implicit responses to objects that arouse motives for behavior.

**Attitudes have a behavioral component.** Attitudes imply a predisposition to behave in an evaluative way. However, both researchers and practitioners have found frequently that people's attitudes toward some class of objects fail to predict their behavior toward a member of that class in some *particular* situation. Thus, a person who holds a negative attitude toward police may nevertheless behave very courteously toward an officer who stops his/her car. Behavior is multiply determined. Any particular act is the product of a blend of several personal predispositions (only one of which is attitude) and of the demands the particular situation places upon the performer. Actually, many theorists prefer to exclude action tendencies from the concept of attitude.

**Attitudes have a cognitive component.** Attitudes toward police, for example, may involve beliefs about the honesty, effectiveness, and attitudes of police officers. Such cognitions are, of course, teachable, and attitudes are learned. People are not born with a set of attitude structures. However, it has often been observed that information alone may not be sufficient to change attitudes. Also, researchers have been puzzled by the repeated failure to obtain a correlation between people's recall of the information in a persuasive message and their agreement with the conclusions of the message. Perhaps, as Greenwald (see Insko, Lind, & LaTour, 1976) suggests, people's retention from a persuasive message is not of the information per se, but of their cognitive reactions that were aroused by the message.

**Attitudes are relatively stable and enduring.** An individual's attitude toward the police does not shift from day to day and is relatively resistant to change. While, again, definitions vary widely, it is on the dimension of durability that attitudes may be differentiated from opinions. Opinions are more transitory and subject to change. For example, the individual may have only an opinion about

Officer Smith, a policeman with whom the individual has had little contact. This distinction between attitudes and opinions lies in the importance the object holds for the individual, and in his/her involvement with the issue.

The distinction between attitudes and values is less clear. Values seem to deal with higher-order concepts such as security and freedom, and are considered to be formed from clusters of attitudes. They are generally even more stable and resistant to change than attitudes. Finally, motives are drive states that may be aroused by attitudes, but which appear and disappear with given circumstances. Newcomb *et al.*, 1965, cited in Martin & Briggs (1986), consider attitude to be "at a crucial intersection between cognitive processes (such as thought and memory) and motivational processes (involving emotion and striving)" (p. 40).

If the goal is to change attitude, three approaches emerge from the theoretical literature (Martin & Briggs, 1986): providing a persuasive message; modeling and reinforcing appropriate behavior; and inducing dissonance between the cognitive, affective, and behavioral components of the attitude. These approaches are ideally used in tandem; as Martin and Briggs observe, "...there is one condition that supersedes all others: *use a variety of approaches*" (Martin & Briggs, 1986, p. 137).

# 1. Designing Persuasive Messages

Persuasive messages can be viewed as an example of a basic communication in which a SOURCE presents a MESSAGE through a CHANNEL to a RECEIVER. In this section, principles of attitude change for each of these components are introduced in the order named. It should be noted, however, that the research in attitude change over the past ten years has demonstrated the complex interactions which occur between these variables. While using a similar communication model as one dimension in his review of the attitude research in 1985, McGuire proposed a matrix which had twelve output steps (e.g., tuning in that produces exposure to the communication; attending to it; liking, interest in it; comprehending in content; etc.). Any step might be differentially affected by any variation in the source, message, channel, or receiver. A positive effect on step one and a negative effect on step five have a potential net effect of canceling out each other.

## The Source

Whether designing a persuasive message or developing a lesson based on modeling, the likelihood that a receiver will accept the conclusions advocated in a given lesson is in part a function of the receiver's perception of the source's or model's credibility. Note the phrase "the receiver's perception." Source credibility is not a constant property of a source; rather, it is an attribution that is conferred upon the source by the receiver.

### 1.1. High-credibility sources exert more persuasive influence than low-credibility sources.

A wide variety of characteristics contributes to perceptions of credibility. For example, Singletary (1976) told subjects to imagine the most credible or believable news source they could, and then to describe that source. The person imagined was described as being knowledgeable, attractive, trustworthy, articulate, satirical, and stable. Other investigators have identified additional characteristics, but two characteristics have been identified and studied repeatedly: expertise and trustworthiness.

Expertise relates to the credentials of the communicator. Does the receiver believe that the source or model has the information, experience, and intelligence to know the correct stand on an issue? Generally the expertise of a source is content-specific. That is, a person may be viewed as being an expert on topic A, but not on topic B. Some persons who are perceived as highly intelligent and generally well-informed may be accorded high credibility over a wide range of issues. In the study of the diffusion of innovations, for example, opinion leaders are individuals who frequently influence others in their social system or group; this influence seems to be generalizable across content rather than content-specific (Rogers, 1983).

If a source or model is perceived as being biased or insincere, attempts at attitude change may be ineffective. When the source's or model's motives are suspect, trustworthiness suffers. Communicators who are judged to be arguing in their own self-interest or who are thought to have ulterior motives may be viewed with skepticism. Communicators who appear to be arguing against their own self-interest are rated as being particularly believable, such as an owner of a manufacturing plant who argues for stronger environmental controls in spite of the potential additional costs to her or his business. The trustworthiness of the source appears to be a less important matter than the source's expertise, particularly when the basis for persuasion is the legitimacy of the factual content in a persuasive message. Even so, it is generally to the source's advantage to be rated high in trustworthiness.

Some factors may reduce the importance of source credibility as an element of a persuasive message. There is evidence that the effects of source credibility diminish with the passage of time so that individuals who judge the conclusions of a message initially based on the credibility or lack of credibility of the source may later change their views. The hypothesis used to explain these findings is that consideration of the merit of the message itself is the intervening factor. Contributing to the confusion is the finding that receivers learn more of the factual content of a message when the source is of uncertain credibility; perhaps people feel a greater need to understand the arguments when they lack the cue of high or low source credibility to guide them in judging the acceptability of the conclusion. If the learning goal is for learners to consider an issue and make their own decision regarding the issue, then source credibility may hamper rather than contribute to that goal. Certainly this is an issue regarding teaching toward affective goals.

Source credibility tends to be topic specific. The receiver evaluates the source's expertise and trustworthiness relative to the particular issue involved. There are, however, other characteristics which are largely irrelevant to topical concerns that may enhance the source's persuasive effectiveness. These characteristics are usually grouped under the rubric of "attractiveness."

### 1.2.  Sources perceived by the receiver as attractive are more influential.

A variety of factors appears to contribute to attractiveness, among them similarity, familiarity, and appearance. These characteristics overlap and are mutually reinforcing. Often it is difficult to specify exactly why we are attracted to other people. Even so, some factors may be isolated—at least conceptually. For example, people are more likely to accept influence from sources with which they can identify. It is particularly effective if the receiver perceives the source as holding similar values and beliefs. Considerable research has been conducted comparing the effectiveness of source-receiver similarity in belief (for example, political beliefs) versus some demographic characteristic (race, age, etc.). Although the evidence is not one-sided, ideological similarity appears to be more critical. Additionally, it appears that the more relevant the nature of the shared belief is to the attitude issue in question, the more effective the source will be in persuading the receiver.

A different kind of contributory factor to the positive effect of similarity in natural communications situations is that there is greater fidelity of communication between people with similar backgrounds. Rogers and Shoemaker (1971) note that when the source and receiver "share common meanings, a mutual subcultural language, and are alike in personal and social characteristics, the communication of ideas is likely to have greater effects in terms of knowledge gain, attitude formation and change, and overt behavior change" (p. 14). Communication failure can often be traced to a dissimilarity between the implicit assumptions held by the two parties. The extreme difficulties experienced in cross-cultural communication forcefully demonstrate the problem.

As might be expected, physical appearance also affects ratings of attractiveness and sincerity. In this area there are two competing concepts: how closely a person physically resembles the receiver's ideal image of a male or female and how closely the source's physical appearance matches the expectations the receiver has for an individual expressing a certain set of views. So, for example, a "liberal" appearing source (longer hair and a beard) was judged as being more sincere when he argued in favor of granting amnesty to draft evaders, whereas a "conservative" appearing source (short hair, no beard) was judged as more sincere when arguing against amnesty (Miller, 1976).

Given credibility and attractiveness both as positive factors, what are the alternatives when it is not possible to identify a source which is both credible and attractive (similar) to the audience? The effectiveness of source credibility lies in the receiver's belief that the source has the ability to know the proper stand on an issue and the objectivity to communicate that stand truthfully. By accepting influence from a high-credibility source, the receiver could be said to be engaging in a rational decision-making process. Attractive sources exert influence simply through their association with a particular point of view. The rationale for the receiver's acceptance is on a more emotional level. These two types of influence may hold implications for the design of the message.

### 1.3. The quality and structure of the arguments in a persuasive message are more critical for credible sources than for attractive sources (see Figure 7.1).

If the receiver is inclined to accept a source's conclusions because of the source's attractiveness, providing supporting arguments will be of minor importance. However, if the receiver is inclined to accept a source's conclusions because of the source's expertise, supporting arguments may be of considerable importance (see Figure 7.1). The converse of this principle implies that when your message includes complicated argumentation, use an expert source; when the message consists of little more than the conclusion, use an attractive source. Stone and Hoyt (1974) found that attractiveness alone was not effective in changing attitudes on a complicated, controversial issue. They also found that expertise was effective only when coupled with attractiveness (and presumably trustworthiness). Thus follows the obvious conclusion that the best approach is to employ sources who are both credible and attractive. The identification of such sources is a problem in cases when expertise implies a lack of similarity to the receiver.

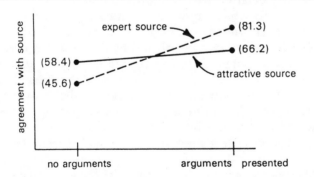

**Figure 7.1.** Norman (1976) found that a message containing no arguments was ineffective when attributed to an expert source (a score of 45.6 as compared to a score of 43.5 for a control group who received no message). On the other hand, subjects showed considerable agreement with an attractive source presenting the message without arguments (58.4) and agreement did not improve significantly with the inclusion of arguments.

The relative effectiveness of credibility and attractiveness may also be related to the nature of the source-receiver relationship and the context of the behavior related to the attitude. Kelman (1961) has identified three persuasion situations based upon the social relationship between the source and receiver: compliance, identification, and internalization. In *compliance*, acceptance is based on a system of rewards and punishments. The credibility and attractiveness of the source are of only minor importance, since the receiver exhibits compliant behavior in hopes of attaining some reward. On such occasions people often say and do things they do not really believe. In general, opinions expressed in compliant situations will terminate when the source is no longer in a position of control. In *identification*, acceptance is based on a personal relationship. It is especially strong when the identification is an affiliation with a group. Acceptance will continue only as long as the receiver obtains satisfaction from the relationship. In *internalization*, the source has no leverage over the receiver. Acceptance is based on how intrinsically appealing the message is, rather than on reasons extrinsic to the topic. The credibility of the source is of prime importance.

It might be argued that in education the ethical position is to attempt to exert influence in the context of internalization rather than compliance or identification. The content itself, and consequently the expertise and trustworthiness of the source, should predominate. Also, if the teacher is interested in finding out what the learner's true beliefs are, care must be taken to avoid situations of compliance, or the learners will simply tell the teacher what they think the teacher wants to hear.

## The Message—WHAT to Say

The second major component of a persuasive communication is the message. Given that the communicators have decided on the conclusion for the receiver to adopt, how can they determine what information to present? Which arguments will be convincing and which arguments will be unconvincing? One means of determining the most effective message is to pretest alternative messages. However, extensive pretesting is not always feasible. Furthermore, how can the communicator think up potentially effective arguments in the first place?

One kind of message content that is frequently overlooked is information about the source. Often, particularly in education, the information provided about the source is sparse. If attitude change is an objective, and if the source is not well known by the learners but possesses characteristics that may facilitate attitude change, then this information should be made part of the message.

### 1.4. Be sure the receiver is informed of the expertise of a high-credibility communicator.

While it has often been shown that communicators who are perceived as being experts on a topic are more persuasive, exactly what constitutes expertise for a given receiver may not be obvious. For example, Cantor, Alfonso, and Zillman (1976) found that a tape-recorded message recommending the use of an intrauterine device was more effective when attributed to a source who had used the IUD herself than a source who had not. However, the same message was not affected by manipulating the level of medical experience of the source. In another study, Shrigley (1976) asked third-year elementary education students to indicate the characteristics of instructors for elementary science methods courses that relate to teaching credibility. He found that practical teaching experience was rated high, while involvement in research and authoring science textbooks was rated low. As noted earlier, credibility, including the factors that are associated with expertise, are *percepts of the receiver* and not properties of the source.

Since the source's attractiveness can also enhance the message's effectiveness, one technique is to increase the perceived similarity of the source by establishing belief congruence between the source and receiver as part of the message.

### 1.5. To enhance communicator attractiveness, establish belief congruence with the receiver by arguing in favor of positions the receiver is known to hold.

Research has shown that establishing co-orientation between source and receiver on one topic can increase the source's effectiveness on another topic. This tactic is known as "flogging a dead horse." Praise the things the receiver likes ("freedom and peace") and criticize the things the receiver dislikes ("crime and taxes").

Once the relationship between the source and the receiver has been enhanced by establishing credibility or similarity with the receiver, one should begin teaching the content where the student *is* in terms of relevant needs. An early learner analysis will help to determine where the student is at in relation to the content.

### 1.6. Arguments are more effective if they are relevant to the receiver's needs.

Show the receiver how an existing need can be satisfied by adopting your point of view. Kamradt and Kamradt (manuscript in preparation) view an attitude as a tool used in fulfilling needs and a feeling as a signal of a need. Changing an attitude is helping the learner see that a new tool (i.e., a new attitude) may be more effective in meeting that need than the old tool.

Often the need that an attitude can serve is quite basic: security, love, etc. Because of the complexity of human needs, often the need which an attitude is serving is not so obvious, and extensive analysis as well as pretesting of message components will be necessary. One of the criticisms of attitude research is that the categorization of attitudes in relation to psychological needs has not produced a consistent set of categories. For example, Katz (1960) describes four functions which attitudes can serve, while Kamradt and Kamradt (manuscript in preparation) have six or seven which cut across Katz's categories rather than simply being additions to those categories.

Once the needs of the receiver are understood, the persuasive message can address those needs in either of two ways: by demonstrating that the object of the attitude has potential to affect satisfaction of the receiver's needs; or, by changing the receiver's estimate of the importance of satisfying those needs. An argument that would produce attitude change is one which enhances the receiver's perception that the object can promote need satisfaction. Another effective argument is one that increases the importance of the needs.

In considering attitudes and the issues to which they relate, there are usually at least two sides to every issue. In a debate, the advocates can be expected to state the arguments that support their views. Sometimes, however, a communicator will also introduce arguments that appear to favor the opposition—and then refute them. This may be a good idea in some cases, but in other cases, it only raises doubts and questions. When should a communicator introduce opposing arguments?

### 1.7.   *Generally two-sided arguments are slightly more effective than one-sided messages.*

Introducing and refuting opposing arguments may be facilitative when the receiver: is already familiar with the issue, initially disagrees with the communicator's position, is highly intelligent and may seek out opposing arguments before making a decision, and is likely to hear the opposing viewpoint later. The cases in which ignoring opposing arguments is advisable are the obverse of the above, namely, when the receiver: is not familiar with the issue, initially agrees with the communicator, is not highly intelligent and inquisitive about the issue, and will not be likely to hear opposing arguments later. In addition, to reinforce existing attitudes it is a good idea to expose receivers to weak forms of opposing arguments so that they have to defend and thereby strengthen their view.

When the decision has been made to use a two-sided rather than a single-sided argument, a second decision must be made—whether to present the "pro" or "con" arguments first. When the receiver is unfamiliar with the controversy, introduce the "pro" arguments first and be sure the receiver clearly understands them before introducing and refuting "con" arguments. However, when faced with a hostile audience which is familiar with the issue, it is better to acknowledge and attempt to refute the "con" before presenting the "pro" arguments.

Is it more effective to let an audience come to its own conclusion or to make the conclusion of your arguments explicit? While it has been suggested that people do not like to be told what to think and are usually more persuaded by their own conclusions, the opposite had been demonstrated by research.

### 1.8.   *It is almost always advisable to state the conclusion explicitly rather than to allow receivers to draw their own conclusions.*

The main problem with leaving the conclusion implicit is that receivers may not come to the right conclusion. In fact, they may not come to any conclusion at all. When the issue is the least bit complex, or when receivers have low motivation or low intelligence, explicitly stating the conclusion is safer and better. Exactly when you state the conclusion and how you order your arguments (weakest or strongest first) depends on the receiver's initial stand and interest in the issue. When the receiver has relatively little interest in the issue but may be favorable to your viewpoint, present your conclusions first and use an anticlimactic order in presenting your arguments. When the receiver is involved in the issue and is initially opposed to your viewpoint, present your arguments in a climactic order and then present your conclusion. When people are not interested in a topic, holding their attention presents a major problem. Disinterested receivers, if they attend to the message at all, may stop attending before you have presented your entire case. Hence it is advisable to get your most critical information across in the early parts of the message. On the other hand, when full attention is likely, a presentation that "builds" may be preferred, particularly when the receiver is antagonistic. Approaching antagonistic receivers with a mild threat to their belief is less likely to produce hostile reactions and total rejection of the message than using a strong initial attack.

Finally, learning research shows that repetition of information aids retention. Does the repetition of a persuasive message help in persuasion?

### 1.9. Repetition helps, but only one or two repetitions are likely to have any additional effect.

Repetition helps, but only up to a certain point. Laboratory experiments in persuasion and field studies of advertising in mass media demonstrate the positive effects of repetition. However, it appears that the gain achieved reaches an asymptote rather rapidly. For a given receiver little gain is likely after one or two repetitions. A greater number of repetitions in mass media channels may be productive if different members of a changing audience are exposed to the different repetitions of the message.

## The Channel

The term "channel," the third major component of a persuasive communication, can be used in at least two ways. In can refer to the type of medium used: film, television, radio, and so forth. It can also refer to human sensory capabilities such as vision, hearing, and touch. When the term "channel" is used in the literature on attitude change, authors are usually referring to some media type, such as film, television, radio, or print. Sometimes the author is implicitly coupling a medium with its distribution-reception system. That is, when the term "television" is used, the author may be thinking of a network broadcast in which million of people are *simultaneously* exposed to the same message in the context of their home viewing environments. That concept is quite different from "closed-circuit instructional television." Also, there are vast differences between messages presented over any given television system. For example, if, in attempting to assess the "persuasive impact of television," television is taken to include the nightly news, music shows, children's programming, deodorant commercials, and televised Presidential debates, the results may be of little or no descriptive or predictive value.

Even so, terms such as "television," "newspapers," and "radio" are frequently used in the literature, and many people have rather definite ideas about the relative effectiveness of these types in attitude change. What does the research say about the differential persuasive effectiveness of different types of media?

> **1.10.** *No one media type has been explicitly shown to have greater persuasive effectiveness than any other media type. Face-to-face communication, however, is more effective in promoting acceptance than mediated communication, particularly in difficult cases.*

Studies of political campaigns and research in the diffusion of innovations show that when attitudes were changed on important issues, it was usually the influence of another person rather than of the media that was primarily responsible. McGuire (1985) reports that audio-visual communications are about as effective as audio-only presentations at changing attitudes, but are not as effective as face-to-face communications.

The effectiveness of face-to-face communication has little to do with the type of information presented, but rather appears to be the result of factors associated with the physical presence of the source. For example, the live source can apply "social pressure," relying upon the receiver's reluctance to directly contradict a person. After all, it is harder to say "No" to a person standing right in front of you than it is to refuse impersonal requests. Also, face-to-face communication may be more effective because the source can tailor the message to each receiver and alter it on-the-spot if necessary. So comprehension may be better. Finally, face-to-face communication has the advantage of increasing the likelihood that the message will be attended to. With regard to this last point, one of the main reasons that media campaigns fail is that the target audience simply does not attend to the message.

## The Receiver

The simple SOURCE-MESSAGE-CHANNEL-RECEIVER communication model encourages the impression that the receiver, the fourth major component of a persuasive communication, is an empty vessel into which the source pours the message. Semiotics, however, presents a totally different view of the receiver in a communication process. From a semiotic sense, receivers make meaning from their environments, one aspect of which may be a persuasive message. The receiver's active role in interpreting has been well substantiated in the research.

A frustrating aspect of receivers for attitude researchers and for practicing communicators is their heterogeneity. A message which has one effect on some individuals will have a different or no effect on others. One factor which seems especially important is understanding the receiver's existing position on the particular attitude issue of concern. Earlier principles demonstrated that the design of the message may depend on the receiver's present stand on the issue. Considering the characteristics of an attitude described early in the chapter, the degree of involvement the receiver has in the issue is especially important.

***1.11.*** *It is very difficult to change the attitudes of receivers who are highly committed to their positions on an issue.*

While two individuals may hold the same attitude related to an attitude object, their commitment to that position may vary greatly. Because of that, attitude research also considers the range of positions an individual is willing to accept (called the latitude of acceptance) and the range of positions the individual rejects (called the latitude of rejection). In changing an individual's attitude, the desired position must fall within the latitude of acceptance (Kiesler, Collins, & Miller, 1969; Sherif, Sherif, & Nebergall, 1965). Martin and Briggs (1986) suggest that the use of successive approximations can expand the latitude of acceptance and thereby permit greater attitude change than might otherwise be possible.

Studies involving most other receiver characteristics, whether demographic, personality type, etc., have reported either inconsistent findings or have been criticized for inadequate research methodology. Even when the findings have been credible, they have been of such small magnitude as to be impractical as a guide for decision making in the design of persuasive messages.

## 2. Modeling Appropriate Behaviors

Emotional responses as well as overt behavior can be learned by observing others. Gagné and Briggs (1979) consider modeling to be a fundamental strategy in attitude change lessons. Bandura (1977) includes modeling as a technique to facilitate attitude change.

As with the design of a persuasive message, when modeling is used as an instructional strategy, the credibility of the model is important.

### 2.1. *High-credibility models exert more persuasive influence than low-credibility models.*

As with the source in a persuasive message, credibility implies expertise and trustworthiness. Moreover, since it is likely that a learner may have closer contact with a model than with a source in a persuasive message, the model must engender the personal respect of the learner. Again, as with the source in a persuasive message, it is important that the model be a person with whom the learner can identify.

Frequently the model is a local source, well known to the learners. It may well be the classroom teacher. However, it is possible for the modeling lesson to be delivered through use of media, "...on film, by television, in a novel or through other vicarious means" (Martin & Briggs, 1986). In those circumstances the means used to establish the model's credibility will be most similar to those used with a persuasive message.

When using modeling as a strategy, it is important that the learners attend to the message. Those principles which apply to attention with any type of lesson apply here. Moreover, it is important that the learners focus on and understand the model's exhibition of the desired behaviors. If they are attending to other aspects of the model's performance, the point of the lesson will be missed.

**2.2.** *In order for modeling to be effective, the learners must comprehend the presentation as a demonstration of specific behaviors.*

Strategies consistent with effective use of any media in a lesson are applicable here. If the instructor introduces the lesson in a way which establishes set, preparing the learners to focus on the point of the lesson and thereby achieve the learning objective, the demonstration will increase in effectiveness. In such a lesson, in addition to the introduction, the lesson should include some means of debriefing to check that the learners have observed and understood the desired behaviors.

**2.3.** *In addition to observing the model demonstrating the behavior, learners should observe the model being reinforced for that behavior.*

Whether viewed from a behavioral point of view or from that of attribution theory in motivation research, what occurs following the performance of any behavior is important. If the model receives a reward (praise, social acceptance, etc.) after performing the demonstrated behavior, and that reward is valuable to the learner, the learner may choose to perform the behavior to gain the reward. As will be observed in Principle 3.2, in changing attitudes it is important that the reward be a contributing factor to encourage performance, but not enough to constitute a moral buy-out. If the learner can rationalize that the behavior was performed strictly to get the reward, then the attitude is not likely to change.

Once the model has demonstrated the behavior, there is greater likelihood of attitude change occurring if the learner has the opportunity to publicly practice the new behavior.

**2.4.** *Role-playing can have powerful persuasive impact.*

In role-playing, participants are asked to behave as they think a certain kind of person would behave in a particular situation. Janis and Mann (1965) told subjects that they were studying certain aspects of human behavior which are difficult to observe in real life, and that consequently they were using role-playing as a technique for observing how people might behave. Subjects were asked to imagine that they were visiting their doctor who had been treating them for a persistent cough. The role-playing session proceeded something like this:

> Doctor: "Well, last time you were here you asked for the whole truth, so I'm going to give it to you. This X-ray (pointing to it) shows there is a small malignant mass on your right lung. Moreover, results of the sputum test confirm this diagnosis."
> Role player: "What you're saying, doctor, is that I have lung cancer, right?"

"Unfortunately, the tests leave no doubt about the diagnosis."

"What next?"

"Immediate surgery is necessary. I've arranged for you to report to the hospital tomorrow morning. Plan on spending at least six weeks there, because chest surgery requires a long convalescence."

"I dread asking this question, but how are my chances?"

"I wish I could be totally encouraging; however, frankness dictates that I tell you there is only a moderate chance for a successful outcome from surgery for this condition."

"Is there anything I can do to improve my chances?"

"We've discussed this before, but I'd like you to refresh my memory on your smoking habits."*

The session continued with a discussion of cigarette smoking and its consequences. The role-playing subjects showed marked attitude changes and reduced their cigarette smoking much more than a control group who merely listened to a recording of one of the role-playing sessions. Even 18 months after the experiment, the role-players continued to smoke fewer cigarettes than control subjects. Since the control subjects were exposed to the same information as the role-players, it must have been something about the active involvement that was so effective.

### 2.5. Active participation produces more attitude change than passive reception of information.

Several researchers have found that participants in role-playing are affected more than observers. In related research, subjects who participated in group discussions about an issue changed attitudes more than subjects who just listened. The active participant is apparently more aroused, more involved, and more able to experience the emotions that might occur in reality. It should be noted, however, that these findings, like many others in attitude research, are not consistent across studies.

## 3. Creating and Managing Dissonance

Many approaches to persuasion focus upon changing attitudes by changing the cognitive component of the attitude structure, believing that changes in understanding will lead to changes in behavior. A different approach focuses upon inducing dissonance, which results from inconsistency in an individual's cognitive structure, on the assumption that the presence of dissonance will be so uncomfortable that the individual will act to resolve the dissonance and that, perhaps, a change in attitude will result. By far the most influential statement of this approach is Leon Festinger's (1957) theory of cognitive dissonance. It deals with pairs of cognitions: an individual's cognition that he or she has behaved in a

---

* From Miller & Burgoon (1973), p. 45.

certain way and his or her attitude about that behavioral act. When there is a conflict between such cognitions as "I smoke" and "Smoking causes cancer," an uncomfortable psychological tension is aroused. Dissonance can also occur when inconsistency exists between attitudes and behavior or between present and past experiences or interpretations of those experiences (Martin & Briggs, 1986). This tension, or cognitive dissonance, can be resolved in a number of ways (see Figure 7.2)

> **3.1.** *If a person can be induced to perform an important act that is counter to the person's own private attitude, attitude change may result.*

To some degree, proponents of school bussing to achieve reduction of racial prejudice are applying dissonance theory. If individuals who feel prejudice toward another group are put in close interaction with that group and induced to behave civilly, dissonance theory would predict that their attitude toward the other racial group might change. Of course, the forces at work in such complex situations are not simple; many factors relate to the success of inducing dissonance and then reducing it again to achieve the desired attitude change. One element is the element of free choice in the decision-making process.

> **3.2.** *When a person is induced to perform an attitudinally-discrepant act because of promise of reward or punishment, attitude change will occur only to the extent that the person feels the magnitude of the reward or punishment was insufficient to justify the attitudinally-discrepant behavior.*

Cognitive dissonance can be thought of as a theory of rationalization. When people can rationalize their behavior by an appeal to external forces, attitude change is not likely. For example, students and their parents involved in forced bussing could protect their prejudices by rationalizing that they were coerced into complying with the program. However, students and their parents who felt some measure of free will in engaging in the act probably experienced some dissonance.

Because of this factor, it is important that the desired alternative in a free-choice situation be made attractive, but not so attractive that the learner feels bought out—making the decision strictly for the reward. Ideally, a change agent would like to offer the minimum inducement that will produce the attitude-discrepant behavior. The dilemma, as Calder and Ross (1976) note, is that the very conditions that are mostly likely to produce the desired behavior (large rewards and severe punishments) work against the internalization of the desired attitude. A sufficient level of reward or punishment to induce the behavior must be applied, but it should be the minimum amount necessary to achieve this end. A delicate balance is required. One such reward may be social approval.

a. Dissonance arousal because of the conflict between a behavior and a cognition.

b. Dissonance elimination by changing a behavior.

c. Dissonance elimination by changing a cognition.

d. Dissonance reduction by modifying a behavior and bolstering a cognition.

**Figure 7.2.** Models of dissonance arousal and reduction.

### 3.3.   Demonstrate the social acceptability of the desired attitude and the reward available socially for behavior consistent with the attitude.

Inherent in this principle is the assumption that the societal group used as a referent is one to which the receiver seeks membership. It may be society as a whole or a sub-group. Whichever, social acceptability is an especially forceful reward for attitude change because it carries with it the secondary rewards inherent in being part of the mainstream of a cultural group or society. These secondary rewards are usually distant enough from the attitude-discrepant behavior that the issue of acting only for the reward is not a problem.

Once it has been possible to induce a behavior which is inconsistent with a previously held belief, it is possible to increase the magnitude of the dissonance experienced by providing information which is discrepant with the already-held beliefs.

### 3.4.   Alternate between presenting information discrepant with existing beliefs and inducing behaviors discrepant with existing attitudes to maximize dissonance.

Once dissonance has been induced, providing additional information which conflicts with the original attitude may make that attitude less tenable. Given the alternative of the new behavior, the receiver may adopt the desired attitude in light of the cognitive information. In turn, to provide avenues for resolution of the dissonance with the appropriate attitude change, provide information consistent with the desired attitude. It was observed above that providing information is not enough to cause attitude change, but providing information after inducing dissonance is helpful. Working on all the elements of the attitude—cognitive, affective, and behavioral—is advised.

### 3.5.   Structure attitude-change lessons so that attention is paid to the cognitive (information), affective (feeling) and behavioral (acting) elements of the attitude.

Kamradt and Kamradt (manuscript in preparation), proponents of what they are calling "Structured Design for Attitude Development," suggest a strategy of achieving attitude change by moving back and forth within instruction between parts of lessons addressing the cognitive aspects of an attitude, its behavioral component, and its feelings. They see an attitude as a tool used to meet needs within the environment. Feelings are a system which signals the need. Attitude-change lessons, then, consist of exposing the learner to the possibility that a new attitude may be more effective in meeting a given need than the old attitude. Following complex attitudinal analysis, the lessons consist of interacting sequences moving from inducing behavioral change, to arguing a new cognition, to creating a situation to move the feeling.

Like Martin and Briggs (1986), Kamradt and Kamradt (manuscript in preparation) indicate the importance of successive approximations.

### 3.6. *Use successive approximations to move attitudes gradually between a current status and a desired state.*

Akin to needs analysis, analysis of the attitude in the instructional design process might begin by identifying the old attitude, the desired state, and the gap between. Further analysis reveals stages within the gap where the three dimensions of the attitude could be internally consistent. The lesson gradually moves the learners from the old attitude, through the intermediate stages where attitude components achieve temporary stability, to the desired attitude. To achieve the small step moves, Kamradt and Kamradt use the technique of "parallel stepping around the triangle," where the triangle refers to the three attitude dimensions.

Analysis of an attitude will reveal several levels at which a cognitive system can be stable or balanced. If instruction alternates between components with the goal of moving the learners from one stable state to the next still unacceptable but closer-to-acceptable stable state, by moving through successive approximations the lesson can gradually draw the learner closer and closer to the desired attitude.

When the desired attitude is adopted, Kamradt and Kamradt add a significant new element to the lesson, a transfer event. The purpose of the transfer event is to teach the learners strategies which will support their maintenance of the new attitude.

## Instructional Design Processes for Attitude-Change Lessons

The process of designing an attitude-change unit can be much like designing a unit of instruction with any outcome: analysis to determine the preset conditions under which the instruction must be delivered (including the characteristics of the learners, the structure of the content, and the constraints of the delivery environment); synthesis to select appropriate instructional strategies and to design an effective message to achieve the specified learning outcomes; and evaluation to assess the effectiveness of the unit at achieving its goals. This close parallel to the instructional design process for lessons with cognitive outcomes is acknowledged by Martin and Briggs (1986), whose approach to dealing with affective outcomes is to specify internal and external conditions for learning so that development of affective units can parallel that of cognitive units when applying Gagné and Briggs' model for instructional design. The main distinction is in the necessity to attend to and appropriately sequence lesson elements which deal with each component of an attitude: cognitive, affective, and behavioral.

The earlier part of this chapter dealt with the principles which might be applied in designing an appropriate message to achieve affective outcomes. In closing, we will pay some attention to the issue of instructional strategies for affective outcomes. Use of group process seems to be especially effective in attitude change. It gives learners the opportunity to view other perspectives (e.g., models of different attitudes), assume an alternative perspective and try it out, take overt action in a safe environment, articulate their own position, and apply the attitude in a problem-solving context. "Use of group processes and social interaction, self-directed learning, providing for success, giving learners a chance to take overt action, and modeling appropriate behavior are the mainstays of affective instructional procedures" (Martin, 1989). Allender (1982) lists a variety of strategies and instructional settings which research has shown facilitate affective outcomes: e.g., cooperative learning environments, use of moral and ethical dilemmas, experiential learning, and open classrooms. Common to all of these are opportunities for free choice and control by students, opportunities for success, and lessons which present and confront alternative perspectives.

## Chapter Conclusion

In closing, Barbara Martin, one of the leading authors in the area of designing instruction for affective outcomes, has observed: "Designing instruction in the affective domain is not an easy task. It is not a science and probably never will be due to the nature of the behaviors under consideration. In addition to it being a difficult task, there is no consensus about whether instruction should be designed in this domain." The purpose of this chapter is to provide some guidelines for those educators who do choose to design instruction for affective outcomes, including attitudinal change.

## References

Allender, J. S. (1982). Affective education. In H. E. Mitzel (Ed.), *Encyclopedia of educational research* (5th ed.). New York: The Free Press.

Bandura, A. (1977). *Social learning theory*. Englewood Cliffs, NJ: Prentice-Hall.

Bloom, B. S. (Ed.) (1956). *Taxonomy of educational objectives: The classification of educational goals. Handbook I: Cognitive domain*. New York: Longman.

Boyer, E. (1983). *High school: A report on secondary education in America* (Carnegie Foundation for the Advancement of Teaching). New York: Harper and Row.

Brandhorst, A. R. (1978). *Reconceptualizing the affective domain*. (ERIC Document Reproduction Service No. ED153891.)

Breckler, S. J. (1984). Empirical validation of affect, behavior, and cognition as distinct components of attitude. *Journal of Personality and Social Psychology, 47*, 1191–1205.

Briggs, L. J. (1984). Whatever happened to motivation and the affective domain? *Educational Technology, 24*(5), 33–34.

Calder, B. J., & Ross, M. (1976). Attitudes: Theories and issues. In J. W. Thibaut, J. R. Spence, and R. C. Carson (Eds.), *Contemporary topics in social psychology.* Morristown, NJ: General Learning Press.

Cantor, J. R., Alfonso, H., & Zillman, D. (1976). The persuasive effectiveness of the peer appeal and a communicator's first-hand experience. *Communication Research, 3*, 293–309.

Festinger, L. (1957). *A theory of cognitive dissonance.* Stanford: Stanford University Press.

Fishbein, M., & Ajzen, T. (1975). *Belief, attitude, intention, and behavior: An introduction to theory and research.* Reading, MA: Addison-Wesley.

Foshay, W. R. (1978). An alternative for task analysis in the affective domain. *Journal of Instructional Development, 1*(2), 22–24.

Gagné, R. M., & Briggs, L. J. (1979). *Principles of instructional design* (2nd ed.). New York: Holt, Rinehart, & Winston.

Gordon, I. J. (1970). Affect and cognition: A reciprocal relationship. *Educational Leadership, 27*, 661–664.

Hovland, C. I., Janis, I. L., & Kelley, H. H. (1953). *Communication and persuasion.* New Haven, CT: Yale University Press.

Hurst, B. L. (1980). An integrated approach to the hierarchical order of the cognitive and affective domains. *Journal of Educational Psychology, 72*, 293–303.

Insko, C. A., Lind, E. A., & LaTour, S. (1976). Persuasion, recall, and thoughts. *Representative Research in Social Psychology, 7*, 66–78.

Janis, I. L., & Mann, L. (1965). Effectiveness of emotional role-playing in modifying smoking habits and attitudes. *Journal of Experimental Research in Personality, 1*, 84–90.

Kamradt, E. J., & Kamradt, T. F. (manuscript in preparation). *Structured design for affective development.* Public seminar sponsored by Indiana University, School of Education, Department of Instructional Systems Technology, May 22–23, 1992.

Katz, D. (1960). The functional approach to the study of attitudes. *Public Opinion Quarterly, 14*, 163–204.

Kelman, H. C. (1961). Three processes of social influence. *Public Opinion Quarterly, 25*, 57–78.

Kiesler, C. A., Collins, B. E., & Miller, N. (1969). *Attitude change: A critical analysis of theoretical approaches.* New York: John Wiley & Sons.

Krathwohl, D. R., Bloom, B. S., & Masia, B. B. (1964). *Taxonomy of educational objectives: The classification of educational goals. Handbook II: Affective domain.* New York: Longman.

Lewy, A. (1968). The empirical validity of major properties of a taxonomy of affective educational objectives. *Journal of Experimental Education, 36*, 70–77.

Martin, B. L. (1989). A checklist for designing instruction in the affective domain. *Educational Technology, 29*(8), 7–15.

Martin, B. L., & Briggs, L. J. (1986). *The affective and cognitive domains: Integration for instruction and research.* Englewood Cliffs, NJ: Educational Technology Publications.

McGuire, W. J. (1969). Nature of attitudes and attitude change. In G. Lindzey & E. Aronson (Eds.), *Handbook of social psychology* (2nd ed., Vol. 3). Reading, MA: Addison-Wesley.

McGuire, W. J. (1973) Persuasion, resistance, and attitude change. In I. S. Pool (Ed.), *Handbook of communication*. Chicago: Rand-McNally.

McGuire, W. J. (1985) Attitudes and attitude change. In G. Lindzey & E. Aronson (Eds.), *Handbook of social psychology* (3rd ed., Vol. 2). New York: Random House.

Miller, A. G. (1976). Constraint and target effects in the attribution of attitudes. *Journal of Experimental Social Psychology, 12,* 325–339.

Miller, G. R., & Burgoon, M. (1973). *New techniques of persuasion.* New York: Harper and Row.

*A nation at risk.* (1983). The National Commission on Excellence in Education. Washington, DC: U.S. Government Printing Office.

Newcomb, T. M., Turner, R. H., & Converse, P. E. (1965). *Social psychology: The study of human interaction.* New York: Holt, Rinehart, & Winston.

Norman, R. (1976). When what is said is important: A comparison of expert and attractive sources. *Journal of Experimental Social Psychology, 12,* 294–300.

Ringness, T. A. (1975). *The affective domain in education.* Boston: Little, Brown and Company.

Rogers, E. M. (1983). *Diffusion of innovations.* New York: The Free Press.

Rogers, E. M., & Shoemaker, F. F. (1971). *Communication of innovations.* New York: The Free Press.

Romiszowski, A. J. (1989). Attitudes and affect in learning and instruction. *Educational Media International, 26*(2), 85–100.

Sherif, C. W., Kelly, M., Rogers, H. L., Sarup, G., & Tettler, B. I. (1973). Personal involvement, social judgment, and action. *Journal of Personality and Social Psychology, 27,* 311–327.

Sherif, C. W., Sherif, M., & Nebergall, R. E. (1965). *Attitude and attitude change.* Philadelphia: W. B. Saunders, 1965.

Shrigley, R. L. (1976). Credibility of the elementary science methods course instructor as perceived by students: A model for attitude modification. *Journal of Research in Science Teaching, 13,* 449–453.

Singletary, M. W. (1976). Components of credibility of a favorable news source. *Journalism Quarterly, 53,* 316–319.

Stone, V. A., & Hoyt, J. L. (1974). Effect of likability and relevance of expertness. *Journalism Quarterly, 51,* 314–317.

Taber, G. (1984). The affective domain and a nation at risk. *NASSP Bulletin, 68,* 49–52.

Wiggins, T., & Chapman, L. M. (1987). The affective context of classroom interaction. *Journal of Humanistic Education and Development, 26,* 64–71.

Zimbardo, P. G., Ebbesen, E. B., & Maslach, C. (1977). *Influencing attitudes and changing behavior* (2nd ed.). Menlo Park, CA: Addison-Wesley.

# Author Index

# Subject Index